Accessing the WAN

CCNA Exploration Labs and Study Guide

John Rullan

Cisco Press

00 East 96th Street

ndianapolis, Indiana 46240 USA

Accessing the WAN
CCNA Exploration Labs and Study Guide

John Rullan

Published by:
Cisco Press
800 East 96th Street
Indianapolis, IN 46240 USA

Printed in the United States of America

Sixth Printing January 2013

Library of Congress Cataloging-in-Publication Data

Rullan, John.
Accessing the WAN : CCNA exploration labs and study guide / John Rullan.
p. cm.
ISBN-13: 978-1-58713-201-8 (pbk. w/cd)
ISBN-10: 1-58713-201-X (pbk. w/cd)
1. Wide area networks (Computer networks)—Examinations—Study guides. I. Cisco Systems,
Inc. II. Title.
TK5105.87.R85 2008
004.67—dc22
2008013029

ISBN-13: 978-1-58713-201-8

ISBN-10: 1-58713-201-x

Publisher
Paul Boger

Associate Publisher
Dave Dusthimer

Cisco Representative
Anthony Wolfenden

Cisco Press Program Manager
Jeff Brady

Executive Editor
Mary Beth Ray

Production Manager
Patrick Kanouse

Senior Development Editor
Christopher Cleveland

Project Editor
Seth Kerney

Copy Editors
Keith Cline
Gayle Johnson

Technical Editors
Roderick Douglas
Lee Hilliard
Wayne Jarvimaki

Editorial Assistant
Vanessa Evans

Book and Cover Designer
Louisa Adair

Composition
Bronkella Publishing, Inc.

Proofreaders
Water Crest Publishing, Inc.
Debbie Williams

This book is part of the Cisco Networking Academy® series from Cisco Press. The products in this series support and complement the Cisco Networking Academy curriculum. If you are using this book outside the Networking Academy, then you are not preparing with a Cisco trained and authorized Networking Academy provider.

CISCO

For more information on the Cisco Networking Academy or to locate a Networking Academy, please visit www.cisco.com/edu.

Warning and Disclaimer

This book is designed to provide information about the Accessing the WAN course of the Cisco Networking Academy CCNA Exploration curriculum. Every effort has been made to make this book as complete and accurate as possible, but no warranty or fitness is implied.

The information is provided on an "as is" basis. The authors, Cisco Press and Cisco Systems, Inc. shall have neither liability nor responsibility to any person or entity with respect to any loss or damages arising from the information contained in this book or from the use of the discs or programs that may accompany it.

The opinions expressed in this book belong to the authors and are not necessarily those of Cisco Systems, Inc.

Trademark Acknowledgments

All terms mentioned in this book that are known to be trademarks or service marks have been appropriately capitalized. Cisco Press or Cisco Systems, Inc. cannot attest to the accuracy of this information. Use of a term in this book should not be regarded as affecting the validity of any trademark or service mark.

Corporate and Government Sales

The publisher offers excellent discounts on this book when ordered in quantity for bulk purchases or special sales, which may include electronic versions and/or custom covers and content particular to your business, training goals, marketing focus, and branding interests. For more information, please contact:

U.S. Corporate and Government Sales
1-800-382-3419
corpsales@pearsontechgroup.com

For sales outside the United States please contact:

International Sales
international@pearsoned.com

Feedback Information

At Cisco Press, our goal is to create in-depth technical books of the highest quality and value. Each book is crafted with care and precision, undergoing rigorous development that involves the unique expertise of members of the professional technical community.

Reader feedback is a natural continuation of this process. If you have any comments about how we could improve the quality of this book, or otherwise alter it to better suit your needs, you can contact us through e-mail at feedback@ciscopress.com. Please be sure to include the book title and ISBN in your message.

We greatly appreciate your assistance.

About the Author

John Rullan has been teaching at Thomas Edison High School in Jamaica, New York for the past 13 years and has been a part of the Cisco Networking Academy since 1998. He is the director of the Cisco Academy for the New York City Department of Education and is the citywide trainer. He provides support to the academy community and has presented at academy conferences throughout the country while working on the Instructional Support and Curriculum Maintenance teams. He also has taught CCNA, CCNP, and network security for the Borough of Manhattan Community College since 2000. He currently holds the Network+, CCNA, CCNP, and CCAI certifications.

About the Contributing Author

Sonya Coker received her undergraduate degree in secondary education from the University of South Alabama. She worked in the public school system for five years as a Title 1 Project Coordinator serving at-risk students. She joined the Cisco Academy program in 1998 when she started a local CCNA Academy at Murphy High School in Mobile, Alabama. She now works as a full-time developer in the Cisco Networking Academy program. She has worked on a variety of Academy curriculum projects, including CCNA, CCNP, Fundamentals of Wireless LANs, and Network Security. She has taught instructor training classes throughout the world.

About the Technical Reviewers

Roderick Douglas, Senior Lecturer with the IT Foundry at Sheffield Hallam University in the UK, has been an active Cisco Certified Academy Instructor since 2002. He is committed to delivering high-quality, flexible, and innovative training through the Cisco Academy Program. He has an MSc in computing from Sheffield Hallam University, Sheffield, UK. He holds CCNA and Wireless certifications from Cisco, as well as Microsoft MCSE/MCT, Novell CNE/CNI/Linux, CompTIA Linux+, and Security+, CWNA, Wireless# certifications.

Lee Hilliard is a professor and department chair for Computer Networking at College of the Canyons in Santa Clarita, California. He has been involved in the Cisco Networking Academy program since 2000 and is a CCAI and CATC instructor for CREATE CATC. He has structured the Computer Networking department to foster a spirit of community involvement by having students work with local businesses and nonprofit organizations. These efforts include soliciting surplus equipment from local businesses when they upgrade, having the students in the program refurbish the equipment as part of their hands-on lab activities, and then redistributing the equipment to nonprofit organizations. This is a win-win-win situation in which the students get practical application of the skills learned, the distribution of the equipment to underprivileged youth helps address the "digital divide," and keeping usable equipment in service supports a sustainability effort. Hilliard has a master of science degree in industrial technology from California State University, Fresno.

Wayne Jarvimaki is a Main Contact/Lead Instructor for North Seattle Cisco Area Training Center (CATC) and has been training instructors in North America and Asia/Pac since 1998. Wayne serves on the Board of SeaKay, a nonprofit organization that helps Cisco Academies and low-income housing. He is the Senior Network Designer for CNS, a provider of bridged wireless campus networks for Digital Divide communities, and currently holds CCNA and CCAI certifications.

Dedications

I would like to dedicate this book to all my past and present students, whose dedication has inspired me to make this book the best that it can be. I would like to give special thanks to Emil Prysak, Alroy Lam, and Nabil El Bakhar, my current students, and Jalil Khan, a graduate, who still lends a hand and is always around to help.

—John Rullan

For all the students and instructors who have challenged and inspired me throughout my career in the Cisco Networking Academy Program. Your enthusiasm and curiosity remind me that there's always something new to learn.

—Sonya Coker

Acknowledgments

Sonya Coker, coauthor, for giving me the pleasure of working with her on various support teams. I couldn't think of anyone else I would like to write this book with. Her input and lab activities are sure to make this Study Guide much more educational and challenging.

Mary Beth Ray, executive editor, for allowing me to share my thoughts and ideas and putting them in this book. She is always there for me and helps keep me on track and on time!

Christopher Cleveland, development editor, for his patience, creativity, and support in making this book possible.

—John Rullan

Thanks to the Exploration development team for making me a part of the process of creating, editing, and improving the course that this book has been written to support. Knowing what you wanted for our students helped set the focus for this Study Guide.

Thanks to Mary Beth Ray and the whole team at Cisco Press for their patience and encouragement. Thanks Chris Cleveland for bearing with me during my learning curve.

—Sonya Coker

Contents at a Glance

Contents

Icons Used in This Book

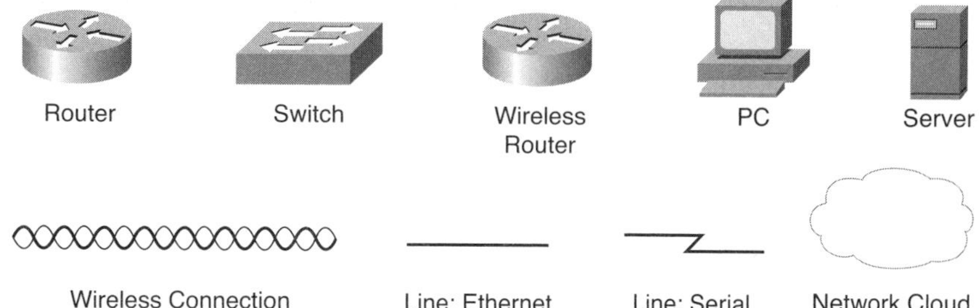

Command Syntax Conventions

The conventions used to present command syntax in this book are the same conventions used in the IOS Command Reference. The Command Reference describes these conventions as follows:

- **Bold** indicates commands and keywords that are entered literally as shown. In actual configuration examples and output (not general command syntax), bold indicates commands that the user enters (such as a **show** command).
- *Italic* indicates arguments for which you supply actual values.
- Vertical bars (|) separate alternative, mutually exclusive elements.
- Square brackets ([ ]) indicate an optional element.
- Braces ({ }) indicate a required choice.
- Braces within brackets ([{ }]) indicate a required choice within an optional element.

Introduction

The Cisco Networking Academy is a comprehensive e-learning program that provides students with Internet technology skills. A Networking Academy delivers web-based content, online assessment, student performance tracking, and hands-on labs to prepare students for industry-standard certifications. The CCNA curriculum includes four courses oriented around the topics on the Cisco Certified Network Associate (CCNA) certification.

Accessing the WAN, CCNA Exploration Labs and Study Guide is a supplement to your classroom and laboratory experience with the Cisco Networking Academy. To succeed on the exam and achieve your CCNA certification, you should do everything in your power to arm yourself with a variety of tools and training materials to support your learning efforts. This Labs and Study Guide is just such a collection of tools. Used to its fullest extent, it will help you acquire the knowledge and practice the skills associated with the content area of the CCNA Exploration Accessing the WAN course. Specifically, this book helps you work on these main areas:

- WAN technology concepts
- PPP concepts and configuration
- Frame Relay concepts and configuration
- Network security threats and mitigation techniques
- Access control list operation and configuration
- Broadband services and technologies
- Network Address Translation concepts and configuration
- DHCP operation and configuration
- IPv6 concepts
- Troubleshooting methodologies and tools

Labs and Study Guides similar to this one are also available for the other three courses: *Network Fundamentals, CCNA Exploration Labs and Study Guide*; *Routing Protocols and Concepts, CCNA Exploration Labs and Study Guide*; and *LAN Switching and Wireless, CCNA Exploration Labs and Study Guide*.

Audience for This Book

This book's main audience is anyone taking the CCNA Exploration Accessing the WAN course of the Cisco Networking Academy curriculum. Many Academies use this book as a required tool in the course, and other Academies recommend the Labs and Study Guides as an additional source of study and practice materials.

Goals and Methods

The most important goal of this book is to help you pass the CCNA exam (640-802). Passing this foundation exam means that you not only have the required knowledge of the technologies covered by the exam, but that you can plan, design, implement, operate, and troubleshoot these technologies. In other words, these exams are rigorously application-based. You can view the exam topics any time at **http://www.cisco.com/go/certifications**. The topics are divided into eight categories:

- Describe how a network works
- Configure, verify, and troubleshoot a switch with VLANs and interswitch communications
- Implement an IP addressing scheme and IP Services to meet network requirements in a medium-size Enterprise branch office network
- Configure, verify, and troubleshoot basic router operation and routing on Cisco devices
- Explain and select the appropriate administrative tasks required for a WLAN
- Identify security threats to a network, and describe general methods to mitigate those threats
- Implement, verify, and troubleshoot NAT and ACLs in a medium-size Enterprise branch office network
- Implement and verify WAN links

The Accessing the WAN course focuses on the third, fifth, sixth, seventh, and eighth topics.

The Study Guide portion of each chapter offers exercises that help you learn the Accessing the WAN concepts as well as the configurations crucial to your success as a CCNA exam candidate. Each chapter is slightly different and includes some or all of the following types of exercises:

- Vocabulary matching and completion
- Skill-building activities and scenarios
- Configuration scenarios
- Concept questions
- Internet research

In the configuration chapters, you'll find many Packet Tracer Activities that work with the Cisco Packet Tracer tool. Packet Tracer allows you to create networks, visualize how packets flow in the network, and use basic testing tools to determine whether the network would work. When you see this icon, you can use Packet Tracer with the listed file to perform a task suggested in this book. The activity files are available on this book's CD-ROM; Packet Tracer software, however, is available through the Academy Connection website. Ask your instructor for access to Packet Tracer.

The Labs and Activities portion of each chapter includes all the online Curriculum Labs, some additional supplemental labs that you can perform with Packet Tracer, and a Packet Tracer Skills Integration Challenge Activity. The Curriculum Labs are divided into three categories:

- **Basic**: The Basic Labs are procedural in nature and assume that you have no experience configuring the technologies that are the topic of the lab.
- **Challenge**: The Challenge Labs cover implementations and assume that you have a firm-enough grasp on the technologies to "go it alone." These labs often give you only a general requirement that you must implement fully without the details of each small step. In other words, you must use the knowledge and skills you gained in the chapter text, activities, and Basic Lab to successfully complete the Challenge Lab. Avoid the temptation to work through the Challenge Lab by flipping back through the Basic Lab when you are unsure of a command. Do not try to short-circuit your CCNA training. You need a deep understanding of CCNA knowledge and skills to ultimately be successful on the CCNA exam.
- **Troubleshooting**: The Troubleshooting Labs ask you to fix a broken network. These labs include corrupted scripts that you purposely load onto the routers. Then you use troubleshooting techniques to isolate problems and implement the solution. By the end of the lab, you should have a functional network with full end-to-end connectivity.

Most of the Hands-on Labs include Packet Tracer Companion Activities, in which you can use Packet Tracer to complete a simulation of the lab.

Each chapter ends with a Packet Tracer Skills Integration Challenge. These activities require you to pull together several skills learned from the chapter—as well as previous chapters and courses—to successfully complete one comprehensive exercise.

A Word About Packet Tracer

Packet Tracer is a self-paced, visual, interactive teaching and learning tool developed by Cisco. Lab activities are an important part of networking education. However, lab equipment can be a scarce resource. Packet Tracer provides a visual simulation of equipment and network processes to offset the challenge of limited equipment. Students can spend as much time as they like completing standard lab exercises through Packet Tracer, and they have the option to work from home. Although Packet Tracer is not a substitute for real equipment, it allows students to practice using a command-line interface. This "e-doing" capability is a fundamental component of learning how to configure routers and switches from the command line.

Packet Tracer version 4.*x* is available only to Cisco Networking Academies through the Academy Connection website.

How This Book Is Organized

Because the content of this book and the online curriculum is sequential, you should work through this book in order, beginning with Chapter 1.

The book covers the major topic headings in the same sequence as the online curriculum for the CCNA Exploration Accessing the WAN course. This book has eight chapters with the same numbers and names as the online course chapters.

If necessary, a chapter uses a single topology for the exercises in the Study Guide portion. This single topology allows for better continuity and easier understanding of switching commands, operations, and outputs. However, the topology is different from the one used in the online curriculum and the Companion Guide. A different topology affords you the opportunity to practice your knowledge and skills without just simply recording the information you find in the text.

- **Chapter 1, "Introduction to WANs"**: The exercises in the Study Guide portion of this chapter focus on LAN design concepts, including vocabulary and the three-layer hierarchical model. The Lab portion of the chapter includes a Basic Lab, a Challenge Lab, a Troubleshooting Lab, and a Packet Tracer Skills Integration Challenge activity.
- **Chapter 2, "PPP"**: The exercises in the first part of this chapter help you understand basic Ethernet and switching concepts, including building the MAC address table and collision and broadcast domains. Then the Packet Tracer exercises cover, in detail, how to configure a switch, including basic switch management and configuring switch security. The Lab portion of the chapter includes two Basic Labs, a Challenge Lab, and a Packet Tracer Skills Integration Challenge activity.

- **Chapter 3, "Frame Relay"**: The exercises in the first portion of this chapter focus on the concepts of VLANs, including benefits of VLANs and types of VLANs. The exercises then cover VLAN trunking concepts before moving into a section devoted to a VLAN and trunk configuration Packet Tracer exercise. The Lab portion of the chapter includes a Basic Lab, a Challenge Lab, a Troubleshooting Lab, and a Packet Tracer Skills Integration Challenge activity.
- **Chapter 4, "Network Security"**: The exercises in this chapter focus on key network security threats, tools, and mitigation techniques for Cisco routers. Configuration practice is provided for router security tasks. The Lab portion of the chapter includes a Basic Lab, a Challenge Lab, a Troubleshooting Lab, and a Packet Tracer Skills Integration Challenge activity.
- **Chapter 5, "ACLs"**: Exercises in this chapter focus on the concept of redundant LAN topologies, using STP and its variants to stop loops, and the commands to manipulate root bridge elections. The Lab portion of the chapter includes a Basic Lab, a Challenge Lab, a Troubleshooting Lab, and a Packet Tracer Skills Integration Challenge activity.
- **Chapter 6, "Teleworker Services"**: This short chapter focuses on how to configure inter-VLAN routing, including two Packet Tracer exercises. The Lab portion of the chapter includes a Basic Lab, a Challenge Lab, a Troubleshooting Lab, and a Packet Tracer Skills Integration Challenge activity.
- **Chapter 7, "IP Addressing Services"**: The exercises in this chapter include several matching term activities, multiple choice questions, fill-in-the-blank exercises, and concept questions that test your knowledge on DHCP and scaling IP addresses with the use of NAT and PAT. It also tests your knowledge of IPv6 and routing using the next generation of RIP. The Lab portion of this chapter includes all the online curriculum labs for DHCP and NAT as well as four additional Packet Tracer activities that test your knowledge and skills in complex configurations using DHCP, Static NAT, PAT, and double NAT. A Packet Tracer Skills Integration Challenge ties all of these concepts together.
- **Chapter 8, "Network Troubleshooting"**: The exercises in this chapter begin with wireless LAN concepts, including standards, operation, and security. The exercises then cover wireless configuration for LAN access using a Linksys WRT300N, including a Packet Tracer exercise. The Lab portion of the chapter includes a Basic Lab, a Challenge Lab, a Troubleshooting Lab, and a Packet Tracer Skills Integration Challenge activity.
- **Appendix, "How to Install SDM"**: Cisco Router and Security Device Manager (SDM) is used in the security labs for this course. This appendix describes and illustrates how to install SDM on a Cisco router or PC.

About the CD-ROM

Packet Tracer Activity

Packet Tracer Companion

Packet Tracer Challenge

The CD-ROM included with this book contains all the Packet Tracer Activity, Packet Tracer Companion, and Packet Tracer Challenge files that are referenced throughout the book, as indicated by the Packet Tracer Activity, Packet Tracer Companion, and Packet Tracer Challenge icons.

You can find updates to these files on this book's website at **http://www.ciscopress.com/title/9781587132018**.

About the Cisco Press Website for This Book

Cisco Press may provide additional content that you can access by registering your book at the ciscopress.com website. Becoming a member and registering is free, and you then gain access to exclusive deals on other resources from Cisco Press.

To register this book, go to **http://www.ciscopress.com/bookstore/register.asp** and log into your account, or create a free account if you do not have one already. Then enter this book's ISBN, located on the back cover.

After you register your book, it appears on your Account page under Registered Products, and you can access any online material from there.

CHAPTER 1

Introduction to WANs

The Study Guide portion of this chapter uses a combination of matching and multiple-choice question exercises to test your knowledge and skills of basic wide-area networks (WAN).

The Labs and Activities portion of this chapter includes all the online curriculum labs. The challenge labs are added to ensure that you have mastered the practical, hands-on skills needed to understand material learned in previous semesters of the Exploration curriculum.

Understanding a router's place and function in the Internet is necessary for moving further in your studies of WANs. You learned how routers communicate within an autonomous system using interior gateway protocols in the Routing Protocols and Concepts CCNA Exploration curriculum. This section tests your knowledge in WAN concepts, technologies, and connection types.

As you work through this chapter, use Chapter 1 in the *Accessing the WAN, CCNA Exploration Companion Guide* or use the corresponding Chapter 1 in the Accessing the WAN online curriculum for assistance.

Study Guide

Providing Integrated Services to the Enterprise

Up until now, the curriculum has focused on LANs, their devices, and how communication occurs using various protocols and services. The focal point of this chapter is on WANs, their devices, and how communication occurs using various encapsulation methods and WAN connections. This section discusses the importance of designing a WAN in a hierarchical structure to ensure a reliable network infrastructure. The Cisco Enterprise Architecture was designed to help a business's network grow as the company grows. This architecture assists network designers with a template to support data centers, branch offices, and teleworkers.

Review Question

You are an engineer in charge of a network that has grown in size from a LAN to a metropolitan-area network (MAN). The network now supports a campus network, multiple offsite offices, data centers, and teleworkers. How can the Cisco Enterprise Architecture help your network to grow parallel to your company? Write an essay of no more than 250 words. Make sure to include WAN connections, wireless mobility, and IP communications. To assist with your answer, use the curriculum and the following URL: **http://www.cisco.com/en/US/solutions/collateral/ns340/ns517/ns477/net_brochure0900aecd802843ce.pdf.**

Exercise 1-1: Browsing Through Internet Routing Tables

Lab exercises from previous chapters required you to configure various routing protocols to route traffic within an autonomous system. The size of the routing table varied, depending on the number of routers in each exercise. The number of locations a "real" company has will most often determine the actual size of their routing table. A static default route is used to route traffic to networks not listed in the routing table (autonomous system) and usually points to your ISP. An ISP's router, which routes traffic to the Internet, may have hundreds of thousands of routes in its routing table. Looking Glass Sites offers publicly available route servers to view current Internet routing tables.

1. Log on to **http://www.nanog.org/lookingglass.html**.
2. Under Routing-Related (Route Servers, etc.), you will notice that there are nine options to choose from. These are companies that allow access to their route servers. In this activity, you access them to view their routing tables.
3. Click the **ATT (US)** link.
4. HyperTerminal will open or a command box will appear asking you to enter a username (see Figure 1-1). Enter the username **rviews**. Note that the username is *not* misspelled.
5. The hostname of route server should appear in User Exec mode.

Figure 1-1 HyperTerminal Login

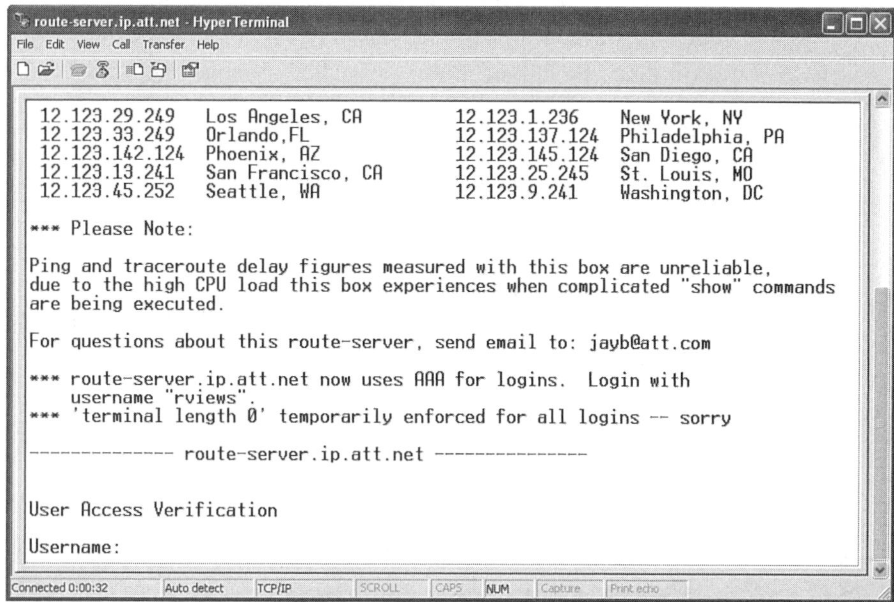

6. Use the **show ip route** command to display the current routing tables. Use the Enter key or spacebar to scroll through the table. The size of the table is "mind boggling!" Can you imagine troubleshooting a network of this magnitude?
7. Open another web browser and log on to **http://www.arin.net/index.shtml**. This site is the American Registry for Internet Numbers (ARIN). This site serves many important purposes; you are going to use it to determine who owns (leases) a particular network address.
8. The 206.107.185.0 network address was taken from the routing table. Enter this address into the Search WHOIS box in the upper-right corner (see Figure 1-2) and press **Enter**.

Figure 1-2 Checking the American Registry for Internet Numbers

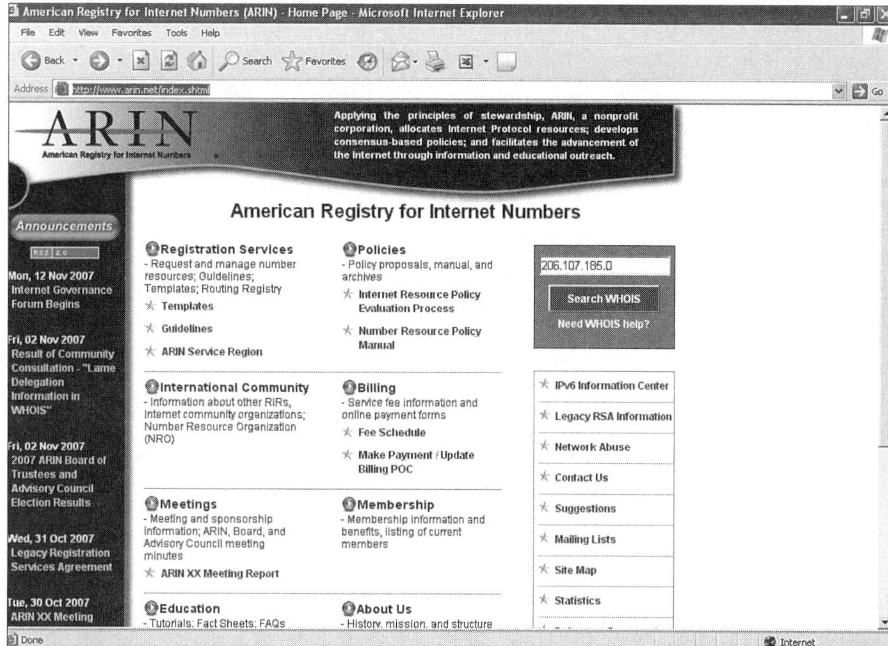

9. The company that leases this address happens to be another ISP. In this case, it belongs to Sprint (see Figure 1-3). Sprint then subleases the address to Rocky Mountain Communications, which in turn subleases the address to Pacific Press Publishing. What this means is that ATT and Sprint route Internet traffic through each other's networks.

Figure 1-3 ARIN WHOIS Results

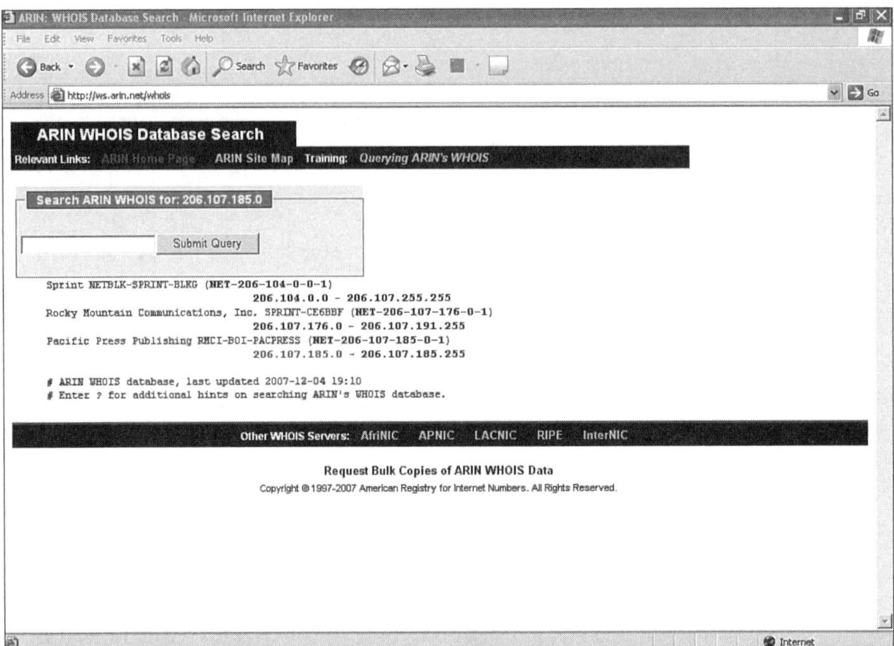

10. Look through the routing table again, and this time on a piece of paper write down several of the IP addresses listed. Go back to ARIN and place the address in the WHOIS box and see which other companies you will find that ATT routes traffic for.

Exercise 1-2: Tracing a Path Through the Internet

The Looking Glass route servers located at **http://www.nanog.org/lookingglass.html** can also be used to trace a path through the Internet from a route server back to your PC:

1. This time, let's use the CERFnet route server.
2. HyperTerminal will open or a command box will appear. No username or password is required.
3. Enter the **show ip int brief** command. This will display all the interfaces on a router. The only interface configured with an IP address is the Ethernet 1/0 interface with the 12.129.193.235 IP address (see Figure 1-4).
4. On your PC, open the command box using the **Start**, **Run** and enter **cmd**.
5. When the command box opens, enter **tracert 12.129.193.235**.
6. This will trace the path from your PC, through your network, through the Internet to the route server whose IP address you entered.

Figure 1-4 Displaying Router Interfaces

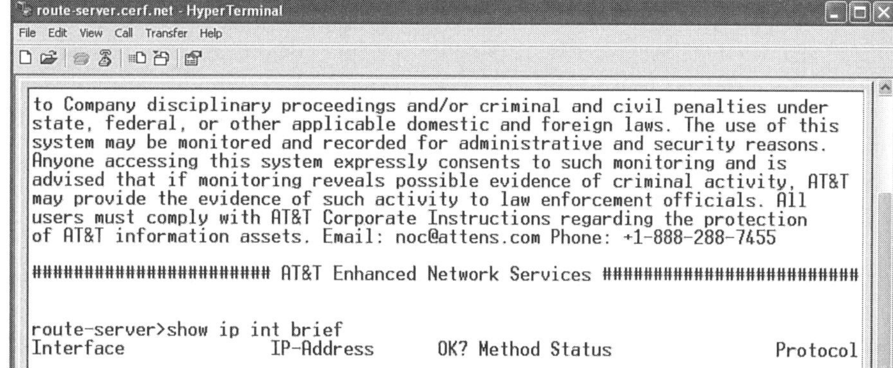

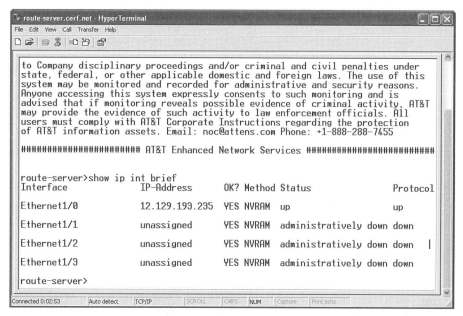

7. This will display the name of the domain and IP addresses of each router you pass through. Depending on where you are in the world will determine how many routers you pass through and the names of the domains in between (see Figure 1-5).

Figure 1-5 Displaying Router Domains and IP Addresses

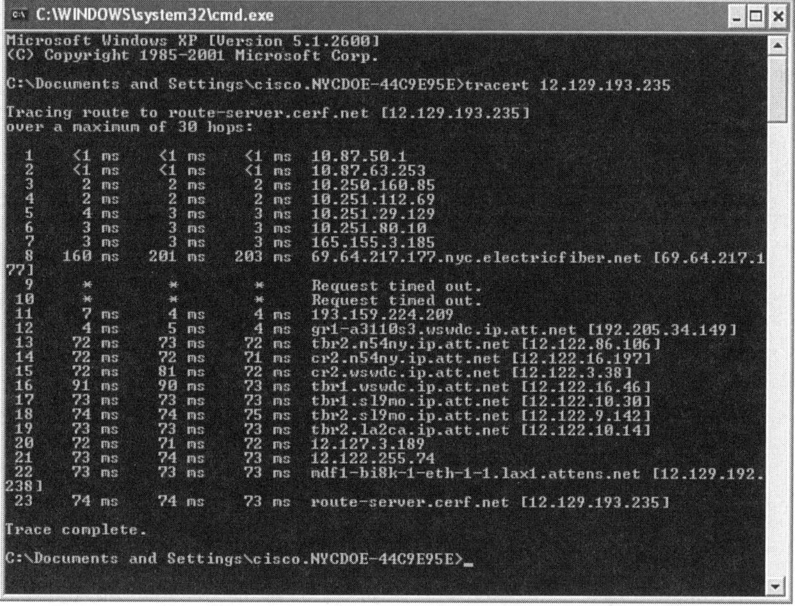

Tracert might not always work because the computers you are using might be behind a firewall that blocks Internet Control Message Protocol (ICMP) traffic. However, if you enter the command **traceroute www.cisco.com** on the CERFnet router you just connected to by Telnet, you see the same results.

WAN Technology Concepts

WANs typically function on Layers 1 and 2 of the OSI model. Layer 1 describes the interface between the DTE and DCE and uses various protocols based on connection speeds. The protocols determine the parameters that devices use to communicate. Layer 2 is concerned with how data is encapsulated before it crosses the WAN. HDLC, PPP, Frame Relay, and ATM are some of the more common data link layer protocols. It is important to remember that a router strips the LAN header from a frame and inserts a WAN header in its place before forwarding the packet across the WAN.

WANs also use several fundamental devices that differ from LANs. These devices are identified based on their location either on the customer or carrier side of the connection. customer premises equipment (CPE) and the data terminal equipment (DTE) are located on the customer side. The data communication equipment (DCE) is located on the carrier's side of the network. The local loop or subscriber line connects the customer at the demarc to the carrier's network. A router, CSU/DSU, modem, WAN switch, and access server are typical WAN devices.

Circuit switching such as ISDN is a dedicated circuit that requires call setup and termination. ISDN uses time-division multiplexing (TDM), which allows voice, video, and data to share the available bandwidth, allocating fixed timeslots for each. Packet switching does not require call setup and termination and generally uses leased lines that are always on. Frame Relay and X.25 are examples of packet-switched technologies. An ISP uses virtual circuits to connect multiple locations. These circuits are brought up on demand using Layer 2 identifiers called data link connection identifiers (DLCI).

Review Question

When a packet goes from a LAN to a WAN, the router strips the Layer 2 LAN header from the packet and replaces it with a Layer 2 WAN header. Explain the reason for doing this and how a WAN header differs from a LAN header.

____

____

____

____

WAN Connection Options

A network administrator has many connection options and speeds to choose from when connecting to an ISP. These options include analog dialup, ISDN, cable, DSL, Frame Relay, ATM, and leased lines such as a T1. Speeds can range from a 56-kbps dialup connection to an OC-768 fiber line of up to 39.81312 Gbps. Of course you realize the more bandwidth there is, the more money it will cost. A point-to-point leased line is an option instead of using a shared connection such as Frame Relay. Dedicated leased lines are more expensive, but dedicated output and limiting latency and delay far outweigh the cost. Analog dialup connections still exist; they are located where high-speed connectivity isn't yet available. Now throw in the cost factor, and analog connections are still a viable option for businesses to transmit small files.

ISDN BRI is twice the speed of dialup (128 kbps) and uses existing phone lines to transmit digital signals. It provides faster call setup and transfer of data than traditional analog dialup. ISDN uses two B channels for data transfer and a separate channel (D channel) for call setup and termination. ISDN PRI uses 23 B channels and provides 1.544 Mbps of throughput (the same as a T1).

Packet-switched connection options include X.25, Frame Relay, and ATM. X.25 operates on Layer 3 and uses switched virtual circuits (SVC) with low-speed connections and extensive error checking. Frame Relay is similar to X.25, but has several differences. It operates at Layer 2 only and uses permanent virtual circuits (PVC), which are identified using DLCIs.

ATM forwards data in fixed-length cells of 53 bytes. It requires 20 percent more bandwidth than Frame Relay and can support connection speeds of up to 622 Mbps (OC-12) and up.

DSL, cable, and wireless are broadband connection options. DSL is an always-on connection that uses existing phone lines to transport data. It provides customers with a dedicated line to the carrier's switch. Cable connections use coaxial cable from a carrier that provides cable television service. Most cable subscribers can now get their television, Internet, and phone service from their carrier through the same coaxial cable. Each signal is sent through the line using a different frequency.

Wireless technology is becoming more and more common, especially in home networks. Municipal WiFi and WiMax are some of the newer developments in broadband wireless. They are designed to travel longer distances and provide greater bandwidth speeds. Virtual private networks (VPN) enable businesses to create secured tunnels through an unsecure network called the Internet. Benefits of using VPN technology include scalability, cost savings, compatibility with broadband services, and of course, security. Metro Ethernet is a maturing technology that uses multilayer switches. These switches operate at Layers 2 and 3 and have routing capabilities. The connection type is Ethernet or fiber, but the use of a router is not necessary with this type of connection. It can provide faster connection speeds at lower costs through a switch that can route packets much faster than a router.

Review Questions

Take a survey of the network of the educational institution that you are currently enrolled in as a student. Ask the instructor or network administrator whether a tour of the school's main distribution facility (MDF) is possible. If the answer is no, ask whether you could ask the following questions without seeing it:

1. Which devices are used for WAN connectivity?

   ____

   ____

2. What type of connection do they use (T1–T3 Frame Relay, and so forth)?

   ____

   ____

3. Do they have offsite campuses, and if yes, how do they connect to them and at what speeds?

   ____

   ____

4. Do they monitor their WAN the same way they monitor their LAN?

   ____

   ____

Chapter Review Vocabulary Exercise: Matching

Match the definition on the right with the correct term on the left.

Field

- **a.** Hierarchical Network Model
- **b.** WAN
- **c.** Distribution layer
- **d.** Leased line
- **e.** Cable modem
- **f.** Demarcation point
- **g.** Data terminal equipment
- **h.** Campus
- **i.** Customer premises equipment
- **j.** ISDN
- **k.** CSU/DSU
- **l.** Central office
- **m.** Virtual private network (VPN)
- **n.** Multiplexing
- **o.** DLCI
- **p.** Frame Relay
- **q.** Data communications equipment
- **r.** Circuit switching
- **s.** DSL
- **t.** Packet switching

Definition

__ Subscriber devices and inside wiring

__ Secure remote connection through the Internet

__ Customer devices that pass the data from a customer network for transmission over the WAN

__ Permanent, shared, medium-bandwidth connectivity that carries voice and data traffic

__ Always-on connection that uses existing phone lines

__ A dedicated circuit between nodes

__ Allows the transmission of data across immense geographic remoteness

__ The location in a building that separates the customer's equipment with the service provider's equipment

__ Preestablished WAN connection

__ Provides an always-on connection that uses coaxial cable

__ High-level tool for designing a reliable network infrastructure

__ Terminates the digital signal and ensures connection integrity

__ A device that sits between the data terminal equipment and transmission circuit

__ A network that consists of multiple LANs or subnetworks each devoted to a separate department

__ Aggregates WAN connections at the edge of the campus

__ Routes packets over a shared network

__ Facility or building where local telephone cables link communication lines through a system of switches and other equipment

__ Identifies a predetermined route for a packet

__ Used as a backup if the leased line fails

__ A method for sending multiple signals along a single communication path

Chapter Review Multiple-Choice Questions

Choose the best answer for each of the questions that follow.

1. Which packet-switched connection uses low-capacity speeds but offers error correction?

A. Frame Relay

B. X.25

C. ISDN

D. ATM

E. PSTN

2. Which of the following are characteristics of the core layer of a hierarchical design? (Choose all that apply.)

A. Rapid convergence

B. Aggregates WAN connections at the edge of the campus

C. High availability

D. Connects users

E. Connects remote sites

F. Fast packet switching

3. Which packet-switched technology use cells that are always a fixed length of 53 bytes?

A. Frame Relay

B. x.25

C. ISDN

D. ATM

4. Which of the following describes virtual private networks?

A. An encrypted connection between public networks over the Internet

B. An encrypted connection between private networks over a public network

C. An encrypted connection between public networks over a private network

D. An encrypted network between a private network using the Internet

5. Which of the following best describes an SVC?

A. Permanently established circuit

B. Configured by the service provider

C. Decreases bandwidth and increases costs

D. Releases the circuit when done which results in reduced costs

6. Which three are WAN physical layer standards?

A. EIA/TIA 449

B. X.21 male

C. X.25 female

D. V.35

E. IEEE 802.11G

7. What are devices that put data on the local loop called? (Choose all that apply.)

   A. Data circuit-terminating equipment

   B. Data communications equipment

   C. Data connection equipment

   D. Data terminal equipment

8. Which of the following best describes WAN physical layer protocols?

   A. Defines how data is encapsulated

   B. Converts packets into frames

   C. Provides flow control

   D. Provides functional connections to the ISP

9. Which of the following are examples of packet-switched communication links? (Choose all that apply.)

   A. ATM

   B. ISDN

   C. PSTN

   D. X.25

   E. Frame Relay

   F. POTS

10. Which of the following uses two bearer channels and one delta channel for sending data over existing phone lines?

    A. BRI

    B. PRI

    C. PSTN

    D. POTS

11. Which of the following devices converts analog signals to digital signals and vice versa?

    A. Modem

    B. CSU/DSU

    C. Access server

    D. WAN switch

    E. CPE

12. Which of the following authorities define WAN access standards? (Choose all that apply.)

    A. International Organization for Standardization

    B. Internetwork Operating Systems

    C. American Registry for Internet Numbers

    D. Telecommunication Industry Association

    E. Electronic Industries Alliance

    F. Electrical Industries Association

13. Which of the following are benefits of using VPNs? (Choose all that apply)

A. Eliminates the need for expensive dedicated WAN links
B. Uses advanced encryption and authentication protocols
C. Supports DSL and cable
D. Cost savings using ISDN and PSTN connections
E. Easy to add new users
F. Cost savings using PVCs

14. Which of the following are the three major characteristics of WANS?

A. Use serial connections
B. Require the services of telephone companies
C. Connect remote devices that are on the same LAN
D. Connect devices on remote LANs
E. Use the Internet rather than a carrier

15. What is another name for the local loop? (Choose two.)

A. Subscriber line
B. Demarc
C. Last mile
D. Telecommunications carrier signal line

16. The unlicensed radio spectrum is available to anyone who has which two things?

A. License
B. Wireless router
C. Wireless device
D. Security access code
E. Permission to access the spectrum

17. Which two things best describe a router's role in a WAN?

A. A multiport internetworking device used in carrier networks
B. Can support multiple telecommunications interfaces
C. Concentrates dial-in and dial-out user communications
D. Converts carrier-line frames into frames that the LAN can interpret
E. Needs a CSU/DSU or modem to connect to the POP

18. Which of the following describe the characteristics of a point-to-point link? (Choose all that apply.)

A. Provides a preestablished LAN communications path to a remote site
B. Provides a preestablished WAN communications path to a remote site
C. Uses leased lines to provide a dedicated connection
D. Uses leased lines to provide a temporary connection

19. Which layer of the OSI reference model does MPLS reside on?

A. Layer 1

B. Layer 2

C. Layer 3

D. Between Layers 2 and 3

20. Which of the following fields can be found in LAN and WAN headers? (Choose all that apply.)

A. Enter

B. FCS

C. Data

D. Flags

E. Protocol

F. Control

Labs and Activities

Lab 1-1: Challenge Review Lab (1.4.1)

Upon completion of this lab, you will be able to

- Cable a network according to the topology diagram in Figure 1-6.
- Erase the startup configuration and reload a router to the default state.
- Perform basic configuration tasks on a router.
- Configure and activate interfaces.
- Configure Spanning Tree Protocol.
- Configure trunk ports on all switches.
- Configure VTP servers and client.
- Configure VLANS on the switches.
- Configure RIP routing on all the routers.
- Configure OSPF routing on all routers.
- Configure EIGRP routing on all the routers.

Figure 1-6 shows the network topology for this lab, and Table 1-1 provides the IP addresses, subnet masks, and default gateways (where applicable) for all devices in the topology.

Figure 1-6 Network Topology for Lab 1-1

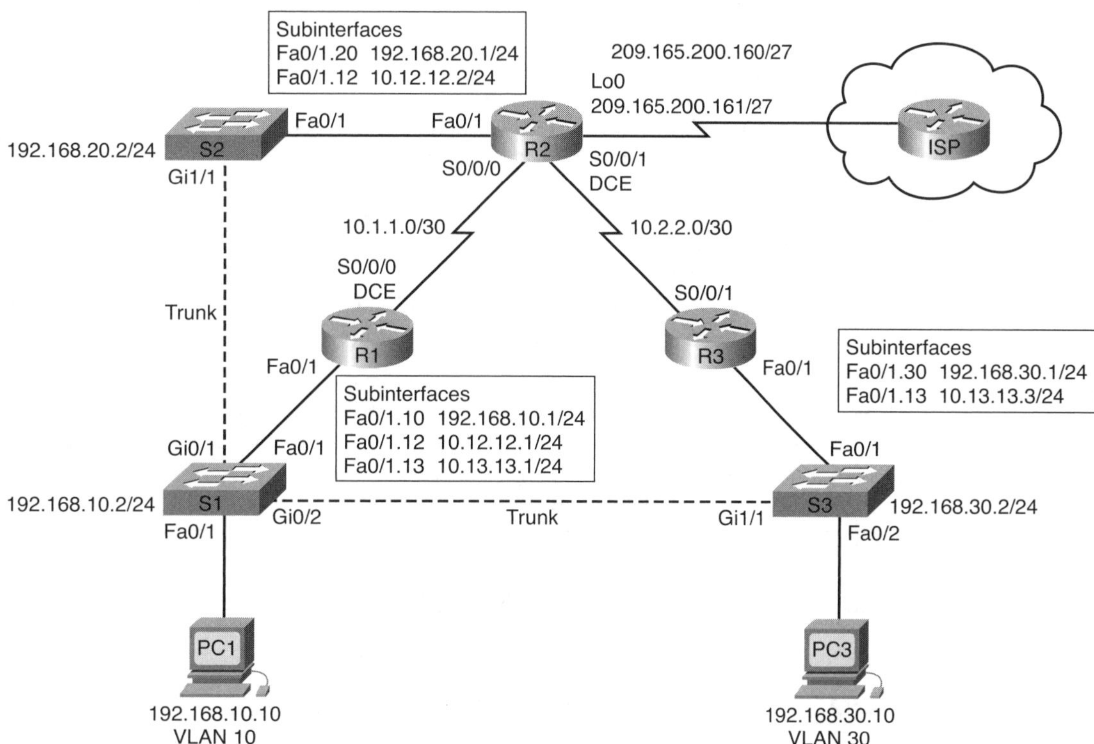

Table 1-1 Lab 1-1 Addressing Table

Device	Interface	IP Address	Subnet Mask	Default Gateway
R1	Fa0/1	N/A	N/A	N/A
	Fa0/1.10	192.168.10.1	255.255.255.0	N/A
	Fa0/1.12	10.12.12.1	255.255.255.0	N/A
	Fa0/1.13	10.13.13.1	255.255.255.0	N/A
	S0/0/0	10.1.1.1	255.255.255.252	N/A
R2	Fa0/1	N/A	N/A	N/A
	Fa0/1.12	10.12.12.2	255.255.255.0	N/A
	Fa0/1.20	192.168.20.1	255.255.255.0	N/A
	S0/0/0	10.1.1.2	255.255.255.252	N/A
	S0/0/1	10.2.2.1	255.255.255.252	N/A
	Lo0	209.165.200.161	255.255.255.224	N/A
R3	Fa0/1	N/A	N/A	N/A
	Fa0/1.13	10.13.13.3	255.255.255.0	N/A
	Fa0/1.30	192.168.30.1	255.255.255.0	N/A
	S0/0/1	10.2.2.2	255.255.255.252	N/A
S1	VLAN10	192.168.10.2	255.255.255.0	192.168.10.1
S2	VLAN20	192.168.20.2	255.255.255.0	192.168.20.1
S3	VLAN30	192.168.30.2	255.255.255.0	192.168.30.1
PC1	NIC	192.168.10.10	255.255.255.0	192.168.10.1
PC3	NIC	192.168.30.10	255.255.255.0	192.168.30.1

Scenario

In this lab, you review basic routing and switching concepts. Try to do as much on your own as possible. Refer back to previous material when you cannot proceed on your own.

Note: Configuring three separate routing protocols (RIP, OSPF, and EIGRP) to route the same network is emphatically *not* a best practice. It should be considered a worst practice and is not something that would be done in a production network. It is done here so that you can review the major routing protocols before proceeding, and so that you can see a dramatic illustration of the concept of administrative distance.

Task 1: Prepare the Network

Step 1. Cable a network similar to the one in Figure 1-6.

Step 2. Clear any existing configurations on the routers.

Task 2: Perform Basic Device Configurations

Configure the R1, R2, and R3 routers and the S1, S2, S3 switches according to the following guidelines:

- Configure the hostname.
- Disable DNS lookup.
- Configure an EXEC mode password.
- Configure a message-of-the-day banner.
- Configure a password for console connections.
- Configure synchronous logging.
- Configure a password for vty connections.

Task 3: Configure and Activate Serial and Ethernet Addresses

Step 1. Configure interfaces on R1, R2, and R3.

Step 2. Verify IP addressing and interfaces.

Step 3. Configure the Management VLAN interface on S1, S2, and S3.

Step 4. Configure the PC1 and PC3 Ethernet interfaces.

Step 5. Test connectivity between each PC and their default gateway.

Task 4: Configure STP

Step 1. Configure S1 to always be root.

Step 2. Verify that S1 is root.

Task 5: Configure VTP

Step 1. Configure S1 as the VTP server and create a domain name and password.

Step 2. Configure S2 and S3 as VTP clients as assign domain names and passwords.

Step 3. Verify the configuration.

Task 6: Configure VLANs

Step 1. Configure S1 with VLANs.

Step 2. Verify that S2 and S3 received VLAN configurations from S1.

Step 3. Assign ports to the appropriate VLANs.

Task 7: Configure RIP Routing

Step 1. Configure RIP routing on R1, R2, and R3.

Step 2. Test connectivity with ping.

Step 3. Verify the routing table.

Task 8: Configure OSPF Routing

Step 1. Configure OSPF routing on R1, R2, and R3.

Step 2. Verify that OSPF routes have replaced RIP routes because of lower administrative distance.

How are the routing decisions different now that OSPF is running?

____

____

____

____

Step 3. Verify that RIP is still running.

Task 9: Configure EIGRP Routing

Step 1. Configure EIGRP routing on R1, R2, and R3.

Step 2. Verify that EIGRP routes have replaced OSPF routes because of lower administrative distance.

Step 3. Verify that OSPF is still running.

Task 10: Document the Router Configurations

Task 11: Clean Up

Erase the configurations and reload the routers. Disconnect and store the cabling. For PC hosts that are normally connected to other networks (such as the school LAN or to the Internet), reconnect the appropriate cabling and restore the TCP/IP settings.

Packet Tracer Exercise: Comprehensive WAN Fundamentals

Open the file lsg04-101.pka on the CD-ROM that accompanies this book to perform a comprehensive activity using Packet Tracer. Remember, however, that Packet Tracer is not a substitute for a hands-on lab experience with real equipment.

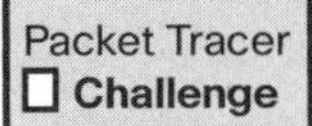

Packet Tracer Skills Integration Challenge

Open file LSG04-PTSkills1.pka on the CD-ROM that accompanies this book to perform this exercise using Packet Tracer. Upon completion of this skills integration challenge, you will be able to

- Configure static and default routing.
- Add and connect the BRANCH router.
- Add and connect the switches.
- Add and connect the PCs.
- Perform basic device configuration.

- Configure OSPF routing.
- Configure STP.
- Configure VTP.
- Configure VLANs.
- Verify end-to-end connectivity.

This activity covers many of the skills you acquired in the first three Exploration courses. Skills include building a network; applying an addressing scheme; configuring routing, VLANs, STP, and VTP; and testing connectivity. You should review those skills before proceeding. In addition, this activity provides you an opportunity to review the basics of the Packet Tracer program. Packet Tracer is integrated throughout this course. You must know how to navigate the Packet Tracer environment to complete this course. Use the tutorials if you need a review of Packet Tracer fundamentals. The tutorials are located in the Packet Tracer Help menu.

Note: This activity contains more than 150 assessed items. Therefore, you might not see the completion percentage increase every time you enter a command. The user EXEC password is **cisco**, and the privileged EXEC password is **class**.

Figure 1-7 shows the network topology for this challenge, and Table 1-2 provides the IP addresses, subnet masks, and default gateways (where applicable) for all devices in the topology.

Figure 1-7 Network Topology for Skills Integration Challenge

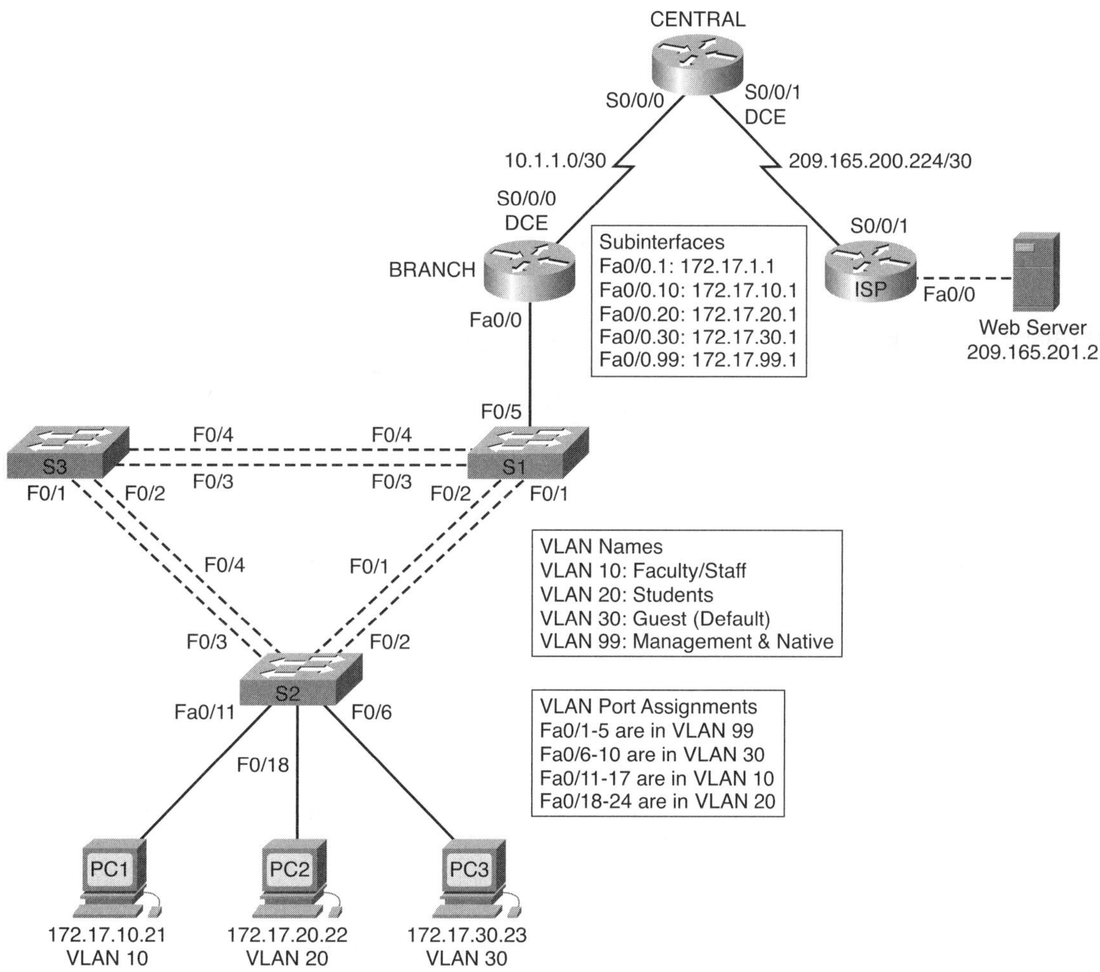

Table 1-2 Skills Integration Challenge Addressing Table

Device	Interface	IP Address	Subnet Mask	Default Gateway
ISP	S0/0/1	209.165.200.225	255.255.255.252	N/A
	Fa0/0	209.165.201.1	255.255.255.252	N/A
CENTRAL	S0/0/0	10.1.1.2	255.255.255.252	N/A
	S0/0/1	209.165.200.226	255.255.255.252	N/A
BRANCH	S0/0/0	10.1.1.1	255.255.255.252	N/A
	Fa0/0.1	172.17.1.1	255.255.255.0	N/A
	Fa0/0.10	172.17.10.1	255.255.255.0	N/A
	Fa0/0.20	172.17.20.1	255.255.255.0	N/A
	Fa0/0.30	172.17.30.1	255.255.255.0	N/A
	Fa0/0.99	172.17.99.1	255.255.255.0	N/A
S1	VLAN 99	172.17.99.11	255.255.255.0	172.17.99.1
S2	VLAN 99	172.17.99.12	255.255.255.0	172.17.99.1
S3	VLAN 99	172.17.99.13	255.255.255.0	172.17.99.1
PC1	NIC	172.17.10.21	255.255.255.0	172.17.10.1
PC2	NIC	172.17.20.22	255.255.255.0	172.17.20.1
PC3	NIC	172.17.30.23	255.255.255.0	172.17.30.1
Web Server	NIC	209.165.201.2	255.255.255.252	209.165.201.1

Task 1: Configure Static and Default Routing

Step 1. Configure static routing from ISP to CENTRAL.

Refer to Figure 1-7 to configure ISP with static routes to all networks. Each network is reachable via S0/0/1 from ISP. Use the exit interface parameter to configure static routes to the following networks:

- 10.1.1.0/30
- 172.17.1.0/24
- 172.17.10.0/24
- 172.17.20.0/24
- 172.17.30.0/24
- 172.17.99.0/24

Step 2. Configure default routing from CENTRAL to ISP.

Configure a default route on CENTRAL using the exit interface parameter to send all default traffic to ISP.

Step 3. Test connectivity to the Web Server.

CENTRAL should now be able to successfully ping the Web Server at 209.165.201.2.

Step 4. Check the results.

Your completion percentage should be 4 percent. If not, click **Check Results** to see which required components are not yet completed.

Task 2: Add and Connect the BRANCH Router

Step 1. Add the BRANCH router.

Click **Custom Made Devices** and add an 1841 router to the topology. Use the Config tab to change the display name and hostname to BRANCH. Display names are case-sensitive.

Note: Using the Physical tab, turn off the power on the router and add the WIC-2T module by clicking the WIC-2T tab and dragging the module picture to Slot 0 on the router. Then, turn the power back on.

Step 2. Connect BRANCH to CENTRAL.

- Connect the BRANCH router's S0/0/0 interface (DCE) to the CENTRAL router's S0/0/0 interface (DTE).
- Configure the link between BRANCH and CENTRAL.
- Use a clock rate of 64000 bps.

Step 3. Check the results.

Your completion percentage should be 8 percent. If not, click **Check Results** to see which required components are not yet completed.

Task 3: Add and Connect the Switches

Refer to the topology illustrated in Figure 1-7 for placement, switch names, and interfaces.

Step 1. Using the 2960 model, add the S1, S2, and S3 switches.

Step 2. Connect S1 to BRANCH.

Step 3. Connect S1 to S2.

Step 4. Connect S1 to S3.

Step 5. Connect S2 to S3.

Step 6. Check the results.

Your completion percentage should be 28 percent. If not, click **Check Results** to see which required components are not yet completed.

Task 4: Add and Connect the PCs

Use the interfaces specified in Figure 1-7 and Table 1-2.

Step 1. Add PC1, PC2, and PC3.

Step 2. Connect PC1, PC2, and PC3 to S2.

Step 3. Configure PCs.

Step 4. Check the results.

Your completion percentage should be 41 percent. If not, click **Check Results** to see which required components are not yet completed.

Task 5: Perform Basic Device Configuration

Step 1. Configure the basic commands on BRANCH, S1, S2, and S3.

Basic configuration commands should include the hostname, EXEC password, banner, console, and vty lines.

Step 2. Configure Fast Ethernet subinterfaces on BRANCH.

Remember to configure 802.1q encapsulation and VLAN settings for each subinterface. The third octet for each subinterface address corresponds to VLAN number. For example, subinterface Fa0/0.30 uses the IP address 172.17.**30**.1 and belongs to VLAN 30. VLAN 99 is the native VLAN.

Step 3. Configure the switches.

- Configure the VLAN 99 interface.
- Configure the default gateway.

Step 4. Check the results.

Your completion percentage should be 59 percent. If not, click **Check Results** to see which required components are not yet completed.

Task 6: Configure OSPF Routing

Step 1. Configure OSPF on CENTRAL and propagate the default route.

- Configure OSPF using the process ID 1.
- Use OSPF Area 0.
- Add only the network shared with BRANCH.
- Propagate the default route to OSPF neighbors.

Step 2. Configure OSPF on BRANCH.

- Configure OSPF using the process ID 1.
- Use OSPF Area 0.
- Add all networks that BRANCH routes.

Step 3. Disable OSPF updates on the appropriate interfaces on both CENTRAL and BRANCH.

Disable OSPF updates on all LAN interfaces and to ISP.

Step 4. Test connectivity.

BRANCH should be able to successfully ping Web Server at 209.165.201.2

Step 5. Check the results.

Your completion percentage should be 69 percent. If not, click **Check Results** to see which required components are not yet completed.

Task 7: Configure STP

Step 1. Ensure that S1 is the root bridge.

Set priorities to 4096.

Step 2. Verify that S1 is the root bridge.

Step 3. Check the results.

Your completion percentage should be 72 percent. If not, click **Check Results** to see which required components are not yet completed.

Task 8: Configure VTP

Step 1. Configure the VTP mode on all three switches.

Configure S1 as the server. Configure S2 and S3 as clients.

Step 2. Configure the VTP domain name on all three switches.

Use **CCNA** as the VTP domain name.

Step 3. Configure the VTP domain password on all three switches.

Use **cisco** as the VTP domain password.

Step 4. Check the results.

Your completion percentage should be 77 percent. If not, click **Check Results** to see which required components are not yet completed.

Task 9: Configure Trunking

Step 1. Configure trunking on S1, S2, and S3.

Configure the appropriate interfaces in trunking mode and assign VLAN 99 as the native VLAN.

Step 2. Check the results.

Your completion percentage should be 94 percent. If not, click **Check Results** to see which required components are not yet completed.

Task 10: Configure VLANs

Step 1. Configure S1 with VLANs.

VLAN names are case sensitive. Add and name the four VLANs using the following specifications:

- VLAN 10: Faculty/Staff
- VLAN 20: Students
- VLAN 30: Guest(Default)
- VLAN 99: Management&Native

Step 2. Verify that S2 and S3 received VLAN configurations from S1.

Step 3. Configure the ports attached to PCs on S2 for access, and assign each port the appropriate VLAN.

Step 4. Check the results.

Your completion percentage should be 100 percent. If not, click **Check Results** to see which required components are not yet completed.

Task 11: Verify End-to-End Connectivity

Step 1. Verify that PC1, PC2, and PC3 can ping each other.

Step 2. Verify that PC1, PC2, and PC3 can ping the Web Server.

CHAPTER 2

PPP

The Study Guide portion of this chapter uses a combination of matching, fill-in-the-blank, multiple-choice, and open-ended question exercises to test your knowledge of Point-to-Point Protocol (PPP) and authentication protocols such as Password Authentication Protocol (PAP) and Challenge Handshake Authentication Protocol (CHAP).

The Labs portion of this chapter includes all the online curriculum labs. The challenge and troubleshooting labs are added to ensure that you have mastered the practical, hands-on skills needed to understand PPP and authentication configurations.

As you work through this chapter, use Chapter 2 in the *Assessing the WAN, CCNA Exploration Companion Guide* or use the corresponding Chapter 2 in the Assessing the WAN online curriculum for assistance.

Study Guide

Serial Point-to-Point Links

Although parallel connections send bits across more lines than serial connections, serial connections have higher data rates and are more suitable for connecting to a WAN. Crosstalk is not as significant with serial cables, allowing WANs to extend to greater distances. The RS-232, V.35, and HSSI are common serial communication standards that use different signaling methods. The V.35 can be found in most Cisco Academy labs and is identified by the male and female pin connections identifying the DTE and DCE connections. An HSSI can support up to 52 Mbps with a maximum cable length of 50 feet. Serial connections can transmit only 1 bit over a link at a time. Time-division multiplexing (TDM) can be used to organize the data transmission through the use of channels. TDM divides the bandwidth into multiple channels and gives each channel a different timeslot. This allows TDM to increase the capacity of a link while allowing data from multiple sources to transmit simultaneously. In other words, this will allow your voice, video, and data to be sent across the link at the same time. However, the disadvantage to this is that if a device does not have any data to send the timeslot remains empty and is not filled by other sources. Statistical time-division multiplexing (STDM) allows channels to compete for empty timeslots when a source has no data to send at a particular period of time. This provides more efficient use of bandwidth and allows empty timeslots to be filled by various sources. SONET and ISDN are examples of WAN technologies that use TDM. The demarcation point is where a carrier brings their line into a customer site. An example of this is in the basement of a house where the telephone company installs the jack for the phone lines. This marks the point where the two networks join and is where responsibility changes hands when a failure occurs. The line leading up to the jack is the telco's responsibility. The lines leading to and including all the jacks in your house are your responsibility. The demarcation point is where the DTE at the customer site connects to DCE, commonly a modem or CSU/DSU on the telco network. WAN serial connections use several connection options such as a null modem cable. This is used when connecting two DTE devices. Just like a LAN, WANs require data to be encapsulated into frames before they are sent across a link. High-Level Data Link Control (HDLC), PPP, Serial Line Internet Protocol (SLIP), and Frame Relay are some of the more common WAN encapsulation protocols, just to name a few. SLIP, at one point, was the default encapsulation protocol on Cisco synchronous serial interfaces and has since been replaced by HDLC. HDLC is a vendor-specific protocol, but Cisco has allowed other vendors to implement their version, which allows more than one protocol to operate on the same serial line. The Protocol field is used to identify the protocol type encapsulated within the frame. HDLC is configured on the interface using the following command:

```
Router(config-if)# encapsulation hdlc
```

One important note is that for both routers to communicate, the same encapsulation protocol must be used at the other end.

Review Questions

1. A V.25 DTE cable can be used to connect the customer's serial interface to the telco's CSU/DSU. Newer CSU/DSUs also support different connect types such as a Category 5 patch cord. If this were true, which type of WAN interface card (WIC) would be needed to connect a patch cord from the router to the CSU/DSU?

____

____

2. A point-to-point connection with different vendor routers using HDLC as the encapsulation type cannot establish a connection. When you change the encapsulation type on both routers to PPP, the connection is established. Why did the routers establish a connection with PPP and not with HDLC?

____

____

____

3. You are troubleshooting a connection from a remote location and notice the serial interface is down. What command will tell you whether the router is receiving a clock rate?

____

4. You enter the **show ip interface brief** command and notice that the status of an interface is as follows: Serial 0/0/0 is up, line protocol down (looped). How would you troubleshoot this issue?

____

____

____

PPP Concepts

HDLC is used when connecting two devices manufactured from the same vendor. PPP is an open standard encapsulation that is used in a multivendor environment. It can be used across synchronous or asynchronous lines, high-speed serial interfaces, and ISDN. PPP provides link configuration, link-quality testing, error detection, and authentication for security. On top of the physical layer, PPP uses Link Control Protocol (LCP) to establish, configure, and test the data-link connection before data can be sent. When configured, link parameters are negotiated here and may include the negotiation of bandwidth, maximum transmission unit (MTU), compression, and authentication. Network Control Protocol (NCP) is used to establish and configure the different network layer protocols that can cross the link at the same time. PPP uses a separate NCP for every network layer protocol crossing the link. When there is no more data being sent across the link, LCP terminates the connection.

Vocabulary Exercise: Matching

Match the definition on the right with the correct term on the left.

Field

- **a.** Address field
- **b.** Control
- **c.** Establishment Phase 1
- **d.** Protocol
- **e.** Multilink
- **f.** HDLC
- **g.** Synchronous serial
- **h.** Datagram
- **i.** Authentication
- **j.** LCP
- **k.** Link quality
- **l.** Establishment Phase 2
- **m.** Algorithm
- **n.** FCS
- **o.** Code field
- **p.** NCP
- **q.** Flag
- **r.** Establishment Phase 3
- **s.** Multiplexing
- **t.** Compression

Definition

__ Value is set to 0x7E.

__ 0 or more bytes that makes up the datagram for the protocol in the Protocol field.

__ Data.

__ Requires a timing mechanism.

__ Link quality.

__ Not used by PPP.

__ Value is set to 0xFF.

__ Checksum.

__ NCP brings up network layer protocols.

__ Combines two or more channels to increase WAN bandwidth.

__ Where multiple signals or data streams are combined into one signal over a shared media.

__ LCP must first open the connection and then configure options.

__ Determines whether line quality is sufficient to bring up network layer protocols.

__ PAP and CHAP.

__ Establishes and negotiates connection.

__ Rule or process for arriving at a solution.

__ Identifies the network layer payload.

__ Identifies the type of LCP packet.

__ Stacker and Predictor.

__ Vendor-specific protocol.

Configuring PPP

PPP is configured with the Router(config-if)# **encapsulation ppp** command. Optional PPP configuration parameters include authentication, compression, multilink, and callback. Authentication uses PAP or CHAP and creates a secure connection between communicating devices. Compression options are Stacker and Predictor. Stacker is more CPU intensive, whereas Predictor is memory intensive. Error detection identifies fault conditions, and Link Quality Monitoring (LQM) monitors line quality. LQM is enabled on an interface using the Router(config-if)# **ppp quality** *percentage* command. If the quality of the link drops below the percentage configured, the router shuts down the interface. Magic numbers are used to detect loops. If a router sees its own magic number in a packet, the line is looped. A router may shut down a link if a loop is detected. If it sees its peer's magic number, the connection is good. The **ppp multilink** command fragments packets across multiple lines. This is similar to the way routers load balance across equal-cost paths, except multilink breaks the frame into fragments and then reassembles it at the other end of the link. PPP callback creates a client/server relationship between communicating devices. It controls access between routers by requiring a router to provide authentication information to a remote router. When the information is checked and determined to be authentic, the remote router (server) calls back the dialing router (client) and establishes a connection.

Review Questions

1. You are the network technician of a company that configured an ISDN connection using PPP as the encapsulation type. When testing the network, you notice that data is being sent across only one of the two ISDN B channels. What PPP configuration command will fragment data across both channels?

   ____

2. Explain the purpose of Link Quality Monitoring (LQM) when configured on a serial interface running PPP.

   ____

   ____

3. You are troubleshooting two routers that will not establish a PPP connection. How will the **debug ppp negotiation** and the **debug ppp authentication** commands assist you?

   ____

   ____

   ____

   ____

Configuring PPP with Authentication

PPP authentication verifies the identity of a router that is trying to establish a connection. PPP supports two authentication protocols: PAP and CHAP. PAP uses a two-way handshake to identify itself to a peer router. Although PAP uses a username and password for authentication, it is not considered a secure authentication protocol. When authentication occurs, the passwords are sent across the link in plain text, and PAP does not protect against playback or repeated trial-and-error attacks. PAP uses bidirectional authentication, meaning each side sends an authentication request and waits to receive an authentication acknowledgment. CHAP uses a three-way handshake to identify authenticating peer routers. CHAP is a secure authentication protocol that uses message digest algorithm 5 (MD5) to encrypt the passwords, which are sent randomly across the link. This protects against playback because each hash is unique. Two-way authentication can be used if the same "secret" is set for mutual authentication. To configure PPP authentication on the interface of the WAN link, use the following command:

```
Router(config-if)# ppp authentication [chap ¦ chap/pap ¦ pap/chap ¦ pap]
```

The configuration options are as follows:

- **chap**: The router authenticates using CHAP only.
- **chap/pap**: The router authenticates using CHAP first; if authentication is not successful, it tries using PAP.
- **pap/chap**: The router authenticates using PAP first; if authentication is not successful, it tries using CHAP.
- **pap**: The router authenticates using PAP only.

The **debug ppp authentication** command verifies whether authentication was successful and, if not, the reasons for the failure.

Review Questions

1. Explain the PAP authentication two-way handshake.

____

____

____

____

2. You notice that a router is configured to use CHAP/PAP as the authentication method. Explain how a router will authenticate using this method.

____

____

3. When configuring a router to use PAP or CHAP as the authentication protocol, what should the username and password be configured as?

____

____

Chapter Review: Multiple-Choice Questions

Note: These questions are identical to the questions in Chapter 1, except #15.

Choose the best answer for each of the questions that follow.

1. Which packet-switched connection uses low-capacity speeds but offers error correction?

A. Frame Relay

B. X.25

C. ISDN

D. ATM

E. PSTN

2. Which of the following are characteristics of the core layer of a hierarchical design? (Choose all that apply.)

A. Rapid convergence
B. Aggregates WAN connections at the edge of the campus
C. High availability
D. Connects users
E. Connects remote sites
F. Fast packet switching

3. Which packet-switched technology uses cells that are always a fixed length of 53 bytes?

A. Frame Relay
B. x.25
C. ISDN
D. ATM

4. Which of the following describes virtual private networks?

A. An encrypted connection between public networks over the Internet
B. An encrypted connection between private networks over a public network
C. An encrypted connection between public networks over a private network
D. An encrypted network between a private network using the Internet

5. Which of the following best describes an SVC?

A. Permanently established circuit
B. Configured by the service provider
C. Decreases bandwidth and increases costs
D. Releases the circuit when done, which results in reduced costs

6. Which three of the following are WAN physical layer standards?

A. EIA/TIA 449
B. X.21 Male
C. X.25 female
D. V.35
E. IEEE 802.11G

7. Devices that put data on the local loop are called _______________? (Choose all that apply.)

A. Data circuit-terminating equipment
B. Data communications equipment
C. Data connection equipment
D. Data terminal equipment

8. Which of the following best describes WAN physical layer protocols?

A. Defines how data is encapsulated
B. Converts packets into frames
C. Provides flow control
D. Provides functional connections to the ISP

9. Which of the following are examples of packet-switched communication links? (Choose all that apply.)

A. ATM

B. ISDN

C. PSTN

D. X.25

E. Frame Relay

F. POTS

10. Which of the following uses two bearer channels and one delta channel for sending data over existing phone lines?

A. BRI

B. PRI

C. PSTN

D. POTS

11. A __________ has analog and digital interfaces.

A. Modem

B. CSU/DSU

C. Access server

D. WAN Switch

12. Which of the following authorities define WAN access standards? (Choose all that apply.)

A. International Organization for Standardization

B. Internetwork Operating Systems

C. American Registry for Internet Numbers

D. Telecommunication Industry Association

E. Electronic Industries Alliance

F. Electrical Industries Association

13. Which of the following are benefits of using VPNs? (Choose all that apply.)

A. Eliminates the need for expensive dedicated WAN links

B. Uses advanced encryption and authentication protocols

C. Supports DSL and cable

D. Cost savings using ISDN and PSTN connections

E. Easy to add new users

F. Cost savings using PVCs

14. Which of the following are the three major characteristics of WANS?

A. Use serial connections

B. Require the services of telephone companies

C. Connect remote devices that are on the same LAN

D. Connect devices on remote LANs

E. Use the Internet rather than a carrier

15. Which of the following puts data on the local loop?

A. CPE

B. DTE

C. DCE

D. CO

16. The unlicensed radio spectrum is available to anyone who has which two things?

A. License

B. Wireless router

C. Wireless device

D. Security access code

E. Permission to access the spectrum

17. Which two statements best describe a router's role in a WAN?

A. A multiport internetworking device used in carrier networks

B. Supports multiple telecommunications interfaces

C. Concentrates dial-in and dial-out user communications

D. Converts carrier line frames into frames that the LAN can interpret

E. Needs a CSU/DSU or modem to connect to the POP

18. A point-to-point link ________________. (Choose all that apply.)

A. Provides a preestablished LAN communications path to a remote site

B. Provides a preestablished WAN communications path to a remote site

C. Uses leased lines to provide a dedicated connection

D. Uses leased lines to provide a temporary connection

19. On which layer of the OSI reference model does MPLS reside?

A. Layer 1

B. Layer 2

C. Layer 3

D. Between Layers 2 and 3

20. Which of the following fields can be found in LAN and WAN headers? (Choose all that apply.)

A. Type

B. FCS

C. Data

D. Flags

E. Protocol

F. Control

Chapter Review Exercise

Fill in the blanks with the correct word from the word bank. There are more words than needed, so choose your words wisely.

Smart Serial cable	HSSI	DB60	RJ-45
RS-423	AAA/TACACS	TDM	STDM
WAN	echo reply	DCE	channels
data circuit-terminating equipment	CPU	EIA	frame check sequence
	Category 5E	DTR	T3-Plus
X.25	EIA/TIA-530	ITU-T	DCD
Fast Ethernet	data communications equipment	RS-232	PIU
CSU/DSU		transmission	XID packet
T1	DSR	memory-specific address	NCP
ATM	NTU	UART broadcast address	asynchronous serial
PPP	serial connection	HDLC	synchronous serial
error detection	HDLC	CHAP	ISDN
PAP	SLIP	Stacker	SIP
Frame Relay	V.35	LCP	Novell
CPE	SDH	MUX	IPX Control Protocol
data link layer	FCS	NCP	IPCP
synchronous serial	group address	ISDN	multiplexing
protocol compression	network layer	debug	Network Control Protocol
RS-422	serial port	PPP	
Predictor	echo request authentication	SDH	flag
Category 6		serial port	PPP callback

A router-to-WAN point-to-point connection is also referred to as a ________________ or leased-line connection. In the United States, _____ is the interface standard used by most routers and DSUs that connect to T1 carriers. Engineers use ______ to connect routers on LANs with WANs over high-speed lines such as T3 lines. A ____________ is a general-purpose interface that can be used for almost any type of device, including modems, mouse devices, and printers. ________ transmits two or more channels over the same link by allocating a different time interval for the transmission of each channel. In effect, the channels take turns using the link. The _______ puts each segment into a single channel by inserting each segment into a timeslot. ________ uses a variable-timeslot length, allowing __________ to compete for any free slot space. The ______, commonly a modem or CSU/DSU, is the device used to convert the user data from the DTE into a form acceptable to the WAN service provider transmission link. The EIA refers to the DCE as ________________________, and the ______ refers to the DTE as __________________________. A null modem is a communication method to directly connect two DTEs, such as a computer, terminal, or printer, using an ________ serial cable. The router interface end of the ___________ is a 26-pin connector that is significantly more compact than the DB-60 connector. When a DTE and DCE are connected, the ___________ on a router is the DTE end of the connection by default, and the clock signal is typically provided by a _________ or similar DCE device. The _____ chip converts the groups of bits in parallel to a serial stream of bits. ______ is now the basis for synchronous _______ used by many servers to connect to a WAN, most commonly the Internet. _____________ eliminates some of the time-consuming processes used in X.25. HDLC uses _________________________ to provide error-free communication between two points. The Address field contains the HDLC address of the secondary station. This address can contain a ______________, a ____________, or a _____________. PPP supports ______ and _____ authentication. CHAP uses a _________________, and CHAP sends the username and password in _____________. The _______ sets up the PPP connection and its parameters, and the ______ handles higher-layer protocol configurations. Two ____________ protocols available in Cisco routers are _______, which is _____intensive, and _________, which is _________ intensive. Use the _______ **ppp** command to display information about the operation of PPP. ______________ is a dedicated server used to authenticate users.

Labs and Activities

Lab 2-1: Basic PPP Configuration Lab (2.5.1)

Upon completion of this lab, you will be able to

- Cable a network according to the topology diagram.
- Erase the startup configuration and reload a router to the default state.
- Perform basic configuration tasks on a router.
- Configure and activate interfaces.
- Configure OSPF routing on all routers.
- Configure PPP encapsulation on all serial interfaces.
- Learn about the **debug ppp negotiation** and **debug ppp packet** commands.
- Learn how to change the encapsulation on the serial interfaces from PPP to HDLC.
- Intentionally break and restore PPP encapsulation.
- Configure PPP PAP and CHAP authentication.
- Intentionally break and restore PPP PAP and CHAP authentication.

Figure 2-1 shows the network topology for this lab, and Table 2-1 provides the IP addresses, subnet masks, and default gateways (where applicable) for all devices in the topology.

Figure 2-1 Network Topology for Lab 2-1

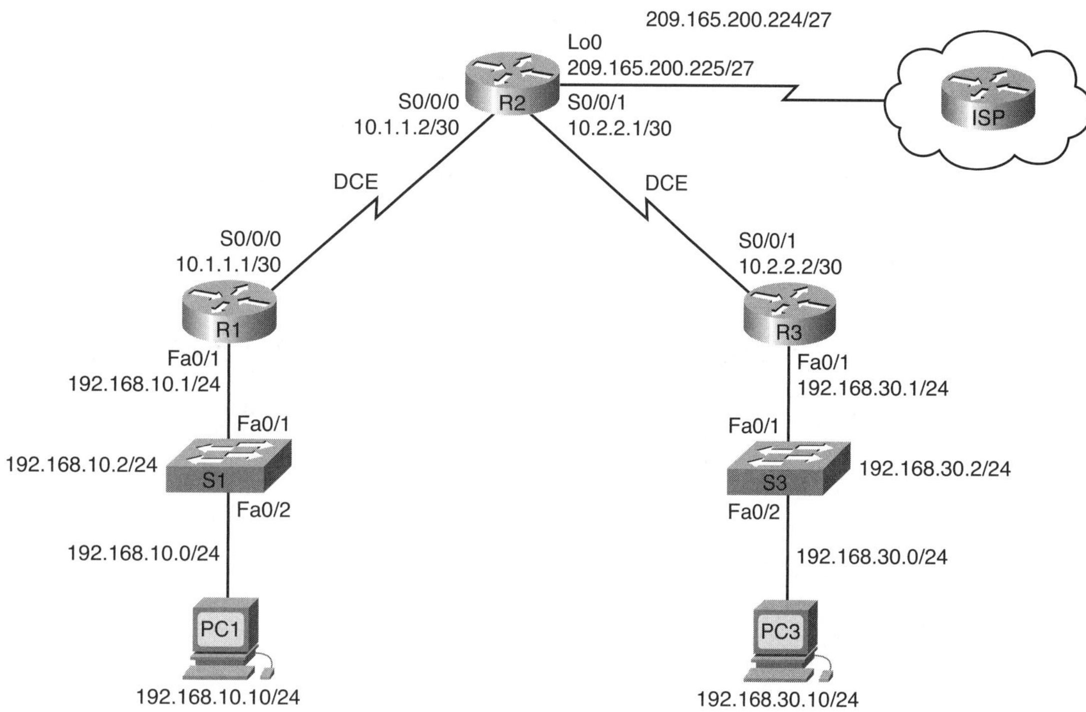

Table 2-1 Lab 2-1 Addressing Table

Device	Interface	IP Address	Subnet Mask	Default Gateway
R1	Fa0/1	192.168.10.1	255.255.255.0	N/A
	S0/0/0	10.1.1.1	255.255.255.252	N/A
R2	Lo0	209.165.200.225	255.255.255.224	N/A
	S0/0/0	10.1.1.2	255.255.255.252	N/A
	S0/0/1	10.2.2.1	255.255.255.252	N/A
R3	Fa0/1	192.168.30.1	255.255.255.0	N/A
	S0/0/1	10.2.2.2	255.255.255.252	N/A
PC1	NIC	192.168.10.10	255.255.255.0	192.168.10.1
PC3	NIC	192.168.30.10	255.255.255.0	192.168.30.1

Scenario

In this lab, you learn how to configure PPP encapsulation on serial links using the network shown in the topology diagram in Figure 2-1. You also learn how to restore serial links to their default HDLC encapsulation. Pay special attention to what the output of the router looks like when you intentionally break PPP encapsulation. This will assist you with Lab 2-3, later in this chapter. Finally, you configure PPP PAP authentication and PPP CHAP authentication.

Task 1: Prepare the Network

Step 1. Cable a network similar to that shown in Figure 2-1.

You can use any current router in your lab as long as it has the required interfaces shown in the topology diagram.

Note: If you use 1700, 2500, or 2600 routers, the router outputs and interface descriptions appear differently.

Step 2. Clear any existing configurations on the routers.

Task 2: Perform Basic Router Configuration

Configure the R1, R2, and R3 routers according to the following guidelines:

- Configure the router hostname.
- Disable DNS lookup.
- Configure an EXEC mode password.
- Configure a message-of-the-day banner.
- Configure a password for console connections.
- Configure synchronous logging.
- Configure a password for vty connections.

Task 3: Configure and Activate Serial and Ethernet Addresses

Step 1. Configure interfaces on R1, R2, and R3.

Configure the interfaces on the R1, R2, and R3 routers with the IP addresses from the addressing table at the beginning of the lab. Be sure to include the clock rate on the serial DCE interfaces.

Step 2. Verify IP addressing and interfaces.

Use the **show ip interface brief** command to verify that the IP addressing is correct and that the interfaces are active.

When you have finished, be sure to save the running configuration to the NVRAM of the router.

Step 3. Configure the Ethernet interfaces of PC1 and PC3.

Configure the Ethernet interfaces of PC1 and PC3 with the IP addresses and default gateways from the addressing table.

Step 4. Test the configuration by pinging the default gateway from the PC.

Task 4: Configure OSPF on the Routers

If you need to review the OSPF commands, see Exploration 2, Module 11.

Step 1. Enable OSPF routing on R1, R2, and R3.

Use the **router ospf** command with a process ID of 1. Be sure to advertise the networks:

```
R1(config)# router ospf 1
R1(config-router)# network 192.168.10.0 0.0.0.255 area 0
R1(config-router)# network 10.1.1.0 0.0.0.3 area 0
R1(config-router)#
```

```
R2(config)# router ospf 1
R2(config-router)# network 10.1.1.0 0.0.0.3 area 0
*Aug 17 17:48:40.645: %OSPF-5-ADJCHG: Process 1, Nbr 192.168.10.1 on
Serial0/0/0 from LOADING to FULL, Loading Done
R2(config-router)# network 10.2.2.0 0.0.0.3 area 0
R2(config-router)# network 209.165.200.224 0.0.0.31 area 0
R2(config-router)#
R2(config-router)#
```

```
R3(config)# router ospf 1
R3(config-router)# network 10.2.2.0 0.0.0.3 area 0
*Aug 17 17:58:02.017: %OSPF-5-ADJCHG: Process 1, Nbr 209.165.200.225 on
Serial0/0/1 from LOADING to FULL, Loading Done
R3(config-router)# network 192.168.30.0 0.0.0.255 area 0
R3(config-router)#
```

Step 2. Verify that you have full network connectivity.

Use the **show ip route** and **ping** commands to verify connectivity:

```
R1# show ip route

<output omitted>

O    192.168.30.0/24 [110/1563] via 10.1.1.2, 00:33:56, Serial0/0/0
C    192.168.10.0/24 is directly connected, FastEthernet0/1
     209.165.200.0/32 is subnetted, 1 subnets
O       209.165.200.225 [110/782] via 10.1.1.2, 00:33:56, Serial0/0/0
     10.0.0.0/8 is variably subnetted, 3 subnets, 2 masks
C       10.1.1.2/32 is directly connected, Serial0/0/0
O       10.2.2.0/30 [110/1562] via 10.1.1.2, 00:33:56, Serial0/0/0
C       10.1.1.0/30 is directly connected, Serial0/0/0

R1# ping 192.168.30.1

Type escape sequence to abort.
Sending 5, 100-byte ICMP Echos to 192.168.30.1, timeout is 2 seconds:
!!!!!
Success rate is 100 percent (5/5), round-trip min/avg/max = 32/32/32 ms
R1#
```

```
R2# show ip route

<output omitted>

O    192.168.30.0/24 [110/782] via 10.2.2.2, 00:33:04, Serial0/0/1
O    192.168.10.0/24 [110/782] via 10.1.1.1, 00:33:04, Serial0/0/0
     209.165.200.0/27 is subnetted, 1 subnets
C       209.165.200.224 is directly connected, Loopback0
     10.0.0.0/8 is variably subnetted, 4 subnets, 2 masks
C       10.2.2.2/32 is directly connected, Serial0/0/1
C       10.2.2.0/30 is directly connected, Serial0/0/1
C       10.1.1.0/30 is directly connected, Serial0/0/0
C       10.1.1.1/32 is directly connected, Serial0/0/0

R2# ping 192.168.30.1

Type escape sequence to abort.
Sending 5, 100-byte ICMP Echos to 192.168.30.1, timeout is 2 seconds:
!!!!!
```

```
Success rate is 100 percent (5/5), round-trip min/avg/max = 16/16/16 ms
R2# ping 192.168.10.1

Type escape sequence to abort.
Sending 5, 100-byte ICMP Echos to 192.168.10.1, timeout is 2 seconds:
!!!!!
Success rate is 100 percent (5/5), round-trip min/avg/max = 16/16/16 ms
R2#
```

```
R3# show ip route

<output omitted>

C      192.168.30.0/24 is directly connected, FastEthernet0/1
O      192.168.10.0/24 [110/1563] via 10.2.2.1, 00:32:01, Serial0/0/1
       209.165.200.0/32 is subnetted, 1 subnets
O         209.165.200.225 [110/782] via 10.2.2.1, 00:32:01, Serial0/0/1
       10.0.0.0/8 is variably subnetted, 3 subnets, 2 masks
C         10.2.2.0/30 is directly connected, Serial0/0/1
O         10.1.1.0/30 [110/1562] via 10.2.2.1, 00:32:01, Serial0/0/1
C         10.2.2.1/32 is directly connected, Serial0/0/1

R3# ping 209.165.200.225

Type escape sequence to abort.
Sending 5, 100-byte ICMP Echos to 209.165.200.225, timeout is 2 seconds:
!!!!!
Success rate is 100 percent (5/5), round-trip min/avg/max = 16/16/16 ms
R3# ping 192.168.10.1

Type escape sequence to abort.
Sending 5, 100-byte ICMP Echos to 192.168.10.1, timeout is 2 seconds:
!!!!!
Success rate is 100 percent (5/5), round-trip min/avg/max = 32/32/32 ms
R3#
```

Task 5: Configure PPP Encapsulation on Serial Interfaces

Step 1. Use the **show interface** command to check whether HDLC is the default serial encapsulation:

```
R1# show interface serial 0/0/0
Serial0/0/0 is up, line protocol is up
  Hardware is GT96K Serial
```

```
  Internet address is 10.1.1.1/30
  MTU 1500 bytes, BW 128 Kbit, DLY 20000 usec,
     reliability 255/255, txload 1/255, rxload 1/255
  Encapsulation HDLC, loopback not set

<output omitted>
```

```
R2# show interface serial 0/0/0
Serial0/0/0 is up, line protocol is up
  Hardware is GT96K Serial
  Internet address is 10.1.1.2/30
  MTU 1500 bytes, BW 128 Kbit, DLY 20000 usec,
     reliability 255/255, txload 1/255, rxload 1/255
  Encapsulation HDLC, loopback not set

<output omitted>

R2# show interface serial 0/0/1
Serial0/0/1 is up, line protocol is up
  Hardware is GT96K Serial
  Internet address is 10.2.2.1/30
  MTU 1500 bytes, BW 128 Kbit, DLY 20000 usec,
     reliability 255/255, txload 1/255, rxload 1/255
  Encapsulation HDLC, loopback not set

<output omitted>
```

```
R3# show interface serial 0/0/1
Serial0/0/1 is up, line protocol is up
  Hardware is GT96K Serial
  Internet address is 10.2.2.2/30
  MTU 1500 bytes, BW 128 Kbit, DLY 20000 usec,
     reliability 255/255, txload 1/255, rxload 1/255
  Encapsulation HDLC, loopback not set

<output omitted>
```

Step 2. Use **debug** commands on R1 and R2 to see the effects of configuring PPP:

```
R1# debug ppp negotiation
PPP protocol negotiation debugging is on
R1# debug ppp packet
PPP packet display debugging is on
R1#
```

```
R2# debug ppp negotiation
PPP protocol negotiation debugging is on
```

```
R2# debug ppp packet
PPP packet display debugging is on
R2#
```

Step 3. Change the encapsulation of the serial interfaces from HDLC to PPP.

Change the encapsulation type on the link between R1 and R2, and observe the effects. If you start to receive too much debug data, use the **undebug all** command to turn debugging off:

```
R1(config)# interface serial 0/0/0
R1(config-if)# encapsulation ppp
R1(config-if)#
*Aug 17 19:02:53.412: %OSPF-5-ADJCHG: Process 1, Nbr 209.165.200.225 on
Serial0/0/0 from FULL to DOWN, Neighbor Down: Interface down or detached
R1(config-if)#
*Aug 17 19:02:53.416: Se0/0/0 PPP: Phase is DOWN, Setup
*Aug 17 19:02:53.416: Se0/0/0 PPP: Using default call direction
*Aug 17 19:02:53.416: Se0/0/0 PPP: Treating connection as a dedicated line
*Aug 17 19:02:53.416: Se0/0/0 PPP: Session handle[E4000001] Session id[0]
*Aug 17 19:02:53.416: Se0/0/0 PPP: Phase is ESTABLISHING, Active Open
*Aug 17 19:02:53.424: Se0/0/0 LCP: O CONFREQ [Closed] id 1 len 10
*Aug 17 19:02:53.424: Se0/0/0 LCP:    MagicNumber 0x63B994DE (0x050663B994DE)
R1(config-if)#
*Aug 17 19:02:55.412: Se0/0/0 PPP: Outbound cdp packet dropped
*Aug 17 19:02:55.432: Se0/0/0 LCP: TIMEout: State REQsent
*Aug 17 19:02:55.432: Se0/0/0 LCP: O CONFREQ [REQsent] id 2 len 10
*Aug 17 19:02:55.432: Se0/0/0 LCP:    MagicNumber 0x63B994DE (0x050663B994DE)
*Aug 17 19:02:56.024: Se0/0/0 PPP: I pkt type 0x008F, datagramsize 24
link[illegal]
*Aug 17 19:02:56.024: Se0/0/0 UNKNOWN(0x008F): Non-NCP packet, discarding
R1(config-if)#
*Aug 17 19:02:57.252: Se0/0/0 PPP: I pkt type 0x000F, datagramsize 84
link[illegal]
*Aug 17 19:02:57.252: Se0/0/0 UNKNOWN(0x000F): Non-NCP packet, discarding
*Aug 17 19:02:57.448: Se0/0/0 LCP: TIMEout: State REQsent
*Aug 17 19:02:57.448: Se0/0/0 LCP: O CONFREQ [REQsent] id 3 len 10
*Aug 17 19:02:57.448: Se0/0/0 LCP:    MagicNumber 0x63B994DE (0x050663B994DE)
R1(config-if)#
*Aug 17 19:02:58.412: %LINEPROTO-5-UPDOWN: Line protocol on Interface
Serial0/0/0, changed state to down
```

```
R2(config)# interface serial 0/0/0
R2(config-if)# encapsulation ppp
R2(config-if)#
*Aug 17 19:06:48.848: Se0/0/0 PPP: Phase is DOWN, Setup
*Aug 17 19:06:48.848: Se0/0/0 PPP: Using default call direction
*Aug 17 19:06:48.848: Se0/0/0 PPP: Treating connection as a dedicated line
*Aug 17 19:06:48.848: Se0/0/0 PPP: Session handle[C6000001] Session id[0]
```

```
*Aug 17 19:06:48.848: Se0/0/0 PPP: Phase is ESTABLISHING, Active Open
*Aug 17 19:06:48.856: Se0/0/0 LCP: O CONFREQ [Closed] id 1 len 10
*Aug 17 19:06:48.856: Se0/0/0 LCP:    MagicNumber 0x63BD388C (0x050663BD388C)
*Aug 17 19:06:48.860: Se0/0/0 PPP: I pkt type 0xC021, datagramsize 14
link[ppp]
*Aug 17 19:06:48.860: Se0/0/0 LCP: I CONFACK [REQsent] id 1 len 10
R2(config-if)#
*Aug 17 19:06:48.860: Se0/0/0 LCP:    MagicNumber 0x63BD388C (0x050663BD388C)
R2(config-if)#
*Aug 17 19:06:50.864: Se0/0/0 LCP: TIMEout: State ACKrcvd
*Aug 17 19:06:50.864: Se0/0/0 LCP: O CONFREQ [ACKrcvd] id 2 len 10
*Aug 17 19:06:50.864: Se0/0/0 LCP:    MagicNumber 0x63BD388C (0x050663BD388C)
*Aug 17 19:06:50.868: Se0/0/0 PPP: I pkt type 0xC021, datagramsize 14
link[ppp]
*Aug 17 19:06:50.868: Se0/0/0 LCP: I CONFREQ [REQsent] id 61 len 10
*Aug 17 19:06:50.868: Se0/0/0 LCP:    MagicNumber 0x63BDB9A8 (0x050663BDB9A8)
*Aug 17 19:06:50.868: Se0/0/0 LCP: O CONFACK [REQsent] id 61 len 10
*Aug 17 19:06:50.868: Se0/0/0 LCP:    MagicNumber 0x63BDB9A8 (0x050663BDB9A8)
*Aug 17 19:06:50.868: Se0/0/0 PPP: I pkt type 0xC021, datagramsize 14
link[ppp]
*Aug 17 19:06:50.868: Se0/0/0 LCP: I CONFACK [ACKsent] id 2 len 10
*Aug 17 19:06:50.868: Se0/0/0 LCP:    MagicNumber 0x63BD388C (0x050663BD388C)
*Aug 17 19:06:50.868: Se0/0/0 LCP: State is Open
*Aug 17 19:06:50.872: Se0/0/0 PPP: Phase is FORWARDING, Attempting Forward
*Aug 17 19:06:50.872: Se0/0/0 PPP: Phase is ESTABLISHING, Finish LCP
*Aug 17 19:06:50.872: Se0/0/0 PPP: Phase is UP
*Aug 17 19:06:50.872: Se0/0/0 IPCP: O CONFREQ [Closed] id 1 len 10
*Aug 17 19:06:50.872: Se0/0/0 IPCP:    Address 10.1.1.2 (0x03060A010102)
*Aug 17 19:06:50.872: Se0/0/0 CDPCP: O CONFREQ [Closed] id 1 len 4
*Aug 17 19:06:50.872: Se0/0/0 PPP: Process pending ncp packets
*Aug 17 19:06:50.876: Se0/0/0 PPP: I pkt type 0x8021, datagramsize 14
link[ip]
*Aug 17 19:06:50.876: Se0/0/0 IPCP: I CONFREQ [REQsent] id 1 len 10
*Aug 17 19:06:50.876: Se0/0/0 IPCP:    Address 10.1.1.1 (0x03060A010101)
*Aug 17 19:06:50.876: Se0/0/0 PPP: I pkt type 0x8207, datagramsize 8
link[cdp]
*Aug 17 19:06:50.876: Se0/0/0 IPCP: O CONFACK [REQsent] id 1 len 10
*Aug 17 19:06:50.876: Se0/0/0 IPCP:    Address 10.1.1.1 (0x03060A010101)
*Aug 17 19:06:50.876: Se0/0/0 CDPCP: I CONFREQ [REQsent] id 1 len 4
*Aug 17 19:06:50.876: Se0/0/0 CDPCP: O CONFACK [REQsent] id 1 len 4
*Aug 17 19:06:50.876: Se0/0/0 PPP: I pkt type 0x8021, datagramsize 14
link[ip]
```

```
*Aug 17 19:06:50.876: Se0/0/0 IPCP: I CONFACK [ACKsent] id 1 len 10
*Aug 17 19:06:50.876: Se0/0/0 IPCP:    Address 10.1.1.2 (0x03060A010102)
*Aug 17 19:06:50.876: Se0/0/0 IPCP: State is Open
*Aug 17 19:06:50.876: Se0/0/0 PPP: I pkt type 0x8207, datagramsize 8
link[cdp]
*Aug 17 19:06:50.876: Se0/0/0 IPCP: Install route to 10.1.1.1
*Aug 17 19:06:50.880: Se0/0/0 CDPCP: I CONFACK [ACKsent] id 1 len 4
*Aug 17 19:06:50.880: Se0/0/0 CDPCP: State is Open
*Aug 17 19:06:50.880: Se0/0/0 PPP: O pkt type 0x0021, datagramsize 80
*Aug 17 19:06:50.880: Se0/0/0 IPCP: Add link info for cef entry 10.1.1.1
*Aug 17 19:06:50.884: Se0/0/0 PPP: I pkt type 0x0021, datagramsize 80
link[ip]
*Aug 17 19:06:51.848: %LINEPROTO-5-UPDOWN: Line protocol on Interface
Serial0/0/0, changed state to up
R2(config-if)#
*Aug 17 19:06:51.888: Se0/0/0 LCP-FS: I ECHOREQ [Open] id 1 len 12 magic
0x63BDB9A8
*Aug 17 19:06:51.888: Se0/0/0 LCP-FS: O ECHOREP [Open] id 1 len 12 magic
0x63BD388C

<output omitted>

*Aug 17 19:07:00.936: %OSPF-5-ADJCHG: Process 1, Nbr 192.168.10.1 on
Serial0/0/0 from LOADING to FULL, Loading Done
```

What happens when one end of the serial link is encapsulated with PPP and the other end of the link is encapsulated with HDLC?

____

____

____

____

What steps does PPP go through when the other end of the serial link on R2 is configured with PPP encapsulation?

____

____

____

____

____

What happens when PPP encapsulation is configured on each end of the serial link?

____

Step 4. Turn off debugging.

Turn off debugging if you have not already used the **undebug all** command:

```
R1# undebug all
Port Statistics for unclassified packets is not turned on.

All possible debugging has been turned off
R1#
```

```
R2# undebug all
Port Statistics for unclassified packets is not turned on.

All possible debugging has been turned off
R2#
```

Step 5. Change the encapsulation from HDLC to PPP on both ends of the serial link between R2 and R3:

```
R2(config)# interface serial0/0/1
R2(config-if)# encapsulation ppp
R2(config-if)#
*Aug 17 20:02:08.080: %OSPF-5-ADJCHG: Process 1, Nbr 192.168.30.1 on Ser-
ial0/0/1 from FULL to DOWN, Neighbor Down: Interface down or detached
R2(config-if)#
*Aug 17 20:02:13.080: %LINEPROTO-5-UPDOWN: Line protocol on Interface Ser-
ial0/0/1, changed state to down
R2(config-if)#
*Aug 17 20:02:58.564: %LINEPROTO-5-UPDOWN: Line protocol on Interface
Serial0/0/1, changed state to up
R2(config-if)#
*Aug 17 20:03:03.644: %OSPF-5-ADJCHG: Process 1, Nbr 192.168.30.1 on
Serial0/0/1 from LOADING to FULL, Loading Done
R2(config-if)#

*Aug 17 20:03:46.988: %LINEPROTO-5-UPDOWN: Line protocol on Interface
Serial0/0/1, changed state to down
```

```
R3(config)# interface serial 0/0/1
R3(config-if)# encapsulation ppp
R3(config-if)#
*Aug 17 20:04:27.152: %LINEPROTO-5-UPDOWN: Line protocol on Interface
Serial0/0/1, changed state to up
```

```
*Aug 17 20:04:30.952: %OSPF-5-ADJCHG: Process 1, Nbr 209.165.200.225 on
Serial0/0/1 from LOADING to FULL, Loading Done
```

When does the line protocol on the serial link come up, and when is OSPF adjacency restored?

____

Step 6. Verify that PPP is now the encapsulation on the serial interfaces:

```
R1# show interface serial0/0/0
Serial0/0/0 is up, line protocol is up
  Hardware is GT96K Serial
  Internet address is 10.1.1.1/30
  MTU 1500 bytes, BW 128 Kbit, DLY 20000 usec,
     reliability 255/255, txload 1/255, rxload 1/255
  Encapsulation PPP, LCP Open
  Open: CDPCP, IPCP, loopback not set

<output omitted>
```

```
R2# show interface serial 0/0/0
Serial0/0/0 is up, line protocol is up
  Hardware is GT96K Serial
  Internet address is 10.1.1.2/30
  MTU 1500 bytes, BW 128 Kbit, DLY 20000 usec,
     reliability 255/255, txload 1/255, rxload 1/255
  Encapsulation PPP, LCP Open
  Open: CDPCP, IPCP, loopback not set

<output omitted>

R2# show interface serial 0/0/1
Serial0/0/1 is up, line protocol is up
  Hardware is GT96K Serial
  Internet address is 10.2.2.1/30
  MTU 1500 bytes, BW 128 Kbit, DLY 20000 usec,
     reliability 255/255, txload 1/255, rxload 1/255
  Encapsulation PPP, LCP Open
  Open: CDPCP, IPCP, loopback not set

<output omitted>
```

```
R3# show interface serial 0/0/1
Serial0/0/1 is up, line protocol is up
```

```
  Hardware is GT96K Serial
  Internet address is 10.2.2.2/30
  MTU 1500 bytes, BW 128 Kbit, DLY 20000 usec,
     reliability 255/255, txload 1/255, rxload 1/255
  Encapsulation PPP, LCP Open
  Open: CDPCP, IPCP, loopback not set

<output omitted>
```

Task 6: Break and Restore PPP Encapsulation

By intentionally breaking PPP encapsulation, you will learn about the error messages that are generated. This will help you later in Lab 2-3.

Step 1. Return both serial interfaces on R2 to their default HDLC encapsulation:

```
R2(config)# interface serial 0/0/0
R2(config-if)# encapsulation hdlc
R2(config-if)#
*Aug 17 20:36:48.432: %OSPF-5-ADJCHG: Process 1, Nbr 192.168.10.1 on Serial0/0/0 from FULL to DOWN, Neighbor Down: Interface down or detached
*Aug 17 20:36:49.432: %LINEPROTO-5-UPDOWN: Line protocol on Interface Serial0/0/0, changed state to down
R2(config-if)#
*Aug 17 20:36:51.432: %LINEPROTO-5-UPDOWN: Line protocol on Interface Serial0/0/0, changed state to up
R2(config-if)# interface serial 0/0/1
*Aug 17 20:37:14.080: %LINEPROTO-5-UPDOWN: Line protocol on Interface Serial0/0/0, changed state to down
R2(config-if)# encapsulation hdlc
R2(config-if)#
*Aug 17 20:37:17.368: %OSPF-5-ADJCHG: Process 1, Nbr 192.168.30.1 on Serial0/0/1 from FULL to DOWN, Neighbor Down: Interface down or detached
*Aug 17 20:37:18.368: %LINEPROTO-5-UPDOWN: Line protocol on Interface Serial0/0/1, changed state to down
R2(config-if)#
*Aug 17 20:37:20.368: %LINEPROTO-5-UPDOWN: Line protocol on Interface Serial0/0/1, changed state to up
R2(config-if)#
*Aug 17 20:37:44.080: %LINEPROTO-5-UPDOWN: Line protocol on Interface Serial0/0/1, changed state to down
R2(config-if)#
```

Why is it useful to intentionally break a configuration?

____

____

Why do both serial interfaces go down, come back up, and then go back down?

____

____

____

Can you think of another way to change the encapsulation of a serial interface from PPP to the default HDLC encapsulation other than using the **encapsulation hdlc** command? (Hint: It has to do with the **no** command.)

____

____

____

____

Step 2. Return both serial interfaces on R2 to PPP encapsulation:

```
R2(config)# interface s0/0/0
R2(config-if)# encapsulation ppp
*Aug 17 20:53:06.612: %LINEPROTO-5-UPDOWN: Line protocol on Interface
Serial0/0/0, changed state to up
R2(config-if)# interface s0/0/1
*Aug 17 20:53:10.856: %OSPF-5-ADJCHG: Process 1, Nbr 192.168.10.1 on
Serial0/0/0 from LOADING to FULL, Loading Done
R2(config-if)# encapsulation ppp
*Aug 17 20:53:23.332: %LINEPROTO-5-UPDOWN: Line protocol on Interface
Serial0/0/1, changed state to up
R2(config-if)#
*Aug 17 20:53:24.916: %OSPF-5-ADJCHG: Process 1, Nbr 192.168.30.1 on
Serial0/0/1 from LOADING to FULL, Loading Done
R2(config-if)#
```

Task 7: Configure PPP Authentication

Step 1. Configure PPP PAP authentication on the serial link between R1 and R2:

```
R1(config)# username R1 password cisco
R1(config)# int s0/0/0
R1(config-if)# ppp authentication pap
R1(config-if)#
*Aug 22 18:58:57.367: %LINEPROTO-5-UPDOWN: Line protocol on Interface Ser-
ial0/0/0, changed state to down
R1(config-if)#
*Aug 22 18:58:58.423: %OSPF-5-ADJCHG: Process 1, Nbr 209.165.200.225 on Ser-
ial0/0/0 from FULL to DOWN, Neighbor Down: Interface down or detached
R1(config-if)# ppp pap sent-username R2 password cisco
```

What happens when PPP PAP authentication is configured on only one end of the serial link?

____

____

```
R2(config)# username R2 password cisco
R2(config)# interface Serial0/0/0
R2(config-if)# ppp authentication pap
R2(config-if)# ppp pap sent-username R1 password cisco
R2(config-if)#
*Aug 23 16:30:33.771: %LINEPROTO-5-UPDOWN: Line protocol on Interface
Serial0/0/0, changed state to up
R2(config-if)#
*Aug 23 16:30:40.815: %OSPF-5-ADJCHG: Process 1, Nbr 192.168.10.1 on
Serial0/0/0 from LOADING to FULL, Loading Done
R2(config-if)#
```

What happens when PPP PAP authentication is configured on both ends of the serial link?

____

____

Step 2. Configure PPP CHAP authentication on the serial link between R2 and R3.

In PAP authentication, the password is not encrypted. Although this is certainly better than no authentication at all, it is still highly preferable to encrypt the password that is being sent across the link. CHAP encrypts the password.

```
R2(config)# username R3 password cisco
R2(config)# int s0/0/1
R2(config-if)# ppp authentication chap
R2(config-if)#
*Aug 23 18:06:00.935: %LINEPROTO-5-UPDOWN: Line protocol on Interface
Serial0/0/1, changed state to down
R2(config-if)#
*Aug 23 18:06:01.947: %OSPF-5-ADJCHG: Process 1, Nbr 192.168.30.1 on
Serial0/0/1 from FULL to DOWN, Neighbor Down: Interface down or detached
R2(config-if)#
```

```
R3(config)# username R2 password cisco
*Aug 23 18:07:13.074: %LINEPROTO-5-UPDOWN: Line protocol on Interface
Serial0/0/1, changed state to up
R3(config)# int s0/0/1
R3(config-if)#
*Aug 23 18:07:22.174: %OSPF-5-ADJCHG: Process 1, Nbr 209.165.200.225 on
Serial0/0/1 from LOADING to FULL, Loading Done
R3(config-if)# ppp authentication chap
R3(config-if)#
```

Notice that the line protocol on interface Serial 0/0/1 changes state to up even before the interface is configured for CHAP authentication. Can you guess why this is the case?

____

____

Step 3. Review the debug output.

To better understand the CHAP process, view the output of the **debug ppp authentication** command on R2 and R3. Then, shut down interface Serial 0/0/1 on R2, and issue the **no shutdown** command on interface Serial 0/0/1 on R2:

```
R2# debug ppp authentication
PPP authentication debugging is on
R2# conf t
Enter configuration commands, one per line.  End with CNTL/Z.
R2(config)# int s0/0/1
R2(config-if)# shutdown
R2(config-if)#
*Aug 23 18:19:21.059: %OSPF-5-ADJCHG: Process 1, Nbr 192.168.30.1 on
Serial0/0/1 from FULL to DOWN, Neighbor Down: Interface down or detached
R2(config-if)#
*Aug 23 18:19:23.059: %LINK-5-CHANGED: Interface Serial0/0/1, changed state
to administratively down
*Aug 23 18:19:24.059: %LINEPROTO-5-UPDOWN: Line protocol on Interface
Serial0/0/1, changed state to down
R2(config-if)# no shutdown

*Aug 23 18:19:55.059: Se0/0/1 PPP: Using default call direction
*Aug 23 18:19:55.059: Se0/0/1 PPP: Treating connection as a dedicated line
*Aug 23 18:19:55.059: Se0/0/1 PPP: Session handle[5B000005] Session id[49]
*Aug 23 18:19:55.059: Se0/0/1 PPP: Authorization required
*Aug 23 18:19:55.063: %LINK-3-UPDOWN: Interface Serial0/0/1, changed state
to up
*Aug 23 18:19:55.063: Se0/0/1 CHAP: O CHALLENGE id 48 len 23 from "R2"
*Aug 23 18:19:55.067: Se0/0/1 CHAP: I CHALLENGE id 2 len 23 from "R3"
*Aug 23 18:19:55.067: Se0/0/1 CHAP: Using hostname from unknown source
*Aug 23 18:19:55.067: Se0/0/1 CHAP: Using password from AAA
*Aug 23 18:19:55.067: Se0/0/1 CHAP: O RESPONSE id 2 len 23 from "R2"
*Aug 23 18:19:55.071: Se0/0/1 CHAP: I RESPONSE id 48 len 23 from "R3"
*Aug 23 18:19:55.071: Se0/0/1 PPP: Sent CHAP LOGIN Request
*Aug 23 18:19:55.071: Se0/0/1 PPP: Received LOGIN Response PASS
*Aug 23 18:19:55.071: Se0/0/1 PPP: Sent LCP AUTHOR Request
*Aug 23 18:19:55.075: Se0/0/1 PPP: Sent IPCP AUTHOR Request
*Aug 23 18:19:55.075: Se0/0/1 LCP: Received AAA AUTHOR Response PASS
*Aug 23 18:19:55.075: Se0/0/1 IPCP: Received AAA AUTHOR Response PASS
*Aug 23 18:19:55.075: Se0/0/1 CHAP: O SUCCESS id 48 len 4
*Aug 23 18:19:55.075: Se0/0/1 CHAP: I SUCCESS id 2 len 4
```

```
*Aug 23 18:19:55.075: Se0/0/1 PPP: Sent CDPCP AUTHOR Request
*Aug 23 18:19:55.075: Se0/0/1 CDPCP: Received AAA AUTHOR Response PASS
*Aug 23 18:19:55.079: Se0/0/1 PPP: Sent IPCP AUTHOR Request
*Aug 23 18:19:56.075: %LINEPROTO-5-UPDOWN: Line protocol on Interface
Serial0/0/1, changed state to up
R2(config-if)#
*Aug 23 18:20:05.135: %OSPF-5-ADJCHG: Process 1, Nbr 192.168.30.1 on
Serial0/0/1 from LOADING to FULL, Loading Done
```

```
R3# debug ppp authentication
PPP authentication debugging is on
R3#
*Aug 23 18:19:04.494: %LINK-3-UPDOWN: Interface Serial0/0/1, changed state
to down
R3#
*Aug 23 18:19:04.494: %OSPF-5-ADJCHG: Process 1, Nbr 209.165.200.225 on
Serial0/0/1 from FULL to DOWN, Neighbor Down: Interface down or detached
*Aug 23 18:19:05.494: %LINEPROTO-5-UPDOWN: Line protocol on Interface
Serial0/0/1, changed state to down
R3#
*Aug 23 18:19:36.494: %LINK-3-UPDOWN: Interface Serial0/0/1, changed state
to up
*Aug 23 18:19:36.494: Se0/0/1 PPP: Using default call direction
*Aug 23 18:19:36.494: Se0/0/1 PPP: Treating connection as a dedicated line
*Aug 23 18:19:36.494: Se0/0/1 PPP: Session handle[3C000034] Session id[52]
*Aug 23 18:19:36.494: Se0/0/1 PPP: Authorization required
*Aug 23 18:19:36.498: Se0/0/1 CHAP: O CHALLENGE id 2 len 23 from "R3"
*Aug 23 18:19:36.502: Se0/0/1 CHAP: I CHALLENGE id 48 len 23 from "R2"
*Aug 23 18:19:36.502: Se0/0/1 CHAP: Using hostname from unknown source
*Aug 23 18:19:36.506: Se0/0/1 CHAP: Using password from AAA
*Aug 23 18:19:36.506: Se0/0/1 CHAP: O RESPONSE id 48 len 23 from "R3"
*Aug 23 18:19:36.506: Se0/0/1 CHAP: I RESPONSE id 2 len 23 from "R2"
R3#
*Aug 23 18:19:36.506: Se0/0/1 PPP: Sent CHAP LOGIN Request
*Aug 23 18:19:36.506: Se0/0/1 PPP: Received LOGIN Response PASS
*Aug 23 18:19:36.510: Se0/0/1 PPP: Sent LCP AUTHOR Request
*Aug 23 18:19:36.510: Se0/0/1 PPP: Sent IPCP AUTHOR Request
*Aug 23 18:19:36.510: Se0/0/1 LCP: Received AAA AUTHOR Response PASS
*Aug 23 18:19:36.510: Se0/0/1 IPCP: Received AAA AUTHOR Response PASS
*Aug 23 18:19:36.510: Se0/0/1 CHAP: O SUCCESS id 2 len 4
*Aug 23 18:19:36.510: Se0/0/1 CHAP: I SUCCESS id 48 len 4
```

```
*Aug 23 18:19:36.514: Se0/0/1 PPP: Sent CDPCP AUTHOR Request
*Aug 23 18:19:36.514: Se0/0/1 PPP: Sent IPCP AUTHOR Request
*Aug 23 18:19:36.514: Se0/0/1 CDPCP: Received AAA AUTHOR Response PASS
R3#
*Aug 23 18:19:37.510: %LINEPROTO-5-UPDOWN: Line protocol on Interface
Serial0/0/1, changed state to up
R3#
*Aug 23 18:19:46.570: %OSPF-5-ADJCHG: Process 1, Nbr 209.165.200.225 on
Serial0/0/1 from LOADING to FULL, Loading Done
R3#
```

Task 8: Intentionally Break and Restore PPP CHAP Authentication

Step 1. Break PPP CHAP authentication.

On the serial link between R2 and R3, change the authentication protocol on interface Serial 0/0/1 to PAP:

```
R2# conf t
Enter configuration commands, one per line.  End with CNTL/Z.
R2(config)# int s0/0/1
R2(config-if)# ppp authentication pap
R2(config-if)# ^Z
R2#
*Aug 24 15:45:47.039: %SYS-5-CONFIG_I: Configured from console by console
R2# copy run start
Destination filename [startup-config]?
Building configuration...
[OK]
R2# reload
```

Does changing the authentication protocol to PAP on interface Serial 0/0/1 break authentication between R2 and R3?

____

____

Step 2. Restore PPP CHAP authentication on the serial link.

Notice that it is not necessary to reload the router for this change to take effect:

```
R2# conf t
Enter configuration commands, one per line.  End with CNTL/Z.
R2(config)# int s0/0/1
```

```
R2(config-if)# ppp authentication chap
R2(config-if)#
*Aug 24 15:50:00.419: %LINEPROTO-5-UPDOWN: Line protocol on Interface
Serial0/0/1, changed state to up
R2(config-if)#
*Aug 24 15:50:07.467: %OSPF-5-ADJCHG: Process 1, Nbr 192.168.30.1 on
Serial0/0/1 from LOADING to FULL, Loading Done
R2(config-if)#
```

Step 3. Intentionally break PPP CHAP authentication by changing the password on R3:

```
R3# conf t
Enter configuration commands, one per line.  End with CNTL/Z.
R3(config)# username R2 password ciisco
R3(config)# ^Z
R3#
*Aug 24 15:54:17.215: %SYS-5-CONFIG_I: Configured from console by console
R3# copy run start
Destination filename [startup-config]?
Building configuration...
[OK]
R3# reload
```

After reloading, what is the status of the line protocol on Serial 0/0/1?

____

____

____

____

____

____

____

Step 4. Restore PPP CHAP authentication by changing the password on R3:

```
R3# conf t
Enter configuration commands, one per line.  End with CNTL/Z.
R3(config)# username R2 password cisco
R3(config)#
*Aug 24 16:11:10.679: %LINEPROTO-5-UPDOWN: Line protocol on Interface
Serial0/0/1, changed state to up
R3(config)#
*Aug 24 16:11:19.739: %OSPF-5-ADJCHG: Process 1, Nbr 209.165.200.225 on
Serial0/0/1 from LOADING to FULL, Loading Done
R3(config)#
```

Task 9: Document the Router Configurations

On each router, issue the **show run** command and capture the configurations:

```
R1# show run
!<output omitted>
!
hostname R1
!
!
enable secret class
!
!
!
no ip domain lookup
!
username R1 password 0 cisco
!
!
!
interface FastEthernet0/1
 ip address 192.168.10.1 255.255.255.0
 no shutdown
!
!
interface Serial0/0/0
 ip address 10.1.1.1 255.255.255.252
 encapsulation ppp
 clockrate 64000
 ppp authentication pap
 ppp pap sent-username R2 password 0 cisco
 no shutdown
!
!
!
router ospf 1
 network 10.1.1.0 0.0.0.3 area 0
 network 192.168.10.0 0.0.0.255 area 0
!
!
banner motd ^CCUnauthorized access strictly prohibited and prosecuted to the full
extent of the law^C
!
line con 0
 exec-timeout 0 0
 password cisco
```

```
 logging synchronous
 login
line aux 0
line vty 0 4
 password cisco
 login
!
end
```

```
R2# show run
!<output omitted>

!
hostname R2
!
!
enable secret class
!
!
no ip domain lookup
!
username R3 password 0 cisco
username R2 password 0 cisco
!
!
!
interface Loopback0
 ip address 209.165.200.225 255.255.255.224
!
!
!
interface Serial0/0/0
 ip address 10.1.1.2 255.255.255.252
 encapsulation ppp
 ppp authentication pap
 ppp pap sent-username R1 password 0 cisco
 no shutdown
!
interface Serial0/0/1
 ip address 10.2.2.1 255.255.255.252
 encapsulation ppp
 clockrate 64000
 ppp authentication chap
 no shutdown
!
```

```
!
router ospf 1
 network 10.1.1.0 0.0.0.3 area 0
 network 10.2.2.0 0.0.0.3 area 0
 network 209.165.200.224 0.0.0.31 area 0
!
!
banner motd ^CUnauthorized access strictly prohibited and prosecuted to the full
extent of the law^C
!
line con 0
 exec-timeout 0 0
 password cisco
 logging synchronous
 login
line aux 0
line vty 0 4
 password cisco
 login
!
end
```

```
R3# show run
!<output omitted>

!
hostname R3
!
!
enable secret class
!
!
!
no ip domain lookup
!
username R2 password 0 cisco
!
!
!
interface FastEthernet0/1
 ip address 192.168.30.1 255.255.255.0
 no shutdown
```

```
!
!
interface Serial0/0/1
 ip address 10.2.2.2 255.255.255.252
 encapsulation ppp
 ppp authentication chap
 no shutdown
!
router ospf 1
 network 10.2.2.0 0.0.0.3 area 0
 network 192.168.30.0 0.0.0.255 area 0
!
!
banner motd ^CUnauthorized access strictly prohibited and prosecuted to the full
extent of the law^C
!
line con 0
 exec-timeout 0 0
 password cisco
 logging synchronous
 login
line aux 0
line vty 0 4
 password cisco
 login
!
end
```

Task 10: Clean Up

Erase the configurations and reload the routers. Disconnect and store the cabling. For PC hosts that are normally connected to other networks, such as the school LAN or the Internet, reconnect the appropriate cabling and restore the TCP/IP settings.

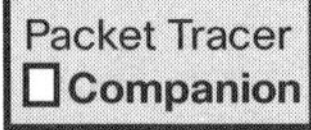

Packet Tracer Companion: Basic PPP Configuration (2.5.1)

You can now open the file LSG04-Lab251.pka on the CD-ROM that accompanies this book to repeat this hands-on lab using Packet Tracer. Remember, however, that Packet Tracer is not a substitute for a hands-on lab experience with real equipment.

Lab 2-2: Challenge PPP Configuration (2.5.2)

Upon completion of this lab, you will be able to

- Cable a network according to the topology diagram.
- Erase the startup configuration and reload a router to the default state.
- Perform basic configuration tasks on a router.
- Configure and activate interfaces.
- Configure OSPF routing on all routers.
- Configure PPP encapsulation on all serial interfaces.
- Change the encapsulation on the serial interfaces from PPP to HDLC.
- Intentionally break and restore PPP encapsulation.
- Configure PPP CHAP authentication.
- Intentionally break and restore PPP CHAP authentication.

Figure 2-2 shows the network topology for this lab, and Table 2-2 provides the IP addresses, subnet masks, and default gateways (where applicable) for all devices in the topology.

Figure 2-2 Network Topology for Lab 2-2

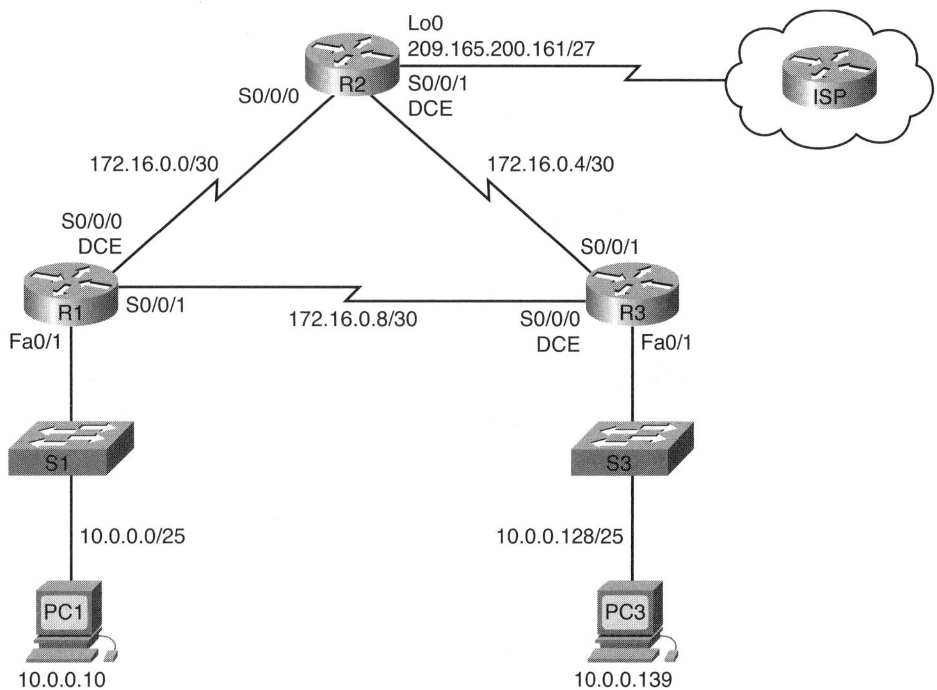

Table 2-2 Lab 2-2 Addressing Table

Device	Interface	IP Address	Subnet Mask	Default Gateway
R1	Fa0/1	10.0.0.1	255.255.255.128	N/A
	S0/0/0	172.16.0.1	255.255.255.252	N/A
	S0/0/1	172.16.0.9	255.255.255.252	N/A
R2	Lo0	209.165.200.161	255.255.255.224	N/A
	S0/0/0	172.16.0.2	255.255.255.252	N/A
	S0/0/1	172.16.0.5	255.255.255.252	N/A
R3	Fa0/1	10.0.0.129	255.255.255.128	N/A
	S0/0/0	172.16.0.10	255.255.255.252	N/A
	S0/0/1	172.16.0.6	255.255.255.252	N/A
PC1	NIC	10.0.0.10	255.255.255.128	10.0.0.1
PC3	NIC	10.0.0.139	255.255.255.128	10.0.0.129

Scenario

In this lab, you learn how to configure PPP encapsulation on serial links using the network shown in Figure 2-2. You also configure PPP CHAP authentication. If you need assistance, refer back to Lab 2-1, but try to do as much on your own as possible.

Task 1: Prepare the Network

Step 1. Cable a network similar to the one in Figure 2-2.

Step 2. Clear any existing configurations on the routers.

Task 2: Perform Basic Router Configuration

Configure the R1, R2, and R3 routers according to the following guidelines:

- Configure the router hostname.
- Disable DNS lookup.
- Configure an EXEC mode password.
- Configure a message-of-the-day banner.
- Configure a password for console connections.
- Configure synchronous logging.
- Configure a password for vty connections.

Task 3: Configure and Activate Serial and Ethernet Addresses

Step 1. Configure interfaces on R1, R2, and R3.

Step 2. Verify IP addressing and interfaces.

Step 3. Configure the Ethernet interfaces of PC1 and PC3.

Step 4. Test connectivity between the PCs.

Task 4: Configure OSPF on Routers

Step 1. Enable OSPF routing on the routers.

Step 2. Verify that you have full network connectivity.

Task 5: Configure PPP Encapsulation on Serial Interfaces

Step 1. Configure PPP on the serial interfaces of all three routers.

Step 2. Verify that all serial interfaces are using PPP encapsulation.

Task 6: Intentionally Break and Restore PPP Encapsulation

Step 1. Choose a way to break PPP encapsulation on the network.

Step 2. Restore full connectivity to your network.

Step 3. Verify full connectivity to your network.

Task 7: Configure PPP CHAP Authentication

Step 1. Configure PPP CHAP authentication on all serial links.

Step 2. Verify PPP CHAP authentication on all serial links.

Task 8: Intentionally Break and Restore PPP CHAP Authentication

Step 1. Choose a way to break PPP CHAP authentication on one or more serial links.

Step 2. Verify that PPP CHAP authentication is broken.

Step 3. Restore PPP CHAP authentication on all serial links.

Step 4. Verify PPP CHAP authentication on all serial links.

Task 9: Document the Router Configurations

Task 10: Clean Up

Erase the configurations and reload the routers. Disconnect and store the cabling. For PC hosts that are normally connected to other networks, such as the school LAN or the Internet, reconnect the appropriate cabling and restore the TCP/IP settings.

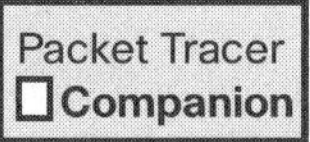

Packet Tracer Companion: Challenge PPP Configuration (2.5.2)

You can now open the file LSG04-Lab252.pka on the CD-ROM that accompanies this book to repeat this hands-on lab using Packet Tracer. Remember, however, that Packet Tracer is not a substitute for a hands-on lab experience with real equipment.

Lab 2-3: Troubleshooting PPP Configuration (2.5.3)

Upon completion of this lab, you will be able to

- Cable a network according to the topology diagram in Figure 2-3.
- Erase the startup configuration and reload a router to the default state.
- Load routers with scripts.
- Find and correct network errors.
- Document the corrected network.

Figure 2-3 shows the network topology for this lab, and Table 2-3 provides the IP addresses, subnet masks, and default gateways (where applicable) for all devices in the topology.

Figure 2-3 Network Topology for Lab 2-3

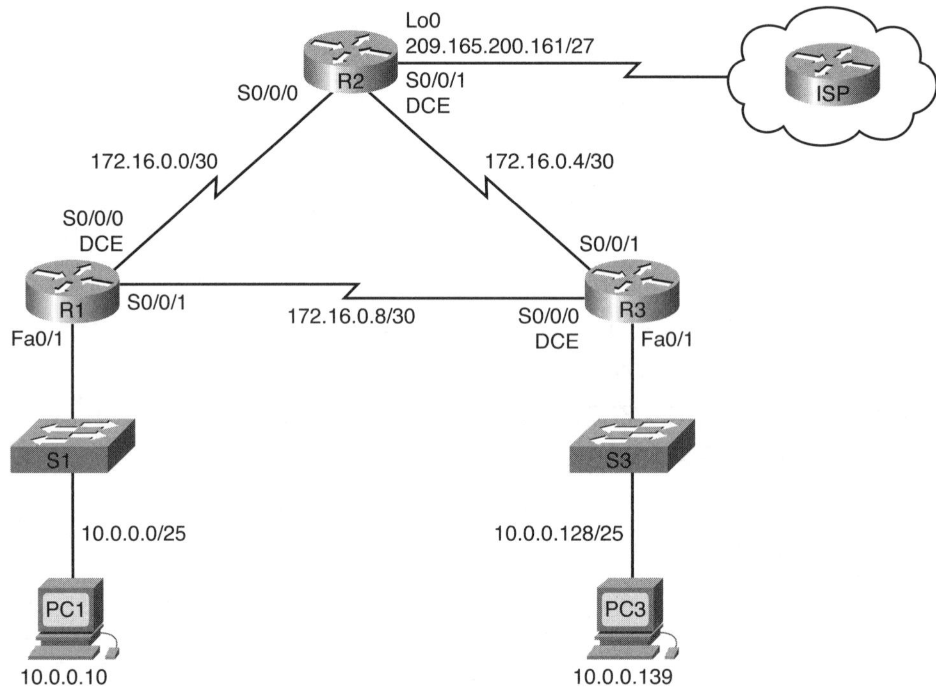

Table 2-3 Lab 2-3 Addressing Table

Device	Interface	IP Address	Subnet Mask	Default Gateway
R1	Fa0/1	10.0.0.1	255.255.255.128	N/A
	S0/0/0	172.16.0.1	255.255.255.252	N/A
	S0/0/1	172.16.0.9	255.255.255.252	N/A
R2	Lo0	209.165.200.161	255.255.255.224	N/A
	S0/0/0	172.16.0.2	255.255.255.252	N/A
	S0/0/1	172.16.0.5	255.255.255.252	N/A

Device	Interface	IP Address	Subnet Mask	Default Gateway
R3	Fa0/1	10.0.0.129	255.255.255.128	N/A
	S0/0/0	172.16.0.10	255.255.255.252	N/A
	S0/0/1	172.16.0.6	255.255.255.252	N/A
PC1	NIC	10.0.0.10	255.255.255.128	10.0.0.1
PC3	NIC	10.0.0.139	255.255.255.128	10.0.0.129

Scenario

The routers at your company were configured by an inexperienced network engineer. Several errors in the configuration have resulted in connectivity issues. Your boss has asked you to troubleshoot and correct the configuration errors and document your work. Using your knowledge of PPP and standard testing methods, find and correct the errors. Make sure that all the serial links use PPP CHAP authentication and that all the networks are reachable.

Task 1: Load Routers with the Supplied Scripts

```
R1

enable
configure terminal
!
hostname R1
!
!
enable secret class
!
!
!
no ip domain lookup
!
username R2 password 0 cisco
!
!
!
interface FastEthernet0/0
 ip address 10.0.0.1 255.255.255.128
```

```
 shutdown
 duplex auto
 speed auto
!
interface FastEthernet0/1
 ip address 10.0.0.1 255.255.255.128
 duplex auto
 speed auto
!
interface Serial0/0/0
 ip address 172.16.0.1 255.255.255.248
 no fair-queue
 clockrate 64000
!
interface Serial0/0/1
 ip address 172.16.0.9 255.255.255.252
 encapsulation ppp
 ppp authentication pap
!
router ospf 1
 log-adjacency-changes
 network 10.0.0.0 0.0.0.127 area 0
 network 172.16.0.4 0.0.0.3 area 0
 network 172.16.0.8 0.0.0.3 area 0
!
ip classless
!
ip http server
!
!
control-plane
!
banner motd ^CUnauthorized access strictly prohibited and prosecuted to the full
extent of the law^C
!
line con 0
 exec-timeout 0 0
 password cisco
 logging synchronous
```

```
 login
line aux 0
line vty 0 4
 password cisco
 login
!
end
```

R2

```
enable
configure terminal
!
hostname R2
!
!
enable secret class
!
!
no ip domain lookup
!
username R11 password 0 cisco
username R3 password 0 class
!
!
!
interface Loopback0
!
!
interface FastEthernet0/0
 no ip address
 shutdown
 duplex auto
 speed auto
!
interface FastEthernet0/1
 ip address 209.165.200.161 255.255.255.224
 shutdown
 duplex auto
 speed auto
!
```

```
interface Serial0/0/0
 ip address 172.16.0.2 255.255.255.252
 encapsulation ppp
 no fair-queue
 ppp authentication chap
!
interface Serial0/0/1
 ip address 172.16.0.5 255.255.255.252
!
router ospf 1
 log-adjacency-changes
 network 172.16.0.0 0.0.0.3 area 0
 network 172.16.0.4 0.0.0.3 area 0
 network 209.165.200.128 0.0.0.31 area 0
ip classless
!
ip http server
!
!
control-plane
!
banner motd ^CUnauthorized access strictly prohibited and prosecuted to the full
extent of the law^C
!
line con 0
 exec-timeout 0 0
 password cisco
 logging synchronous
 login
line aux 0
line vty 0 4
 password cisco
 login
!
end
```

R3

```
enable
configure terminal
!
hostname R3
```

```
!
!
enable secret class
!
!
no ip domain lookup
!
username R1 password 0 cisco
username R3 password 0 ciscco
!
!
interface FastEthernet0/0
 no ip address
 shutdown
 duplex auto
 speed auto
!
interface FastEthernet0/1
 ip address 10.0.0.129 255.255.255.0
duplex auto
 speed auto
!
interface Serial0/0/0
 ip address 172.16.0.10 255.255.255.252
 no fair-queue
 clockrate 64000
!
interface Serial0/0/1
 no ip address
 encapsulation ppp
 ppp authentication pap
!
router ospf 1
 log-adjacency-changes
 network 10.0.0.128 0.0.0.127 area 0
 network 192.16.0.4 0.0.0.3 area 0
 network 192.16.0.8 0.0.0.3 area 0
!
ip classless
!
ip http server
!
```

```
!
control-plane
!
banner motd ^CUnauthorized access strictly prohibited and prosecuted to the full
extent of the law^C
!
line con 0
 exec-timeout 0 0
 password cisco
 logging synchronous
 login
line aux 0
line vty 0 4
 password cisco
 login
!
end
```

Task 2: Find and Correct Network Errors

Using standard troubleshooting methods, find, document, and correct each error.

Task 3: Document the Corrected Network

Now that you have corrected all errors and tested connectivity throughout the network, document the final configuration for each device.

Task 4: Clean Up

Erase the configurations and reload the routers. Disconnect and store the cabling. For PC hosts that are normally connected to other networks, such as the school LAN or the Internet, reconnect the appropriate cabling and restore the TCP/IP settings.

Packet Tracer Companion: Troubleshooting PPP Configuration (2.5.3)

You can now open the file LSG04-Lab253.pka on the CD-ROM that accompanies this book to repeat this hands-on lab using Packet Tracer. Remember, however, that Packet Tracer is not a substitute for a hands-on lab experience with real equipment.

Packet Tracer Exercise 2-1: PPP

Here is an extra activity on PPP configuration to run using Packet Tracer. Open the file lsg04-201.pka on the CD-ROM that accompanies this book to do this Packet Tracer exercise. Detailed instructions are provided within the activity file.

Packet Tracer Exercise 2-2: PPP Troubleshooting

Here is an extra activity on PPP troubleshooting to run using Packet Tracer. Open the file lsg04-202.pka on the CD-ROM that accompanies this book to do this Packet Tracer exercise. Detailed instructions are provided within the activity file

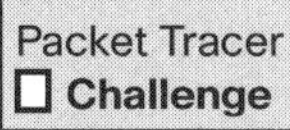

Packet Tracer Skills Integration Challenge

Open file LSG04-PTSkills2.pka on the CD-ROM that accompanies this book to perform this exercise using Packet Tracer. Upon completion of this skills integration challenge, you will be able to

- Configure static and default routing.
- Add and connect a router.
- Design and document an addressing scheme.
- Add and connect devices in an address space.
- Configure basic device settings.
- Configure PPP encapsulation with CHAP.
- Configure OSPF routing.
- Configure VLANs.
- Verify connectivity.

Figure 2-4 shows the network topology for this challenge, and Table 2-4 provides the IP addresses, subnet masks, and default gateways (where applicable) for all devices in the topology.

Figure 2-4 Network Topology for Skills Integration Challenge

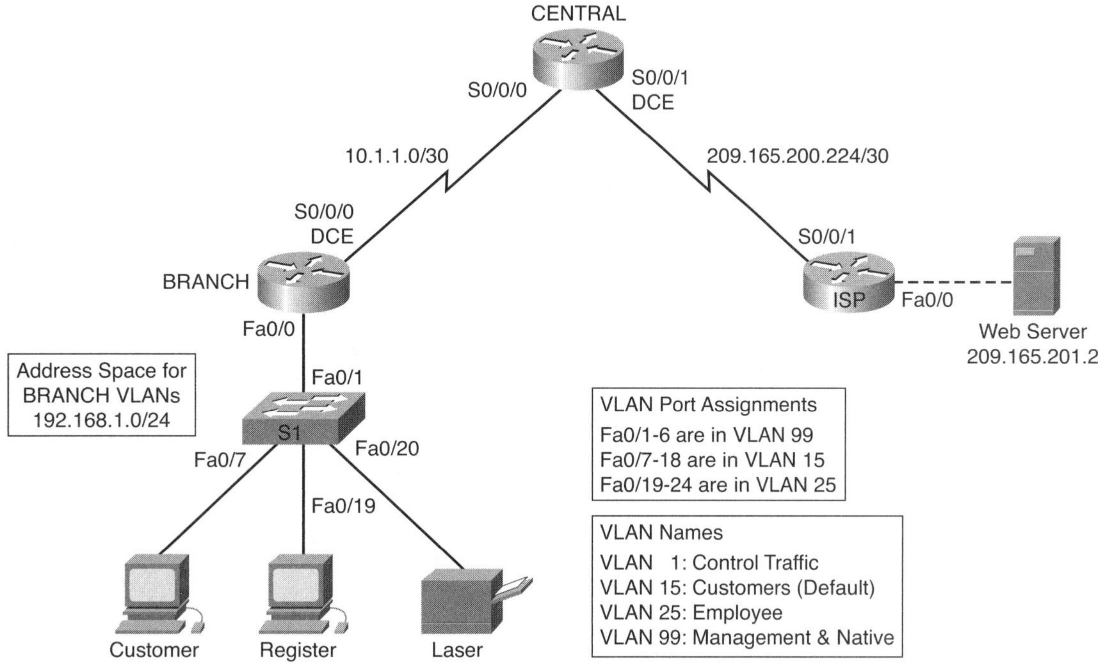

Table 2-4 Skills Integration Challenge Addressing Table

Device	Interface	IP Address	Subnet Mask	Default Gateway
CENTRAL	S0/0/0	10.1.1.2	255.255.255.252	N/A
	S0/0/1	209.165.200.226	255.255.255.252	N/A
ISP	S0/0/1	209.165.200.225	255.255.255.252	N/A
	Fa0/0	209.165.201.1	255.255.255.252	N/A
BRANCH	Fa0/0.1			N/A
	Fa0/0.15			N/A
	Fa0/0.25			N/A
	Fa0/0.99			N/A
	S0/0/0	10.1.1.1	255.255.255.252	N/A
S1	VLAN99			
Customer	NIC			
Register	NIC			
Laser	NIC			
Web Server	NIC	209.165.201.2	255.255.255.252	209.165.201.1

Task 1: Configure Static and Default Routing

Step 1. Configure static routing from ISP to CENTRAL.

Use the passwords **cisco** and **class** to access EXEC modes of the CLI for routers. Configure two static routes on ISP using the **exit interface** argument to the following networks:

- 10.1.1.0/30
- 192.168.1.0/24

Step 2. Configure default routing from CENTRAL to ISP.

Configure a default route on CENTRAL using the **exit interface** argument to send all default traffic to ISP.

Step 3. Test connectivity to Web Server.

CENTRAL should be able to successfully ping Web Server at 209.165.201.2.

Step 4. Check the results.

Your completion percentage should be 4 percent. If not, click **Check Results** to see which required components are not yet completed.

Task 2: Add and Connect a Router

Step 1. Add the BRANCH router.

Click **Custom Made Devices** and add an 1841 router to the topology. Use the Config tab to change the display name to BRANCH. Display names are case sensitive. Do not change the hostname yet.

Step 2. Connect BRANCH to CENTRAL.

Choose the correct cable and connect BRANCH to CENTRAL according to the interfaces shown in the topology.

Step 3. Check the results.

Your completion percentage should be 9 percent. If not, click **Check Results** to see which required components are not yet completed. If you changed the hostname in Step 2, your percentage will be higher.

Task 3: Design and Document an Addressing Scheme

Step 1. Design an addressing scheme.

Using the topology in Figure 2-4 and the following requirements, design an addressing scheme:

- Addressing is provided for all WAN links.
- For the VLANs attached to BRANCH, use the address space 192.168.1.0/24. Starting with the largest host requirement, assign subnets in the following order for all VLANs:

  VLAN 15 needs space for 100 hosts: ________________

  VLAN 25 needs space for 50 hosts: ________________

  VLAN 1 needs space for 20 hosts: ________________

  VLAN 99 needs space for 20 hosts: ________________

Step 2. Document the addressing scheme.

Complete the addressing table in Table 2-4 using the following guidelines. You add the remaining devices in the next task.

- Assign the first address in each VLAN to the corresponding BRANCH subinterface. The subinterface numbers match the VLAN numbers.
- Assign the second address in VLAN 99 to S1.
- Assign the second address in VLAN 15 to the Customer PC.
- Assign the second address in VLAN 25 to the Register PC.
- Assign the last address in VLAN 25 to the laser printer.

Be sure you record the appropriate subnet mask and default gateway for each address.

Task 4: Add and Connect the Devices in the Address Space

Step 1. Add S1, Customer PC, Register PC, and the laser printer in the 192.168.1.0/24 address space.

- S1 is a 2960 switch. Add it to the topology and change the display name to S1. Display names are case sensitive. Do not change the hostname yet.
- The PCs and printer are listed under End Devices. Add two PCs and a printer. Change the display names of the PCs and printer according to the topology.

Step 2. Connect S1 to BRANCH.

Choose the correct cable and connect S1 to BRANCH according to the interfaces shown in the topology.

Step 3. Connect Customer PC, Register PC, and the laser printer to S1.

Choose the correct cable and connect the PCs and printer to S1 according to the interfaces shown in the topology.

Step 4. Check the results.

Your completion percentage should be 22 percent. If not, click **Check Results** to see which required components are not yet completed. If you changed the hostname of S1 in Step 1, your percentage will be higher.

Task 5: Configure Basic Device Settings

Step 1. Configure BRANCH and S1.

Using your documentation, set the basic configuration for BRANCH and S1, including addressing. Use **cisco** as the line password and **class** as the secret password. Use 64000 as the clock rate. Graded portions of the basic configuration include the following:

- Hostnames, which are case sensitive.
- Interface addressing and activation. Set clocking to 64000 bps.
- For interface Fa0/0.99, configure VLAN 99 as the native VLAN.
- Interface VLAN 99 creation and addressing on S1. Activating VLAN 99 is done after the trunk is configured later in the activity.

Step 2. Configure the remaining devices.

Using your documentation, configure the PCs and printer with the correct addressing.

Step 3. Test connectivity between BRANCH and CENTRAL.

CENTRAL should now be able to successfully ping BRANCH. S1 cannot ping until trunking is configured.

Step 4. Check the results.

Your completion percentage should be 63 percent. If not, click **Check Results** to see which required components are not yet completed.

Task 6: Configure PPP Encapsulation with CHAP Authentication

Step 1. Configure CENTRAL to use PPP with CHAP for the link to BRANCH.

The password for CHAP authentication is **cisco123**. The link goes down.

Step 2. Configure BRANCH to use PPP with CHAP for the link to CENTRAL.

The password for CHAP authentication is **cisco123**. The link comes back up.

Step 3. Test the connectivity between BRANCH and CENTRAL.

It might take Packet Tracer a little longer than real equipment to bring the interfaces back up. When the interfaces come up, CENTRAL should be able to successfully ping BRANCH.

Step 4. Check the results.

Your completion percentage should be 71 percent. If not, click **Check Results** to see which required components are not yet completed.

Task 7: Configure OSPF Routing

Step 1. Configure OSPF on CENTRAL.

- Configure OSPF using the process ID 1.
- Add only the network shared with BRANCH.
- Propagate the default route to OSPF neighbors.
- Disable OSPF updates to ISP.

Step 2. Configure OSPF on BRANCH.

- Configure OSPF using the process ID 1.
- Add all active networks that BRANCH routes.
- Disable OSPF updates to the VLANs.

Step 3. Test connectivity to Web Server.

BRANCH should now be able to successfully ping Web Server at 209.165.201.2.

Step 4. Check the results.

Your completion percentage should be 86 percent. If not, click **Check Results** to see which required components are not yet completed.

Task 8: Configure VLANs

Step 1. Add VLANs to S1.

VLAN names are case sensitive. Add and name the four VLANs using the following specifications:

- VLAN 15; name is **Customers(Default)**
- VLAN 25; name is **Employee**
- VLAN 99; name is **Management&Native**

Step 2. Assign ports to the appropriate VLANs and activate interface VLAN 99.

- Using the VLAN port assignments shown in the topology diagram in Figure 2-4, configure the access ports attached to the end devices and assign each to the correct VLAN.
- Enable trunking on the Fa0/1 port and configure it to use VLAN 99 as the native VLAN.
- Activate interface VLAN 99, if necessary. It should already be up.

Step 3. Check the results.

Your completion percentage should be 100 percent. If not, click **Check Results** to see which required components are not yet completed.

Task 9: Verify Connectivity

Step 1. Verify that Customer PC, Register PC, and the laser printer can ping each other.

Step 2. Verify that Customer PC, Register PC, and the laser printer can ping Web Server.

CHAPTER 3

Frame Relay

The Study Guide portion of this chapter uses a combination of matching, multiple-choice, and open-ended question exercises to test your knowledge of Frame Relay, map statements, Inverse ARP, and LMI extensions.

The Labs and Activities portion of this chapter includes all the online curriculum labs. The Challenge and Troubleshooting labs ensure that you have mastered the practical, hands-on skills needed to understand and configure Frame Relay maps, subinterface configurations, and troubleshooting.

As you work through this chapter, use Chapter 3 in the *Accessing the WAN, CCNA Exploration Companion Guide*, or use the corresponding Chapter 3 in the *Accessing the WAN* online curriculum, for assistance.

Study Guide

Basic Frame Relay Concepts

Frame Relay is a packet-switched WAN technology that operates at the physical and data link layers of the OSI model. Originally designed by Sprint to be used across ISDN, it is now used across a variety of interfaces. Although it offers no error checking, Frame Relay does offer flow control and congestion control mechanisms (FECN and BECN). Due to its low cost and flexibility, Frame Relay has become the most commonly used WAN technology used in today's networks, no matter how big or small. Very little equipment is needed, and the cost of the connection varies, depending on the amount of bandwidth you require. This helps keep the price down and makes Frame Relay more cost-effective than implementing dedicated lines.

Virtual circuits (VC) are used to connect multiple LANs, regardless of their locations, as if they were directly connected. These virtual circuits are logical connections between two DTE devices connecting through the cloud. A different circuit in the carrier's network is used to connect each remote location and is uniquely identified using a Data Link Connection Identifier (DLCI). Two types of circuits can be used—switched or permanent. Switched virtual circuits (SVC) are temporary and require call setup and termination, similar to dialup or ISDN connections. They are commonly used when data transfer is sporadic. The cost is reduced because you pay only when the line is in use. Permanent virtual circuits (PVC) are permanently established circuits that do not require call setup and termination. They are always on and are mainly used when you have steady data transfers. It is important to remember that these so-called permanent circuits are shared connections and are not dedicated. Dedicated means that you and only you have access to them, which is why they are so expensive.

Frame Relay encapsulates data before it enters the WAN, similar to how Ethernet prepares data for transport across the LAN. The Frame Relay strips the LAN header and reencapsulates the data with a WAN header, which includes a DLCI number located in the address field, and a checksum.

The flexibility in Frame Relay allows you to add more connections as you add more locations to your network without adding more equipment. The only cost would be the additional circuit in your carrier's network. The hub-and-spoke topology could be used to connect multiple locations. Each connection would require a separate interface and DLCI.

A single Frame Relay physical interface can send data to multiple destinations identified by the outgoing DLCI. All incoming frames have the same DLCI. You also can create multiple subinterfaces that are logical interfaces on a single Frame Relay physical interface. You identify the logical interfaces by assigning them different DLCIs. Logical interfaces are more flexible, because they can be defined on different subnets with different IP addresses and allow you to create point-to-point links within the Frame Relay "cloud." This has some advantages for routing protocols subject to the "split horizon" rule, discussed later.

As mentioned, virtual circuits are used to connect remote locations through a carrier's network. These circuits are identified using DLCI numbers. To accomplish this, you have to identify the endpoint of this circuit by mapping the DLCI at your end to the IP address of the remote router. You can do this manually using map statements, or you can dynamically associate them using Inverse ARP. Inverse ARP is a protocol that allows you to dynamically learn the IP address of the remote site that you are connecting to. It does this in conjunction with Local Management Interface (LMI) status messages. LMI status messages are used to communicate and synchronize the connection between end devices, as well as report on the status of virtual circuits, thereby allowing the LMI global addressing extension to identify a specific interface on a Frame Relay network. If you are using Cisco IOS software

Release 11.2 or higher, no configuration is necessary except enabling Frame Relay on the appropriate interface. Inverse ARP does the rest. Unfortunately, most carriers disable Inverse ARP and require that you manually configure the connection using map statements. Configuring static map statements is covered in the next section.

Review Questions

1. A DLCI is used to identify a virtual circuit in the carrier's network. What is the range of numbers used for DLCIs, and which ones are reserved? Also, briefly describe how DLCIs are used in Frame Relay networks.

____

____

____

____

____

____

____

2. Explain what statistically multiplexed switching means and how Frame Relay uses it.

____

____

Configuring Frame Relay

All Frame Relay configurations are done on the serial interface connected to the carrier's network. Minimum requirements include encapsulating the interface as well as dynamic or static mapping of the DLCI to the remote device's IP address. The default Frame Relay encapsulation type on Cisco serial interfaces is **cisco**, which is the recommended type if you're connecting to another Cisco router. Remember, encapsulation occurs between the two communicating devices, and the carrier's network has no bearing on this. Although many vendors now support the Cisco option, use the **ietf** option when connecting to non-Cisco devices that do not. To configure encapsulation on an interface, use the following command:

```
Router(config-if)# encapsulation frame relay [cisco ¦ ietf]
```

Because Frame Relay connections are always on, routing protocols can send updates across the line without incurring additional charges. With that said, it is sensible to configure the correct link bandwidth to allow routing protocols such as EIGRP or OSPF to calculate the accurate metric for determining the best path. Use the following command:

```
Router(config-if)# bandwidth kbps
```

If you're using an older IOS version, you must specify the correct LMI type using the following command:

```
Router(config-if)# frame-relay lmi-type [cisco ¦ q933a ¦ ansi]
```

The command gives you three options to choose from: **cisco**, **q933a**, and **ansi**. By now you must have guessed that the default LMI type on Cisco serial interfaces is **ansi** (just kidding; it's **cisco**). Frame Relay map statements are used when Inverse ARP is unavailable. Use the following command:

```
Router(config-if)# frame-relay map [protocol][network address][dlci] broadcast
```

protocol is the network layer protocol, such as IP. *network address* is the IP address of the remote router. This is the address of the interface that connects to the WAN on the remote router. **dlci** is the DLCI number of the virtual circuit that is provided by your ISP; it is used to connect the remote router. Nonbroadcast multiaccess networks such as Frame Relay and X.25 do not support broadcast traffic, thereby preventing routing updates from being sent across the connection. The **broadcast** keyword added at the end of the **frame-relay map** statement allows routing updates to be sent and received.

Vocabulary Exercise: Matching Terms

In Table 3-1, match the term on the left with its definition on the right.

Table 3-1 Frame Rely Command Review

Field	Definition
a. SVC	____ Overrides Inverse ARP
b. Inverse ARP	____ Configured only when you're using IOS version 11.2 or earlier
c. DLCI	____ A preconfigured circuit identified with a unique DLCI number
d. Local Management Interface	____ An optional configuration that uses FECNs and BECNs
e. Frame Relay encapsulation	____ Statically mapped with a next-hop protocol address
f. Traffic shaping	____ A dynamically established circuit
g. **broadcast** keyword	____ A dynamic address mapping
h. Static map	____ Used by come routing protocols to calculate and determine a metric
i. Bandwidth configuration	____ A simplified way to forward routing updates
j. PVC	____ Uses the **cisco** or **ietf** options

Advanced Frame Relay Concepts

Split horizon prevents routing loops by not allowing routes that are advertised to a neighbor to be sent back on the same interface. The split horizon rule tells a neighboring router to remove this route from any routing update it sends to the device that it learned the route from. Unfortunately, when a router has multiple connections on a single physical interface that are all on the same subnet, the split horizon rule prevents routing updates from being forwarded. This is when the subinterfaces are configured as multipoint using full- or partial-mesh topologies. Configuring subinterfaces as point-to-point allows each virtual circuit to be configured on a separate subnet with a separate DLCI for each circuit. This also allows you to configure a different encapsulation option for each VC should the need arise. In this case, the router treats each subinterface as if is a separate physical interface and allows updates to be forwarded to its neighbors.

ISPs offer Frame Relay with various options, including access rates. The access rate is the speed at which you connect to your ISP's Frame Relay network. Typical speeds range from 56 kbps to as much as 45 Mbps. The Committed Information Rate (CIR) is the amount of bandwidth that the ISP guarantees when congestion occurs. Line speed (access rate) may not be achieved due to congestion, but the ISP agrees not to drop any packets at or below the CIR. Bits that exceed the CIR during congestion are marked as Discard Eligible (DE) and are dropped first if throughput cannot be achieved.

One of the benefits of using Frame Relay is that any unused bandwidth can be shared, allowing customers to exceed their CIR. ISPs normally oversubscribe Frame Relay connections because most customers do not use the link's full capacity. Unfortunately, when they do, congestion usually occurs. Congestion notification mechanisms notify the router when congestion occurs in the Frame Relay cloud. Forward Explicit Congestion Notification (FECN) is an indirect notification that informs the receiving device that the frame experienced congestion while reaching its destination. Backward Explicit Congestion Notification (BECN) is a direct notification sent from DCEs in the Frame Relay cloud to the transmitting device. BECN notifies the device that the Frame Relay network is congested and that the device should slow its rate of transmission. Flow control can be achieved by lowering transmission rates when multiple BECNs are received and raising transmission rates when fewer BECNs are received.

Fill-in-the-Blank Exercise

________________ prevents routing loops but causes ______________ issues on NBMA networks. ______________ split horizon is an option, but doing so may cause a _____________. A physical interface can be ______________ partitioned into multiple virtual interfaces called subinterfaces. Subinterfaces can be configured in either point-to-point or multipoint mode. Each point-to-point connection is on its own _________ and uses a unique ________. ______________ subinterfaces use a single subnet and do not resolve the split horizon issue. Frame Relay can be ordered at different speeds. Access rate is the speed of the ____________. The ________ is the amount of ____________ throughput. Frames that exceed the CIR are marked as _______ and are dropped first when ___________ occurs. Any unused bandwidth can be shared by all customers. This additional throughput allows customers to ________ above their CIR for no additional cost. When congestion does occur, flow control can be initiated using _________ and _________. This process prevents frames from filling a _________ and being dropped when congestion thwarts them from being delivered.

Configuring Advanced Frame Relay

Advanced Frame Relay configurations consist of configuring subinterfaces on a router as point-to-point. Frame Relay encapsulation is done on the physical interface, which must also be administratively enabled. Each subinterface acts as a separate virtual circuit and must be on a separate subnet, with each having a unique DLCI. To map the specific DLCI to each virtual circuit, you must execute the following command on each subinterface:

```
frame-relay interface-dlci [dlci number]
```

This is all done on the router that acts as the hub. The spoke routers are not configured as subinterfaces and require dynamic or static map statements. You can check the PVC status using the following command, which also displays the number of FECNs and BECNs sent and received by the router:

```
show frame-relay pvc
```

To verify the remote network address to local DLCI mapping, use the following command:

```
show frame-relay map
```

To display the LMI type, LMI DLCI, and Frame Relay DTE/DCE type, use the following command:

```
show interface
```

To troubleshoot a Frame Relay connection to see if the router is communicating with the Frame Relay switch in your carrier's network, use the following command:

debug frame-relay lmi

Vocabulary Exercise: Matching Commands

In the following table, write in the command that could be used to produce the output shown.

Command	Output
____________	PVC Statistics for interface Serial2/1 (Frame Relay DTE) Active Inactive Deleted Static Local 115 0 0 0 Switched 0 0 0 0 Unused 0 0 0 0 DLCI = 100, DLCI USAGE = LOCAL, PVC STATUS = ACTIVE, INTERFACE = Serial2/1 input pkts 12 output pkts 7 in bytes 4406 out bytes 1366 dropped pkts 0 in FECN pkts 0 in BECN pkts 0 out FECN pkts 0 out BECN pkts 0 in DE pkts 0 out DE pkts 0 out bcast pkts 7 out bcast bytes 1366 pvc create time 1d04h, last time pvc status changed 00:30:32
____________	*Mar 1 01:16:39.235: Serial1/2: FR ARP input *Mar 1 01:16:39.235: datagramstart = 0x7D0DE6E, datagramsize = 34 *Mar 1 01:16:39.235: FR encap = 0x64110300 *Mar 1 01:16:39.235: 80 00 00 00 08 06 00 0F 08 00 02 04 00 08 00 00 *Mar 1 01:16:39.239: AC 10 01 04 18 51 00 00 00 00 01 02 00 00 *Mar 1 01:16:39.239: *Mar 1 01:16:44.899: Serial1/2: FR ARP input *Mar 1 01:16:44.899: datagramstart = 0x7D0E0EE, datagramsize = 34 *Mar 1 01:16:44.899: FR encap = 0x30910300 *Mar 1 01:16:44.899: 80 00 00 00 08 06 00 0F 08 00 02 04 00 09 00 00 *Mar 1 01:16:44.899: AC 10 01 02 30 91 AC 10 01 01 01 02 00 00 *Mar 1 01:17:44.911: Serial1/2: FR ARP input *Mar 1 01:17:44.911: datagramstart = 0x7D0CCEE, datagramsize = 34 *Mar 1 01:17:44.911: FR encap = 0x48D10300 *Mar 1 01:17:44.911: 80 00 00 00 08 06 00 0F 08 00 02 04 00 09 00 00 *Mar 1 01:17:44.911: AC 10 01 02 48 D1 AC 10 01 01 01 02 00 00
____________	Serial 1 (administratively down): ip 131.108.177.177 dlci 177 (0xB1,0x2C10), static, broadcast, CISCO TCP/IP Header Compression (inherited), passive (inherited)

Command	Output
	LMI Statistics for interface Serial1 (Frame Relay DTE) LMI TYPE = ANSI Invalid Unnumbered info 0 Invalid Prot Disc 0 Invalid dummy Call Ref 0 Invalid Msg Type 0 Invalid Status Message 0 Invalid Lock Shift 0 Invalid Information ID 0 Invalid Report IE Len 0 Invalid Report Request 0 Invalid Keep IE Len 0 Num Status Enq. Sent 9 Num Status msgs Rcvd 0 Num Update Status Rcvd 0 Num Status Timeouts 9
	Serial1/2 is up, line protocol is up Hardware is CD2430 in sync mode Internet address is 172.16.1.1/24 MTU 1500 bytes, BW 128 Kbit, DLY 20000 usec, reliability 255/255, txload 1/255, rxload 1/255 Encapsulation FRAME-RELAY, loopback not set Keepalive set (10 sec) LMI enq sent 131, LMI stat recvd 116, LMI upd recvd 0, DTE LMI up LMI enq recvd 0, LMI stat sent 0, LMI upd sent 0 LMI DLCI 1023 LMI type is CISCO frame relay DTE FR SVC disabled, LAPF state down Broadcast queue 0/64, broadcasts sent/dropped 9/0, interface broadcasts 0 Last input 00:00:03, output 00:00:03, output hang never Last clearing of "show interface" counters 00:24:10 Input queue: 0/75/0/0 (size/max/drops/flushes); Total output drops: 0 Queueing strategy: fifo Output queue :0/40 (size/max) 5 minute input rate 0 bits/sec, 0 packets/sec 5 minute output rate 0 bits/sec, 0 packets/sec 241 packets input, 8933 bytes, 0 no buffer Received 0 broadcasts, 0 runts, 0 giants, 0 throttles 0 input errors, 0 CRC, 0 frame, 0 overrun, 0 ignored, 0 abort 164 packets output, 2865 bytes, 0 underruns 0 output errors, 0 collisions, 10 interface resets 0 output buffer failures, 0 output buffers swapped out 2 carrier transitions DCD=up DSR=up DTR=up RTS=up CTS=up

Chapter Review Multiple-Choice Questions

Choose the best answer(s) for each of the following questions.

1. Which command allows you to view the number of FECN and BECN messages exchanged between the carrier's switch and your router?

A. **show frame-relay**

B. **show frame-relay map**

C. **show frame-relay lmi**

D. **show frame-relay pvc**

2. Access rate ________________.

A. Is the capacity of the local loop

B. Is guaranteed

C. Is marked as discard eligible

D. Notifies the DTE that the Frame Relay network is congested

3. What three basic components are needed when connecting sites through the WAN? (Choose three.)

A. A device to convert signals and to provide coding and line clocking

B. A device to convert information into signals

C. A device to convert signals into information

D. A transmission circuit

4. Which three LMIs do Cisco routers support? (Choose three.)

A. IETF

B. Cisco

C. ANSI

D. q933a

E. TIA

F. EIA

5. What is the capacity of the local loop that is guaranteed by the ISP called?

A. Congestion Information Rate

B. Control Information Rate

C. Committed Information Rate

D. Conformed Information Rate

6. Which of the following are true of split horizon? (Choose two.)

A. It prevents updates received on one interface from being forwarded out other interfaces.

B. It prevents updates received on one interface from being forwarded out the same interface.

C. It is used with distance vector routing protocols.

D. It cannot be disabled.

7. Which of the following commands creates a static Frame Relay map from R3 to R2 in the topology shown in Figure 3-1?

Figure 3-1 Topology for Question 7

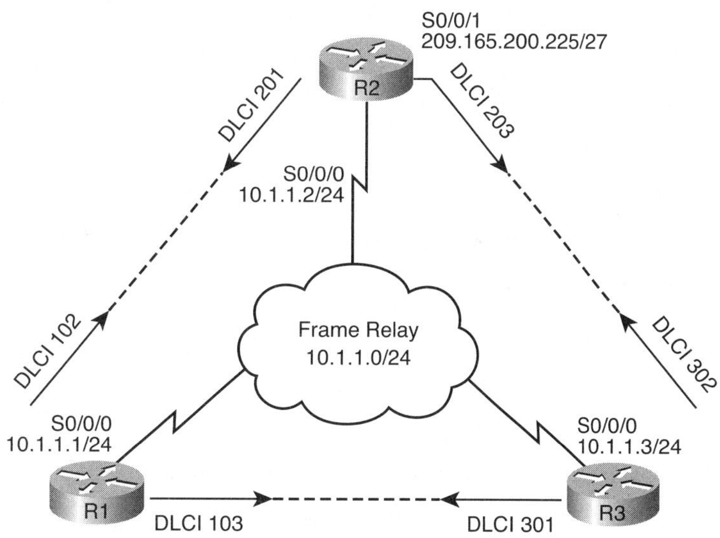

A. **frame-relay map ip 10.1.1.2 102 broadcast**

B. **frame-relay map ip 10.1.1.1 201 broadcast**

C. **frame-relay map ip 10.1.1.2 203 broadcast**

D. **frame-relay map ip 10.1.1.2 302 broadcast**

E. **frame-relay map ip 10.1.1.1 301 broadcast**

8. Which keyword allows multicast traffic to be sent across an NBMA network?

A. **cisco**

B. **ansi**

C. **broadcast**

D. **ietf**

E. **multicast**

9. DTEs receiving frames with the __________ bits set try to reduce the flow of frames until congestion clears.

A. DE

B. CIR

C. CBIR

D. BECN

10. Which of the following are required tasks when you configure Frame Relay? (Choose two.)

A. Configure the LMI

B. Configure static or dynamic address mapping

C. Enable Frame Relay encapsulation on an interface

D. Configure Frame Relay SVCs

E. Configure Frame Relay traffic shaping

11. Which of the following are LMI extensions? (Choose all that apply.)

A. Multicasting

B. Keepalives

C. Local addressing

D. Global addressing

E. Clock synchronization

F. VC status messages

G. Broadcasting

12. Which command displays the number of FECNs and BECNs received by a router?

A. **show interface serial 0/0/0**

B. **show frame-relay pvc**

C. **show frame-relay map**

D. **show frame-relay lmi**

13. The **show interfaces** command displays how the encapsulation is set up, along with Layer 1 and 2 information, including _______________. (Choose three.)

A. PVC statistics

B. LMI DLCI

C. LMI type

D. Current map entries

E. Frame Relay DTE/DCE type

14. How often is the Frame Relay keepalive sent on Cisco serial interfaces?

A. Every second

B. Every 5 seconds

C. Every 10 seconds

D. Every 30 seconds

15. Which of the following are displayed when you use the **show frame-relay lmi** command? (Choose two.)

A. LMI type

B. DLCI number

C. The number of status messages sent and received

D. Current map entries

16. Which of the following helps isolate a problem between your router and the carrier's frame switch?

A. Any nonzero "invalid" items

B. Any zero "invalid" items

C. Any nonzero "valid" items

D. Any zero "valid" items

17. A PVC status could be which of the following? (Choose three.)

A. Passive

B. Active

C. Inactive

D. Valid

E. Deleted

18. What are the two Frame Relay encapsulation options?

A. IETF

B. Cisco

C. ANSI

D. ITU

E. TIA

F. EIA

19. What are Cisco, ANSI, and Q933a?

A. Encapsulation types

B. PVCs

C. LMI types

D. DLCIs

20. Which of the following are optional tasks when you're configuring Frame Relay? (Choose all that apply.)

A. Configure the LMI

B. Configure static or dynamic address mapping

C. Enable Frame Relay encapsulation on an interface

D. Configure Frame Relay SVCs

E. Configure Frame Relay traffic shaping

Labs and Activities

Lab 3-1: Basic Frame Relay (3.5.1)

Upon completion of this lab, you will be able to

- Cable a network according to the topology diagram shown in Figure 3-2
- Erase the startup configuration and reload a router to the default state
- Perform basic configuration tasks on a router
- Configure and activate interfaces
- Configure EIGRP routing on all routers
- Configure Frame Relay encapsulation on all serial interfaces
- Configure a router as a Frame Relay switch
- Understand the output of the **show frame-relay** commands
- Learn the effects of the **debug frame-relay lmi** command
- Intentionally break and restore a Frame Relay link
- Change the Frame Relay encapsulation type from the Cisco default to IETF
- Change the Frame Relay LMI type from Cisco to ANSI
- Configure a Frame Relay subinterface

Figure 3-2 shows the network topology for this lab. Table 3-2 provides the IP addresses, subnet masks, and default gateways (where applicable) for all devices in the topology.

Table 3-2 Lab 3-1 Addressing Table

Device	Interface	IP Address	Subnet Mask	Default Gateway
R1	Fa0/0	192.168.10.1	255.255.255.0	—
	S0/0/1	10.1.1.1	255.255.255.252	—
R2	S0/0/1	10.1.1.2	255.255.255.252	—
	Lo 0	209.165.200.225	255.255.255.224	—
S1	VLAN1	192.168.10.2	255.255.255.0	192.168.10.1
PC1	NIC	192.168.10.10	255.255.255.0	192.168.10.1

Figure 3-2 Network Topology for Lab 3-1

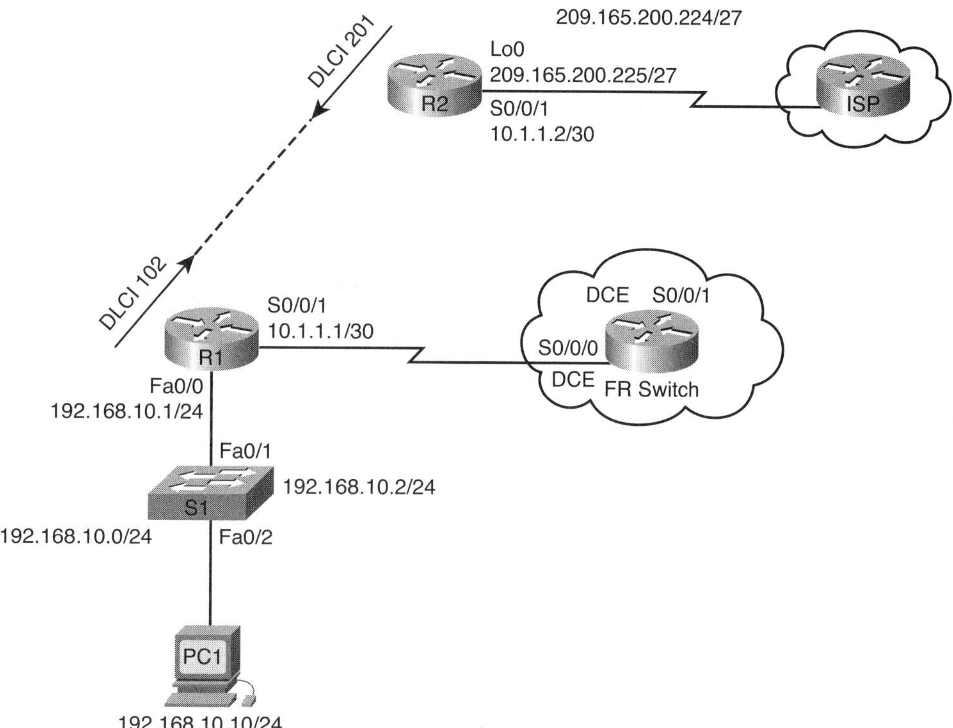

Scenario

In this lab, you will learn how to configure Frame Relay encapsulation on serial links using the network shown in Figure 3-2. You will also learn how to configure a router as a Frame Relay switch. Both Cisco standards and open standards apply to Frame Relay. You will learn both. Pay special attention in the Lab section, where you will intentionally break the Frame Relay configurations. This will help you in the troubleshooting lab associated with this chapter.

Task 1: Prepare the Network

Step 1. Cable a network that is similar to the one shown in Figure 3-2.

You can use any current router in your lab as long as it has the required interfaces shown in the topology. The Frame Relay labs, unlike any of the other labs in Exploration 4, have two DCE links on the same router. Be sure to change your cabling to reflect the topology diagram.

Note: If you use 1700, 2500, or 2600 routers, the router output and interface descriptions appear differently.

Step 2. Clear any existing configurations on the routers.

Task 2: Perform Basic Router Configuration

Configure the R1 and R2 routers and the S1 switch according to the following guidelines:

- Configure the router hostname.
- Disable DNS lookup.
- Configure an EXEC mode password.
- Configure a message-of-the-day banner.
- Configure a password for console connections.
- Configure a password for vty connections.
- Configure IP addresses on R1 and R2.
- Important: Leave serial interfaces shut down.
- Enable EIGRP AS 1 on R1 and R2 for all networks.

```
enable
configure terminal
no ip domain-lookup
enable secret class
banner motd ^CUnauthorized access strictly prohibited, violators will be
  prosecuted to the full extent of the law^C
!
!
!
line console 0
logging synchronous
 password cisco
 login
!
line vty 0 4
password cisco
login
end
copy running-config startup-config
```

```
!R1
interface serial 0/0/1
ip address 10.1.1.1 255.255.255.252
shutdown
!The serial interfaces should remain shut down until the Frame Relay
!switch is configured

interface fastethernet 0/0
ip address 192.168.10.1 255.255.255.0
no shutdown
router eigrp 1
```

```
no auto-summary
network 10.0.0.0
network 192.168.10.0
!
!R2
interface serial 0/0/1
ip address 10.1.1.2 255.255.255.252
shutdown
!The serial interfaces should remain shut down until the Frame Relay
!switch is configured

interface loopback 0
ip address 209.165.200.225 255.255.255.224
router eigrp 1
no auto-summary
network 10.0.0.0
network 209.165.200.0
!
```

Task 3: Configure Frame Relay

You will now set up a basic point-to-point Frame Relay connection between routers 1 and 2. You first need to configure FR Switch as a Frame Relay switch and create DLCIs.

What does DLCI stand for?

____

What is a DLCI used for?

____

What is a PVC, and how is it used?

____

____

____

Step 1. Configure FR Switch as a Frame Relay switch, and create a PVC between R1 and R2.

This command enables Frame Relay switching globally on the router, allowing it to forward frames based on the incoming DLCI rather than on an IP address basis:

```
FR-Switch(config)# frame-relay switching
```

Change the interface encapsulation type to Frame Relay. Like HDLC or PPP, Frame Relay is a data link layer protocol that specifies the framing of Layer 2 traffic.

```
FR-Switch(config)# interface serial 0/0/0
FR-Switch(config)# clock rate 64000
FR-Switch(config-if)# encapsulation frame-relay
```

Changing the interface type to DCE tells the router to send LMI keepalives and allows Frame Relay route statements to be applied. You cannot set up PVCs using the **frame-relay route** command between two Frame Relay DTE interfaces.

```
FR-Switch(config-if)# frame-relay intf-type dce
```

Note: Frame Relay interface types do not need to match the underlying physical interface type. A physical DTE serial interface can act as a Frame Relay DCE interface, and a physical DCE interface can act as a logical Frame Relay DTE interface.

Configure the router to forward incoming traffic on interface serial 0/0/0 with DLCI 102 to serial 0/0/1 with an output DLCI of 201:

```
FR-Switch(config-if)# frame-relay route 102 interface serial 0/0/1 201
FR-Switch(config-if)# no shutdown
```

This configuration creates two PVCs: one from R1 to R2 (DLCI 102), and one from R2 to R1 (DLCI 201). You can verify the configuration using the **show frame-relay pvc** command:

```
FR-Switch(config-if)# interface serial 0/0/1
FR-Switch(config)# clock rate 64000
FR-Switch(config-if)# encapsulation frame-relay
FR-Switch(config-if)# frame-relay intf-type dce
FR-Switch(config-if)# frame-relay route 201 interface serial 0/0/0 102
FR-Switch(config-if)# no shutdown


FR-Switch# show frame-relay pvc


PVC Statistics for interface Serial0/0/0 (Frame Relay DCE)


              Active     Inactive      Deleted       Static
  Local          0           0            0             0
  Switched       0           1            0             0
  Unused         0           0            0             0


DLCI = 102, DLCI USAGE = SWITCHED, PVC STATUS = INACTIVE, INTERFACE = Ser-
  ial0/0/0

  input pkts 0              output pkts 0             in bytes 0
  out bytes 0               dropped pkts 0            in pkts dropped 0
  out pkts dropped 0        out bytes dropped 0
  in FECN pkts 0            in BECN pkts 0            out FECN pkts 0
  out BECN pkts 0           in DE pkts 0              out DE pkts 0
  out bcast pkts 0          out bcast bytes 0
  30 second input rate 0 bits/sec, 0 packets/sec
  30 second output rate 0 bits/sec, 0 packets/sec
  switched pkts 0
  Detailed packet drop counters:
  no out intf 0             out intf down 0           no out PVC 0
```

```
  in PVC down 0            out PVC down 0            pkt too big 0
  shaping Q full 0         pkt above DE 0            policing drop 0
  pvc create time 00:03:33, last time pvc status changed 00:00:19

PVC Statistics for interface Serial0/0/1 (Frame Relay DCE)

              Active     Inactive      Deleted       Static
  Local          0          0             0             0
  Switched       0          1             0             0
  Unused         0          0             0             0

DLCI = 201, DLCI USAGE = SWITCHED, PVC STATUS = INACTIVE, INTERFACE =
  Serial0/0/1

  input pkts 0             output pkts 0             in bytes 0
  out bytes 0              dropped pkts 0            in pkts dropped 0
  out pkts dropped 0                out bytes dropped 0
  in FECN pkts 0           in BECN pkts 0            out FECN pkts 0
  out BECN pkts 0          in DE pkts 0              out DE pkts 0
  out bcast pkts 0         out bcast bytes 0
  30 second input rate 0 bits/sec, 0 packets/sec
  30 second output rate 0 bits/sec, 0 packets/sec
  switched pkts 0
  Detailed packet drop counters:
  no out intf 0            out intf down 0           no out PVC 0
  in PVC down 0            out PVC down 0            pkt too big 0
  shaping Q full 0         pkt above DE 0            policing drop 0
  pvc create time 00:02:02, last time pvc status changed 00:00:18
```

Notice the 1 in the Inactive column. The PVC you have created does not have any endpoints configured. The Frame Relay switch knows this and has marked the PVC as Inactive.

Issue the **show frame-relay route** command. This command shows any existing Frame Relay routes, their interfaces, DLCIs, and status. This is the Layer 2 route that Frame Relay traffic takes through the network. Do not confuse this with Layer 3 IP routing.

```
FR-Switch# show frame-relay route

Input Intf      Input Dlci      Output Intf     Output Dlci     Status
Serial0/0/0     102             Serial0/0/1     201             inactive
Serial0/0/1     201             Serial0/0/0     102             inactive
```

Step 2. Configure R1 for Frame Relay.

Inverse ARP allows distant ends of a Frame Relay link to dynamically discover each other and provides a dynamic method of mapping IP addresses to DLCIs. Although Inverse ARP is useful, it is not always reliable. The best practice is to statically map IP addresses to DLCIs and to disable Inverse ARP.

```
R1(config)# interface serial 0/0/1
R1(config-if)# encapsulation frame-relay
R1(config-if)# no frame-relay inverse-arp
```

Why would you want to map an IP address to a DLCI?

____

____

____

____

The command **frame-relay map** statically maps an IP address to a DLCI. In addition to mapping IP to a DLCI, Cisco IOS software allows several other Layer 3 protocol addresses to be mapped. The **broadcast** keyword in the following command sends any multicast or broadcast traffic destined for this link over the DLCI. Most routing protocols require the **broadcast** keyword to properly function over Frame Relay. You can use the **broadcast** keyword on multiple DLCIs on the same interface. The traffic is replicated to all PVCs.

```
R1(config-if)# frame-relay map ip 10.1.1.2 102 broadcast
```

Is the DLCI mapped to the local IP address or the IP address at the other end of the PVC?

____

```
R1(config-if)# no shutdown
```

Why is the **no shutdown** command used after the **no frame-relay inverse-arp** command?

____

____

____

____

Step 3. Configure R2 for Frame Relay:

```
R2(config)# interface serial 0/0/1
R2(config-if)# encapsulation frame-relay
R2(config-if)# no frame-relay inverse-arp
R2(config-if)# frame-relay map ip 10.1.1.1 201 broadcast
R2(config-if)# no shutdown
```

At this point, you receive messages indicating that the interfaces have come up and that EIGRP neighbor adjacency has been established:

```
R1#*Sep  9 17:05:08.771: %DUAL-5-NBRCHANGE: IP-EIGRP(0) 1: Neighbor 10.1.1.2
  (Serial0/0/1) is up: new adjacency
R2#*Sep  9 17:05:47.691: %DUAL-5-NBRCHANGE: IP-EIGRP(0) 1: Neighbor 10.1.1.1
  (Serial0/0/1) is up: new adjacency
```

The **show ip route** command shows complete routing tables:

```
R1:
R1# show ip route

Codes: C - connected, S - static, R - RIP, M - mobile, B - BGP
       D - EIGRP, EX - EIGRP external, O - OSPF, IA - OSPF inter area
       N1 - OSPF NSSA external type 1, N2 - OSPF NSSA external type 2
       E1 - OSPF external type 1, E2 - OSPF external type 2
       i - IS-IS, su - IS-IS summary, L1 - IS-IS level-1, L2 - IS-IS
  level-2
       ia - IS-IS inter area, * - candidate default, U - per-user     static
  route
       o - ODR, P - periodic downloaded static route

Gateway of last resort is not set

C    192.168.10.0/24 is directly connected, FastEthernet0/0
     209.165.200.0/27 is subnetted, 1 subnets
D       209.165.200.224 [90/20640000] via 10.1.1.2, 00:00:07, Serial0/0/1
     10.0.0.0/30 is subnetted, 1 subnets
C       10.1.1.0 is directly connected, Serial0/0/1
```

```
R2:
R2# show ip route

Codes: C - connected, S - static, R - RIP, M - mobile, B - BGP
       D - EIGRP, EX - EIGRP external, O - OSPF, IA - OSPF inter area
       N1 - OSPF NSSA external type 1, N2 - OSPF NSSA external type 2
       E1 - OSPF external type 1, E2 - OSPF external type 2
       i - IS-IS, su - IS-IS summary, L1 - IS-IS level-1, L2 - IS-IS level-2
       ia - IS-IS inter area, * - candidate default, U - per-user static
  route
       o - ODR, P - periodic downloaded static route

Gateway of last resort is not set

D    192.168.10.0/24 [90/20514560] via 10.1.1.1, 00:26:03, Serial0/0/1
     209.165.200.0/27 is subnetted, 1 subnets
C       209.165.200.224 is directly connected, Loopback0
     10.0.0.0/30 is subnetted, 1 subnets
C       10.1.1.0 is directly connected, Serial0/0/1
```

Task 4: Verify the Configuration

You should now be able to ping from R1 to R2. After you bring up the interfaces, it may take several seconds for the PVC to become active. You can also see EIGRP routes for each router.

Step 1. **Ping R1 and R2.**

Ensure that you can ping router R2 from router R1:

```
R1# ping 10.1.1.2

Type escape sequence to abort.
Sending 5, 100-byte ICMP Echos to 10.1.1.2, timeout is 2 seconds:
!!!!!
Success rate is 100 percent (5/5), round-trip min/avg/max = 28/29/32 ms
```

```
R2# ping 10.1.1.1

Type escape sequence to abort.
Sending 5, 100-byte ICMP Echos to 10.1.1.1, timeout is 2 seconds:
!!!!!
Success rate is 100 percent (5/5), round-trip min/avg/max = 28/29/32 ms
```

Step 2. **Get PVC information.**

The **show frame-relay pvc** command displays information on all PVCs configured on the router. The output also includes the associated DLCI.

```
R1:
R1# show frame-relay pvc

PVC Statistics for interface Serial0/0/1 (Frame Relay DTE)

              Active     Inactive      Deleted       Static
  Local          1            0            0            0
  Switched       0            0            0            0
  Unused         0            0            0            0

DLCI = 102, DLCI USAGE = LOCAL, PVC STATUS = ACTIVE, INTERFACE = Serial0/0/1

  input pkts 5             output pkts 5            in bytes 520
  out bytes 520            dropped pkts 0           in pkts dropped 0
  out pkts dropped 0                out bytes dropped 0
  in FECN pkts 0           in BECN pkts 0           out FECN pkts 0
  out BECN pkts 0          in DE pkts 0             out DE pkts 0
  out bcast pkts 0         out bcast bytes 0
  5 minute input rate 0 bits/sec, 0 packets/sec
  5 minute output rate 0 bits/sec, 0 packets/sec
  pvc create time 10:26:41, last time pvc status changed 00:01:04
```

```
R2:
R2# show frame-relay pvc

PVC Statistics for interface Serial0/0/1 (Frame Relay DTE)

              Active     Inactive      Deleted       Static
  Local          1           0            0             0
  Switched       0           0            0             0
  Unused         0           0            0             0

DLCI = 201, DLCI USAGE = LOCAL, PVC STATUS = ACTIVE, INTERFACE = Serial0/0/1

  input pkts 5             output pkts 5            in bytes 520
  out bytes 520            dropped pkts 0           in pkts dropped 0
  out pkts dropped 0                out bytes dropped 0
  in FECN pkts 0           in BECN pkts 0           out FECN pkts 0
  out BECN pkts 0          in DE pkts 0             out DE pkts 0
  out bcast pkts 0         out bcast bytes 0
  5 minute input rate 0 bits/sec, 0 packets/sec
  5 minute output rate 0 bits/sec, 0 packets/sec
  pvc create time 10:25:31, last time pvc status changed 00:00:00
```

```
FR Switch:
FR-Switch# show frame-relay pvc

PVC Statistics for interface Serial0/0/0 (Frame Relay DCE)

              Active     Inactive      Deleted       Static
  Local          0           0            0             0
  Switched       1           0            0             0
  Unused         0           0            0             0

DLCI = 102, DLCI USAGE = SWITCHED, PVC STATUS = ACTIVE, INTERFACE =
  Serial0/0/0

  input pkts 0             output pkts 0            in bytes 0
  out bytes 0              dropped pkts 0           in pkts dropped 0
  out pkts dropped 0                out bytes dropped 0
  in FECN pkts 0           in BECN pkts 0           out FECN pkts 0
  out BECN pkts 0          in DE pkts 0             out DE pkts 0
  out bcast pkts 0         out bcast bytes 0
  30 second input rate 0 bits/sec, 0 packets/sec
  30 second output rate 0 bits/sec, 0 packets/sec
  switched pkts 0
```

```
  Detailed packet drop counters:
  no out intf 0            out intf down 0          no out PVC 0
  in PVC down 0            out PVC down 0           pkt too big 0
  shaping Q full 0         pkt above DE 0           policing drop 0
  pvc create time 10:28:31, last time pvc status changed 00:03:57

PVC Statistics for interface Serial0/0/1 (Frame Relay DCE)

              Active     Inactive      Deleted       Static
  Local          0           0            0             0
  Switched       1           0            0             0
  Unused         0           0            0             0

DLCI = 201, DLCI USAGE = SWITCHED, PVC STATUS = ACTIVE, INTERFACE =
  Serial0/0/1

  input pkts 0             output pkts 0            in bytes 0
  out bytes 0              dropped pkts 0           in pkts dropped 0
  out pkts dropped 0                out bytes dropped 0
  in FECN pkts 0           in BECN pkts 0           out FECN pkts 0
  out BECN pkts 0          in DE pkts 0             out DE pkts 0
  out bcast pkts 0         out bcast bytes 0
  30 second input rate 0 bits/sec, 0 packets/sec
  30 second output rate 0 bits/sec, 0 packets/sec
  switched pkts 0
  Detailed packet drop counters:
  no out intf 0            out intf down 0          no out PVC 0
  in PVC down 0            out PVC down 0           pkt too big 0
  shaping Q full 0         pkt above DE 0           policing drop 0
  pvc create time 10:27:00, last time pvc status changed 00:04:03
```

Step 3. Verify Frame Relay mappings.

The **show frame-relay map** command displays information on the static and dynamic mappings of Layer 3 addresses to DLCIs. Because Inverse ARP has been turned off, only static maps exist.

```
R1:
R1# show frame-relay map

Serial0/0/1 (up): ip 10.1.1.2 dlci 102(0x66,0x1860), static,
              CISCO, status defined, active
```

```
R2:
R2# show frame-relay map
```

```
Serial0/0/1 (up): ip 10.1.1.1 dlci 201(0xC9,0x3090), static,
              CISCO, status defined, active
```

FR Switch acts as a Layer 2 device, so there is no need to map Layer 3 addresses to Layer 2 DLCIs.

Step 4. **Debug the Frame Relay LMI.**

What purpose does the LMI serve in a Frame Relay network?

____

____

____

____

What are the three different types of LMI?

____

What DLCI does the LMI operate on?

____

Issue the **debug frame-relay lmi** command. The output gives detailed information on all LMI data. Keepalives are sent every 10 seconds, so you may have to wait before seeing any output.

The **debug** output shows two LMI packets: the first outgoing, and the second incoming:

```
R1# debug frame-relay lmi

Frame Relay LMI debugging is on
Displaying all Frame Relay LMI data
R1#
*Aug 24 06:19:15.920: Serial0/0/1(out): StEnq, myseq 196, yourseen 195, DTE
up
*Aug 24 06:19:15.920: datagramstart = 0xE73F24F4, datagramsize = 13
*Aug 24 06:19:15.920: FR encap = 0xFCF10309
*Aug 24 06:19:15.920: 00 75 01 01 00 03 02 C4 C3
*Aug 24 06:19:15.920:
*Aug 24 06:19:15.924: Serial0/0/1(in): Status, myseq 196, pak size 21
*Aug 24 06:19:15.924: RT IE 1, length 1, type 0
*Aug 24 06:19:15.924: KA IE 3, length 2, yourseq 196, myseq 196
*Aug 24 06:19:15.924: PVC IE 0x7 , length 0x6 , dlci 102, status 0x2 , bw 0
R1# undebug all

Port Statistics for unclassified packets is not turned on.

All possible debugging has been turned off
```

Notice that the output shows an outgoing LMI packet with a sequence number of 196. The last LMI message received from the FR Switch had sequence number 195.

```
*Aug 24 06:19:15.920: Serial0/0/1(out): StEnq, myseq 196, yourseen 195, DTE
  up
```

This line indicates an incoming LMI message from FR Switch to R1 with sequence number 196.

```
*Aug 24 06:19:15.924: Serial0/0/1(in): Status, myseq 196, pak size 21
```

FR Switch sent this as sequence number 196 (myseq), and the last LMI message received by FR Switch from R1 had sequence number 196 (yourseq).

```
*Aug 24 06:19:15.924: KA IE 3, length 2, yourseq 196, myseq 196
```

DLCI 102 is the only DLCI on this link, and it is currently active.

```
*Aug 24 06:19:15.924: PVC IE 0x7 , length 0x6 , dlci 102, status 0x2 , bw 0
```

Task 5: Troubleshoot Frame Relay

A variety of tools are available to troubleshoot Frame Relay connectivity issues. To learn about troubleshooting, you will break the Frame Relay connection established earlier and then reestablish it.

Step 1. Remove the frame map from R1:

```
R1# configure terminal

Enter configuration commands, one per line.  End with CNTL/Z.
R1(config)# interface serial0/0/1
R1(config-if)# encapsulation frame-relay
R1(config-if)# no frame-relay map ip 10.1.1.2 102 broadcast
```

Now that you have removed the frame map statement from R1, try to ping router R1 from router R2. You get no response.

```
R2# ping 10.1.1.1

Type escape sequence to abort.
Sending 5, 100-byte ICMP Echos to 10.1.1.1, timeout is 2 seconds:
.....
Success rate is 0 percent (0/5)
```

Additionally, you should get console messages reporting the EIGRP adjacency going up and down:

```
R1(config-if)#*Sep  9 17:28:36.579: %DUAL-5-NBRCHANGE: IP-EIGRP(0) 1:
  Neighbor
  10.1.1.2 (Serial0/0/1) is down: Interface Goodbye received
R1(config-if)#*Sep  9 17:29:32.583: %DUAL-5-NBRCHANGE: IP-EIGRP(0) 1:
  Neighbor
  10.1.1.2 (Serial0/0/1) is up: new adjacency
R1(config-if)#*Sep  9 17:32:37.095: %DUAL-5-NBRCHANGE: IP-EIGRP(0) 1:
  Neighbor
  10.1.1.2 (Serial0/0/1) is down: retry limit exceeded
R2#*Sep  9 17:29:15.359: %DUAL-5-NBRCHANGE: IP-EIGRP(0) 1: Neighbor 10.1.1.1
  (Serial0/0/1) is down: holding time expired
```

Issue the **debug ip icmp** command on R1:

```
R1# debug ip icmp

ICMP packet debugging is on
```

Now ping the serial interface of R1 again. The following debug message appears on R1:

```
R2# ping 10.1.1.1

Type escape sequence to abort.
Sending 5, 100-byte ICMP Echos to 10.1.1.1, timeout is 2 seconds:
.....
Success rate is 0 percent (0/5)
R1#*Sep  9 17:42:13.415: ICMP: echo reply sent, src 10.1.1.1, dst 10.1.1.2
R1#*Sep  9 17:42:15.411: ICMP: echo reply sent, src 10.1.1.1, dst 10.1.1.2
R1#*Sep  9 17:42:17.411: ICMP: echo reply sent, src 10.1.1.1, dst 10.1.1.2
R1#*Sep  9 17:42:19.411: ICMP: echo reply sent, src 10.1.1.1, dst 10.1.1.2
R1#*Sep  9 17:42:21.411: ICMP: echo reply sent, src 10.1.1.1, dst 10.1.1.2
```

As shown in this debug message, the ICMP packet from R2 is reaching R1.

Why does the ping fail?

____

____

Issuing the **show frame-relay map** command returns a blank line:

```
R1# show frame-relay map
R1#
```

Turn off all debugging with the **undebug all** command, and reapply the **frame-relay map ip** command, but without using the **broadcast** keyword:

```
R1# undebug all

Port Statistics for unclassified packets is not turned on.
All possible debugging has been turned off
R1# configure terminal

Enter configuration commands, one per line.  End with CNTL/Z.
R1(config)# interface serial0/0/1
R1(config-if)# encapsulation frame-relay
R1(config-if)# frame-relay map ip 10.1.1.2 102
```

```
R2# ping 10.1.1.1

Type escape sequence to abort.
Sending 5, 100-byte ICMP Echos to 10.1.1.1, timeout is 2 seconds:
!!!!!
Success rate is 100 percent (5/5), round-trip min/avg/max = 40/41/44 ms
```

Notice that although pings are successful, the EIGRP adjacency continues to "flap" (go up and down):

```
R1(config-if)#*Sep  9 17:47:58.375: %DUAL-5-NBRCHANGE: IP-EIGRP(0) 1: Neighbor
  10.1.1.2 (Serial0/0/1) is up: new adjacency
R1(config-if)#*Sep  9 17:51:02.887: %DUAL-5-NBRCHANGE: IP-EIGRP(0) 1: Neighbor
  10.1.1.2 (Serial0/0/1) is down: retry limit exceeded
R1(config-if)#*Sep  9 17:51:33.175: %DUAL-5-NBRCHANGE: IP-EIGRP(0) 1: Neighbor
  10.1.1.2 (Serial0/0/1) is up: new adjacency
R1(config-if)#*Sep  9 17:54:37.687: %DUAL-5-NBRCHANGE: IP-EIGRP(0) 1: Neighbor
  10.1.1.2 (Serial0/0/1) is down: retry limit exceeded
```

Why does the EIGRP adjacency continue to flap?

____

____

Replace the **frame-relay map** statement, and include the **broadcast** keyword this time. Verify that the full routing table is restored and that you have full end-to-end connectivity.

```
R1# configure terminal

Enter configuration commands, one per line.  End with CNTL/Z.
R1(config)# interface serial0/0/1
R1(config-if)# encapsulation frame-relay
R1(config-if)# frame-relay map ip 10.1.1.2 102 broadcast
R1# show ip route

Codes: C - connected, S - static, R - RIP, M - mobile, B - BGP
       D - EIGRP, EX - EIGRP external, O - OSPF, IA - OSPF inter area
       N1 - OSPF NSSA external type 1, N2 - OSPF NSSA external type 2
       E1 - OSPF external type 1, E2 - OSPF external type 2
       i - IS-IS, su - IS-IS summary, L1 - IS-IS level-1, L2 - IS-IS level-2
       ia - IS-IS inter area, * - candidate default, U - per-user static route
       o - ODR, P - periodic downloaded static route
Gateway of last resort is not set
C     192.168.10.0/24 is directly connected, FastEthernet0/0
      209.165.200.0/27 is subnetted, 1 subnets
D     209.165.200.224 [90/20640000] via 10.1.1.2, 00:00:05, Serial0/0/1
      10.0.0.0/30 is subnetted, 1 subnets
C     10.1.1.0 is directly connected, Serial0/0/1
```

Step 2. **Change the Frame Relay encapsulation type.**

Cisco IOS software supports two types of Frame Relay encapsulation: the default Cisco encapsulation and the standards-based IETF encapsulation. Change the Frame Relay encapsulation on serial0/0/1 on R2 to IETF:

```
R2(config-if)# encapsulation frame-relay ietf
```

Notice that the interface does not go down. You might be surprised by this. Cisco routers can correctly interpret Frame Relay frames that use either the default Cisco Frame Relay encapsulation or the IETF standard Frame Relay encapsulation. If your network is composed entirely of Cisco routers, it does not make any difference whether you use the default Cisco Frame Relay encapsulation or the IETF standard. Cisco routers understand both types of incoming frames. However, if you have routers from different vendors using Frame Relay, the IETF standard must be used. The command **encapsulation frame-relay ietf** forces the Cisco router to encapsulate its outgoing frames using the IETF standard. This standard can be correctly understood by the router of another vendor.

```
R2# show interface serial 0/0/1

Serial0/0/1 is up, line protocol is up
  Hardware is GT96K Serial
  Internet address is 10.1.1.2/30
  MTU 1500 bytes, BW 128 Kbit, DLY 20000 usec,
     reliability 255/255, txload 1/255, rxload 1/255
  Encapsulation FRAME-RELAY IETF, loopback not set

<output omitted>
```

```
FR-Switch# show int s0/0/0

Serial0/0/0 is up, line protocol is up
  Hardware is GT96K Serial
  MTU 1500 bytes, BW 128 Kbit, DLY 20000 usec,
     reliability 255/255, txload 1/255, rxload 1/255
  Encapsulation FRAME-RELAY, loopback not set
```

Note the difference in output between the two **show interface** commands. Also notice that the EIGRP adjacency is still up. Although FR Switch and R2 are using different encapsulation types, they are still passing traffic.

Change the encapsulation type back to the default:

```
R2(config-if)# encapsulation frame-relay
```

Step 3. Change the LMI type.

On R2, change the LMI type to ANSI:

```
R2# configure terminal

Enter configuration commands, one per line.  End with CNTL/Z.
R2(config)# interface serial 0/0/1
R2(config-if)# encapsulation frame-relay
R2(config-if)# frame-relay lmi-type ansi
R2(config-if)# ^Z
R2# copy run start

Destination filename [startup-config]?
Building configuration...
```

```
[OK]
*Sep  9 18:41:08.351: %LINEPROTO-5-UPDOWN: Line protocol on Interface
  Serial0/0/1,
  changed state to down
*Sep  9 18:41:08.351: %DUAL-5-NBRCHANGE: IP-EIGRP(0) 1: Neighbor 10.1.1.1
  (Serial0/0/1) is down: interface down
R2# show interface serial 0/0/1

Serial0/0/1 is up, line protocol is down
R2# show frame-relay lmi

LMI Statistics for interface Serial0/0/1 (Frame Relay DTE) LMI TYPE = ANSI
  Invalid Unnumbered info 0             Invalid Prot Disc 0
  Invalid dummy Call Ref 0              Invalid Msg Type 0
  Invalid Status Message 0              Invalid Lock Shift 0
  Invalid Information ID 0              Invalid Report IE Len 0
  Invalid Report Request 0              Invalid Keep IE Len 0
  Num Status Enq. Sent 1391             Num Status msgs Rcvd 1382
  Num Update Status Rcvd 0              Num Status Timeouts 10
  Last Full Status Req 00:00:27         Last Full Status Rcvd 00:00:27
```

If you continue issuing the **show frame-relay lmi** command, you will notice the highlighted times incrementing. When 60 seconds have passed, the interface changes its state to up down, because R2 and FR Switch are no longer exchanging keepalives or any other link-state information.

Issue the **debug frame-relay lmi** command. Notice that LMI packets are no longer showing up in pairs. Although all outgoing LMI messages are logged, no incoming messages are shown. This is because R2 is expecting ANSI LMI, and FR Switch is sending Cisco LMI.

```
R2# debug frame-relay lmi

*Aug 25 04:34:25.774: Serial0/0/1(out): StEnq, myseq 20, yourseen 0, DTE
  down
*Aug 25 04:34:25.774: datagramstart = 0xE73F2634, datagramsize = 14
*Aug 25 04:34:25.774: FR encap = 0x00010308
*Aug 25 04:34:25.774: 00 75 95 01 01 00 03 02 14 00
*Aug 25 04:34:25.774:
```

Leave debugging on, and restore the LMI type to Cisco on R2:

```
R2(config-if)# frame-relay lmi-type cisco

*Aug 25 04:42:45.774: Serial0/0/1(out): StEnq, myseq 2, yourseen 1, DTE down
*Aug 25 04:42:45.774: datagramstart = 0xE7000D54, datagramsize = 13
*Aug 25 04:42:45.774: FR encap = 0xFCF10309
*Aug 25 04:42:45.774: 00 75 01 01 01 03 02 02 01
*Aug 25 04:42:45.774:
```

```
*Aug 25 04:42:45.778: Serial0/0/1(in): Status, myseq 2, pak size 21
*Aug 25 04:42:45.778: RT IE 1, length 1, type 0
*Aug 25 04:42:45.778: KA IE 3, length 2, yourseq 2 , myseq 2
*Aug 25 04:42:45.778: PVC IE 0x7 , length 0x6 , dlci 201, status 0x2 , bw 0
*Aug 25 04:42:55.774: Serial0/0/1(out): StEnq, myseq 3, yourseen 2, DTE up
*Aug 25 04:42:55.774: datagramstart = 0xE7001614, datagramsize = 13
*Aug 25 04:42:55.774: FR encap = 0xFCF10309
*Aug 25 04:42:55.774: 00 75 01 01 01 03 02 03 02
*Aug 25 04:42:55.774:
*Aug 25 04:42:55.778: Serial0/0/1(in): Status, myseq 3, pak size 21
*Aug 25 04:42:55.778: RT IE 1, length 1, type 0
*Aug 25 04:42:55.778: KA IE 3, length 2, yourseq 1 , myseq 3
*Aug 25 04:42:55.778: PVC IE 0x7 , length 0x6 , dlci 201, status 0x2 , bw 0
*Aug 25 04:42:56.774: %LINEPROTO-5-UPDOWN: Line protocol on Interface
  Serial0/0/1,
  changed state to up
```

As you can see, the LMI sequence number was reset to 1, and R2 began to understand the LMI messages coming in from FR Switch. After FR Switch and R2 successfully exchanged LMI messages, the interface changed state to up.

Task 6: Configure a Frame Relay Subinterface

Frame Relay supports two types of subinterfaces: point-to-point and point-to-multipoint. Point-to-multipoint subinterfaces support nonbroadcast multiaccess topologies. For example, a hub-and-spoke topology would use a point-to-multipoint subinterface. In this lab, you will create a point-to-point subinterface.

Step 1. **On FR Switch, create a new PVC between R1 and R2:**

```
FR-Switch(config)# interface serial 0/0/0
FR-Switch(config-if)# frame-relay route 112 interface serial 0/0/1 212
FR-Switch(config-if)# interface serial 0/0/1
FR-Switch(config-if)# frame-relay route 212 interface serial 0/0/0 112
```

Step 2. **Create and configure a point-to-point subinterface on R1.**

Create subinterface 112 as a point-to-point interface. Frame Relay encapsulation must be specified on the physical interface before subinterfaces can be created.

```
R1(config)# interface serial 0/0/1.112 point-to-point
R1(config-subif)# ip address 10.1.1.5 255.255.255.252
R1(config-subif)# frame-relay interface-dlci 112
```

Step 3. **Create and configure a point-to-point subinterface on R2:**

```
R2(config)# interface serial 0/0/1.212 point-to-point
R2(config-subif)# ip address 10.1.1.6 255.255.255.252
R2(config-subif)# frame-relay interface-dlci 212
```

Step 4. **Verify connectivity.**

You should be able to ping across the new PVC:

```
R1# ping 10.1.1.6
```

```
Type escape sequence to abort.
Sending 5, 100-byte ICMP Echos to 10.1.1.6, timeout is 2 seconds:
!!!!!
Success rate is 100 percent (5/5), round-trip min/avg/max = 28/28/32 ms
```

```
R2# ping 10.1.1.5

Type escape sequence to abort.
Sending 5, 100-byte ICMP Echos to 10.1.1.5, timeout is 2 seconds:
!!!!!
Success rate is 100 percent (5/5), round-trip min/avg/max = 28/28/32 ms
```

You can also verify the configuration using the **show frame-relay pvc** and **show frame-relay map** commands from Task 4:

```
R1:
R1# show frame-relay pvc

PVC Statistics for interface Serial0/0/1 (Frame Relay DTE)

              Active     Inactive      Deleted       Static
  Local          2           0             0            0
  Switched       0           0             0            0
  Unused         0           0             0            0

DLCI = 102, DLCI USAGE = LOCAL, PVC STATUS = ACTIVE, INTERFACE = Serial0/0/1

  input pkts 319            output pkts 279           in bytes 20665
  out bytes 16665           dropped pkts 0            in pkts dropped 0
  out pkts dropped 0                 out bytes dropped 0
  in FECN pkts 0            in BECN pkts 0            out FECN pkts 0
  out BECN pkts 0           in DE pkts 0              out DE pkts 0
  out bcast pkts 193        out bcast bytes 12352
  5 minute input rate 0 bits/sec, 0 packets/sec
  5 minute output rate 0 bits/sec, 0 packets/sec
  pvc create time 04:43:35, last time pvc status changed 01:16:05

DLCI = 112, DLCI USAGE = LOCAL, PVC STATUS = ACTIVE, INTERFACE =
  Serial0/0/1.112

  input pkts 15             output pkts 211           in bytes 2600
  out bytes 17624           dropped pkts 0            in pkts dropped 0
  out pkts dropped 0                 out bytes dropped 0
  in FECN pkts 0            in BECN pkts 0            out FECN pkts 0
  out BECN pkts 0           in DE pkts 0              out DE pkts 0
  out bcast pkts 200        out bcast bytes 16520
  5 minute input rate 0 bits/sec, 0 packets/sec
```

```
  5 minute output rate 0 bits/sec, 0 packets/sec
  pvc create time 00:19:16, last time pvc status changed 00:18:56
```

```
R2:
R2# show frame-relay pvc

PVC Statistics for interface Serial0/0/1 (Frame Relay DTE)

              Active     Inactive      Deleted       Static
  Local          2           0             0            0
  Switched       0           0             0            0
  Unused         0           0             0            0

DLCI = 201, DLCI USAGE = LOCAL, PVC STATUS = ACTIVE, INTERFACE = Serial0/0/1

  input pkts 331          output pkts 374          in bytes 19928
  out bytes 24098         dropped pkts 0           in pkts dropped 0
  out pkts dropped 0               out bytes dropped 0
  in FECN pkts 0          in BECN pkts 0           out FECN pkts 0
  out BECN pkts 0         in DE pkts 0             out DE pkts 0
  out bcast pkts 331      out bcast bytes 21184
  5 minute input rate 0 bits/sec, 0 packets/sec
  5 minute output rate 0 bits/sec, 0 packets/sec
  pvc create time 05:22:55, last time pvc status changed 01:16:36

DLCI = 212, DLCI USAGE = LOCAL, PVC STATUS = ACTIVE, INTERFACE =
  Serial0/0/1.212

  input pkts 217          output pkts 16           in bytes 18008
  out bytes 2912          dropped pkts 0           in pkts dropped 0
  out pkts dropped 0               out bytes dropped 0
  in FECN pkts 0          in BECN pkts 0           out FECN pkts 0
  out BECN pkts 0         in DE pkts 0             out DE pkts 0
  out bcast pkts 6        out bcast bytes 1872
  5 minute input rate 0 bits/sec, 0 packets/sec
  5 minute output rate 0 bits/sec, 0 packets/sec
  pvc create time 00:19:37, last time pvc status changed 00:18:57
```

```
FR Switch:
FR-Switch# show frame-relay pvc

PVC Statistics for interface Serial0/0/0 (Frame Relay DCE)

              Active     Inactive      Deleted       Static
  Local          0           0             0            0
  Switched       2           0             0            0
  Unused         0           0             0            0
```

```
DLCI = 102, DLCI USAGE = SWITCHED, PVC STATUS = ACTIVE, INTERFACE =
  Serial0/0/0

  input pkts 335          output pkts 376          in bytes 20184
  out bytes 24226         dropped pkts 2           in pkts dropped 2
  out pkts dropped 0               out bytes dropped 0
  in FECN pkts 0          in BECN pkts 0           out FECN pkts 0
  out BECN pkts 0         in DE pkts 0             out DE pkts 0
  out bcast pkts 0        out bcast bytes 0
  30 second input rate 0 bits/sec, 0 packets/sec
  30 second output rate 0 bits/sec, 0 packets/sec
  switched pkts 333
  Detailed packet drop counters:
  no out intf 0           out intf down 0          no out PVC 0
  in PVC down 0           out PVC down 2           pkt too big 0
  shaping Q full 0        pkt above DE 0           policing drop 0
  pvc create time 05:23:43, last time pvc status changed 01:18:32

DLCI = 112, DLCI USAGE = SWITCHED, PVC STATUS = ACTIVE, INTERFACE =
  Serial0/0/0

  input pkts 242          output pkts 18           in bytes 20104
  out bytes 3536          dropped pkts 0           in pkts dropped 0
  out pkts dropped 0               out bytes dropped 0
  in FECN pkts 0          in BECN pkts 0           out FECN pkts 0
  out BECN pkts 0         in DE pkts 0             out DE pkts 0
  out bcast pkts 0        out bcast bytes 0
  30 second input rate 0 bits/sec, 0 packets/sec
  30 second output rate 0 bits/sec, 0 packets/sec
  switched pkts 242
  Detailed packet drop counters:
  no out intf 0           out intf down 0          no out PVC 0
  in PVC down 0           out PVC down 0           pkt too big 0
  shaping Q full 0        pkt above DE 0           policing drop 0
  pvc create time 00:21:41, last time pvc status changed 00:21:22

PVC Statistics for interface Serial0/0/1 (Frame Relay DCE)

              Active     Inactive      Deleted       Static
  Local          0           0             0             0
  Switched       2           0             0             0
  Unused         0           0             0             0

DLCI = 201, DLCI USAGE = SWITCHED, PVC STATUS = ACTIVE, INTERFACE =
  Serial0/0/1
```

```
  input pkts 376          output pkts 333          in bytes 24226
  out bytes 20056         dropped pkts 0           in pkts dropped 0
  out pkts dropped 0               out bytes dropped 0
  in FECN pkts 0          in BECN pkts 0           out FECN pkts 0
  out BECN pkts 0         in DE pkts 0             out DE pkts 0
  out bcast pkts 0        out bcast bytes 0
  30 second input rate 0 bits/sec, 0 packets/sec
  30 second output rate 0 bits/sec, 0 packets/sec
  switched pkts 376
  Detailed packet drop counters:
  no out intf 0           out intf down 0          no out PVC 0
  in PVC down 0           out PVC down 0           pkt too big 0
  shaping Q full 0        pkt above DE 0           policing drop 0
  pvc create time 05:23:14, last time pvc status changed 01:39:39

DLCI = 212, DLCI USAGE = SWITCHED, PVC STATUS = ACTIVE, INTERFACE =
  Serial0/0/1

  input pkts 18           output pkts 243          in bytes 3536
  out bytes 20168         dropped pkts 0           in pkts dropped 0
  out pkts dropped 0               out bytes dropped 0
  in FECN pkts 0          in BECN pkts 0           out FECN pkts 0
  out BECN pkts 0         in DE pkts 0             out DE pkts 0
  out bcast pkts 0        out bcast bytes 0
  30 second input rate 0 bits/sec, 0 packets/sec
  30 second output rate 0 bits/sec, 0 packets/sec
  switched pkts 18
  Detailed packet drop counters:
  no out intf 0           out intf down 0          no out PVC 0
  in PVC down 0           out PVC down 0           pkt too big 0
  shaping Q full 0        pkt above DE 0           policing drop 0
  pvc create time 00:21:36, last time pvc status changed 00:21:20
```

```
R1:
R1# show frame-relay map

Serial0/0/1 (up): ip 10.1.1.2 dlci 102(0x66,0x1860), static,
              broadcast,
              CISCO, status defined, active
Serial0/0/1.112 (up): point-to-point dlci, dlci 112(0x70,0x1C00), broadcast
          status defined, active
```

```
R2:
R2# show frame-relay map

Serial0/0/1 (up): ip 10.1.1.1 dlci 201(0xC9,0x3090), static,
              broadcast,
```

```
          CISCO, status defined, active
Serial0/0/1.212 (up): point-to-point dlci, dlci 212(0xD4,0x3440), broadcast
          status defined, active
```

```
FR Switch:
FR-Switch# show frame-relay route

Input Intf      Input Dlci      Output Intf     Output Dlci     Status
Serial0/0/0     102             Serial0/0/1     201             active
Serial0/0/0     112             Serial0/0/1     212             active
Serial0/0/1     201             Serial0/0/0     102             active
Serial0/0/1     212             Serial0/0/0     112             active
```

Now debug the Frame Relay LMI:

```
R1# debug frame-relay lmi

*Aug 25 05:58:50.902: Serial0/0/1(out): StEnq, myseq 136, yourseen 135, DTE
  up
*Aug 25 05:58:50.902: datagramstart = 0xE7000354, datagramsize = 13
*Aug 25 05:58:50.902: FR encap = 0xFCF10309
*Aug 25 05:58:50.902: 00 75 01 01 00 03 02 88 87
*Aug 25 05:58:50.902:
*Aug 25 05:58:50.906: Serial0/0/1(in): Status, myseq 136, pak size 29
*Aug 25 05:58:50.906: RT IE 1, length 1, type 0
*Aug 25 05:58:50.906: KA IE 3, length 2, yourseq 136, myseq 136
*Aug 25 05:58:50.906: PVC IE 0x7 , length 0x6 , dlci 102, status 0x2 , bw 0
*Aug 25 05:58:50.906: PVC IE 0x7 , length 0x6 , dlci 112, status 0x2 , bw 0
```

Note that two DLCIs are listed in the LMI message from FR Switch to R1.

```
R2# debug frame-relay lmi

*Aug 25 06:08:35.774: Serial0/0/1(out):StEnq, myseq 7,yourseen 4,DTE up
*Aug 25 06:08:35.774: datagramstart = 0xE73F28B4, datagramsize = 13
*Aug 25 06:08:35.774: FR encap = 0xFCF10309
*Aug 25 06:08:35.774: 00 75 01 01 00 03 02 07 04
*Aug 25 06:08:35.774:
*Aug 25 06:08:35.778: Serial0/0/1(in): Status, myseq 7, pak size 29
*Aug 25 06:08:35.778: RT IE 1, length 1, type 0
*Aug 25 06:08:35.778: KA IE 3, length 2, yourseq 5 , myseq 7
*Aug 25 06:08:35.778: PVC IE 0x7,length 0x6, dlci 201, status 0x2, bw 0
*Aug 25 06:08:35.778: PVC IE 0x7,length 0x6, dlci 212, status 0x2, bw 0
```

Lab 3-2: Challenge Frame Relay Configuration (3.5.2)

Upon completion of this lab, you will be able to

- Cable a network according to the topology diagram shown in Figure 3-3
- Erase the startup configuration, and reload a router to the default state
- Perform basic configuration tasks on a router
- Configure and activate interfaces
- Configure EIGRP routing on all routers
- Configure Frame Relay encapsulation on all serial interfaces
- Configure a Frame Relay PVC
- Intentionally break and restore a Frame Relay PVC
- Configure Frame Relay subinterfaces
- Intentionally break and restore the PVC

Figure 3-3 shows the network topology for this lab. Table 3-3 provides the IP addresses, subnet masks, and default gateways (where applicable) for all devices in the topology.

Figure 3-3 Network Topology for Lab 3-2

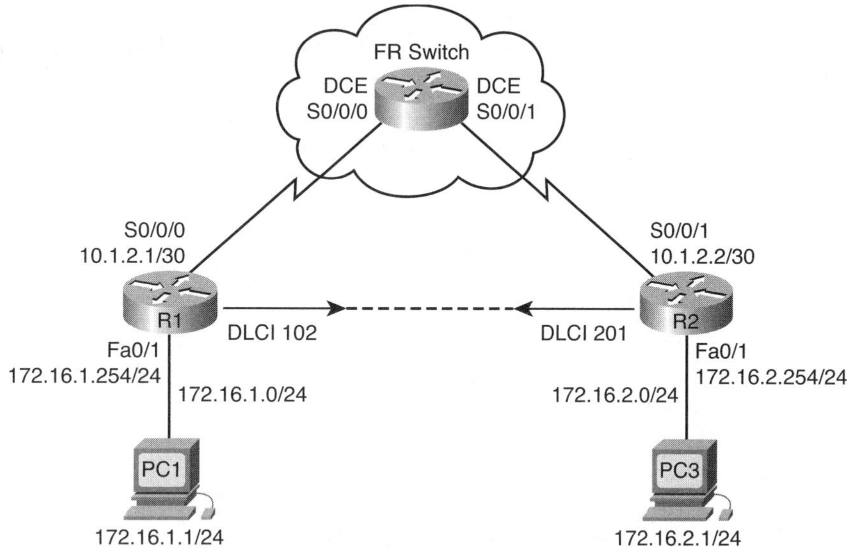

Table 3-3 Lab 3-2 Addressing Table

Device	Interface	IP Address	Subnet Mask	Default Gateway
R1	Fa0/1	172.16.1.254	255.255.255.0	—
	S0/0/0	10.1.2.1	255.255.255.252	—
R2	Fa0/1	172.16.2.254	255.255.255.0	—
	S0/0/1	10.1.2.2	255.255.255.252	—
PC1	NIC	172.16.1.1	255.255.255.0	172.16.1.254
PC3	NIC	172.16.2.1	255.255.255.0	172.16.2.254

Scenario

In this lab, you will configure Frame Relay using the network shown in Figure 3-3. If you need assistance, refer to Lab 3-1. However, try to do as much on your own as possible.

Task 1: Prepare the Network

Step 1. Cable a network that is similar to the one shown in Figure 3-3.

Step 2. Clear any existing configurations on the routers.

Task 2: Perform Basic Router Configuration

Configure the R1, R2, and FR Switch routers according to the following guidelines:

- Configure the router hostname.
- Disable DNS lookup.
- Configure an EXEC mode password.
- Configure a message-of-the-day banner.
- Configure a password for console connections.
- Configure synchronous logging.
- Configure a password for vty connections.

Task 3: Configure IP Addresses

Step 1. Configure IP addresses on all links according to the addressing table.

Step 2. Verify IP addressing and interfaces.

Step 3. Activate the Ethernet interfaces of R1 and R2. Do not activate the serial interfaces.

Step 4. Configure the Ethernet interfaces of PC1 and PC3.

Step 5. Test connectivity between the PCs and their local routers.

Task 4: Configure EIGRP on Routers R1 and R2

Enable EIGRP on R1 and R2 for all subnets, and disable autosummarization.

Task 5: Configure Frame Relay PVC Between R1 and R2

Step 1. Configure interfaces on FR Switch to create the PVC between R1 and R2.

Use the DLCIs shown in Figure 3-3.

Step 2. Configure physical interfaces on R1 and R2 for Frame Relay encapsulation.

Do not automatically discover IP addresses on the far end of links. Activate the link after full configuration.

Step 3. Configure Frame Relay maps on R1 and R2 with proper DLCIs. Enable broadcast traffic on the DLCIs.

Step 4. Verify end-to-end connectivity using PC1 and PC2.

Task 6: Intentionally Break the PVC, and Then Restore It

Step 1. By a means of your choosing, break the PVC between R1 and R2.

Step 2. Restore full connectivity to your network.

Step 3. Verify full connectivity to your network.

Task 7: Configure Frame Relay Subinterfaces

Step 1. Remove the IP address and frame map configuration from the physical interfaces on R1 and R2.

Step 2. Configure Frame Relay point-to-point subinterfaces on R1 and R2 with the same IP addresses and DLCI used earlier on the physical interfaces.

Step 3. Verify full end-to-end connectivity.

Task 8: Intentionally Break the PVC, and Then Restore It

Step 1. Break the PVC using a different method than you used in Task 6.

Step 2. Restore the PVC.

Step 3. Verify full end-to-end connectivity.

Task 9: Document the Router Configurations

On each router, issue the **show run** command, and capture the configurations.

Task 10: Clean Up

Erase the configurations, and reload the routers. Disconnect and store the cabling. For PC hosts that are normally connected to other networks (such as the school LAN or the Internet), reconnect the appropriate cabling, and restore the TCP/IP settings.

Lab 3-3: Troubleshooting Frame Relay (3.5.3)

In this lab, you will practice Frame Relay troubleshooting skills.

Figure 3-4 shows the network topology for this lab, and Table 3-4 provides the IP addresses, subnet masks, and default gateways (where applicable) for all devices in the topology.

Figure 3-4 Network Topology for Lab 3-3

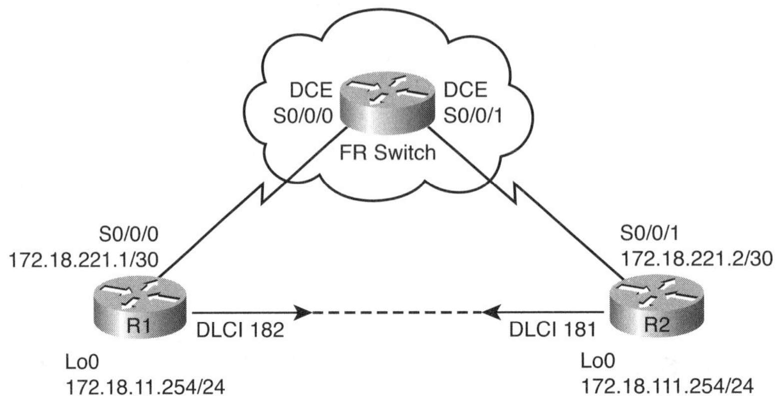

Table 3-4 Lab 3-3 Addressing Table

Device	Interface	IP Address	Subnet Mask	Default Gateway
R1	Lo0	172.18.11.254	255.255.255.0	—
	S0/0/0	172.18.221.1	255.255.255.252	—
R2	Lo0	172.18.111.254	255.255.255.0	—
	S0/0/1	172.18.221.2	255.255.255.252	—

Scenario

In this lab, you will practice troubleshooting a misconfigured Frame Relay environment. Load or have your instructor load the following configurations into your routers. Locate and repair all errors in the configurations, and establish end-to-end connectivity. Your final configuration should match the topology diagram and addressing table. All passwords are set to **cisco** except the enable secret password, which is set to **class**.

Task 1: Prepare the Network

Step 1. Cable a network that is similar to the one shown in Figure 3-4.

Step 2. Clear any existing configurations on the routers.

Step 3. Import the configurations:

```
Router 1
!
hostname R1
!
enable secret class
```

```
!
no ip domain lookup
!
!
!
!
interface Loopback0
 ip address 172.18.11.254 255.255.255.0
!
interface FastEthernet0/0
 no ip address
 shutdown
 duplex auto
 speed auto
!
interface FastEthernet0/1
 no ip address
 shutdown
 duplex auto
 speed auto
!
interface Serial0/0/1
 no ip address
 shutdown
 no fair-queue
 clockrate 125000
!
interface Serial0/0/0
 ip address 172.18.221.1 255.255.255.252
 encapsulation frame-relay
 frame-relay map ip 172.18.221.2 678 broadcast
no frame-relay inverse-arp
 no shutdown
!
router eigrp 1
 network 172.18.221.0 0.0.0.3
 network 172.18.11.0 0.0.0.255
 no auto-summary
!
!
!
line con 0
 password cisco
 logging synchronous
```

```
line aux 0
line vty 0 4
 password cisco
 login
!
end
```

Router 2

```
!
hostname R2
!
enable secret class
!
no ip domain lookup
!
interface Loopback0
 ip address 172.18.111.254 255.255.255.0
!
interface FastEthernet0/0
 no ip address
 shutdown
 duplex auto
 speed auto
!
interface FastEthernet0/1
 no ip address
 shutdown
 duplex auto
 speed auto
!
interface Serial0/0/0
 no ip address
 shutdown
 no fair-queue
!
interface Serial0/0/1
 ip address 172.18.221.2 255.255.255.252
 encapsulation frame-relay
 clockrate 125000
 frame-relay map ip 172.18.221.1 181 broadcast
 no frame-relay inverse-arp
 frame-relay lmi-type ansi
!
router eigrp 1
 network 172.18.221.0 0.0.0.3
```

```
 network 172.18.111.0 0.0.0.255
 no auto-summary
!
!
!
line con 0
 password cisco
 logging synchronous
line aux 0
line vty 0 4
 password cisco
 login
!
end
```

```
FR-Switch:
!
hostname FR-Switch
!
!
enable secret class
!
!
!
no ip domain lookup
frame-relay switching
!
!
!
!
interface FastEthernet0/0
 no ip address
 shutdown
 duplex auto
 speed auto
!
interface FastEthernet0/1
 no ip address
 shutdown
 duplex auto
 speed auto
!
interface Serial0/0/0
 no ip address
 encapsulation frame-relay
```

```
 no fair-queue
 clockrate 125000
 frame-relay intf-type dce
 frame-relay route 182 interface Serial0/0/1 181
 no shutdown
!
interface Serial0/0/1
 no ip address
 clockrate 125000
 encapsulation frame-relay
 frame-relay intf-type dce
 no shutdown
!
!
!
!
line con 0
 password cisco
 logging synchronous
line aux 0
line vty 0 4
 password cisco
 login
!
end
```

Task 2: Troubleshoot and Repair the Frame Relay Connection Between R1 and R2

Task 3: Document the Router Configurations

On each router, issue the **show run** command, and capture the configurations.

Task 4: Clean Up

Erase the configurations, and reload the routers. Disconnect and store the cabling. For PC hosts that are normally connected to other networks, such as the school LAN or the Internet, reconnect the appropriate cabling, and restore the TCP/IP settings.

Lab 3-4: Frame Relay with Subinterfaces

Upon completion of this bonus lab, you will be able to

- Configure point-to-point subinterfaces
- Configure Frame Relay maps
- Configure EIGRP

Figure 3-5 shows the network topology for this lab. Table 3-5 provides the interfaces, IP addresses, and subnet masks for all devices in the topology.

Figure 3-5 Network Topology for Lab 3-4

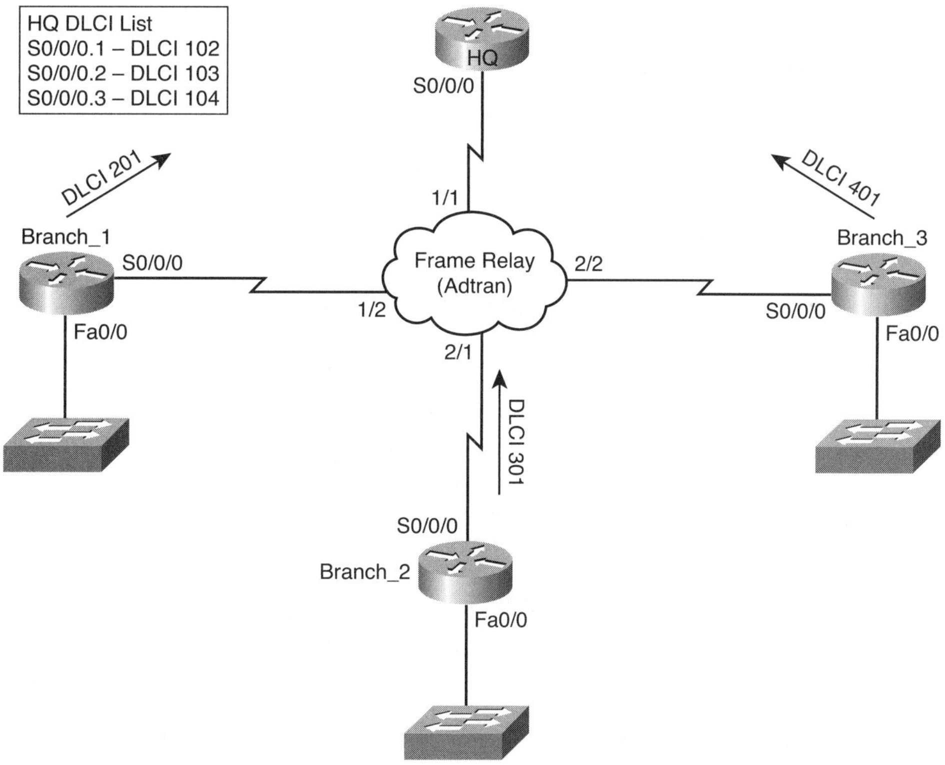

Table 3-5 Lab 3-4 Addressing Table

Router	Interface	IP Address	Subnet Mask
HQ	Serial 0/0/0.102	10.10.10.1	255.255.255.252
	Serial 0/0/0.103	10.10.10.5	255.255.255.252
	Serial 0/0/0.104	10.10.10.9	255.255.255.252
Branch 1	Serial 0/0/0	10.10.10.2	255.255.255.252
	FastEthernet 0/0	172.16.0.1	255.255.240.0
Branch 2	Serial 0/0/0	10.10.10.6	255.255.255.252
	FastEthernet 0/0	172.16.16.1	255.255.248.0
Branch 3	Serial 0/0/0	10.10.10.10	255.255.255.252
	FastEthernet 0/0	172.16.24.1	255.255.252.0

Scenario

You are the network administrator of a company that has three branch offices. In a cost-saving move, you decide to implement a hub-and-spoke design using subinterfaces. Each subinterface will be on a separate subnet, with a unique DLCI number to identify each virtual circuit.

Task 1: Configure the HQ Router

Step 1. Configure Serial 0/0/0 to use Frame Relay encapsulation.

Step 2. Configure the LMI as ANSI.

Step 3. Administratively enable the interface.

Task 2: Configure Subinterfaces on the HQ Router

Step 1. Configure the serial 0/0/0.102 subinterface as point-to-point.

Step 2. Configure the appropriate IP address on the interface.

Step 3. Use the **frame-relay interface-dlci** command to tell the subinterface to use DLCI 102. This tells the router to use this circuit when connecting to the Branch 1 router.

Step 4. Configure the serial 0/0/0.103 subinterface as point-to-point.

Step 5. Configure the appropriate IP address on the interface.

Step 6. Use the **frame-relay interface-dlci** command to tell the subinterface to use DLCI 103. This tells the router to use this circuit when connecting to the Branch 2 router.

Step 7. Configure the serial 0/0/0.104 subinterface as point-to-point.

Step 8. Configure the appropriate IP address on the interface.

Step 9. Use the **frame-relay interface-dlci** command to tell the subinterface to use DLCI 104. This tells the router to use this circuit when connecting to the Branch 3 router.

Task 3: Configure the Serial Interface on the Branch 1 Router

Step 1. Configure the serial 0/0/0 interface with the appropriate IP address.

Step 2. Configure Serial 0/0/0 to use Frame Relay encapsulation.

Step 3. Configure a Frame Relay map to the HQ router using DLCI 201.

Step 4. Administratively enable the interface.

Step 5. Verify connectivity, and ping the corresponding interface on the HQ router.

Task 4: Configure the Serial Interface on the Branch 2 Router

Step 1. Configure the serial 0/0/0 interface with the appropriate IP address.

Step 2. Configure Serial 0/0/0 to use Frame Relay encapsulation.

Step 3. Configure a Frame Relay map to the HQ router using DLCI 301.

Step 4. Administratively enable the interface.

Step 5. Verify connectivity, and ping the corresponding interface on the HQ router.

Task 5: Configure the Serial Interface on the Branch 3 Router

Step 1. Configure the serial 0/0/0 interface with the appropriate IP address.

Step 2. Configure Serial 0/0/0 to use Frame Relay encapsulation.

Step 3. Configure a Frame Relay map to the HQ router using DLCI 401.

Step 4. Administratively enable the interface.

Step 5. Verify connectivity, and ping the corresponding interface on the HQ router.

Task 6: Configure the FastEthernet Interface on the Branch 1 LAN

Step 1. Configure the FastEthernet 0/0 interface with the appropriate IP address.

Step 2. Administratively enable the interface.

Task 7: Configure the FastEthernet Interface on the Branch 2 LAN

Step 1. Configure the FastEthernet 0/0 interface with the appropriate IP address.

Step 2. Administratively enable the interface.

Task 8: Configure the FastEthernet Interface on the Branch 3 LAN

Step 1. Configure the FastEthernet 0/0 interface with the appropriate IP address.

Step 2. Administratively enable the interface.

Task 9: Configure EIGRP

Step 1. Configure EIGRP on each router using Process ID 168.

Step 2. Advertise all directly connected networks as subnets using their respective wildcard masks.

Step 3. Disable autosummarization on each router.

Task 10: Verify the Configurations

Use the **show ip route** command to verify that all networks are visible in the routing table. If not, check your configurations as well as map statements.

Packet Tracer Companion: Frame Relay Full Mesh

You can now open the file LSG04-Lab0335.pka on the CD-ROM that accompanies this book to repeat bonus Lab 3-4 using Packet Tracer. Remember, however, that Packet Tracer is not a substitute for hands-on lab experience with real equipment.

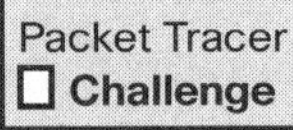

Packet Tracer Skills Integration Challenge

Open file LSG04-PTSkills3.pka on the CD-ROM that accompanies this book to perform this exercise using Packet Tracer. Upon completion of this skills integration challenge, you will be able to

- Configure PPP with CHAP
- Configure full-mesh Frame Relay
- Configure static and default routing
- Configure and test inter-VLAN routing
- Configure VTP and trunking on switches
- Configure VLANs on a switch
- Configure and verify interface VLAN 99
- Configure a switch as root for all spanning trees
- Assign ports to VLANs
- Test end-to-end connectivity

This activity allows you to practice a variety of skills, including configuring Frame Relay, PPP with CHAP, static and default routing, VTP, and VLAN. Because this activity has almost 150 graded components, you may not see the completion percentage increase every time you configure a graded command. You can always click **Check Results** and **Assessment Items** to see if you correctly entered a graded command.

Figure 3-6 shows the network topology for this challenge. Table 3-6 provides the interfaces, IP addresses, and subnet masks for all devices in the topology.

Figure 3-6 Network Topology for Skills Integration Challenge

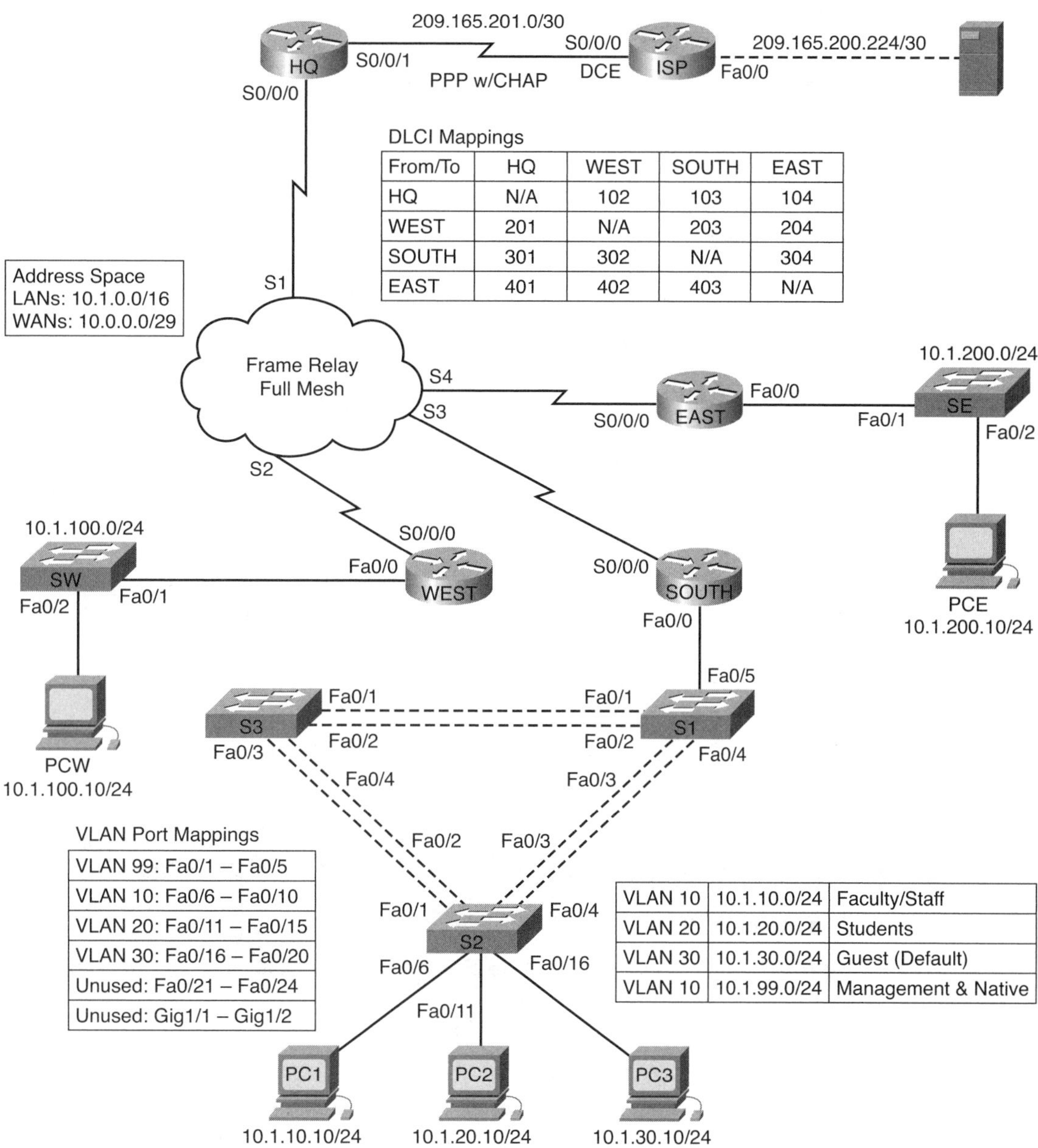

Table 3-6 Skills Integration Challenge Addressing Table

Device	Interface	IP Address	Subnet Mask
HQ	S0/0/1	209.165.201.2	255.255.255.252
	S0/0/0	10.0.0.1	255.255.255.248
WEST	S0/0/0	10.0.0.2	255.255.255.248
	Fa0/0	10.1.100.1	255.255.255.0
SOUTH	S0/0/0	10.0.0.3	255.255.255.248
	Fa0/0.10	10.1.10.1	255.255.255.0
	Fa0/0.20	10.1.20.1	255.255.255.0
	Fa0/0.30	10.1.30.1	255.255.255.0
	Fa0/0.99	10.1.99.1	255.255.255.0
EAST	S0/0/0	10.0.0.4	255.255.255.248
	Fa0/0	10.1.200.1	255.255.255.0
ISP	S0/0/0	209.165.201.1	255.255.255.252
	Fa0/0	209.165.200.225	255.255.255.252
Web Server	NIC	209.165.200.226	255.255.255.252
S1	VLAN99	10.1.99.11	255.255.255.0
S2	VLAN99	10.1.99.12	255.255.255.0
S3	VLAN99	10.1.99.13	255.255.255.0

Task 1: Configure PPP with CHAP Between Devices

Step 1. Configure and activate serial 0/0/1 on HQ.

Step 2. Configure PPP encapsulation on HQ for the link shared with ISP.

Step 3. Configure CHAP authentication on HQ.

Use **cisco** as the password.

Step 4. Verify connectivity between HQ and ISP.

The link between HQ and ISP should now be up, and you should be able to ping ISP. However, the link may take a few minutes to come up in Packet Tracer. To speed up the process, switch between Simulation and Realtime mode three or four times.

Step 5. Check the results.

Your completion percentage should be 4%. If not, click **Check Results** to see which required components are not yet completed.

Task 2: Configure Full-Mesh Frame Relay

The topology diagram shown in Figure 3-6 and the information in Table 3-7 both show the DLCI mappings used in this full-mesh Frame Relay configuration. Read the table from left to right. For example, the DLCI mappings you will configure on HQ are 102 to WEST, 103 to SOUTH, and 104 to EAST.

Table 3-7 DLCI Mappings

From/To	HQ	WEST	SOUTH	EAST
HQ	—	102	103	104
WEST	201	—	203	204
SOUTH	301	302	—	304
EAST	401	402	403	—

HQ, WEST, and SOUTH are all using the default Frame Relay encapsulation **cisco**. However, EAST is using the encapsulation type IETF.

Step 1. Configure and activate the serial 0/0/0 interface on HQ.

Configure the interface with the following information:

- IP address
- Frame Relay encapsulation
- Mappings to WEST, SOUTH, and EAST (EAST uses IETF encapsulation)
- LMI type is ANSI

Step 2. Configure and activate the serial 0/0/0 interface on WEST.

Configure the interface with the following information:

- IP address
- Frame Relay encapsulation
- Mappings to HQ, SOUTH, and EAST (EAST uses IETF encapsulation)
- LMI type is ANSI

Step 3. Configure and activate the serial 0/0/0 interface on SOUTH.

Configure the interface with the following information:

- IP address
- Frame Relay encapsulation
- Mappings to HQ, WEST, and EAST (EAST uses IETF encapsulation)
- LMI type is ANSI

Step 4. Configure and activate the Serial 0/0/0 interface on EAST.

Configure the interface with the following information:

- IP address
- Frame Relay encapsulation using IETF
- Mappings to HQ, WEST, and SOUTH
- LMI type is ANSI

Note: Packet Tracer does not grade your map statements. However, you must still configure the commands. You should now have full connectivity between the Frame Relay routers.

Step 5. Verify connectivity between Frame Relay routers.

The map on HQ should look like the following. Make sure that all routers have full maps.

- **Serial0/0/0 (up)**: ip 10.0.0.2 dlci 102, static, broadcast, CISCO, status defined, active
- **Serial0/0/0 (up)**: ip 10.0.0.3 dlci 103, static, broadcast, CISCO, status defined, active
- **Serial0/0/0 (up)**: ip 10.0.0.4 dlci 104, static, broadcast, IETF, status defined, active

Verify that HQ, WEST, SOUTH, and EAST can now ping each other.

Step 6. Check the results.

Your completion percentage should be 28%. If not, click **Check Results** to see which required components are not yet completed.

Task 3: Configure Static and Default Routing

No routing protocol is used in this topology. All routing is done through static and default routing.

Step 1. Configure static and default routes on HQ.

- HQ needs six static routes to the six remote LANs in the topology. Use the *next-hop-ip* argument in the static route configuration.
- HQ also needs a default route. Use the *exit-interface* argument in the default route configuration.

Step 2. Configure static and default routes on WEST.

- WEST needs five static routes to the five remote LANs in the topology. Use the *next-hop-ip* argument in the static route configuration.
- WEST also needs a default route. Use the *next-hop-ip* argument in the default route configuration.

Step 3. Configure static and default routes on SOUTH.

- SOUTH needs two static routes to the two remote LANs in the topology. Use the *next-hop-ip* argument in the static route configuration.
- SOUTH needs a default route. Use the *next-hop-ip* argument in the default route configuration.

Step 4. Configure static and default routes on EAST.

- EAST needs five static routes to the five remote LANs in the topology. Use the *next-hop-ip* argument in the static route configuration.
- EAST needs a default route. Use the *next-hop-ip* argument in the default route configuration.

Step 5. Verify connectivity from EAST and WEST LANs to the Web Server.

- All routers should now be able to ping the Web Server.
- The WEST PC (PCW) and the EAST PC (PCE) should now be able to ping each other and the Web Server.

Step 6. Check the results.

Your completion percentage should be 43%. If not, click **Check Results** to see which required components are not yet completed.

Task 4: Configure and Test Inter-VLAN Routing

Step 1. Configure inter-VLAN routing on SOUTH.

Using the addressing table, activate Fast Ethernet 0/0 on SOUTH, and configure inter-VLAN routing. The subinterface number corresponds to the VLAN number. VLAN 99 is the native VLAN.

Step 2. Test inter-VLAN routing on SOUTH.

HQ, WEST, and EAST should now be able to ping each of the subinterfaces on SOUTH.

Step 3. Check the results.

Your completion percentage should be 56%. If not, click **Check Results** to see which required components are not yet completed. The routers are now fully configured.

Task 5: Configure VTP and Trunking on the Switches

Step 1. Configure VTP settings on S1, S2, and S3.

S1 is the server. S2 and S3 are clients.

The domain name is **CCNA**.

The password is **cisco**.

Step 2. Configure trunking on S1, S2, and S3.

Trunking ports for S1, S2, and S3 are all ports attached to another switch or router. Set all trunking ports to trunk mode, and assign VLAN 99 as the native VLAN.

Step 3. Check the results.

Your completion percentage should be 81%. If not, click **Check Results** to see which required components are not yet completed.

Task 6: Configure VLANs on the Switch

Step 1. Create and name the VLANs.

Create and name the following VLANs on S1 only:

- VLAN 10, name = Faculty/Staff
- VLAN 20, name = Students
- VLAN 30, name = Guest(Default)
- VLAN 99, name = Management&Native

Step 2. Verify that the VLANs were sent S2 and S3.

What command displays the following output?

```
VTP Version                     : 2
Configuration Revision          : 8
Maximum VLANs supported locally : 64
Number of existing VLANs        : 9
VTP Operating Mode              : Client
VTP Domain Name                 : CCNA
VTP Pruning Mode                : Disabled
VTP V2 Mode                     : Disabled
VTP Traps Generation            : Disabled
MD5 digest                      : 0xF5 0x50 0x30 0xB6 0x91 0x74 0x95 0xD9
Configuration last modified by 0.0.0.0 at 3-1-93 00:12:30
```

____

What command displays the following output?

```
VLAN Name                             Status    Ports
---- -------------------------------- --------- -------------------------------
1    default                          active    Fa0/5, Fa0/6, Fa0/7, Fa0/8
                                                Fa0/9, Fa0/10, Fa0/11, Fa0/12
                                                Fa0/13, Fa0/14, Fa0/15, Fa0/16
                                                Fa0/17, Fa0/18, Fa0/19, Fa0/20
                                                Fa0/21, Fa0/22, Fa0/23, Fa0/24
                                                Gig1/1, Gig1/2
10   Faculty/Staff                    active
20   Students                         active
30   Guest(Default)                   active
99   Management&Native                active
<output omitted>
```

____

Step 3. Check the results.

Your completion percentage should be 84%. If not, click **Check Results** to see which required components are not yet completed.

Task 7: Configure and Verify VLAN 99

Step 1. On S1, S2, and S3, follow these steps:

- Configure and activate VLAN 99.
- Configure the default gateway.
- Verify that S1, S2, and S3 can now ping SOUTH at 10.1.99.1.

Step 2. Check the results.

Your completion percentage should be 92%. If not, click **Check Results** to see which required components are not yet completed.

Task 8: Configure S1 as Root for All Spanning Trees

Step 1. Configure S1 as the root bridge for all spanning trees, including VLANs 1, 10, 20, 30, and 99.

Notice that S3 won the root war and is currently the root bridge for all spanning trees. Set the priority to 4096 on S1 for all spanning trees.

Step 2. Verify that S1 is now the root for all spanning trees.

Only the output for VLAN 1 is shown here. However, S1 should be the root for all spanning trees. What command displays the following output?

```
VLAN0001
  Spanning tree enabled protocol ieee
  Root ID    Priority    4097
             Address     00D0.BC79.4B57
             This bridge is the root
             Hello Time   2 sec  Max Age 20 sec  Forward Delay 15 sec
  Bridge ID  Priority    4097  (priority 4096 sys-id-ext 1)
             Address     00D0.BC79.4B57
             Aging Time 300

Interface        Role Sts Cost      Prio.Nbr Type
---------------- ---- --- --------- -------- --------------------------------
Fa0/1            Desg FWD 19        128.3    Shr
Fa0/2            Desg FWD 19        128.3    Shr
Fa0/3            Desg FWD 19        128.3    Shr
Fa0/4            Desg FWD 19        128.3    Shr
Fa0/5            Desg FWD 19        128.3    Shr
<output omitted>
```

____

Step 3. Check the results.

Your completion percentage should be 96%. If not, click **Check Results** to see which required components are not yet completed.

Task 9: Assign Ports to VLANs

Step 1. Assign ports on S2 to VLANs.

Packet Tracer grades only the ports that are attached to PC1, PC2, and PC3.

- Configure the port for access mode.
- Assign the port to its VLAN.

The VLAN port mappings are as follows:

- VLAN 99: Fa0/1 to Fa0/5
- VLAN 10: Fa0/6 to Fa0/10
- VLAN 20: Fa0/11 to Fa0/15
- VLAN 30: Fa0/16 to Fa0/20
- Unused: Fa0/21 to Fa0/24; Gig1/1; Gig1/2

Unused ports should be shut down for security purposes.

Step 2. Verify VLAN port assignments.

What command was used to get the following output showing the VLAN assignments?

```
VLAN Name                             Status    Ports
---- -------------------------------- --------- -------------------------------
1    default                          active    Fa0/5, Fa0/21, Fa0/22, Fa0/23
                                                Fa0/24, Gig1/1, Gig1/2
10   Faculty/Staff                    active    Fa0/6, Fa0/7, Fa0/8, Fa0/9
                                                Fa0/10
20   Students                         active    Fa0/11, Fa0/12, Fa0/13, Fa0/14
                                                Fa0/15
30   Guest(Default)                   active    Fa0/16, Fa0/17, Fa0/18, Fa0/19
                                                Fa0/20
99   Management&Native                active
1002 fddi-default                     active
1003 token-ring-default               active
1004 fddinet-default                  active
1005 trnet-default                    active
```

____

Step 3. Check the results.

Your completion percentage should be 100%. If not, click **Check Results** to see which required components are not yet completed.

Task 10: Test End-to-End Connectivity

Although Packet Tracer may take some time to converge, pings eventually will succeed from PC1, PC2, and PC3. Test connectivity to PCW, PCE, and the Web Server. If necessary, switch between Simulation and Realtime modes to accelerate convergence.

CHAPTER 4

Network Security

The Study Guide portion of this chapter uses a combination of matching, completion, and short-answer exercises to test and reinforce your knowledge of network security.

The Labs portion of this chapter includes all the online curriculum labs and the Packet Tracer Skills Integration Challenge.

As you work through this chapter, use Chapter 4 in the *Accessing the WAN, CCNA Exploration Companion Guide* or use the corresponding Chapter 4 in the Accessing the WAN online curriculum for assistance.

Study Guide

Introduction to Network Security

A study of network security starts with understanding the types of threats to networks and where those threats come from. It is important to be familiar with the terminology of threats, attacks, and attackers to plan for and mitigate these risks.

Vocabulary Exercise: Matching

Match the description on the left with a security threat or attack on the right. This exercise is not necessarily a one-to-one matching. Some descriptions might be used more than once, and some threats or attacks might have multiple descriptions.

Descriptions

a. The unauthorized discovery and mapping of systems, services, or vulnerabilities
b. Mostly inexperienced individuals using easily available hacking tools, such as shell scripts and password crackers
c. Arise from individuals or organizations working outside of a company who do not have authorized access to the computer systems or network
d. Come from someone who has authorized access to the network with either an account or physical access
e. Can lead to physical damage to servers, routers, switches, cabling plant, and workstations
f. The ability for an intruder to gain access to a device for which the intruder does not have an account or a password
g. Temperature extremes (too hot or too cold) or humidity extremes (too wet or too dry)
h. Involve either crashing the system or slowing it down to the point that it is unusable
i. Poor handling of key electrical components (electrostatic discharge), lack of critical spare parts, poor cabling, and poor labeling
j. Voltage spikes, insufficient supply voltage (brownouts), unconditioned power (noise), and total power loss
k. Malicious software that can be inserted onto a host to damage or corrupt a system, replicate itself, or deny access to networks, systems, or services
l. Come from individuals or groups that are more highly motivated and technically competent

Terms

__ Reconnaissance
__ Access
__ Denial of service
__ Worms, viruses, and Trojan horses
__ Unstructured threats
__ Structured threats
__ External threats
__ Internal threats
__ Hardware threats
__ Environmental threats
__ Electrical threats
__ Maintenance threats

Vocabulary Exercise: Completion

Complete the paragraphs that follow by filling in the appropriate words and phrases.

To help automate IP address information gathering, an attacker may use a _______________ tool, such as fping or gping, which systematically pings all network addresses in a given range or subnet. This is similar to going through a section of a telephone book and calling each number to see who answers.

When the active IP addresses are identified, the intruder uses a ___________________ to determine which network services or _______________ are active on the live IP addresses. Common software utilities can perform this attack (for example, Nmap and Superscan).

Network snooping and packet sniffing are common terms for _______________. The information gathered this way can be used to pose other attacks to the network.

A common method for eavesdropping on communications is to capture TCP/IP or other protocol packets and decode the contents using a _______________ or similar utility.

Password attacks can be implemented using a _______________ to yield user accounts and passwords that are transmitted as clear text. Password attacks usually refer to repeated attempts to log in to a shared resource, such as a server or router, to identify a user account, password, or both. These repeated attempts are called ___________________ attacks or _______________ attacks.

The goal of a__________________ attack is to compromise a trusted host, using it to stage attacks on other hosts in a network.

A ___________________ attack is a type of trust-exploitation attack that uses a compromised host to pass traffic through a firewall that would otherwise be blocked.

A ___________________ attack is carried out by attackers that manage to position themselves between two legitimate hosts. The attacker might allow the normal transactions between hosts to occur, and only periodically manipulate the conversation between the two.

Some common denial-of-service (DoS) attacks include the following:

- ____
- ____
- ____
- ____

Worm attack mitigation requires diligence on the part of system and network administration staff. The following are the recommended steps for worm attack mitigation:

1. _______________: Contain the spread of the worm in and within the network. Compartmentalize uninfected parts of the network.
2. _______________: Start patching all systems and, if possible, scanning for vulnerable systems.
3. _______________: Track down each infected machine inside the network. Disconnect, remove, or block infected machines from the network.
4. _______________: Clean and patch each infected system. Some worms might require complete core system reinstallations to clean the system.

A _______________ is malicious software attached to another program to execute a particular unwanted function on a workstation.

A _______________ is different only in that the entire application was written to look like something else, when in fact it is an attack tool.

The key element that distinguishes a computer _______________ from a computer _______________ is that human interaction is required to facilitate the spread of a _______________.

Securing Cisco Routers

Router security is a critical element in any security deployment. Routers are definite targets for network attackers. If an attacker can compromise and access a router, it can be a potential aid to them. Knowing the roles that routers fulfill in the network helps you understand their vulnerabilities.

Describe Good Password Practices

A strong password is the most fundamental element in controlling secure access to a router. For this reason, strong passwords should always be configured. In your own words, describe some common good password practices.

- ____
  ____
- ____
  ____
- ____
  ____
- ____
  ____
- ____
  ____
- ____
  ____

Configuring Router Passwords

This exercise walks you through some password-configuration tasks that can be used to secure access to your router.

First, enter global configuration mode:

____

Now, configure the password that is to be used to enter privileged EXEC mode. Use the preferred command that uses the MD5 algorithm to protect access to the password. Use **C1sc0r0x** as the password:

____

Enter the command that ensures that no enable password is configured:

____

Ensure that all passwords are hidden from casual observers. Use the command that prevents passwords that are displayed on the screen from being readable:

____

Next, set the minimum character length for all router passwords to 10 characters:

____

How does this last command affect existing passwords?

____

____

Disable logins to the auxiliary port:

____

____

____

Configure the vty lines to support incoming Telnet and SSH sessions only:

____

____

____

Further secure the vty lines by setting the executive timeout to 3 minutes and enabling TCP keepalives:

____

____

____

Secure Router Network Services

Cisco routers support a large number of network services. Some of these services can be restricted or disabled to improve security without degrading the operational use of the router. General security practice for routers should be used to support only the traffic and protocols a network needs.

Routing protocols are also points of vulnerability and must be protected from attacks.

Vulnerable Router Services Exercise

The following table lists some common router services. Complete the table with the missing components.

Service	Description	Default Status	Command to Disable
CDP	Proprietary Cisco Layer 2 protocol.		`no cdp run`
TCP small servers	Standard TCP network services.	IOS version dependent	
UDP small servers	Standard UDP network services.	IOS version dependent	
Finger	UNIX user lookup service.		`no service finger`
HTTP server	Web-based interface for devices.	Varies by device	
BOOTP server	Allows other routers to boot from this one.		`no ip bootp server`
IP source routing	Allows packets to specify their own routes.	Enabled	
Proxy ARP	Router proxies Layer 2 address resolution.		`no ip proxy-arp`
IP directed broadcast	Packets can identify a target LAN for broadcasts.	IOS version dependent	
IP unreachable notifications	Router will explicitly notify senders of incorrect IP addresses.		`no ip unreachable`
IP redirects	Router will send ICMP redirect message in response to certain routed IP packets.		`no ip redirect`
SNMP	Routers support remote query and configuration.	Enabled	
DNS	Routers perform name resolution.		`no ip name-server`

Securing Routing Protocols: Completion

Routing protocols should be protected from attacks using various methods. Complete the paragraphs that follow by filling in the appropriate words and phrases.

Routers are at risk from attack just as much as end-user systems. Anyone with a ______________ can read information propagating between routers. In general, routing systems can be attacked in two ways:

- ______________________________
- ______________________________

A more subtle class of attack targets the information carried within the ______________________. Falsified routing information may generally be used to cause systems to ______________________, cause a DoS, or cause traffic to follow a path it would not normally follow. The consequences of falsifying routing information are as follows:

1. ______________________________
2. ______________________________
3. ______________________________

The best way to protect routing information on the network is to ______________________ routing protocol packets using ______________________________. An algorithm like ___________ allows the routers to compare signatures that should all be the same.

The three components of such a system are as follows:

1. ______________________________
2. ______________________________
3. ______________________________

Using Cisco Security Device Manager

Cisco Security Device Manager (SDM) simplifies router and security configuration through the use of several intelligent wizards to enable efficient configuration of key router virtual private network (VPN) and Cisco IOS firewall parameters. This capability permits administrators to quickly and easily deploy, configure, and monitor Cisco access routers.

Preparing a Router for SDM

A router must be configured to support access to SDM through a web browser on a network client. Fill in the missing commands used to prepare the router for SDM.

Enter global configuration mode:

```
Router# ________________________________
```

Enable both HTTP and HTTPS on the router:

```
Router(config)# ________________________________
Router(config)# ________________________________
```

Create a local user account with privilege level 15 and configure the HTTP server to use this account for authentication. Configure the username to be Student and the password to be **c1sc0R0ck5**:

```
Router(config)# ________________________________
Router(config)# ________________________________
```

Configure SSH and Telnet for local login with privilege level 15:

```
Router(config)# ________________________________
Router(config-line)# ___________________________
Router(config-line)# ___________________________
Router(config-line)# ___________________________
```

Secure Router Management

One of the most critical components of the router is the Cisco IOS Software image. This image is like the operating system on your computer. And, just as your computer will not operate without its operating system, your router will not operate without a valid IOS Software image.

A network manager should have a backup copy of the Cisco IOS Software image for each device on the network. These images should be stored on a TFTP server that can be accessed from the network devices.

Managing Cisco IOS Images: Identify Commands

The Cisco IOS Software **copy** command is used to move configuration files and software images from one component or device to another, such as RAM, NVRAM, or a TFTP server. For each item, describe the effect of the command.

```
R2# copy running-config startup-config
```

____

```
R2# copy running-config tftp:
```

____

```
R2# copy tftp: running-config
```

____

```
R2# copy tftp: startup-config
```

____

```
R2# copy flash: tftp:
```

____

```
R2# copy tftp: flash:
```

____

Managing Cisco IOS Images: Short Answer

The router IOS images should be stored on a TFTP server on the network. A network TFTP server can be used to restore lost or corrupted IOS images to network devices. In your own words, answer the following questions about IOS image management.

What information is required when using the **copy** command to upload or download a system image file?

____

____

How can a new system image file be copied to a router if there is not sufficient flash memory for more than one Cisco IOS image?

____

____

____

What happens to a router when the IOS is deleted from flash?

____

____

____

____

What information and commands must be entered at the ROMmon prompt to retrieve the backup IOS file from a TFTP server?

- ____
- ____
- ____
- ____
- ____
- ____

Why is the **tftpdnld** command preferred over the **xmodem** command when restoring an IOS image?

____

____

____

____

Password-Recovery Exercise

Password recovery might be necessary for a number of reasons. In a production environment, employees might change jobs and leave behind no documentation about device passwords. In a lab environment, such as your classroom, students might misspell a password or configure a password unknown to other students. Fortunately, Cisco routers provide a method for password recovery/reset that allows you to keep the configuration.

Password recovery requires physical access to the router. You connect your PC to the router through a console cable.

Complete the steps that follow, filling in the missing commands and phrases.

Step 1. Connect to the ____________________.

Step 2. Enter ____________________ at the prompt, and record the configuration register setting.

Step 3. Use the ____________________ to turn off the router, and then turn the router back on.

Step 4. Press _______________ on the terminal keyboard within _____ seconds of power up to put the router into ROMmon.

Step 5. Enter ____________________ at the rommon 1> prompt. This causes the router to bypass the startup configuration where the forgotten enable password is stored.

Step 6. Enter _____ at the rommon 2> prompt. The router reboots, but ignores the saved configuration.

Step 7. Enter _____ after each setup question, or press _____ to skip the initial setup procedure.

Step 8. Enter _____________ at the Router> prompt. This puts you into enable mode, and you should be able to see the Router# prompt.

Step 9. Enter _________________________________ to copy the NVRAM into memory. Be careful! Do not enter **copy running-config startup-config**; otherwise, you erase your startup configuration.

Step 10. Enter ____________________ to view the configuration loaded into RAM.

Step 11. Enter ____________________. The hostname(config)# prompt appears.

Step 12. Enter _________________________________ to change the enable secret password.

Step 13. Issue the ____________________ command on every interface that you want to use.

Step 14. Enter _________________________________.

Step 15. Press _____ or type _____ to leave configuration mode. The hostname# prompt appears.

Step 16. Enter _________________________________ to commit the changes.

Labs and Activities

Lab 4-1: Basic Security Configuration (4.6.1)

Upon completion of this lab, you will be able to

- Cable a network according to the topology diagram.
- Erase the startup configuration and reload a router to the default state.
- Perform basic configuration tasks on a router.
- Configure basic router security.
- Disable unused Cisco services and interfaces.
- Protect enterprise networks from basic external and internal attacks.
- Understand and manage Cisco IOS configuration files and Cisco file system.
- Set up and use Cisco SDM (Security Device Manager) and SDM Express to configure basic router security.
- Configure VLANs on the switches.

Scenario

In this lab, you learn how to configure basic network security using the network shown in the topology diagram. You learn how to configure router security three different ways: using the CLI, the AutoSecure feature, and Cisco SDM. You also learn how to manage Cisco IOS Software.

Figure 4-1 shows the topology for this lab, and Table 4-1 shows the IP addressing, subnet, and default gateway information for the devices in the topology.

Table 4-1 Addressing Table for Lab 4-1

Device	Interface	IP Address	Subnet Mask	Default Gateway
R1	Fa0/1	192.168.10.1	255.255.255.0	N/A
	S0/0/0	10.1.1.1	255.255.255.252	N/A
R2	Fa0/1	192.168.20.1	255.255.255.0	N/A
	S0/0/0	10.1.1.2	255.255.255.252	N/A
	S0/0/1	10.2.2.1	255.255.255.252	N/A
	Lo0	209.165.200.225	255.255.255.224	N/A
R3	Fa0/1	192.168.30.1	255.255.255.0	N/A
	S0/0/1	10.2.2.2	255.255.255.252	N/A
S1	VLAN 10	192.168.10.2	255.255.255.0	N/A
S3	VLAN 30	192.168.30.2	255.255.255.0	N/A

continues

Table 4-1 Addressing Table for Lab 4-1 *continued*

Device	Interface	IP Address	Subnet Mask	Default Gateway
PC1	NIC	192.168.10.10	255.255.255.0	192.168.10.1
PC2	NIC	192.168.30.10	255.255.255.0	192.168.30.1
TFTP	NIC	192.168.20.254	255.255.255.0	192.168.20.1

Figure 4-1 Topology Diagram for Lab 4-1

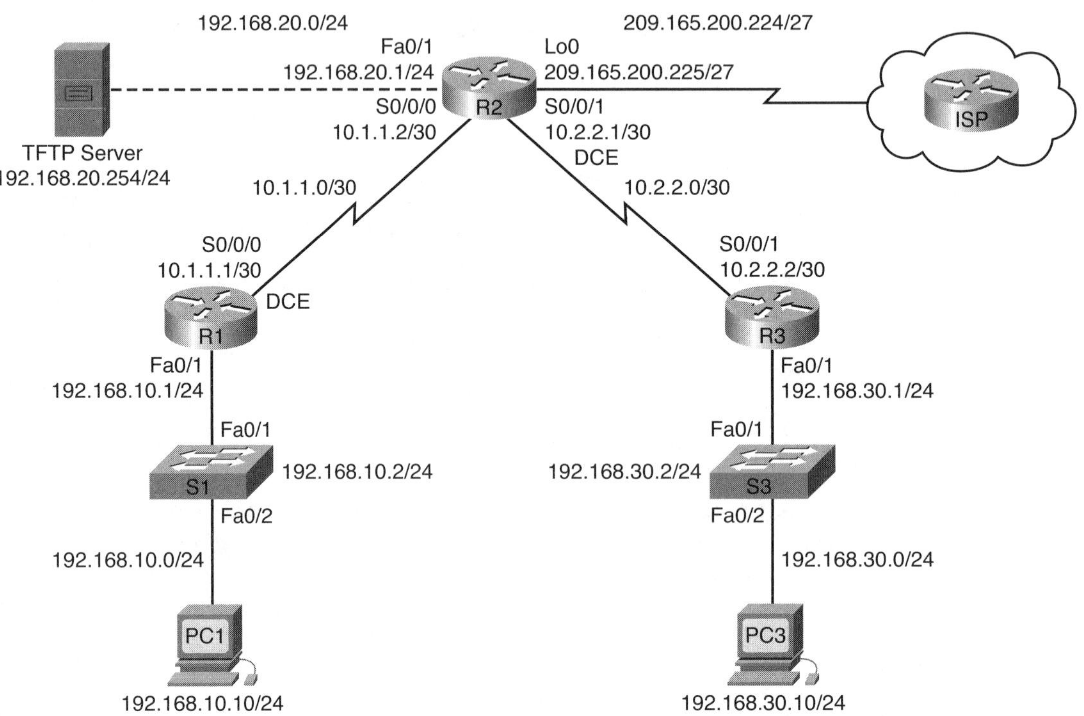

Task 1: Prepare the Network

Step 1. Cable a network similar to the one in the topology diagram in Figure 4-1.

You can use any current router in your lab as long as it has the required interfaces shown in the topology.

Note: This lab was developed and tested using 1841 routers. If you use 1700, 2500, or 2600 series routers, the router outputs and interface descriptions might differ.

Step 2. Clear any existing configurations on the routers.

Task 2: Perform Basic Router Configurations

Step 1. Configure routers.

Configure the R1, R2, and R3 routers according to the following guidelines:

- Configure the router hostname according to the topology diagram in Figure 4-1.
- Disable DNS lookup.
- Configure a message-of-the-day banner.
- Configure IP addresses on R1, R2, and R3.
- Enable RIP Version 2 on all routers for all networks.
- Create a loopback interface on R2 to simulate the connection to the Internet.
- Configure a TFTP server on R2. If you need to download TFTP server software, one option is http://tftpd32.jounin.net/.

Step 2. Configure Ethernet interfaces.

Configure the Ethernet interfaces of PC1, PC3, and TFTP server with the IP addresses and default gateways from the addressing table at the beginning of the lab.

Step 3. Test the PC configuration by pinging the default gateway from each of the PCs and the TFTP server.

Task 3: Secure the Router from Unauthorized Access

Step 1. Configure secure passwords and (authentication, authorization, and accounting) AAA.

Use a local database on R1 to configure secure passwords. Use **ciscoccna** for all passwords in this lab:

```
R1(config)# enable secret ciscoccna
```

How does configuring an enable secret password help protect a router from being compromised by an attack?

____

____

____

____

The **username** command creates a username and password stored locally on the router. The default privilege level of the user is 0 (the least amount of access). You can change the level of access for a user by adding the keyword **privilege** *0–15* before the **password** keyword:

```
R1(config)# username ccna password ciscoccna
```

The **aaa** command enables AAA globally on the router. This is used when connecting to the router:

```
R1(config)# aaa new-model
```

You can create an authentication list that is accessed when someone attempts to log in to the device after applying it to vty and console lines. The **local** keyword indicates that the user database is stored locally on the router:

```
R1(config)# aaa authentication login LOCAL_AUTH local
```

The following commands tell the router that users attempting to connect to the router should be authenticated using the list you just created:

```
R1(config)# line console 0
R1(config-lin)# login authentication LOCAL_AUTH
R1(config-lin)# line vty 0 4
R1(config-lin)# login authentication LOCAL_AUTH
```

What do you notice that is not secure about the following section of the running configuration:

```
R1# show run
<output omitted>
!
enable secret 5 $1$.DB7$DunHvguQH0EvLqzQCqzfr1
!
aaa new-model
!
aaa authentication login LOCAL_AUTH local
!
username ccna password 0 ciscoccna
!
<output omitted>
!
banner motd ^CUnauthorized access strictly prohibited, violators will be
prosecuted to the full extent of the law^C
!
line con 0
 logging synchronous
 login authentication LOCAL_AUTH
line aux 0
line vty 0 4
 login authentication LOCAL_AUTH
!
```

____

____

To apply simple encryption to the passwords, enter the following command in global config mode:

```
R1(config)# service password-encryption
```

Verify this with the **show run** command:

```
R1# show run
service password-encryption
!
enable secret 5 $1$.DB7$DunHvguQH0EvLqzQCqzfr1
!
aaa new-model
!
aaa authentication login LOCAL_AUTH local
!
username ccna password 7 0822455D0A1606141C0A
<output omitted>
!
banner motd ^CCUnauthorized access strictly prohibited, violators will be
prosecuted to the full extent of the law^C
!
line con 0
 logging synchronous
 login authentication LOCAL_AUTH
line aux 0
line vty 0 4
 login authentication LOCAL_AUTH
!
```

Step 2. Secure the console and vty lines.

You can cause the router to log out a line that has been idle for a specified time. If a network engineer was logged in to a networking device and was suddenly called away, this command automatically logs the user out after the specified time. The following commands cause the line to log out after 5 minutes:

```
R1(config)# line console 0
R1(config-lin)# exec-timeout 5 0
R1(config-lin)# line vty 0 4
R1(config-lin)# exec-timeout 5 0
```

The following command hampers brute-force login attempts. The router blocks login attempts for 5 minutes if someone fails five attempts within 2 minutes. This is set especially low for the purpose of this lab. An additional measure is to log each time this happens:

```
R1(config)# login block-for 300 attempt 2 within 120
R1(config)# security authentication failure rate 5 log
```

To verify this, attempt to connect to R1 from R2 via Telnet with an incorrect username and password:

On R2

```
R2# telnet 10.1.1.1
Trying 10.1.1.1 ... Open
Unauthorized access strictly prohibited, violators will be prosecuted to the
full extent of the law


User Access Verification


Username: cisco
Password:


% Authentication failed


User Access Verification


Username: cisco
Password:


% Authentication failed


[Connection to 10.1.1.1 closed by foreign host]
R2# telnet 10.1.1.1
Trying 10.1.1.1 ...
% Connection refused by remote host
```

On R1

```
*Sep 10 12:40:11.211: %SEC_LOGIN-5-QUIET_MODE_OFF: Quiet Mode is OFF,
because block period timed out at 12:40:11 UTC Mon Sep 10 2007
```

Task 4: Secure Access to the Network

Step 1. Prevent RIP routing update propagation.

Who can receive RIP updates on a network segment where RIP is enabled? Is this the most desirable setup?

____

____

____

The **passive-interface** command prevents routers from sending routing updates to all interfaces except those interfaces configured to participate in routing updates. This command is issued as part of the RIP configuration.

The first command puts all interfaces into passive mode (the interface receives only RIP updates). The second command returns specific interfaces from passive to active mode (both sending and receiving RIP updates).

R1

```
R1(config)# router rip
R1(config-router)# passive-interface default
R1(config-router)# no passive-interface s0/0/0
```

R2

```
R2(config)# router rip
R2(config-router)# passive-interface default
R2(config-router)# no passive-interface s0/0/0
R2(config-router)# no passive-interface s0/0/1
```

R3

```
R3(config)# router rip
R3(config-router)# passive-interface default
R3(config-router)# no passive-interface s0/0/1
```

Step 2. Prevent unauthorized reception of RIP updates.

Preventing unnecessary RIP updates to the whole network is the first step to securing RIP. The next is to have RIP updates password protected. To do this, you must first configure a key to use:

```
R1(config)# key chain RIP_KEY
R1(config-keychain)# key 1
R1(config-keychain-key)# key-string cisco
```

This has to be added to each router that is going to receive RIP updates:

```
R2(config)# key chain RIP_KEY
R2(config-keychain)# key 1
R2(config-keychain-key)# key-string cisco
R3(config)# key chain RIP_KEY
R3(config-keychain)# key 1
R3(config-keychain-key)# key-string cisco
```

To use the key, each interface participating in RIP updates needs to be configured. These will be the same interfaces that were enabled using the **no passive-interface** command earlier:

```
R1(config)# int s0/0/0
R1(config-if)# ip rip authentication mode md5
R1(config-if)# ip rip authentication key-chain RIP_KEY
```

At this point, R1 is no longer receiving RIP updates from R2 because R2 is not yet configured to use a key for routing updates. You can view this on R1 using the **show ip route** command and confirm that no routes from R2 appear in the routing table.

Clear out IP routes with **clear ip route** * or wait for routes to time out:

```
R1# show ip route
Codes: C - connected, S - static, R - RIP, M - mobile, B - BGP
       D - EIGRP, EX - EIGRP external, O - OSPF, IA - OSPF inter area
       N1 - OSPF NSSA external type 1, N2 - OSPF NSSA external type 2
       E1 - OSPF external type 1, E2 - OSPF external type 2
       i - IS-IS, su - IS-IS summary, L1 - IS-IS level-1, L2 - IS-IS level-2
       ia - IS-IS inter area, *- candidate default, U - per-user static route
       o - ODR, P - periodic downloaded static route

Gateway of last resort is not set

     10.0.0.0/8 is variably subnetted, 1 subnets, 1 masks
C       10.1.1.0/24 is directly connected, Serial0/0/0
C    192.168.10.0 is directly connected, Serial0/0/0
```

Configure R2 and R3 to use routing authentication. Remember that each active interface must be configured.

R2

```
R2(config)# int s0/0/0
R2(config-if)# ip rip authentication mode md5
R2(config-if)# ip rip authentication key-chain RIP_KEY
R2(config)# int s0/0/1
R2(config-if)# ip rip authentication mode md5
R2(config-if)# ip rip authentication key-chain RIP_KEY
```

R3

```
R3(config)# int s0/0/1
R3(config-if)# ip rip authentication mode md5
R3(config-if)# ip rip authentication key-chain RIP_KEY
```

Step 3. Verify that RIP routing still works.

After all three routers have been configured to use routing authentication, the routing tables should repopulate with all RIP routes. R1 should now have all the routes via RIP. Confirm this with the **show ip route** command:

```
R1# show ip route
Codes: C - connected, S - static, R - RIP, M - mobile, B - BGP
       D - EIGRP, EX - EIGRP external, O - OSPF, IA - OSPF inter area
       N1 - OSPF NSSA external type 1, N2 - OSPF NSSA external type 2
       E1 - OSPF external type 1, E2 - OSPF external type 2
       i - IS-IS, su - IS-IS summary, L1 - IS-IS level-1, L2 - IS-IS level-2
       ia - IS-IS inter area, *-candidate default, U-per-user static route
       o - ODR, P - periodic downloaded static route

Gateway of last resort is not set
```

```
R    192.168.30.0/24 [120/2] via 10.1.1.2, 00:00:16, Serial0/0/0
C    192.168.10.0/24 is directly connected, FastEthernet0/1
R    192.168.20.0/24 [120/1] via 10.1.1.2, 00:00:13, Serial0/0/0
     10.0.0.0/8 is variably subnetted, 2 subnets, 1 masks
R       10.2.2.0/24 [120/1] via 10.1.0.2, 00:00:16, Serial0/0/0
C       10.1.1.0/24 is directly connected, Serial0/0/0
```

Task 5: Logging Activity with SNMP (Simple Network Management Protocol)

Step 1. Configure SNMP logging to the syslog server.

SNMP logging can be useful in monitoring network activity. The captured information can be sent to a syslog server on the network, where it can be analyzed and archived. You should be careful when configuring logging (syslog) on the router. When choosing the designated log host, remember that the log host should be connected to a trusted or protected network or an isolated and dedicated router interface.

In this lab, you configure PC1 as the syslog server for R1. Use the **logging** command to select the IP address of the device to which SNMP messages are sent. In this example, the IP address of PC1 is used:

```
R1(config)# logging 192.168.10.10
```

Note: PC1 should have syslog software installed and running if you want to view syslog messages.

In the next step, you define the level of severity for messages to be sent to the syslog server.

Step 2. Configure the SNMP severity level.

The level of SNMP messages can be adjusted to allow the administrator to determine what kinds of messages are sent to the syslog device. Routers support different levels of logging. The eight levels range from 0 (emergencies), indicating that the system is unstable, to 7 (debugging), which sends messages that include router information. To configure the severity levels, you use the keyword associated with the level, as shown in Table 4-2.

Table 4-2 SNMP Message Severity

Severity Level	Keyword	Description
0	**emergencies**	System unusable
1	**alerts**	Immediate action required
2	**critical**	Critical conditions
3	**errors**	Error conditions
4	**warnings**	Warning conditions
5	**notifications**	Normal but significant condition
6	**informational**	Informational messages
7	**debugging**	Debugging messages

The **logging trap** command sets the severity level. The severity level includes the level specified and anything below it (severity-wise). Set R1 to level 4 to capture messages with severity level 4, 5, 6, and 7.

```
R1(config)# logging trap warnings
```

What is the danger of setting the level of severity too high or too low?

____

____

____

____

Note: If you installed syslog software on PC1, generate and look at syslog software for messages.

Task 6: Disabling Unused Cisco Network Services

Step 1. Disable unused interfaces.

Why should you disable unused interfaces on network devices?

____

____

____

In the topology diagram, you can see that R1 should be using only interface S0/0/0 and Fa0/1. All other interfaces on R1 should be administratively shut down using the **shutdown** interface configuration command:

```
R1(config)# interface fastethernet0/0
R1(config-if)# shutdown
R1(config-if)# interface s0/0/1
R1(config-if)# shutdown
*Sep 10 13:40:24.887: %LINK-5-CHANGED: Interface FastEthernet0/0, changed
state to administratively down
*Sep 10 13:40:25.887: %LINEPROTO-5-UPDOWN: Line protocol on Interface
FastEthernet0/0, changed state to down
```

To verify that R1 has all inactive interfaces shut down, use the **show ip interface brief** command. Interfaces manually shut down are listed as administratively down:

```
R1# show ip interface brief
Interface            IP-Address      OK? Method Status                Protocol
FastEthernet0/0      unassigned      YES unset  administratively down down
FastEthernet0/1      192.168.10.1    YES manual up                    up
Serial0/0/0          10.1.0.1        YES manual up                    up
Serial0/0/1          unassigned      YES unset  administratively down down
```

Step 2. Disable unused global services.

Many services are not needed in most modern networks. Leaving unused services enabled leaves ports open that can be used to compromise a network. Disable each of these services on R1:

```
R1(config)# no service pad
R1(config)# no service finger
R1(config)# no service udp-small-server
R1(config)# no service tcp-small-server
R1(config)# no ip bootp server
R1(config)# no ip http server
R1(config)# no ip finger
R1(config)# no ip source-route
R1(config)# no ip gratuitous-arps
R1(config)# no cdp run
```

Step 3. Disable unused interface services.

These commands are entered at the interface level and should be applied to every interface on R1:

```
R1(config-if)# no ip redirects
R1(config-if)# no ip proxy-arp
R1(config-if)# no ip unreachables
R1(config-if)# no ip directed-broadcast
R1(config-if)# no ip mask-reply
R1(config-if)# no mop enabled
```

What kind of attack does disabling IP redirects, IP unreachables, and IP directed broadcasts mitigate?

____

____

____

____

Step 4. Use AutoSecure to secure a Cisco router.

When you use a single command in CLI mode, the AutoSecure feature enables you to disable common IP services that can be exploited for network attacks and enable IP services and features that can aid in the defense of a network when under attack. AutoSecure simplifies the security configuration of a router and hardens the router configuration.

Using the AutoSecure feature, you can apply the same security features that you just applied (except for securing RIP) to a router much faster. Because you have already secured R1, use the **auto secure** command on R3:

```
R3# auto secure
                --- AutoSecure Configuration ---

*** AutoSecure configuration enhances the security of
the router, but it will not make it absolutely resistant
to all security attacks ***
```

```
AutoSecure will modify the configuration of your device.
All configuration changes will be shown. For a detailed
explanation of how the configuration changes enhance security
and any possible side effects, please refer to Cisco.com for
Autosecure documentation.
At any prompt you may enter '?' for help.
Use ctrl-c to abort this session at any prompt.

Gathering information about the router for AutoSecure

Is this router connected to internet? [no]: yes
Enter the number of interfaces facing the internet [1]: 1

Interface                  IP-Address      OK? Method Status      Protocol
FastEthernet0/0            unassigned      YES unset  down        down
FastEthernet0/1            192.168.30.1    YES manual up          up
Serial0/0/0                unassigned      YES manual down        down
Serial0/0/1                10.2.2.2        YES manual up          up

Enter the interface name that is facing the internet: Serial0/0/1
Securing Management plane services...
Disabling service finger
Disabling service pad
Disabling udp & tcp small servers
Enabling service password encryption
Enabling service tcp-keepalives-in
Enabling service tcp-keepalives-out
Disabling the cdp protocol

Disabling the bootp server
Disabling the http server
Disabling the finger service
Disabling source routing
Disabling gratuitous arp
Enable secret is either not configured or
 Is the same as enable password
Enter the new enable password: ciscoccna
Confirm the enable password: ciscoccna
Enter the new enable password: ccnacisco
Confirm the enable password: ccnacisco

Configuration of local user database
Enter the username: ccna
Enter the password: ciscoccna
```

```
Confirm the password: ciscoccna
Configuring AAA local authentication
Configuring Console, Aux and VTY lines for
local authentication, exec-timeout, and transport
Securing device against Login Attacks
Configure the following parameters

Blocking Period when Login Attack detected: 300

Maximum Login failures with the device: 5

Maximum time period for crossing the failed login attempts: 120

Configure SSH server? Yes
Enter domain-name: cisco.com

Configuring interface specific AutoSecure services
Disabling the following ip services on all interfaces:

 no ip redirects
 no ip proxy-arp
 no ip unreachables
 no ip directed-broadcast
 no ip mask-reply
Disabling mop on Ethernet interfaces

Securing Forwarding plane services...

Enabling CEF (This might impact the memory requirements for your platform)
Enabling unicast rpf on all interfaces connected to internet

Configure CBAC firewall feature: no
Tcp intercept feature is used prevent tcp syn attack
On the servers in the network. Create autosec_tcp_intercept_list
To form the list of servers to which the tcp traffic is to be observed
Enable TCP intercept feature: yes

This is the configuration generated:
no service finger
no service pad
no service udp-small-servers
no service tcp-small-servers
service password-encryption
service tcp-keepalives-in
```

```
service tcp-keepalives-out
no cdp run
no ip bootp server
no ip http server
no ip finger
no ip source-route
no ip gratuitous-arps
no ip identd
security passwords min-length 6
security authentication failure rate 10 log
enable password 7 070C285F4D061A061913
username ccna password 7 045802150C2E4F4D0718
aaa new-model
aaa authentication login local_auth local
line con 0
 login authentication local_auth
 exec-timeout 5 0
 transport output telnet
line aux 0
 login authentication local_auth
 exec-timeout 10 0
 transport output telnet
line vty 0 4
 login authentication local_auth
 transport input telnet
line tty 1
 login authentication local_auth
 exec-timeout 15 0
line tty 192
 login authentication local_auth
 exec-timeout 15 0
login block-for 300 attempts 5 within 120
service timestamps debug datetime msec localtime show-timezone
service timestamps log datetime msec localtime show-timezone
logging facility local2
logging trap debugging
service sequence-numbers
logging console critical
logging buffered
interface FastEthernet0/0
 no ip redirects
 no ip proxy-arp
 no ip unreachables
 no ip directed-broadcast
```

```
 no ip mask-reply
 no mop enabled
interface FastEthernet0/1
 no ip redirects
 no ip proxy-arp
 no ip unreachables
 no ip directed-broadcast
 no ip mask-reply
 no mop enabled
interface Serial0/0/0
 no ip redirects
 no ip proxy-arp
 no ip unreachables
 no ip directed-broadcast
 no ip mask-reply
interface Serial0/0/1
 no ip redirects
 no ip proxy-arp
 no ip unreachables
 no ip directed-broadcast
 no ip mask-reply
interface Serial0/1/0
 no ip redirects
 no ip proxy-arp
 no ip unreachables
 no ip directed-broadcast
 no ip mask-reply
interface Serial0/1/1
 no ip redirects
 no ip proxy-arp
 no ip unreachables
 no ip directed-broadcast
 no ip mask-reply
ip cef
access-list 100 permit udp any any eq bootpc
interface Serial0/0/1
 ip verify unicast source reachable-via rx allow-default 100
ip tcp intercept list autosec_tcp_intercept_list
ip tcp intercept drop-mode random
ip tcp intercept watch-timeout 15
ip tcp intercept connection-timeout 3600
ip tcp intercept max-incomplete low 450
ip tcp intercept max-incomplete high 550
!
```

```
end

Apply this configuration to running-config? [yes]:yes

The name for the keys will be: R3.cisco.com

% The key modulus size is 1024 bits
% Generating 1024 bit RSA keys, keys will be non-exportable...[OK]
R3#
000045: *Nov 16 15:39:10.991 UTC: %AUTOSEC-1-MODIFIED: AutoSecure configura-
tion has been Modified on this device
```

As you can see, the AutoSecure feature is much faster than line-by-line configuration. However, there are advantages to doing it manually, as you will see in the troubleshooting lab. When you use AutoSecure, you might disable a service you need. Always use caution and think about the services that you require before using AutoSecure.

Task 7: Managing Cisco IOS and Configuration Files

Step 1. Show Cisco IOS files.

Cisco IOS is the software that routers use to operate. Your router might have enough memory to store multiple Cisco IOS images. It is important to know which files are stored on your router.

Issue the **show flash** command to view the contents of the flash memory of your router.

Caution: Be very careful when issuing commands that involve the flash memory. Mistyping a command could result in the deletion of the Cisco IOS image.

```
R2# show flash
-#- --length-- -----date/time------ path
1     13937472 May 05 2007 21:25:14 +00:00 c1841-ipbase-mz.124-1c.bin
2         1821 May 05 2007 21:40:28 +00:00 sdmconfig-18xx.cfg
3      4734464 May 05 2007 21:41:02 +00:00 sdm.tar
4       833024 May 05 2007 21:41:24 +00:00 es.tar
5      1052160 May 05 2007 21:41:48 +00:00 common.tar

8679424 bytes available (23252992 bytes used)
```

Just by looking at this list, we can determine the following:

- The image is for an 1841 router (c**1841**-ipbase-mz.124-1c.bin).
- The router is using IP base image (c1841-**ipbase**-mz.124-1c.bin).
- The Cisco IOS is Version 12.4(1c) (c1841-ipbase-mz.**124-1c**.bin).
- SDM is installed on this device (**sdm**config-18xx.cfg, **sdm**.tar).

You can use the **dir all** command to show all files on the router:

```
R2# dir all
Directory of archive:/

No files in directory

No space information available
Directory of system:/

 3  dr-x          0                     <no date>  memory
 1  -rw-        979                     <no date>  running-config
 2  dr-x          0                     <no date>  vfiles

No space information available
Directory of nvram:/

 189  -rw-        979                     <no date>  startup-config
 190  ----          5                     <no date>  private-config
 191  -rw-        979                     <no date>  underlying-config
   1  -rw-          0                     <no date>  ifIndex-table

196600 bytes total (194540 bytes free)
Directory of flash:/

 1 -rw- 13937472  May 05 2007 20:08:50 +00:00  c1841-ipbase-mz.124-1c.bin
 2 -rw-     1821  May 05 2007 20:25:00 +00:00  sdmconfig-18xx.cfg
 3 -rw-  4734464  May 05 2007 20:25:38 +00:00  sdm.tar
 4 -rw-   833024  May 05 2007 20:26:02 +00:00  es.tar
 5 -rw-  1052160  May 05 2007 20:26:30 +00:00  common.tar
 6 -rw-     1038  May 05 2007 20:26:56 +00:00  home.shtml
 7 -rw-   102400  May 05 2007 20:27:20 +00:00  home.tar
 8 -rw-   491213  May 05 2007 20:27:50 +00:00  128MB.sdf
 9 –rw-   398305  May 05 2007 20:29:08 +00:00  sslclient-win-1.1.0.154.pkg
 10 -rw- 1684577  May 05 2007 20:28:32 +00:00  securedesktop-ios-3.1.1.27-
   k9.pkg

31932416 bytes total (8679424 bytes free)
```

Step 2. Transfer files with TFTP.

TFTP is used when archiving and updating the Cisco IOS Software of a device. In this lab, however, we do not use actual Cisco IOS files because any mistakes made in entering the commands could lead to erasing the Cisco IOS image of the device. At the end of this section, there is an example of what a Cisco IOS TFTP transfer looks like.

Why is it important to have an updated version of Cisco IOS Software?

____

____

____

When transferring files via TFTP, it is important to ensure that the TFTP server and the router can communicate. One way to test this is to ping between these devices.

To begin transfer of the Cisco IOS Software, create a file on the TFTP server called **test** in the TFTP root folder. This file can be a blank text file, because this step only serves to illustrate the steps involved. Each TFTP program differs in where files are stored. Consult your TFTP server help file to determine the root folder.

From R1, retrieve the file and save it to the flash memory:

```
R2# copy tftp flash
Address or name of remote host []? 192.168.20.254 (IP address of the TFTP server)
Source filename []? Test (name of the file you created and saved to TFTP server)
Destination filename [test]? test-server (An arbitrary name for the file when saved to the router)
Accessing tftp://192.168.20.254/test...
Loading test from 192.168.20.254 (via FastEthernet0/1): !
[OK - 1192 bytes]

1192 bytes copied in 0.424 secs (2811 bytes/sec)
```

Verify the file's existence in the flash with the **show flash** command:

```
R2# show flash
-#- --length-- -----date/time------ path
1     13937472 May 05 2007 21:13:20 +00:00 c1841-ipbase-mz.124-1c.bin
2         1821 May 05 2007 21:29:36 +00:00 sdmconfig-18xx.cfg
3      4734464 May 05 2007 21:30:14 +00:00 sdm.tar
4       833024 May 05 2007 21:30:42 +00:00 es.tar
5      1052160 May 05 2007 21:31:10 +00:00 common.tar
6         1038 May 05 2007 21:31:36 +00:00 home.shtml
7       102400 May 05 2007 21:32:02 +00:00 home.tar
8       491213 May 05 2007 21:32:30 +00:00 128MB.sdf
9      1684577 May 05 2007 21:33:16 +00:00 securedesktop-ios-3.1.1.27-k9.pkg
10      398305 May 05 2007 21:33:50 +00:00 sslclient-win-1.1.0.154.pkg
11        1192 Sep 12 2007 07:38:18 +00:00 test-server

8675328 bytes available (23257088 bytes used)
```

Routers can also act as TFTP servers. This can prove useful if there is a device that needs an image and you have one that is already using that image. We will make R2 a TFTP server for R1. Remember that Cisco IOS images are specific to router platforms and memory requirements. Use caution when transferring a Cisco IOS image from one router to another.

The command syntax is as follows:

tftp-server nvram: [*filename1* [alias *filename2*]

The following command configures R2 as a TFTP server:

```
R2(config)# tftp-server nvram:startup-config alias test
```

R2 supplies its startup configuration file to devices requesting it via TFTP (we are using the startup configuration for the sake of simplicity and ease). The **alias** keyword allows devices to request the file using the alias **test** rather than the full filename:

```
R2(config)# tftp-server nvram:startup-config alias test
```

Now we can request the file from R2 using R1:

```
R1# copy tftp flash
Address or name of remote host []? 10.1.1.2
Source filename []? test
Destination filename []? test-router
Accessing tftp://10.1.1.2/test...
Loading test from 10.1.1.2 (via Serial0/0/0): !
[OK - 1192 bytes]

1192 bytes copied in 0.452 secs (2637 bytes/sec)
```

Again, verify that the file **test** has been successfully copied with the **show flash** command:

```
R1# show flash
-#- --length-- -----date/time------ path
1     13937472 May 05 2007 21:13:20 +00:00 c1841-ipbase-mz.124-1c.bin
2         1821 May 05 2007 21:29:36 +00:00 sdmconfig-18xx.cfg
3      4734464 May 05 2007 21:30:14 +00:00 sdm.tar
4       833024 May 05 2007 21:30:42 +00:00 es.tar
5      1052160 May 05 2007 21:31:10 +00:00 common.tar
6         1038 May 05 2007 21:31:36 +00:00 home.shtml
7       102400 May 05 2007 21:32:02 +00:00 home.tar
8       491213 May 05 2007 21:32:30 +00:00 128MB.sdf
9      1684577 May 05 2007 21:33:16 +00:00 securedesktop-ios-3.1.1.27-k9.pkg
10      398305 May 05 2007 21:33:50 +00:00 sslclient-win-1.1.0.154.pkg
11        1192 Sep 12 2007 07:38:18 +00:00 test-server
12        1192 Sep 12 2007 07:51:04 +00:00 test-router

8671232 bytes available (23261184 bytes used)
```

Because you do not want unused files occupying precious memory space, delete them now from the flash memory of R1. *Be very careful when doing this!* Accidentally erasing flash memory will mean that you have to reinstall the entire IOS image for the router. If the router prompts you to **erase flash**, something is very wrong. You rarely want to erase the entire flash. The only legitimate time this will happen is when you are upgrading the IOS to a large IOS image. If you see the **erase flash** prompt as in the example, *stop immediately*. Do *not* press Enter. *Immediately* ask for assistance from your instructor.

```
Erase flash: ?[confirm] no

R1# delete flash:test-server
Delete filename [test-server]?
Delete flash:test? [confirm]
R1# delete flash:test-router
Delete filename [test-router]?
Delete flash:test-router? [confirm]
```

Verify that the files have been deleted by issuing the **show flash** command. *This is an example only. Do not complete this task.*

```
R1# show flash
-#- --length-- -----date/time------ path
1      13937472 May 05 2007 21:13:20 +00:00 c1841-ipbase-mz.124-1c.bin
2          1821 May 05 2007 21:29:36 +00:00 sdmconfig-18xx.cfg
3       4734464 May 05 2007 21:30:14 +00:00 sdm.tar
4        833024 May 05 2007 21:30:42 +00:00 es.tar
5       1052160 May 05 2007 21:31:10 +00:00 common.tar
6          1038 May 05 2007 21:31:36 +00:00 home.shtml
7        102400 May 05 2007 21:32:02 +00:00 home.tar
8        491213 May 05 2007 21:32:30 +00:00 128MB.sdf
9       1684577 May 05 2007 21:33:16 +00:00 securedesktop-ios-3.1.1.27-k9.pkg
10       398305 May 05 2007 21:33:50 +00:00 sslclient-win-1.1.0.154.pkg

8679424 bytes available (23252992 bytes used)
```

The following is an example of a TFTP transfer of a Cisco IOS image file.

Do *not* complete on your routers. Only read it.

```
R1# copy tftp flash
Address or name of remote host []? 10.1.1.2
Source filename []? c1841-ipbase-mz.124-1c.bin
Destination filename []? flash:c1841-ipbase-mz.124-1c.bin
Accessing tftp://10.1.1.2/c1841-ipbase-mz.124-1c.bin...
Loading c1841-ipbase-mz.124-1c.bin from 10.1.1.2 (via Serial0/0/0):
!!!!!!!!!!!!!!!!!!!!!!!!!!!!!!!!!!!!!!!!!!!!!!!!!!!!!!!!!!!!!!!!!!!!!!!!!!!!
<output omitted>
!!!!!!!!!!!!!!!!!!!!!!!!!!!!
[OK - 13937472 bytes]

13937472 bytes copied in 1113.948 secs (12512 bytes/sec)
```

Step 3. Recover a password using ROMmon.

If for some reason you can no longer access a device because you do not know, have lost, or have forgotten a password, you can still gain access by changing the configuration register. The configuration register tells the router which configuration to load on boot. In the configuration register, you can instruct the router to boot from a blank configuration that is not password protected.

The first step in changing the configuration register is to view the current setting using the **show version** command. These steps are performed on R3:

```
R3# show version
Cisco IOS Software, 1841 Software (C1841-IPBASE-M), Version 12.4(1c),
RELEASE SOFTWARE (fc1)
Technical Support: http://www.cisco.com/techsupport
Copyright (c) 1986-2005 by Cisco Systems, Inc.
Compiled Tue 25-Oct-05 17:10 by evmiller

ROM: System Bootstrap, Version 12.4(13r)T, RELEASE SOFTWARE (fc1)

R3 uptime is 25 minutes
System returned to ROM by reload at 08:56:50 UTC Wed Sep 12 2007
System image file is "flash:c1841-ipbase-mz.124-1c.bin"

Cisco 1841 (revision 7.0) with 114688K/16384K bytes of memory.
Processor board ID FTX1118X0BN
2 FastEthernet interfaces
2 Low-speed serial(sync/async) interfaces
DRAM configuration is 64 bits wide with parity disabled.
191K bytes of NVRAM.
31360K bytes of ATA CompactFlash (Read/Write)

Configuration register is 0x2102
```

Next, reload the router and send a break during boot. The Break key is different on different computers. Frequently, it is in the upper-right corner of the keyboard. A break causes the device to enter a mode called ROMmon. This mode does not require the device to have access to a Cisco IOS image file:

```
R3# reload
Proceed with reload? [confirm]

*Sep 12 08:27:28.670: %SYS-5-RELOAD: Reload requested by console. Reload
Reason: Reload command.
System Bootstrap, Version 12.4(13r)T, RELEASE SOFTWARE (fc1)
Technical Support: http://www.cisco.com/techsupport
Copyright (c) 2006 by cisco Systems, Inc.
PLD version 0x10
```

```
GIO ASIC version 0x127
c1841 platform with 131072 Kbytes of main memory
Main memory is configured to 64 bit mode with parity disabled

Readonly ROMMON initialized
rommon 1 >
```

Change the configuration register to a value that loads the initial configuration of the router. This configuration does not have a password configured, but supports Cisco IOS commands. Change the value of the configuration register to 0x2142:

```
rommon 1 > confreg 0x2142
```

Now that this is changed we can boot the device with the **reset** command:

```
rommon 2 > reset
program load complete, entry point: 0x8000f000, size: 0xcb80
program load complete, entry point: 0x8000f000, size: 0xcb80

program load complete, entry point: 0x8000f000, size: 0xd4a9a0
Self decompressing the image :
###########################################################

##########################################################################
## [OK]
<output omitted>

         --- System Configuration Dialog ---

Would you like to enter the initial configuration dialog? [yes/no]: no

Press RETURN to get started!
```

Step 4. Restore the router.

Now we copy the startup configuration to the running configuration, restore the configuration, and then change the configuration register back to the default (0x2102).

To copy the startup configuration from NVRAM to running memory, enter **copy startup-config running-config**. Be careful! Do *not* enter **copy running-config startup-config**; otherwise, you will erase your startup configuration.

```
Router# copy startup-config running-config
Destination filename [running-config]? {enter}

2261 bytes copied in 0.576 secs (3925 bytes/sec)

R3#show running-config
<output omitted>
enable secret 5 $1$31P/$cyPgoxc0R9y93Ps/N3/kg.
!
<output omitted>
!
```

```
key chain RIP_KEY
 key 1
  key-string 7 01100F175804
username ccna password 7 094F471A1A0A1411050D
!
interface FastEthernet0/1
 ip address 192.168.30.1 255.255.255.0
 no ip redirects
 no ip unreachables
 no ip proxy-arp
 no ip directed-broadcast
 shutdown
 duplex auto
 speed auto
!
interface Serial0/0/1
 ip address 10.2.2.2 255.255.255.252
 no ip redirects
 no ip unreachables
 no ip proxy-arp
 no ip directed-broadcast
 shutdown
 ip rip authentication mode md5
 ip rip authentication key-chain RIP_KEY
!
<output omitted>
!
line con 0
 exec-timeout 5 0
 logging synchronous
 login authentication
 transport output telnet
line aux 0
 exec-timeout 15 0
 logging synchronous
 login authentication local_auth
 transport output telnet
line vty 0 4
 exec-timeout 15 0
 logging synchronous
 login authentication local_auth
```

```
 transport input telnet
!
end
```

In this configuration, the **shutdown** command appears under all interfaces because all the interfaces are currently shut down. Most important, you can now see the passwords (enable password, enable secret, vty, console passwords) in either an encrypted or unencrypted format. You can reuse unencrypted passwords. You must change encrypted passwords to a new password:

```
R3# configure terminal
Enter configuration commands, one per line.  End with CNTL/Z.
R3(config)# enable secret ciscoccna
R3(config)# username ccna password ciscoccna
```

Issue the **no shutdown** command on every interface that you want to use:

```
R3(config)# interface FastEthernet0/1
R3(config-if)# no shutdown
R3(config)# interface Serial0/0/0
R3(config-if)# no shutdown
```

You can issue a **show ip interface brief** command to confirm that your interface configuration is correct. Every interface that you want to use should display up up:

```
R3# show ip interface brief
Interface            IP-Address      OK? Method Status                Protocol
FastEthernet0/0      unassigned      YES NVRAM  administratively down down
FastEthernet0/1      192.168.30.1    YES NVRAM  up                    up
Serial0/0/0          10.2.2.2        YES NVRAM  up                    up
Serial0/0/1          unassigned      YES NVRAM  administratively down down
```

Enter **config-register** *configuration register value*. The variable configuration register value is either the value you recorded in Step 3 or 0x2102. Save the running configuration:

```
R3(config)# config-register 0x2102
R3(config)# end
R3# copy running-config startup-config
Destination filename [startup-config]?
Building configuration...
[OK]
```

What are the downsides to password recovery?

____

____

____

____

____

Task 8: Using SDM to Secure a Router

In this task, you use Security Device Manager (SDM), the GUI interface, to secure router R2. SDM is faster than typing each command and gives you more control than the AutoSecure feature.

Verify whether SDM is installed on your router:

```
R2# show flash
-#- --length-- -----date/time------ path
1     13937472 Sep 12 2007 08:31:42 +00:00 c1841-ipbase-mz.124-1c.bin
2         1821 May 05 2007 21:29:36 +00:00 sdmconfig-18xx.cfg
3      4734464 May 05 2007 21:30:14 +00:00 sdm.tar
4       833024 May 05 2007 21:30:42 +00:00 es.tar
5      1052160 May 05 2007 21:31:10 +00:00 common.tar
6         1038 May 05 2007 21:31:36 +00:00 home.shtml
7       102400 May 05 2007 21:32:02 +00:00 home.tar
8       491213 May 05 2007 21:32:30 +00:00 128MB.sdf
9      1684577 May 05 2007 21:33:16 +00:00 securedesktop-ios-3.1.1.27-k9.pkg
10      398305 May 05 2007 21:33:50 +00:00 sslclient-win-1.1.0.154.pkg
11        2261 Sep 25 2007 23:20:16 +00:00 Tr(RIP)
12        2506 Sep 26 2007 17:11:58 +00:00 save.txt
```

If SDM is not installed on your router, it must be installed to continue. Consult your instructor for directions.

Step 1. Connect to R2 using the TFTP server.

Create a username and password on R2:

```
R2(config)# username ccna password ciscoccna
```

Enable the HTTP Secure server on R2 and connect to R2 using a web browser on the TFTP server:

```
R2(config)# ip http secure-server
% Generating 1024 bit RSA keys, keys will be non-exportable...[OK]
R2(config)#
*Nov 16 16:01:07.763: %SSH-5-ENABLED: SSH 1.99 has been enabled
*Nov 16 16:01:08.731: %PKI-4-NOAUTOSAVE: Configuration was modified.  Issue
"write memory" to save new certificate
R2(config)# end
R2# copy run start
```

From the TFTP server, open a web browser and navigate to https://192.168.20.1/. Log in with the previously configured username and password.

Username: **ccna**

Password: **ciscoccna**

Select: **Cisco Router and Security Device Manager**

Open Internet Explorer and enter the IP address for R2 in the address bar. A new window opens, as shown in Figure 4-2. Make sure that you have all popup blockers turned off in your browser. Also make sure that Java is installed and updated.

After it is done loading, a new window opens for SDM, as shown in Figure 4-3.

Step 2. Navigate to the Security Audit feature.

Click the **Configure** button in the upper left of the window, as shown in Figure 4-4.

Figure 4-2 Cisco Router and Security Device Manager

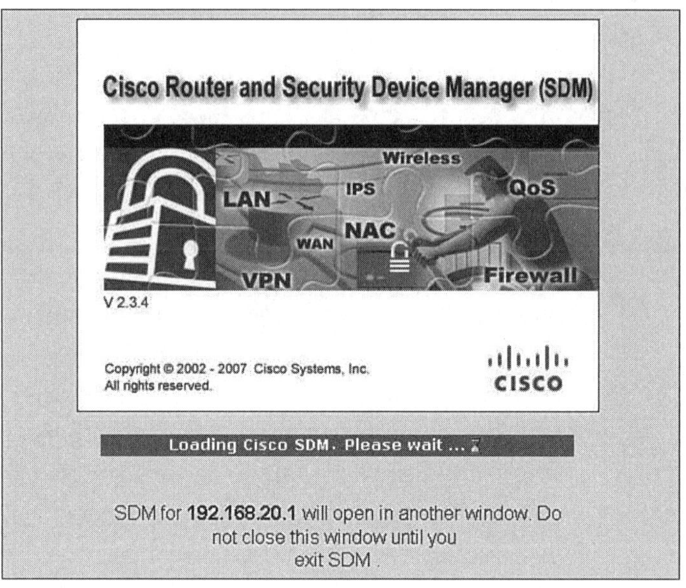

Figure 4-3 SDM Home

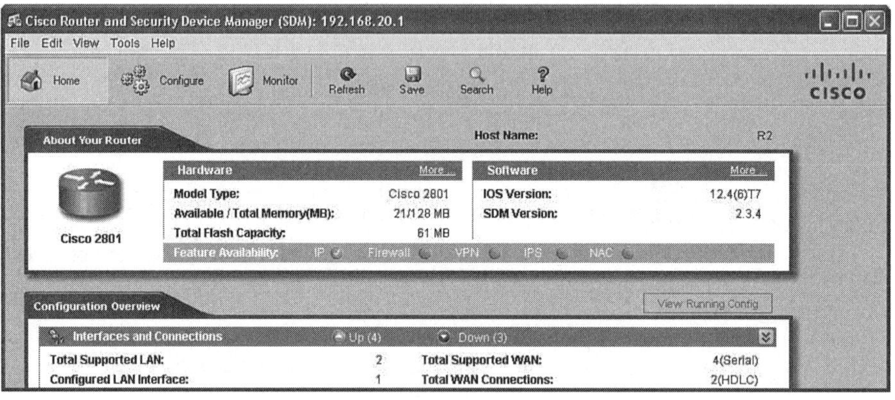

Figure 4-4 SDM Configuration

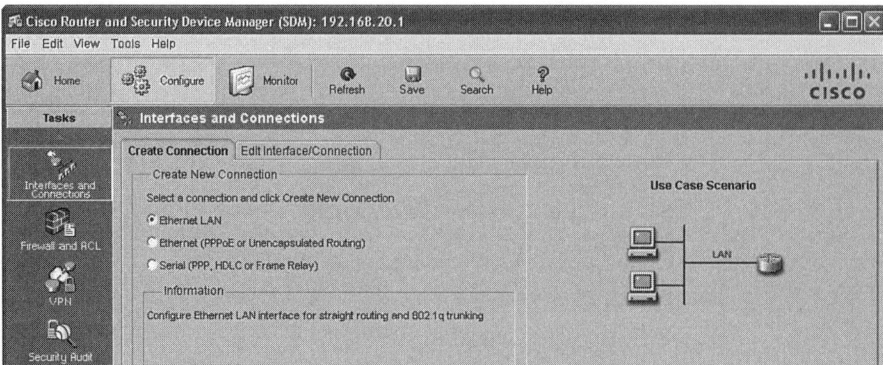

Now, navigate down the left panel to Security Audit and click it, as shown in Figure 4-5.

Figure 4-5 SDM Security Audit

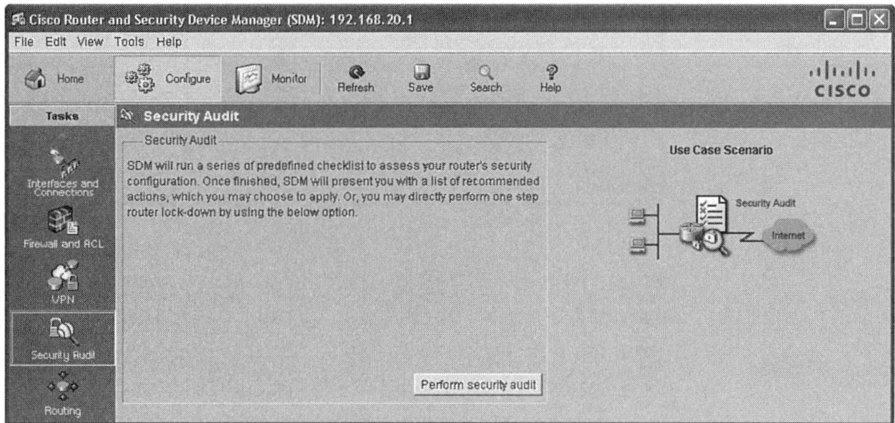

When you click Security Audit, another window opens, as shown in Figure 4-6.

Figure 4-6 Security Audit Wizard

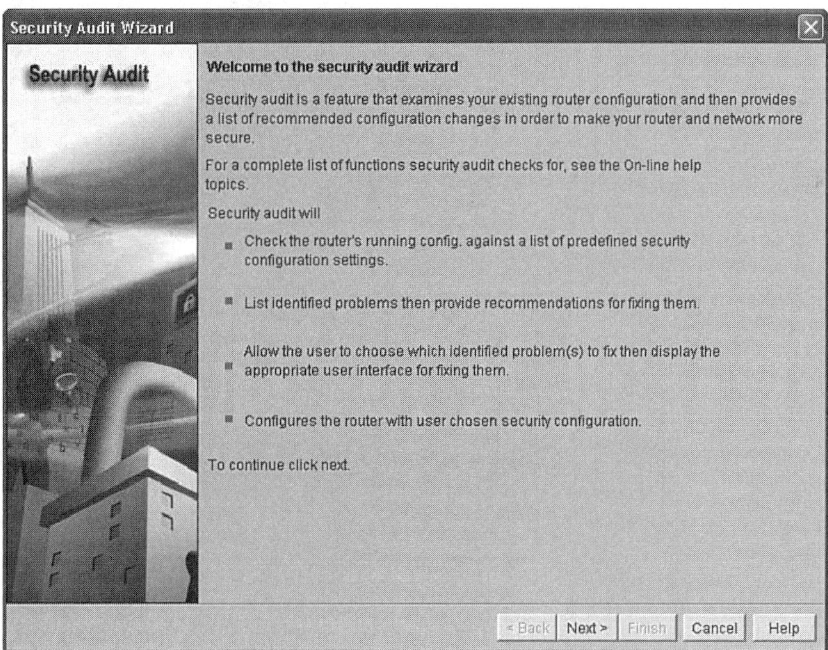

Step 3. Perform a security audit.

This gives a brief explanation of what the Security Audit feature does. Click **Next** to open the Security Audit Interface configuration window, as shown in Figure 4-7.

Figure 4-7 Security Audit Interface Configuration

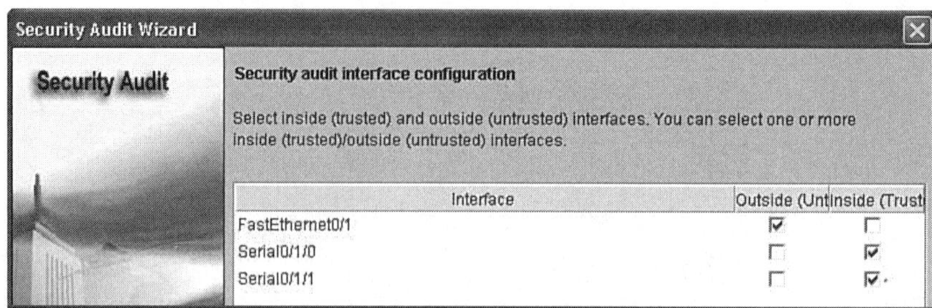

An interface should be classified as outside (untrusted) if you cannot be sure of the legitimacy of the traffic coming into the interface. In this example, both FastEthernet 0/1 and Serial 0/1/0 are untrusted because Serial 0/1/0 is facing the Internet and FastEthernet 0/1 is facing the access part of the network and illegitimate traffic could be generated.

After selecting outside and inside interfaces, click **Next**. A new window opens indicating that SDM is conducting a security audit, as shown in Figure 4-8.

Figure 4-8 Security Audit Check

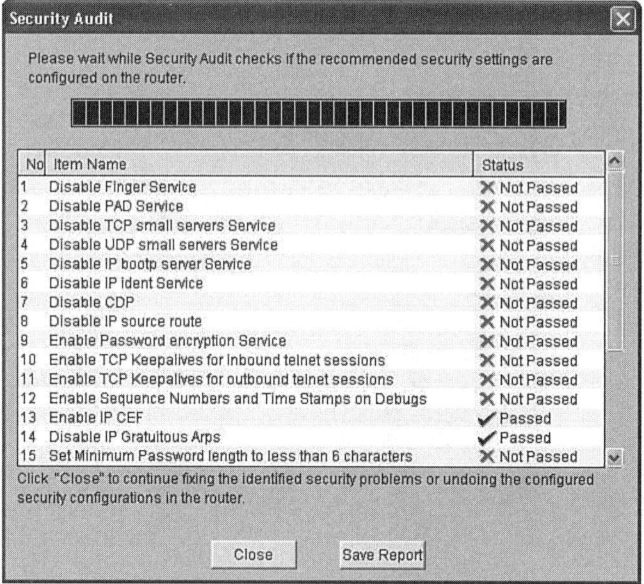

As you can see, the default configuration is not secure. Click the **Close** button to continue.

Step 4. Apply settings to the router.

From the screen shown in Figure 4-9, click the **Fix All** button to make all the suggested security changes. Then, click the **Next** button.

Figure 4-9 Security Audit Suggested Fixes

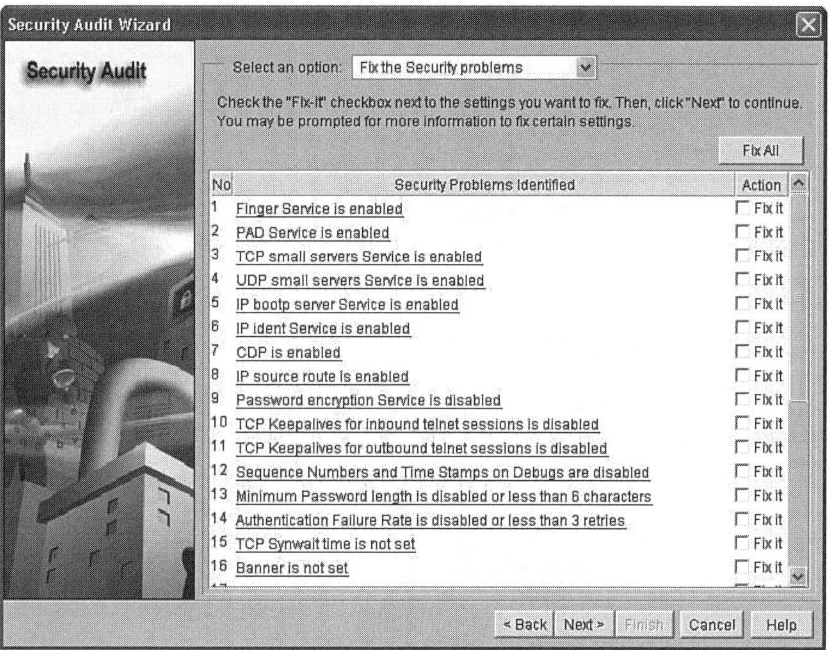

Enter a banner message to use as the message of the day for the router, as shown in Figure 4-10, and then click **Next**.

Figure 4-10 Login Banner Configuration

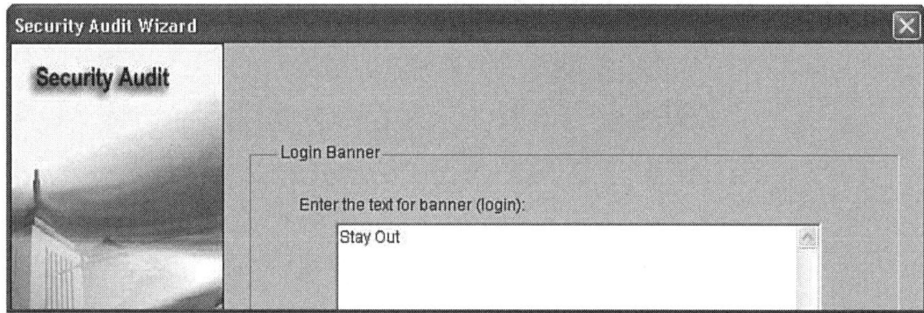

Next, from the screen in Figure 4-11, set the level of severity of log traps that you want the router to send to the syslog server. The severity level is set to debugging for this scenario. Click **Next** to view a summary of the changes about to be made to the router.

Step 5. Commit the configuration to the router.

After reviewing the changes about to be committed as shown in the screen in Figure 4-12, click **Finish**.

Figure 4-11 Logging Level Configuration

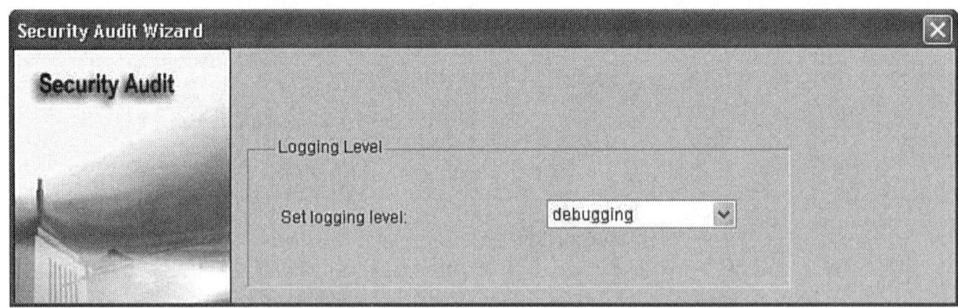

Figure 4-12 Security Audit Summary

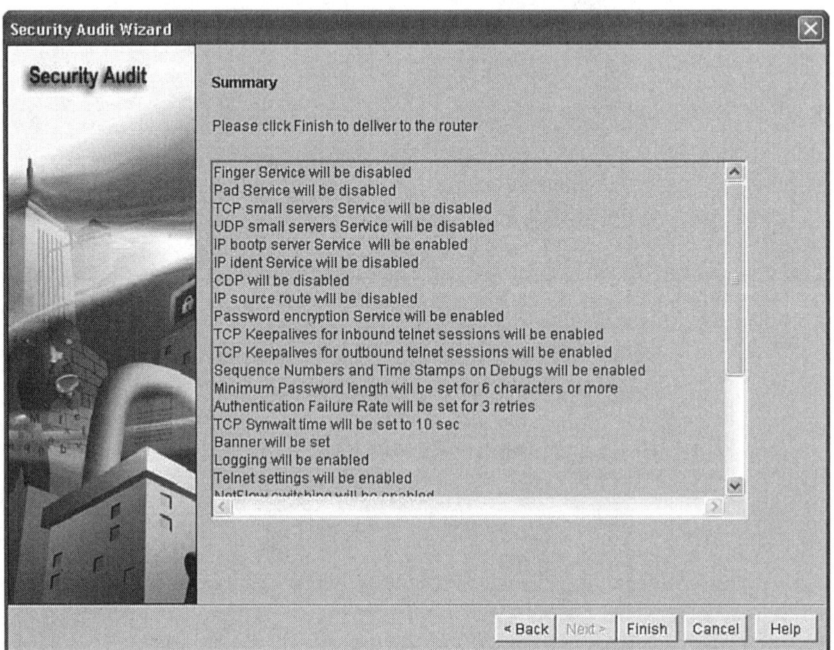

From the screen in Figure 4-13, click **OK** and exit SDM.

Figure 4-13 Command Delivery

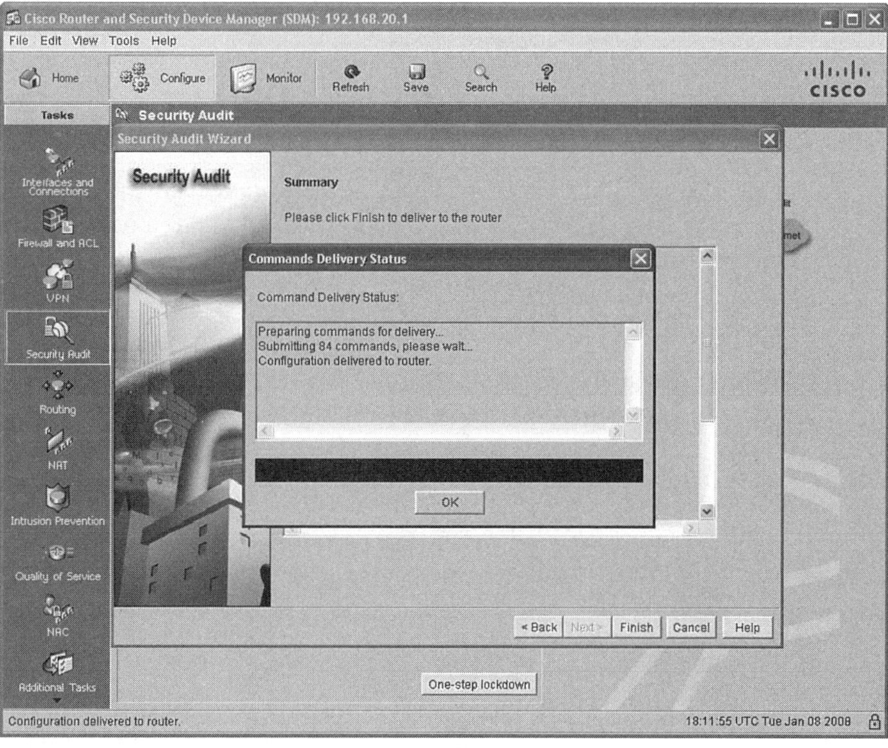

Task 9: Document the Router Configurations

On each router, issue the **show run** command and capture the configurations.

Task 10: Clean Up

Erase the configurations and reload the routers. Disconnect and store the cabling. For PC hosts that are normally connected to other networks (such as the school LAN or to the Internet), reconnect the appropriate cabling and restore the TCP/IP settings.

Lab 4-2: Challenge Security Configuration (4.6.2)

Upon completion of this lab, you will be able to

- Cable a network according to the topology diagram in Figure 4-14.
- Erase the startup configuration and reload a router to the default state.
- Perform basic configuration tasks on a router.
- Configure basic router security.
- Disable unused Cisco services and interfaces.
- Protect enterprise networks from basic external and internal attacks.
- Understand and manage Cisco IOS configuration files and Cisco file system.

- Set up and use Cisco SDM (Security Device Manager) and SDM Express to configure basic router security.
- Configure VLANs on the switches.

Scenario

In this lab, you configure security using the network shown in the topology diagram in Figure 4-14. If you need assistance, see Lab 4-1; however, try to do as much on your own as possible. For this lab, do not use password protection or log in on any console lines, because they might cause accidental logout. However, you should still secure the console line using other means. Use **ciscoccna** for all passwords in this lab.

Table 4-3 provides the IP addresses, subnet masks, and default gateways (where applicable) for all devices in the topology.

Figure 4-14 Topology Diagram for Lab 4-2

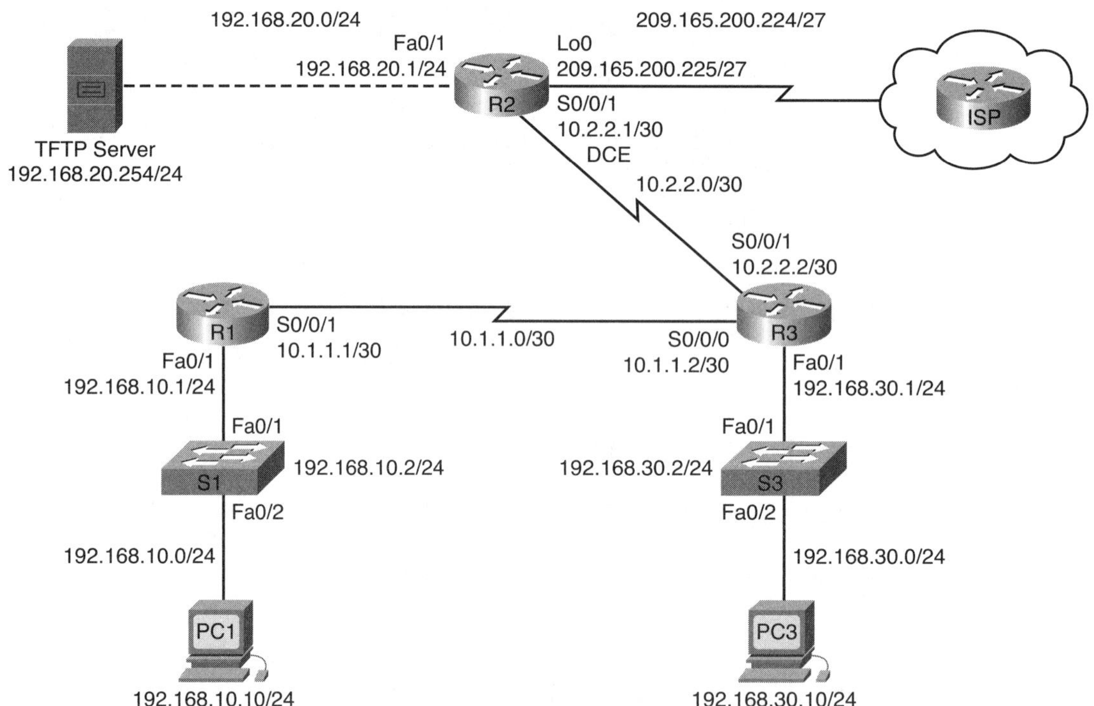

Table 4-3 Addressing Table for Lab 4-2

Device	Interface	IP Address	Subnet Mask	Default Gateway
R1	Fa0/1	192.168.10.1	255.255.255.0	N/A
	S0/0/0	10.1.1.1	255.255.255.252	N/A
R2	Fa0/1	192.168.20.1	255.255.255.0	N/A
	S0/0/0	10.1.1.2	255.255.255.252	N/A

Device	Interface	IP Address	Subnet Mask	Default Gateway
	S0/0/1	10.2.2.1	255.255.255.252	N/A
	Lo0	209.165.200.225	255.255.255.224	N/A
R3	Fa0/1	192.168.30.1	255.255.255.0	N/A
	S0/0/1	10.2.2.2	255.255.255.252	N/A
S1	VLAN 10	192.168.10.2	255.255.255.0	N/A
S3	VLAN 30	192.168.30.2	255.255.255.0	N/A
PC1	NIC	192.168.10.10	255.255.255.0	192.168.10.1
PC2	NIC	192.168.30.10	255.255.255.0	192.168.30.1
TFTP	NIC	192.168.20.254	255.255.255.0	192.168.20.1

Task 1: Prepare the Network

Step 1. Cable a network similar to the one in the topology diagram in Figure 4-14.

Note: This lab was developed and tested using 1841 routers. If you use 1700, 2500, or 2600 series routers, the router outputs and interface descriptions might differ.

Step 2. Clear any existing configurations on the routers.

Task 2: Perform Basic Router Configurations

Step 1. Configure routers.

Configure the R1, R2, and R3 routers according to the following guidelines:

- Configure the router hostname according to the topology diagram.
- Disable DNS lookup.
- Configure a message-of-the-day banner.
- Configure IP addresses on R1, R2, and R3.
- Enable RIP Version 2 on all routers for all networks.
- Create a loopback interface on R2 to simulate the connection to the Internet.
- Create VLANs on switch S1 and S3 and configure the respective interfaces to participate in the VLANs.
- Configure router R3 for SDM secure connectivity.
- Install SDM on either PC3 or R3 if it is not installed already.

Step 2. Configure Ethernet interfaces.

Configure the Ethernet interfaces of PC1, PC3, and the TFTP server with the IP addresses and default gateways from the addressing table at the beginning of the lab.

Step 3. Test the PC configuration by pinging the default gateway from each of the PCs and the TFTP server.

Task 3: Secure Access to Routers

Step 1. Configure secure passwords and AAA using a local database.

Create a secure password for router access. Create the username **ccna** to store locally on the router. Configure the router to use the local authentication database. Remember to use **ciscoccna** for all passwords in this lab.

Step 2. Secure the console and the vty lines.

Configure the console and vty lines to block a user who enters an incorrect username and password five times within 2 minutes. Block additional login attempts for 2 minutes.

Step 3. Verify that connection attempts are denied after the failed attempt limit is reached.

Task 4: Secure Access to the Network

Step 1. Secure the RIP routing protocol.

Do not send RIP updates to non-network routers (any router not in this scenario). Authenticate RIP updates and encrypt them.

Step 2. Verify that RIP routing still works.

Task 5: Logging Activity with SNMP (Simple Network Management Protocol)

Step 1. Configure SNMP logging to the syslog server at 192.168.10.250 on all devices.

Step 2. Log all messages with severity level 4 to the syslog server.

Task 6: Disabling Unused Cisco Network Services

Step 1. Disable unused interfaces on all devices.

Step 2. Disable unused global services on R1.

Step 3. Disable unused interface services on R1.

Step 4. Use AutoSecure to secure R2.

Remember to use **ciscoccna** for all passwords in this lab.

Task 7: Managing Cisco IOS and Configuration Files

Step 1. Identify where the running configuration file is located in router memory.

Step 2. Transfer the running configuration file from R1 to R2 using TFTP.

Step 3. Break R1 and recover it using ROMmon.

Enter the following commands on R1, and then recover R1 using ROMmon.

```
line vty 0 4
 exec-timeout 0 20
line console 0
 exec-timeout 0 20
end
copy run start
exit
```

Step 4. Restore the saved configuration to R1 from R2 using TFTP.

Step 5. Erase the saved configuration from R2.

Task 8: Using SDM to Secure R2

Step 1. Connect to R2 using PC1.

Step 2. Navigate to the Security Audit feature.

Step 3. Perform a security audit.

Step 4. Choose settings to apply to the router.

Step 5. Commit the configuration to the router.

Task 9: Document the Router Configurations

On each router, issue the **show run** command and capture the configurations.

Task 10: Clean Up

Erase the configurations and reload the routers. Disconnect and store the cabling. For PC hosts that are normally connected to other networks (such as the school LAN or to the Internet), reconnect the appropriate cabling and restore the TCP/IP settings.

Lab 4-3: Troubleshooting Security Configuration (4.6.3)

Upon completion of this lab, you will be able to

- Cable a network according to the topology diagram in Figure 4-15.
- Erase the startup configuration and reload a router to the default state.
- Load routers with supplied scripts.
- Find and correct all network errors.
- Disable unused Cisco services and interfaces.
- Document the corrected network.

Scenario

Your company just hired a new network engineer who has created some security issues in the network with misconfigurations and oversights. Your boss has asked you to correct the errors the new engineer has made configuring the routers. While correcting the problems, make sure that all the devices are secure but are still accessible by administrators, and that all networks are reachable. All routers must be accessible with SDM from PC1. Verify that a device is secure by using tools such as Telnet and ping. Unauthorized use of these tools should be blocked, but also ensure that authorized use is permitted. For this lab, do not use login or password protection on any console lines to prevent accidental lockout. Use **ciscoccna** for all passwords in this scenario.

Figure 4-15 shows the network topology for this lab, and Table 4-4 provides the IP addresses, subnet masks, and default gateways (where applicable) for all devices in the topology.

Figure 4-15 Topology Diagram for Lab 4-3

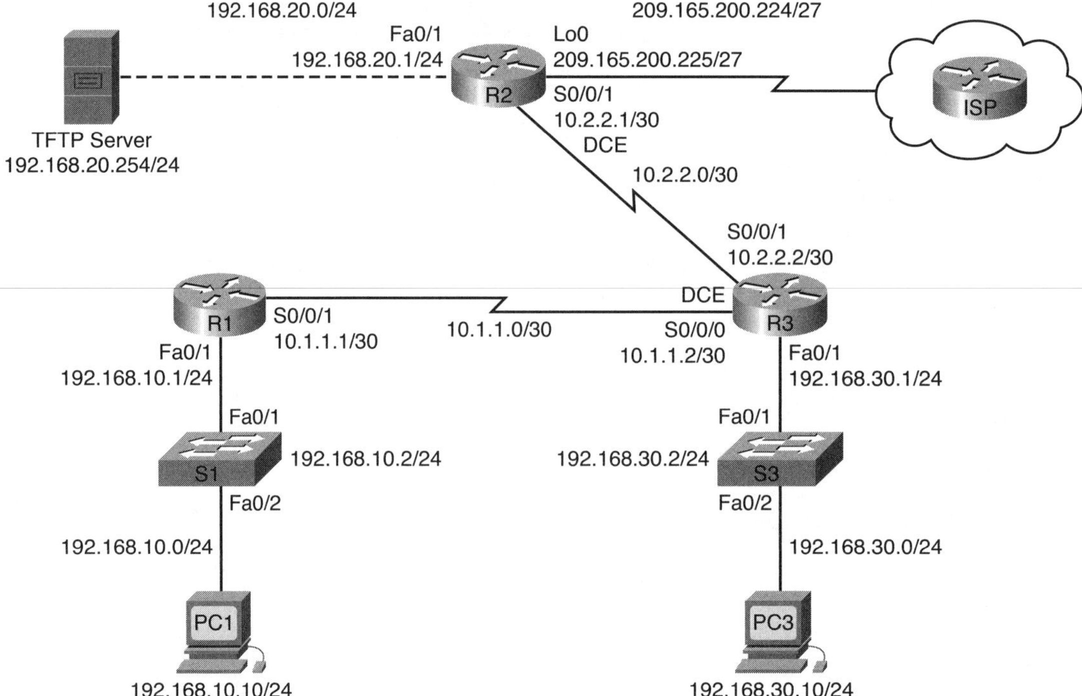

Table 4-4 Addressing Table for Lab 4-3

Device	Interface	IP Address	Subnet Mask	Default Gateway
R1	Fa0/1	192.168.10.1	255.255.255.0	N/A
	S0/0/0	10.1.1.1	255.255.255.252	N/A
R2	Fa0/1	192.168.20.1	255.255.255.0	N/A
	S0/0/0	10.1.1.2	255.255.255.252	N/A
	S0/0/1	10.2.2.1	255.255.255.252	N/A
	Lo0	209.165.200.225	255.255.255.224	N/A
R3	Fa0/1	192.168.30.1	255.255.255.0	N/A
	S0/0/1	10.2.2.2	255.255.255.252	N/A
S1	VLAN 10	192.168.10.2	255.255.255.0	N/A
S3	VLAN 30	192.168.30.2	255.255.255.0	N/A
PC1	NIC	192.168.10.10	255.255.255.0	192.168.10.1
PC2	NIC	192.168.30.10	255.255.255.0	192.168.30.1
TFTP	NIC	192.168.20.254	255.255.255.0	192.168.20.1

Task 1: Load Routers with the Supplied Scripts

Load the following configurations into the devices in the topology.

R1

```
no service pad
service timestamps debug datetime msec
service timestamps log datetime msec
service password-encryption
!
hostname R1
!
boot-start-marker
boot-end-marker
!
security authentication failure rate 10 log
security passwords min-length 6
enable secret ciscoccna
!
aaa new-model
!
```

```
aaa authentication login LOCAL_AUTH local
!
aaa session-id common
!
resource policy
!
mmi polling-interval 60
no mmi auto-configure
no mmi pvc
mmi snmp-timeout 180
ip subnet-zero
no ip source-route
no ip gratuitous-arps
ip cef
!
no ip dhcp use vrf connected
!
no ip bootp server
!
key chain RIP_KEY
 key 1
  key-string cisco
username ccna password ciscoccna
!
 interface FastEthernet0/0
 no ip address
 no ip redirects
 no ip unreachables
 no ip proxy-arp
no shutdown
 duplex auto
 speed auto
!
interface FastEthernet0/1
 ip address 192.168.10.1 255.255.255.0
 no ip redirects
 no ip unreachables
 no ip proxy-arp
 duplex auto
 speed auto
 no shutdown
!
!
```

```
interface Serial0/0/0
 no ip address
 no ip redirects
 no ip unreachables
 no ip proxy-arp
 no shutdown
 no fair-queue
 clockrate 125000
!
interface Serial0/0/1
 ip address 10.1.1.1 255.255.255.252
 no ip redirects
 no ip unreachables
 no ip proxy-arp
 no shutdown
!
interface Serial0/1/0
 no ip address
 no ip redirects
 no ip unreachables
 no ip proxy-arp
 no shutdown
 clockrate 2000000
!
interface Serial0/1/1
 no ip address
 no ip redirects
 no ip unreachables
 no ip proxy-arp
no shutdown
!
router rip
 version 2
 passive-interface default
 no passive-interface Serial0/0/0
 network 10.0.0.0
 network 192.168.10.0
 no auto-summary
!
ip classless
!
no ip http server
```

```
logging 192.168.10.150
no cdp run
!
line con 0
 exec-timeout 5 0
 logging synchronous
 transport output telnet
line aux 0
 exec-timeout 15 0
 logging synchronous
 login authentication local_auth
 transport output telnet
line vty 0 4
 exec-timeout 5 0
 logging synchronous
 login authentication local_auth
!
end
```

R2

```
no service pad
service timestamps debug datetime msec
service timestamps log datetime msec
!
hostname R2
!
security authentication failure rate 10 log
security passwords min-length 6
!
aaa new-model
!
aaa authentication login local_auth local
!
aaa session-id common
!
resource policy
!
mmi polling-interval 60
no mmi auto-configure
no mmi pvc
mmi snmp-timeout 180
no ip source-route
no ip gratuitous-arps
```

```
ip cef
!
no ip dhcp use vrf connected
!
no ip bootp server
!
username ccna password ciscoccna
!
interface FastEthernet0/0
 no ip address
 no ip redirects
 no ip unreachables
 no ip proxy-arp
 no ip directed-broadcast
 shutdown
 duplex auto
 speed auto
!
interface FastEthernet0/1
 ip address 192.168.20.1 255.255.255.0
 no ip redirects
 no ip unreachables
 no ip proxy-arp
 no ip directed-broadcast
 duplex auto
 speed auto
 no shutdown
!
interface Serial0/0/0
 no ip address
 no ip redirects
 no ip unreachables
 no ip proxy-arp
 no ip directed-broadcast
 shutdown
 no fair-queue
!
interface Serial0/0/1
 ip address 10.2.2.1 255.255.255.252
 no ip redirects
```

```
 no ip unreachables
 no ip proxy-arp
 no ip directed-broadcast
 ip rip authentication mode md5
 ip rip authentication key-chain RIP_KEY
 clockrate 128000
 no shutdown
!
interface Serial0/1/0
 ip address 209.165.200.224 255.255.255.224
 no ip redirects
 no ip unreachables
 no ip proxy-arp
 no ip directed-broadcast
 no shutdown
!
interface Serial0/1/1
 no ip address
 no ip redirects
 no ip unreachables
 no ip proxy-arp
 no ip directed-broadcast
 shutdown
 clockrate 2000000
!
router rip
 version 2
 no passive-interface Serial0/0/1
 network 10.0.0.0
 network 192.168.20.0
 no auto-summary
!
ip classless
!
no ip http server
!
logging trap debugging
logging 192.168.10.150
!
line con 0
 exec-timeout 5 0
 logging synchronous
 transport output telnet
line aux 0
```

```
 exec-timeout 15 0
 logging synchronous
 login authentication local_auth
 transport output telnet
line vty 0 4
 exec-timeout 0 0
logging synchronous
 login authentication local_auth
 transport input telnet
!
end
```

R3

```
no service pad
service timestamps debug datetime msec
service timestamps log datetime msec
service password-encryption
!
hostname R3
!
boot-start-marker
boot-end-marker
!
security authentication failure rate 10 log
security passwords min-length 6
enable secret ciscoccna
!
aaa new-model
!
aaa authentication login local_auth local
!
aaa session-id common
!
resource policy
!
mmi polling-interval 60
no mmi auto-configure
no mmi pvc
mmi snmp-timeout 180
ip subnet-zero
no ip source-route
no ip gratuitous-arps
ip cef
!
!
```

```
no ip dhcp use vrf connected
!
no ip bootp server
!
key chain RIP_KEY
 key 1
  key-string Cisco
!
interface FastEthernet0/0
 no ip address
 no ip redirects
 no ip proxy-arp
 no ip directed-broadcast
 duplex auto
 speed auto
 shutdown
!
interface FastEthernet0/1
 ip address 192.168.30.1 255.255.255.0
 no ip redirects
 no ip unreachables
 no ip proxy-arp
 no ip directed-broadcast
 no shutdown
 duplex auto
 speed auto
!
interface Serial0/0/0
 ip address 10.1.1.2 255.255.255.252
 no ip redirects
 no ip unreachables
 no ip proxy-arp
 no ip directed-broadcast
 clockrate 125000
!
interface Serial0/0/1
 ip address 10.2.2.2 255.255.255.252
 no ip redirects
 no ip unreachables
 no ip proxy-arp
 no ip directed-broadcast
```

```
!
router rip
 version 2
 passive-interface default
 passive-interface Serial0/0/0
 passive-interface Serial0/0/1
 network 10.0.0.0
 network 192.168.30.0
 no auto-summary
!
ip classless
!
no ip http server
!
logging trap debugging
logging 192.168.10.150
no cdp run
!
control-plane
!
line con 0
 exec-timeout 5 0
 logging synchronous
 transport output telnet
line aux 0
 exec-timeout 15 0
 logging synchronous
 login authentication local_auth
 transport output telnet
line vty 0 4
 exec-timeout 15 0
 logging synchronous
 login authentication local_auth
 transport input telnet
!
end
```

Task 2: Find and Correct All Network Errors

Using standard troubleshooting methods, find, document, and correct each error.

When troubleshooting a production network that is not working, many very small mistakes can prevent everything from working correctly. The first item to check is the spelling and case of all passwords, keychain names and keys, and authentication list names. It is often a mismatch in case or spelling that causes total failure. The best practice is to start with the most basic and work upward.

First ask whether all the names and keys match up. Next, if the configuration uses a list or keychain and so on, check whether the item referenced actually exists and is the same on all devices. Configuring something once on one device and then copying and pasting into the other device is the best way to ensure that the configuration is exactly the same.

Next, when thinking about disabling or restricting services, ask what the services are used for and whether they are needed. Also ask what information the router should be sending out. Who should and should not receive that information. Finally, ask what the services enable the users to do, and whether you want them to be able to do that. Generally, if you can think of a way that a service can be abused, you should take steps to prevent that.

Task 3: Document the Corrected Network

Task 4: Clean Up

Erase the configurations and reload the routers. Disconnect and store the cabling. For PC hosts that are normally connected to other networks (such as the school LAN or to the Internet), reconnect the appropriate cabling and restore the TCP/IP settings.

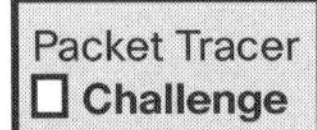

Packet Tracer Skills Integration Challenge

Open file LSG04-PTSkills4.pka on the CD-ROM that accompanies this book to perform this exercise using Packet Tracer. Upon completion of this skills integration challenge, you will be able to

- Configure routing
- Configure OSPF authentication
- Upgrade the Cisco IOS image

This activity is a cumulative review of the chapter covering OSPF routing, authentication, and upgrading the Cisco IOS image.

Open the file LSG04-PTSkills04.pka on the CD-ROM that accompanies this book. You use the topology in Figure 4-16 and the addressing information in Table 4-5 to complete this activity.

Table 4-5 Addressing Table for Packet Tracer Skills Integration Challenge

Device	Interface	IP Address	Subnet Mask
ISP	S0/0/0	209.165.200.226	255.255.255.252
R1	Fa0/1	192.168.10.1	255.255.255.0
	S0/0/0	10.1.1.1	255255.255.252
R2	Fa0/1	192.168.20.1	255.255.255.0
	S0/0/0	10.1.1.2	255.255.255.252
	S0/0/1	10.2.2.1	255.255.255.252
	S0/1/0	209.165.200.225	255.255.255.252

continues

Table 4-5 Addressing Table for Packet Tracer Skills Integration Challenge *continued*

Device	Interface	IP Address	Subnet Mask
R3	Fa0/1	192.168.30.1	255.255.255.0
	S0/0/1	10.2.2.2	255.255.255.252
PC1	NIC	192.168.10.10	255.255.255.0
PC3	NIC	192.168.30.10	255.255.255.0
TFTP server	NIC	192.168.20.254	255.255.255.255

Figure 4-16 Packet Tracer Skills Integration Challenge Topology

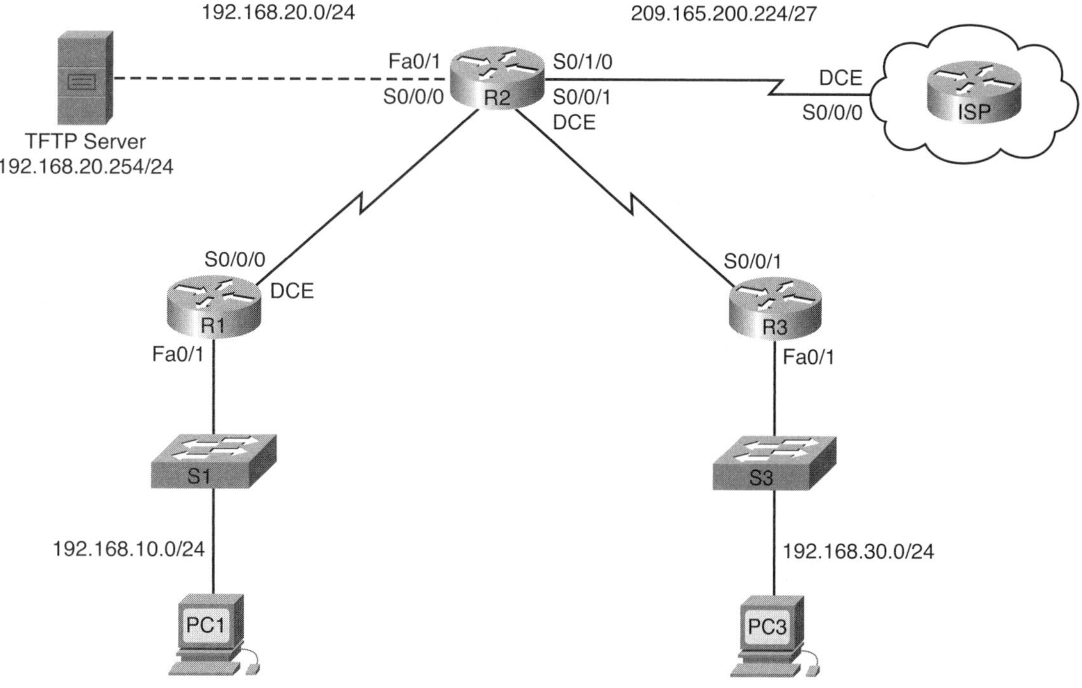

Task 1: Configure Routing

Step 1. Configure a default route to ISP.

On R2, use the **exit interface** argument to configure a default route to ISP.

Step 2. Configure OSPF routing between R1, R2, and R3.

Configure OSPF routing on all three routers. Use process ID 1. Disable OSPF updates on appropriate interfaces.

Step 3. Propagate the default route.

Step 4. Check the results.

Your completion percentage should be 59 percent. If not, click **Check Results** to see which required components are not yet completed.

Task 2: Configure OSPF Authentication

Step 1. Configure MD5 authentication between R1, R2, and R3.

Configure OSPF MD5 authentication between R1, R2, and R3 using **1** as the key value and **cisco123** as the password.

Step 2. Check the results.

Your completion percentage should be 91 percent. If not, click **Check Results** to see which required components are not yet completed.

Task 3: Upgrade the Cisco IOS Image

Step 1. Copy a newer image from the TFTP server to flash on R2.

Look under the Config tab for the TFTP server to determine the name of the newer Cisco IOS image. Then, copy the newer image to flash on R2.

Step 2. Configure R2 to boot with the new image.

Step 3. Save the configuration and reload.

Verify that the new image is loaded in RAM.

Step 4. Check the results.

Your completion percentage should be 100 percent. If not, click **Check Results** to see which required components are not yet completed.

CHAPTER 5

ACLs

The Study Guide portion of this chapter uses a combination of matching, multiple-choice, and open-ended question exercises to test your knowledge of the various types of access control lists (ACL). You will also learn how to configure and where to place ACLs to properly secure and control traffic patterns in and out of networks.

The Labs portion of this chapter includes all the online curriculum labs. The Challenge and Troubleshooting labs are added to ensure that you have mastered the practical, hands-on skills needed to configure, place, and troubleshoot ACLs.

As you work through this chapter, use Chapter 5 in the *Accessing the WAN, CCNA Exploration Companion Guide*, or use the corresponding Chapter 5 in the *Accessing the WAN* online curriculum, for assistance.

Study Guide

Using ACLs to Secure Networks

ACLs are used to secure and control traffic into and out of networks. ACLs filter traffic based on rules you set in your ACL statements. The rules determine if packets are permitted or denied, what service they are allowed to use, and who they can communicate with. An example of this is whether a host is allowed to access the Internet or have access to a particular server on the network.

Access to services is filtered based on port numbers. Ports 0 to 1023 are called well-known ports. These include common services such as Telnet port 23 and HTTP, which uses port 80. Companies may request a port number from IANA between 1024 and 49,151 to identify a specific application. For example, Shockwave uses port number 1626. Ports 49,152 to 65,535 are dynamically assigned to end devices and are temporary, lasting only the duration of a connection.

When configured, an ACL turns a router into a firewall and checks all traffic against each statement before it can be forwarded to its destination. This process controls traffic patterns and helps secure your network but definitely adds latency. Packets are checked against ACL statements in the order in which they are configured, from top to bottom, one statement at a time. When the first match occurs, whether it is permitted or denied, that action occurs. If each statement is a permit action, an implicit "deny any" at the end of the statement list is not seen and does not need to be configured. Any packet that does not match any of the permit statements is automatically denied. Therefore, if all statements are deny actions, a permit any must be the last statement written, or all traffic is denied! This is a very common mistake for novice network administrators to make.

Standard and extended access lists can be named or numbered. Standard ACLS are simple statements that permit or deny traffic based on the source IP address. They should be configured on the router as close to the destination as possible. Extended ACLs can filter traffic using multiple variables such as protocol, source and destination IP address, and port number based on the service or application being filtered. Because they are precise, they are configured on the router closest to the source being filtered. This prevents denied traffic from consuming bandwidth.

Standard and extended ACLs can be configured to be named or numbered. ACLS generally are given a number to identify their type—1 to 99 for standard IP and 100 to 199 for extended IP. Named ACLs have no limit, but, more importantly, they can be modified without starting over from the beginning. Sequence numbers can be used when you want to add a statement to the middle of the list without starting over.

As mentioned, packets are processed against ACLs in the order in which they were created. This means that if you make a mistake and put a statement first that should have been last, you cannot simply remove it; you must start from the beginning. This is why it is recommended that you write out your ACL statements in Notepad and have someone check them over before you drop them into your configuration. If you use named ACLs, you are not limited as to how many statements you can create, and you also can tweak your configuration without removing it and starting over. After you create the access list that serves its purpose, the next and last step is to apply it to an interface. You must apply an ACL to an interface for it to work. Without this, the ACL is useless and is the same as having no security as all.

Multiple-Choice Questions

1. What is the well-known port number range?

A. 0 to 1023

B. 1 to 1023

C. 0 to 1024

D. 1 to 1024

2. Which of the following is a port used by TCP and UDP?

A. 23 Telnet

B. 25 SMTP

C. 53 DNS

D. 69 TFTP

3. Which port is used by secure websites using HTTPS?

A. 161

B. 443

C. 520

D. 694

4. Why are ACL numbers 200 to 1299 skipped?

A. They are reserved.

B. The are used by well-known ACLs.

C. They are reserved for loopbacks.

D. They are used by other protocols.

5. Which criterion *cannot* be used in an ACL rule to match a packet?

A. Source address

B. Source port

C. Destination address

D. Destination port

E. Protocol

F. Direction

6. What are the "Three Ps" when configuring ACLs on a router? (Choose three.)

A. One ACL per port
B. One ACL per protocol
C. One ACL per interface
D. One ACL per direction
E. One ACL per network
F. One ACL per filter

7. Place the following actions in the correct order:

A. The packet is processed by outbound ACL.
B. The packet is processed by inbound ACL.
C. The packet is transmitted on an interface.
D. The packet is received on an interface.
E. The packet is routed to the appropriate interface for transmission.

A. A, B, C, D, E
B. E, D, B, A, C
C. D, B, E, A, C
D. C, A, D, E, B

8. What are the benefits of using named ACLs over numbered? (Choose two.)

A. There is no limit to the number of ACLs you can create.
B. They are not sequential like numbered ACLs.
C. They can be modified without starting over.
D. They are easier to configure.

9. What is the range of numbers used to identify IP standard access lists?

A. 0 to 99
B. 1 to 99
C. 100 to 199
D. 100 to 200

10. At what layer of the OSI Reference Model does packet filtering occur?

A. Data link
B. Network
C. Transport
D. Application

Configuring Standard ACLs: Command Exercise

For question 1, refer to the topology shown in Figure 5-1.

Figure 5-1 Network Topology for Question 1

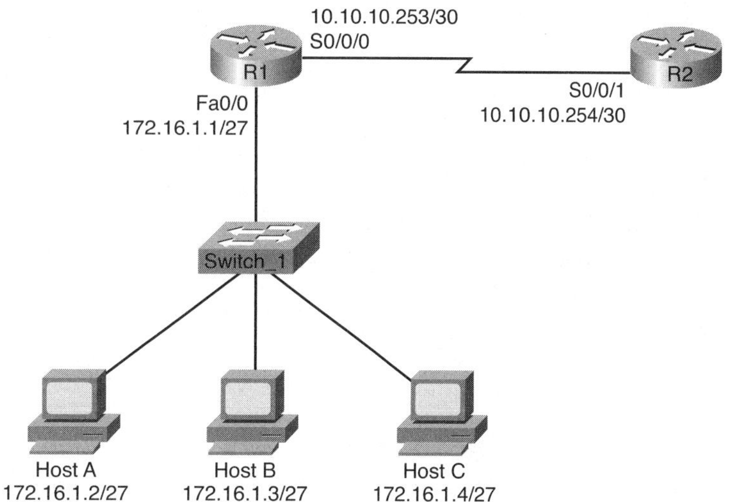

Allow only Host A to telnet to the R2 router, using **cisco** as the password. Use a standard named ACL to accomplish this task, and name the ACL **No_Telnet**. Write all the commands below.

____

____

____

____

____

____

____

For questions 2 through 4, refer to the topology shown in Figure 5-2.

Figure 5-2 Network Topology for Questions 2 Through 4

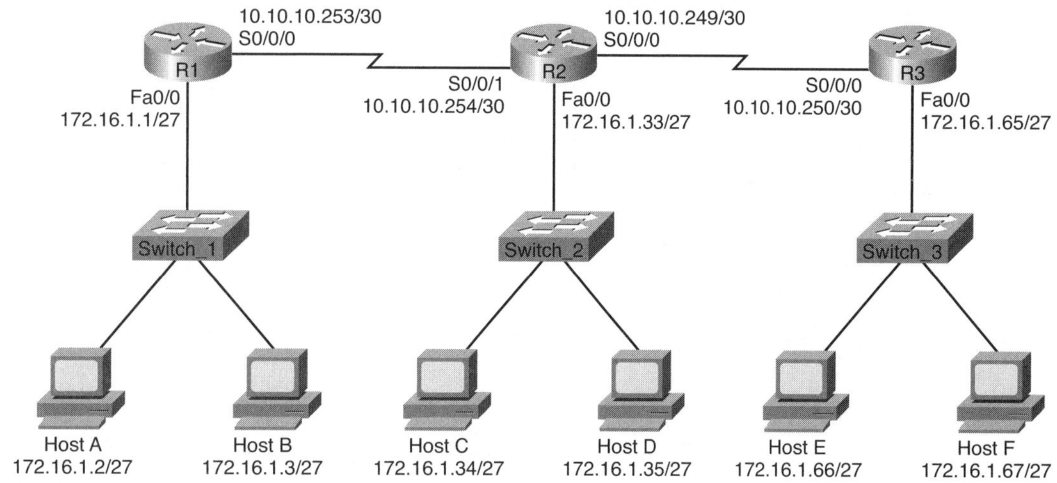

Deny users from the R1 LAN access to the R3 LAN. Use a standard numbered ACL to accomplish this task, and be sure to include the appropriate wildcard mask. Configure a remark that will remind the administrator of the purpose of the ACL. Write all the commands below.

Permit *only* users from the R3 LAN access to the R2 LAN. Use a standard named ACL to accomplish this task, and name the ACL **R3_Only**. Write all the commands below.

Traffic from the R2 LAN should not be permitted to leave the LAN. Create a standard numbered ACL to accomplish this. Use the last usable number in the standard IP ACL number range. Write all the commands below.

Configuring Extended ACLs

Vocabulary Exercise: Matching Terms

Match the parameter on the left with its definition on the right. Use the following command syntax as a basis for your answers:

```
access?list access?list?number [dynamic dynamic?name [timeout minutes]]
  {deny ¦ permit} protocol source source?wildcard destination destination?wildcard
  [precedence precedence] [tos tos] [log ¦ log?input] [time?range time?range?name]
```

Parameter

a. Extended ACL number range

b. Dynamic

c. Protocol

d. Source/destination

e. Wildcard

f. Port

g. Log

h. Operator

i. Host

j. Any

Definition

__ Specifies the different types of traffic

__ Sends an informational message about a packet that matches the entry to be sent to the console

__ The number of the network or host from which the packet is being sent

__ Can be listed as a name or number

__ A number range from 100 to 199 or from 2000 to 2699

__ Used with lock-and-key security

__ An abbreviation for a source or destination wildcard of 0.0.0.0 255.255.255.255

__ A string of binary digits telling the router which parts of the subnet to look at

__ Equal to, not equal to, and less than

__ Abbreviation for a source or destination wildcard of 0.0.0.0

Extended ACL Command Exercise

Refer to Figure 5-3 for all the questions in this command exercise.

Figure 5-3 Network Topology for Questions 1 Through 4

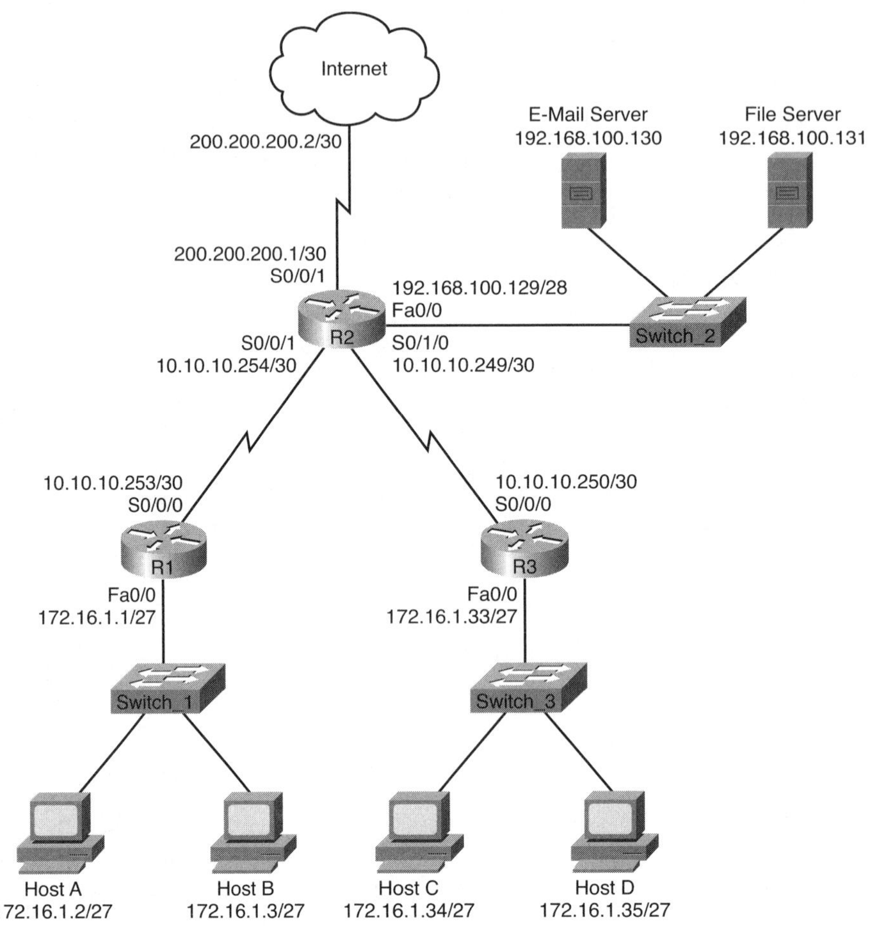

1. Allow only Host A from the 172.16.1.0/27 subnet access to the E-Mail server. Use the last usable number in the extended list range. Host A should not have access to any of the other servers. Write all the commands below.

____

____

____

____

2. Allow only Host B access to the Internet, and deny everyone else. Use an extended named ACL to accomplish this task, and name the ACL **Internet**. Write all the commands below.

____

____

____

____

____

3. No one from the 172.16.1.0/27 subnet is allowed access to the File Server, but all other traffic should be permitted. Use an extended named ACL to accomplish this task, and name the ACL **No_Access**. Write all the commands below.

____

____

____

____

____

____

4. Allow only hosts on the R3 LAN to communicate with hosts on the R1 LAN. They are allowed access to the Internet, but deny them access to the servers on the R2 LAN. Use the first usable number in the extended IP range to accomplish this task. Write all the commands below.

____

____

____

____

Configuring Complex ACLs

Review Questions

Various types of ACLs are available to secure your network and to filter traffic such as standard, extended, numbered, dynamic, lock-and-key, reflexive, and time-based. Below, write the definitions, and give an example of when you would use each kind of ACL.

Lock-and-key:

____

____

____

____

____

____

____

Reflexive:

____

____

____

____

____

____

Time-based:

____

____

____

____

Vocabulary Exercise: Matching Terms

Match the term on the left with its definition on the right.

Field

a. Standard ACL
b. Named ACL
c. Lock-and-key
d. Access class
e. Extended
f. Reflexive
g. IP access group
h. Log
i. Time-based
j. Logical operations

Definition

__ Allows you to add or delete entries within the ACL

__ Shows the ACL number and whether a packet was permitted or denied

__ Applies an ACL to a line

__ This ACL is not applied to an interface or line but is "nested" within an extended ACL

__ Equal to, not equal to, and less than

__ This feature is dependent on Telnet

__ Controls traffic based on the source and destination address

__ Controls traffic based on the source address only

__ Applies an ACL to an interface

__ This feature works best with NTP synchronization

Labs and Activities

Lab 5-1: Basic Access Control Lists (5.5.1)

Upon completion of this lab, you will be able to

- Design named standard and named extended ACLs
- Apply named standard and named extended ACLs
- Test named standard and named extended ACLs
- Troubleshoot named standard and named extended ACLs

Figure 5-4 shows the network topology for this lab. Table 5-1 provides the IP addresses, subnet masks, and default gateways (where applicable) for all devices in the topology.

Figure 5-4 Network Topology for Lab 5-1

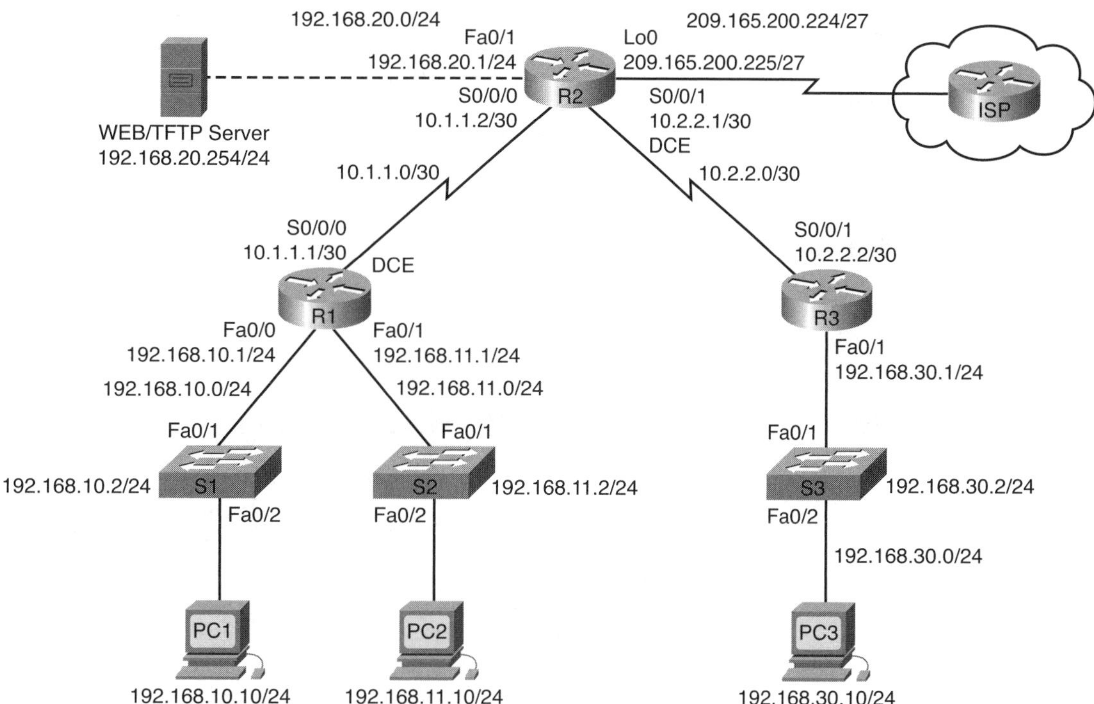

Table 5-1 Lab 5-1 Addressing Table

Device	Interface	IP Address	Subnet Mask	Default Gateway
R1	Fa0/0	192.168.10.1	255.255.255.0	—
	Fa0/1	192.168.11.1	255.255.255.0	—
	S0/0/0	10.1.1.1	255.255.255.252	—

continues

Table 5-1 Lab 5-1 Addressing Table continued

Device	Interface	IP Address	Subnet Mask	Default Gateway
R2	Fa0/1	192.168.20.1	255.255.255.0	—
	S0/0/0	10.1.1.2	255.255.255.252	—
	S0/0/1	10.2.2.1	255.255.255.252	—
	Lo0	209.165.200.225	255.255.255.224	—
R3	Fa0/1	192.168.30.1	255.255.255.0	—
	S0/0/1	10.2.2.2	255.255.255.252	—
S1	Vlan1	192.168.10.2	255.255.255.0	192.168.10.1
S2	Vlan1	192.168.11.2	255.255.255.0	192.168.11.1
S3	Vlan1	192.168.30.2	255.255.255.0	192.168.30.1
PC1	NIC	192.168.10.10	255.255.255.0	192.168.10.1
PC2	NIC	192.168.11.10	255.255.255.0	192.168.11.1
PC3	NIC	192.168.30.10	255.255.255.0	192.168.30.1
Web Server	NIC	192.168.20.254	255.255.255.0	192.168.20.1

Scenario

In this lab, you will learn how to configure basic network security using ACLs. You will apply both standard and extended ACLs.

Task 1: Prepare the Network

Step 1. Cable a network that is similar to the one shown in Figure 5-4.

You can use any current router in your lab as long as it has the required interfaces shown in the topology diagram.

Note: This lab was developed and tested using 1841 routers. If you use 1700, 2500, or 2600 series routers, the router outputs and interface descriptions might be different. On older routers, or those running Cisco IOS software earlier than Release 12.4, some commands may be different or nonexistent.

Step 2. Clear any existing configurations on the routers.

Task 2: Perform Basic Router Configurations

Configure the R1, R2, R3, S1, S2, and S3 routers and switches according to the following guidelines:

- Configure the router hostname to match the topology diagram.
- Disable DNS lookup.

- Configure an EXEC mode password of **class**.
- Configure a message-of-the-day banner.
- Configure a password of **cisco** for console connections.
- Configure a password for VTY connections.
- Configure IP addresses and masks on all devices.
- Enable OSPF area 0 on all routers for all networks.
- Configure a loopback interface on R2 to simulate the ISP.
- Configure IP addresses for the VLAN 1 interface on each switch.
- Configure each switch with the appropriate default gateway.
- Verify full IP connectivity using the **ping** command.

Task 3: Configure a Standard ACL

Standard ACLs can filter traffic based on source IP address only. A typical best practice is to configure a standard ACL as close to the destination as possible. In this task, you are configuring a standard ACL. The ACL is designed to block traffic from the 192.168.11.0/24 network located in a student lab from accessing any local networks on R3.

This ACL will be applied inbound on the R3 serial interface. Remember that every ACL has an implicit "deny all" that causes all traffic that has not matched a statement in the ACL to be blocked. For this reason, add the **permit any** statement to the end of the ACL.

Before configuring and applying this ACL, be sure to test connectivity from PC1 (or the Fa0/1 interface on R1) to PC3 (or the Fa0/1 interface on R3). Connectivity tests should be successful before applying the ACL.

Step 1. Create the ACL on router R3.

In global configuration mode, create a standard named ACL called **STND-1**:

```
R3(config)# ip access-list standard STND-1
```

In standard ACL configuration mode, add a statement that denies any packets with a source address of 192.168.11.0/24 and prints a message to the console for each matched packet:

```
R3(config-std-nacl)# deny 192.168.11.0 0.0.0.255 log
```

Permit all other traffic:

```
R3(config-std-nacl)# permit any
```

Step 2. Apply the ACL.

Apply the ACL **STND-1** as a filter on packets entering R3 through serial interface 0/0/1:

```
R3(config)# interface serial 0/0/1
R3(config-if)# ip access-group STND-1 in
R3(config-if)# end
R3# copy run start
```

Step 3. Test the ACL.

Before testing the ACL, make sure that the console of R3 is visible. This allows you to see the access list log messages when the packet is denied.

Test the ACL by pinging from PC2 to PC3. Because the ACL is designed to block traffic with source addresses from the 192.168.11.0/24 network, PC2 (192.168.11.10) should not be able to ping PC3.

You can also use an extended ping from the Fa0/1 interface on R1 to the Fa0/1 interface on R3:

```
R1# ping ip

Target IP address: 192.168.30.1
Repeat count [5]:
Datagram size [100]:
Timeout in seconds [2]:
Extended commands [n]: y
Source address or interface: 192.168.11.1
Type of service [0]:
Set DF bit in IP header? [no]:
Validate reply data? [no]:
Data pattern [0xABCD]:
Loose, Strict, Record, Timestamp, Verbose[none]:
Sweep range of sizes [n]:
Type escape sequence to abort.
Sending 5, 100-byte ICMP Echos to 192.168.30.1, timeout is 2 seconds:
Packet sent with a source address of 192.168.11.1
U.U.U
Success rate is 0 percent (0/5)
```

You should see the following message on the R3 console:

```
*Sep  4 03:22:58.935: %SEC-6-IPACCESSLOGNP: list STND-1 denied 0 0.0.0.0 ->
192.168.11.1, 1 packet
```

In privileged EXEC mode on R3, issue the **show access-lists** command. You see output similar to the following. Each line of an ACL has an associated counter showing how many packets have matched the rule.

```
Standard IP access list STND-1
    10 deny   192.168.11.0, wildcard bits 0.0.0.255 log (5 matches)
    20 permit any (25 matches)
```

The purpose of this ACL is to block hosts from the 192.168.11.0/24 network. Any other hosts, such as those on the 192.168.10.0/24 network, should be allowed access to the networks on R3. Conduct another test from PC1 to PC3 to ensure that this traffic is not blocked.

You can also use an extended ping from the Fa0/0 interface on R1 to the Fa0/1 interface on R3:

```
R1# ping ip

Target IP address: 192.168.30.1
Repeat count [5]:
Datagram size [100]:
Timeout in seconds [2]:
Extended commands [n]: y
Source address or interface: 192.168.10.1
Type of service [0]:
Set DF bit in IP header? [no]:
Validate reply data? [no]:
Data pattern [0xABCD]:
Loose, Strict, Record, Timestamp, Verbose[none]:
Sweep range of sizes [n]:
Type escape sequence to abort.
Sending 5, 100-byte ICMP Echos to 192.168.30.1, timeout is 2 seconds:
Packet sent with a source address of 192.168.10.1
!!!!!
Success rate is 100 percent (5/5), round-trip min/avg/max = 40/43/44 ms
```

Task 4: Configure an Extended ACL

When greater granularity is required, you should use an extended ACL. Extended ACLs can filter traffic based on more than just source address. Extended ACLs can filter on protocol, source, and destination IP addresses, and source and destination port numbers.

An additional policy for this network states that devices from the 192.168.10.0/24 LAN are permitted to reach only internal networks. Computers on this LAN are not permitted to access the Internet. Therefore, these users must be blocked from reaching the IP address 209.165.200.225. Because this requirement needs to enforce both source and destination, an extended ACL is needed.

In this task, you will configure an extended ACL on R1 that keeps traffic originating from any device on the 192.168.10.0/24 network from accessing the 209.165.200.255 host (the simulated ISP). This ACL will be applied inbound on the R1 FastEthernet 0/0 interface. A typical best practice for applying extended ACLs is to place them as close to the source as possible.

Before beginning, verify that you can ping 209.165.200.225 from PC1.

Step 1. Configure a named extended ACL.

In global configuration mode, create a named extended ACL called **EXTEND-1**.

```
R1(config)# ip access-list extended EXTEND-1
```

Notice that the router prompt changes to indicate that you are now in extended ACL configuration mode. From this prompt, add the necessary statements to block traffic from the 192.168.10.0/24 network to the host. Use the **host** keyword when defining the destination:

```
R1(config-ext-nacl)# deny ip 192.168.10.0 0.0.0.255 host 209.165.200.225
```

Recall that the implicit "deny all" blocks all other traffic without the additional **permit** statement. Add the **permit** statement to ensure that other traffic is not blocked:

```
R1(config-ext-nacl)# permit ip any any
```

Step 2. Apply the ACL.

With standard ACLs, the best practice is to place the ACL as close to the destination as possible. Extended ACLs typically are placed close to the source. The **EXTEND-1** ACL will be placed on the serial interface and will filter outbound traffic.

```
R1(config)# interface serial 0/0/0
R1(config-if)# ip access-group EXTEND-1 out log
R1(config-if)# end
R1# copy run start
```

Step 3. Test the ACL.

From PC1, ping the loopback interface on R2. These pings should fail, because all traffic from the 192.168.10.0/24 network is filtered when the destination is 209.165.200.225. If the destination is any other address, the pings should succeed. Confirm this by pinging R3 from the 192.168.10.0/24 network device.

Note: The extended ping feature on R1 cannot be used to test this ACL, because the traffic will originate within R1 and will never be tested against the ACL applied to the R1 serial interface.

You can further verify this by issuing the **show ip access-list** command on R1 after pinging:

```
R1# show ip access-list

Extended IP access list EXTEND-1
    10 deny ip 192.168.10.0 0.0.0.255 host 209.165.200.225 (4 matches)
    20 permit ip any any
```

Task 5: Control Access to the VTY Lines with a Standard ACL

It is good practice to restrict access to the router VTY lines for remote administration. An ACL can be applied to the VTY lines, allowing you to restrict access to specific hosts or networks. In this task, you will configure a standard ACL to permit hosts from two networks to access the VTY lines. All other hosts are denied.

Verify that you can telnet to R2 from both R1 and R3.

Step 1. Configure the ACL.

Configure a named standard ACL on R2 that permits traffic from 10.2.2.0/30 and 192.168.30.0/24. Deny all other traffic. Call the ACL **TASK-5**:

```
R2(config)# ip access-list standard TASK-5
R2(config-std-nacl)# permit 10.2.2.0 0.0.0.3
R2(config-std-nacl)# permit 192.168.30.0 0.0.0.255
```

Step 2. Apply the ACL.

Enter line configuration mode for VTY lines 0 to 4:

```
R2(config)# line vty 0 4
```

Use the **access-class** command to apply the ACL to the vty lines in the inbound direction. Note that this differs from the command used to apply ACLs to other interfaces:

```
R2(config-line)# access-class TASK-5 in
R2(config-line)# end
R2# copy run start
```

Step 3. Test the ACL.

Telnet to R2 from R1. Note that R1 does not have IP addresses in the address range listed in the ACL TASK-5 permit statements. Connection attempts should fail.

```
R1# telnet 10.1.1.2

Trying 10.1.1.2 ...
% Connection refused by remote host
```

From R3, telnet to R2. You see a prompt for the VTY line password:

```
R3# telnet 10.1.1.2

Trying 10.1.1.2 ... Open
CUnauthorized access strictly prohibited, violators will be prosecuted to
  the full extent of the law.

User Access Verification

Password:
```

Why do connection attempts from other networks fail even though they are not specifically listed in the ACL?

____

____

Task 6: Troubleshoot ACLs

When an ACL is improperly configured or is applied to the wrong interface or in the wrong direction, network traffic may be adversely affected.

Step 1. Remove ACL STND-1 from S0/0/1 of R3.

In an earlier task, you created and applied a named standard ACL on R3. Use the **show running-config** command to view the ACL and its placement. You should see that an ACL named **STND-1** was configured and applied inbound on Serial 0/0/1. Recall that this ACL was designed to block all network traffic with a source address from the 192.168.11.0/24 network from accessing the LAN on R3.

To remove the ACL, go to interface configuration mode for Serial 0/0/1 on R3. Use the **no ip access-group STND-1 in** command to remove the ACL from the interface:

```
R3(config)# interface serial 0/0/1
R3(config-if)# no ip access-group STND-1 in
```

Use the **show running-config** command to confirm that the ACL has been removed from Serial 0/0/1.

Step 2. Apply ACL STND-1 on S0/0/1 outbound.

To test the importance of the ACL filtering direction, reapply the STND-1 ACL to the Serial 0/0/1 interface. This time the ACL filters outbound traffic, rather than inbound traffic. Remember to use the **out** keyword when applying the ACL:

```
R3(config)# interface serial 0/0/1
R3(config-if)# ip access-group STND-1 out
```

Step 3. Test the ACL.

Test the ACL by pinging from PC2 to PC3. As an alternative, use an extended ping from R1. Notice that this time pings succeed, and the ACL counters are not incremented. Confirm this by issuing the **show ip access-list** command on R3.

Step 4. Restore the ACL to its original configuration.

Remove the ACL from the outbound direction and reapply it to the inbound direction:

```
R3(config)# interface serial 0/0/1
R3(config-if)# no ip access-group STND-1 out
R3(config-if)# ip access-group STND-1 in
```

Step 5. Apply TASK-5 to the R2 serial 0/0/0 interface inbound:

```
R2(config)# interface serial 0/0/0
R2(config-if)# ip access-group TASK-5 in
```

Step 6. Test the ACL.

Attempt to communicate with any device connected to R2 or R3 from R1 or its attached networks. Notice that all communication is blocked and that ACL counters are not incremented. This is because of the implicit "deny all" at the end of every ACL. This deny statement prevents all inbound traffic to serial 0/0/0 from any source other than R3. Essentially, this causes routes from R1 to be removed from the routing table.

You should see messages similar to the following printed on the consoles of R1 and R2 (it takes some time for the OSPF neighbor relationship to go down, so be patient):

```
*Sep  4 09:51:21.757: %OSPF-5-ADJCHG: Process 1, Nbr 192.168.11.1 on
  Serial0/0/0 from FULL to DOWN, Neighbor Down: Dead timer expired
```

After you receive this message, issue the command **show ip route** on both R1 and R2 to see which routes have been removed from the routing table.

Remove ACL TASK-5 from the interface, and save your configurations:

```
R2(config)# interface serial 0/0/0
R2(config-if)# no ip access-group TASK-5 in
R2(config)# exit
R2# copy run start
```

Task 7: Document the Router Configurations

Task 8: Clean Up

Erase the configurations and reload the routers. Disconnect and store the cabling. For PC hosts that are normally connected to other networks, such as the school LAN or the Internet, reconnect the appropriate cabling and restore the TCP/IP settings.

Packet Tracer Companion: Basic Access Control Lists (5.5.1)

You can now open the file LSG04-Lab551.pka on the CD-ROM that accompanies this book to repeat this hands-on lab using Packet Tracer. Remember, however, that Packet Tracer is not a substitute for hands-on lab experience with real equipment.

Lab 5-2: Access Control Lists Challenge (5.5.2)

Upon completion of this lab, you will be able to

- Design named standard and named extended ACLs
- Apply named standard and named extended ACLs
- Test named standard and named extended ACLs
- Troubleshoot named standard and named extended ACLs

Figure 5-5 shows the network topology for this lab. Table 5-2 provides the IP addresses, subnet masks, and default gateways (where applicable) for all devices in the topology.

Figure 5-5 Network Topology for Lab 5-2

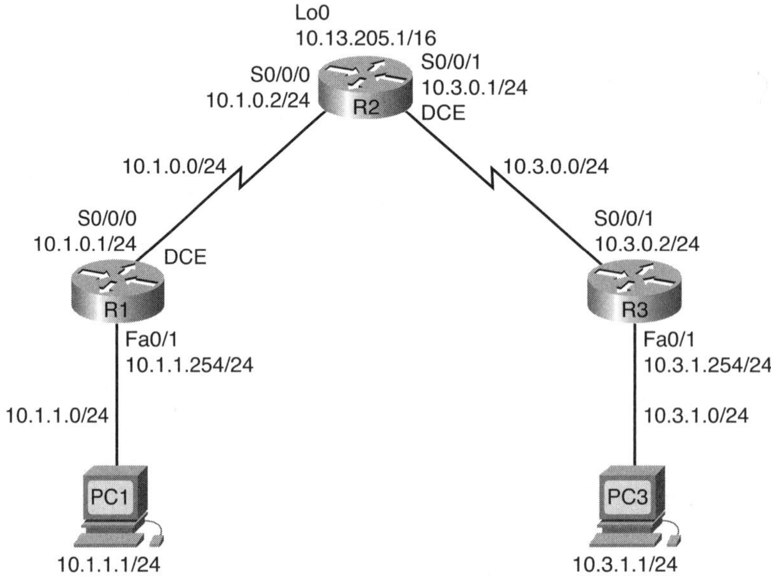

Table 5-2 Lab 5-2 Addressing Table

Device	Interface	IP Address	Subnet Mask	Default Gateway
R1	S0/0/0	10.1.0.1	255.255.255.0	—
	Fa0/1	10.1.1.254	255.255.255.0	—
R2	S0/0/0	10.1.0.2	255.255.255.0	—
	S0/0/1	10.3.0.1	255.255.255.0	—
	Lo 0	10.13.205.1	255.255.0.0	—
R3	S0/0/1	10.3.0.2	255.255.255.0	—
	Fa0/1	10.3.1.254	255.255.255.0	—
PC 1	NIC	10.1.1.1	255.255.255.0	10.1.1.254
PC 3	NIC	10.3.1.1	255.255.255.0	10.3.1.254

Task 1: Prepare the Network

Step 1. Cable a network that is similar to the one shown in Figure 5-5.

You can use any current router in your lab as long as it has the required interfaces shown in the topology diagram.

Note: If you use a 1700, 2500, or 2600 router, the router outputs and interface descriptions may look different.

Step 2. Clear any existing configurations on the routers.

Task 2: Perform Basic Router Configurations

Configure the R1, R2, and R3 routers according to the following guidelines:

- Configure the router hostname.
- Disable DNS lookup.
- Configure an EXEC mode password.
- Configure a message-of-the-day banner.
- Configure a password for console connections.
- Configure a password for VTY connections.
- Configure IP addresses on all devices.
- Create a loopback interface on R2.
- Enable OSPF area 0 on all routers for all networks.
- Verify full IP connectivity using the **ping** command.

Task 3: Configure Standard ACLs

Configure standard named ACLs on the R1 and R3 VTY lines, permitting hosts connected directly to their FastEthernet subnets to gain Telnet access. Deny and log all other connection attempts. Document your testing procedures.

____

____

____

____

Task 4: Configure Extended ACLs

Using extended ACLs on R1 and R3, complete the following requirements:

- The LANs connected to R1 and R3 are used for student computer labs. The network administrator has noticed that students in these labs are playing games across the WAN with the remote students. Make sure that your ACL prevents the LAN attached to R1 from reaching the LAN at R3 and that the LAN on R3 cannot reach the LAN on R1. Be specific in your statements so that any new LANs added to either R1 or R3 are unaffected.

- Permit all OSPF traffic.
- Permit ICMP traffic to the R2 local interfaces.
- All network traffic destined for TCP port 80 should be allowed. Any other traffic should be denied and logged.
- Any traffic not specified here should be denied.

Note: This may require multiple access lists. Verify your configuration, and document your testing procedure.

Why is the order of access list statements so important?

____

____

Task 5: Verify an ACL

Test each protocol that you are trying to block, and make sure that permitted traffic is allowed. This requires testing ping, HTTP, Telnet, and OSPF.

Step 1. Test R1 to R3 traffic and R3 to R1 traffic.

Ping from PC1 to PC3.

Ping from PC3 to PC1.

Both should fail.

Step 2. Test port 80 access.

To test port 80 functionality, enable the HTTP server on R2:

```
R2(config)# ip http server
```

From PC1, open a web browser to the R2 Serial 0/0/0 interface. This should be successful.

Step 3. Verify OSPF routes.

No routes should be lost. Confirm with **show ip route**.

Step 4. Test ping to R2.

Ping to R2 from R1 and PC1.

Ping to R2 from R3 and PC3.

Both should succeed.

Step 5. Perform other ping tests to confirm that all other traffic is denied.

Task 6: Document the Router Configurations

Task 7: Clean Up

Erase the configurations and reload the routers. Disconnect and store the cabling. For PC hosts that are normally connected to other networks, such as the school LAN or the Internet, reconnect the appropriate cabling and restore the TCP/IP settings.

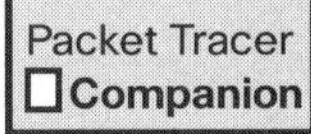

Packet Tracer Companion: Challenge Access Control Lists (5.5.2)

You can now open the file LSG04-Lab552.pka on the CD-ROM that accompanies this book to repeat this hands-on lab using Packet Tracer. Remember, however, that Packet Tracer is not a substitute for hands-on lab experience with real equipment.

Lab 5-3: Troubleshooting Access Control Lists (5.5.3)

Upon completion of this lab, you will be able to

- Cable a network according to the topology diagram shown in Figure 5-6
- Erase the startup configuration and reload a router to the default state
- Load routers with scripts
- Find and correct network errors
- Document the corrected network

Figure 5-6 shows the network topology for this lab. Table 5-3 provides the IP addresses, subnet masks, and default gateways (where applicable) for all devices in the topology.

Figure 5-6 Network Topology for Lab 5-3

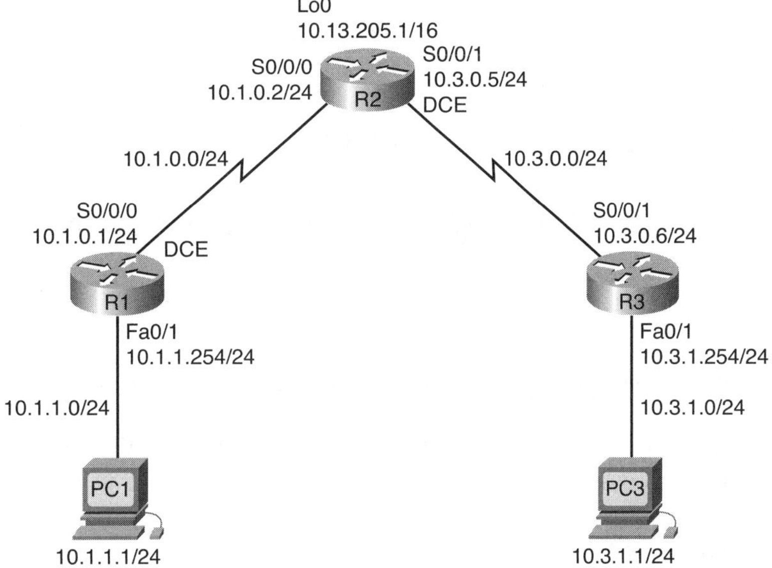

Table 5-3 Lab 5-3 Addressing Table

Device	Interface	IP Address	Subnet Mask	Default Gateway
R1	S0/0/0	10.1.0.1	255.255.255.0	—
	Fa0/1	10.1.1.254	255.255.255.0	—
R2	S0/0/0	10.1.0.2	255.255.255.0	—
	S0/0/1	10.3.0.5	255.255.255.0	—
	Lo 0	10.13.205.1	255.255.0.0	—
R3	S0/0/1	10.3.0.6	255.255.255.0	—
	Fa0/1	10.3.1.254	255.255.255.0	—
PC 1	NIC	10.1.1.1	255.255.255.0	10.1.1.254
PC 3	NIC	10.3.1.1	255.255.255.0	10.3.1.254

Scenario

You work for a regional service provider that has customers who have recently experienced several security breaches. Some security policies have been implemented that haven't addressed the customers' specific needs. Your department has been asked to examine the configuration, conduct tests, and change the configuration as necessary to secure the customer routers.

Ensure that your final configurations implement the following security policies:

- R1 and R3 customers request that only local PCs be able to access VTY lines. Log any attempts by other devices to access the VTY lines.
- R1 and R3 directly connected networks should not be allowed to send or receive traffic to or from each other. All other traffic should be allowed to and from R1 and R3.

A minimum of ACL statements should be used and applied inbound on the R2 serial interfaces. OSPF is used to distribute routing information. All passwords, except the enable secret password, are set to **cisco**. The enable secret password is set to **class**.

Task 1: Load Routers with the Supplied Scripts

Task 2: Find and Correct Network Errors

Find and correct all errors in the configuration. Document the steps you used to troubleshoot the network, and note each error found.

Task 3: Document the Corrected Network

Now that you have corrected all errors and tested connectivity throughout the network, document the final configuration for each device.

Task 4: Clean Up

Erase the configurations and reload the routers. Disconnect and store the cabling. For PC hosts that are normally connected to other networks, such as the school LAN or the Internet, reconnect the appropriate cabling and restore the TCP/IP settings.

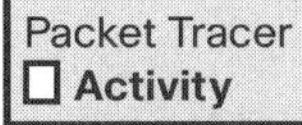

Packet Tracer Exercise 5.1: Named Access Control Lists

You can now open the file LSG04-Lab0554.pka on the CD-ROM that accompanies this book to complete this activity using Packet Tracer. Remember, however, that Packet Tracer is not a substitute for hands-on lab experience with real equipment.

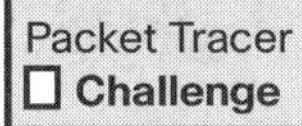

Packet Tracer Exercise 5.2: Access Control Lists

You can now open the file LSG04-Lab0555.pka on the CD-ROM that accompanies this book to complete this activity using Packet Tracer. Remember, however, that Packet Tracer is not a substitute for hands-on lab experience with real equipment.

Packet Tracer Challenge

Packet Tracer Skills Integration Challenge

Open file LSG04-PTSkills5.pka on the CD-ROM that accompanies this book to perform this exercise using Packet Tracer. Upon completion of this skills integration challenge, you will be able to

- Configure PPP with CHAP authentication
- Configure default routing
- Configure OSPF routing
- Implement and verify multiple ACL security policies

Figure 5-7 shows the network topology for this lab. Table 5-4 provides the IP addresses, subnet masks, and default gateways (where applicable) for all devices in the topology.

Table 5-4 Lab 5-6 Addressing Table

Device	Interface	IP Address	Subnet Mask
HQ	S0/0/0	10.1.1.1	255.255.255.252
	S0/0/1	10.1.1.5	255.255.255.252
	S0/1/0	209.165.201.2	255.255.255.252
	Fa0/0	10.1.50.1	255.255.255.0
	Fa0/1	10.1.40.1	255.255.255.0
B1	S0/0/0	10.1.1.2	255.255.255.252
	Fa0/0	10.1.10.1	255.255.255.0
	Fa0/1	10.1.20.1	255.255.255.0
B2	S0/0/0	10.1.1.6	255.255.255.252
	Fa0/0	10.1.80.1	255.255.255.0
	Fa0/1	10.1.70.1	255.255.255.0
ISP	S0/0/0	209.165.201.1	255.255.255.252
	Fa0/0	209.165.202.129	255.255.255.252
Web Server	NIC	209.165.202.130	255.255.255.252

Figure 5-7 Network Topology for Lab 5-6

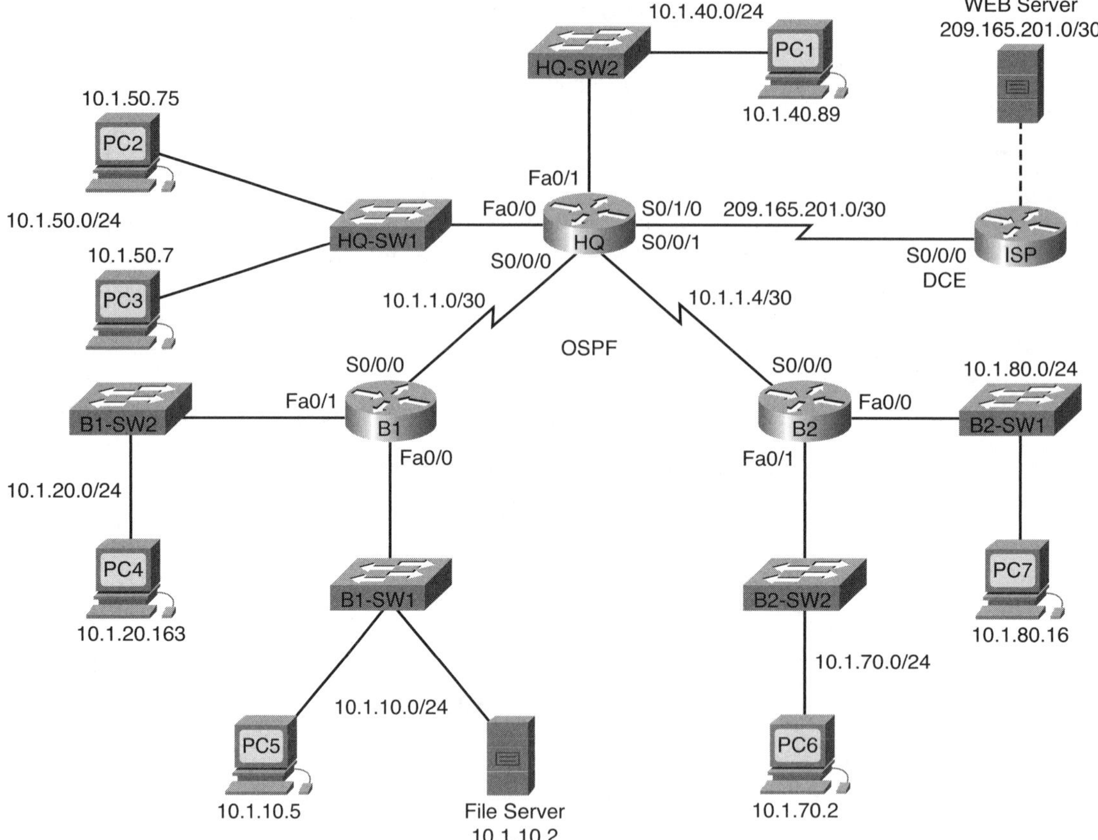

Introduction

In this activity, you will demonstrate your ability to configure ACLs that enforce five security policies. In addition, you will configure PPP and OSPF routing. The devices are already configured with IP addressing. The user EXEC password is **cisco,** and the privileged EXEC password is **class**.

Task 1: Configure PPP with CHAP Authentication

Step 1. Configure the link between HQ and B1 to use PPP encapsulation with CHAP authentication.

The password for CHAP authentication is **cisco123**.

Step 2. Configure the link between HQ and B2 to use PPP encapsulation with CHAP authentication.

The password for CHAP authentication is **cisco123**.

Step 3. Verify that connectivity is restored between the routers.

HQ should be able to ping both B1 and B2. The interfaces may take a few minutes to come back up. You can switch back and forth between Realtime and Simulation modes to speed up the process. Another possible workaround to this Packet Tracer behavior is to use the **shutdown** and **no shutdown** commands on the interfaces.

Note: The interfaces may go down at random points during the activity because of a Packet Tracer bug. The interface normally comes back up on its own if you wait a few seconds.

Step 4. Check the results.

Your completion percentage should be 29%. If not, click **Check Results** to see which required components are not yet completed.

Task 2: Configure Default Routing

Step 1. Configure default routing from HQ to ISP.

Configure a default route on HQ using the *exit interface* argument to send all default traffic to ISP.

Step 2. Test connectivity to Web Server.

HQ should be able to successfully ping Web Server at 209.165.202.130 as long as the ping is sourced from the Serial0/1/0 interface.

Step 3. Check the results.

Your completion percentage should be 32%. If not, click **Check Results** to see which required components are not yet completed.

Task 3: Configure OSPF Routing

Step 1. Configure OSPF on HQ.

Configure OSPF using the process ID 1.

Advertise all subnets except the 209.165.201.0 network.

Propagate the default route to OSPF neighbors.

Disable OSPF updates to ISP and to the HQ LANs.

Step 2. Configure OSPF on B1 and B2.

Configure OSPF using the process ID 1.

On each router, configure the appropriate subnets.

Disable OSPF updates to the LANs.

Step 3. Test connectivity throughout the network.

The network should now have full end-to-end connectivity. All devices should be able to successfully ping all other devices, including Web Server at 209.165.202.130.

Step 4. Check the results.

Your completion percentage should be 76%. If not, click **Check Results** to see which required components are not yet completed.

Task 4: Implement Multiple ACL Security Policies

Step 1. Implement security policy number 1.

Block the 10.1.10.0 network from accessing the 10.1.40.0 network. All other access to 10.1.40.0 is allowed. Configure the ACL on HQ using ACL number 10.

- Use a standard or extended ACL? _______________
- Apply the ACL to which interface? _______________
- Apply the ACL in which direction? _______________

Step 2. Verify that security policy number 1 is implemented.

A ping from PC5 to PC1 should fail.

Step 3. Check the results.

Your completion percentage should be 80%. If not, click **Check Results** to see which required components are not yet completed.

Step 4. Implement security policy number 2.

Host 10.1.10.5 is not allowed to access host 10.1.50.7. All other hosts are allowed to access 10.1.50.7. Configure the ACL on B1 using ACL number 115.

- Use a standard or extended ACL? _______________
- Apply the ACL to which interface? _______________
- Apply the ACL in which direction? _______________

Step 5. Verify that security policy number 2 is implemented.

A ping from PC5 to PC3 should fail.

Step 6. Check the results.

Your completion percentage should be 85%. If not, click **Check Results** to see which required components are not yet completed.

Step 7. Implement security policy number 3.

Hosts 10.1.50.1 through 10.1.50.63 are not allowed web access to the Intranet server at 10.1.80.16. All other access is allowed. Configure the ACL on the appropriate router, and use ACL number 101.

- Use a standard or extended ACL? _______________
- Configure the ACL on which router? _______________
- Apply the ACL to which interface? _______________
- Apply the ACL in which direction? _______________

Step 8. Verify that security policy number 3 is implemented.

To test this policy, click PC3, click the **Desktop** tab, and click **Web Browser**. For the URL, enter the IP address for the Intranet server, 10.1.80.16, and press **Enter**. After a few seconds, you should receive a Request Timeout message. PC2 and any other PC in the network should be able to access the Intranet server.

Step 9. Check the results.

Your completion percentage should be 90%. If not, click **Check Results** to see which required components are not yet completed.

Step 10. Implement security policy number 4.

Use the name **NO_FTP** to configure a named ACL that blocks the 10.1.70.0/24 network from accessing FTP services (port 21) on the file server at 10.1.10.2. All other access should be allowed.

Note: Names are case-sensitive.

- Use a standard or extended ACL? _______________
- Configure the ACL on which router? _______________
- Apply the ACL to which interface? _______________
- Apply the ACL in which direction? _______________

Step 11. Check the results.

Packet Tracer does not support testing FTP access, so you can't verify this policy. However, your completion percentage should be 95%. If not, click **Check Results** to see which required components are not yet completed.

Step 12. Implement security policy number 5.

Because ISP represents connectivity to the Internet, configure a named ACL called **FIREWALL** in the following order:

1. Allow only inbound ping replies from ISP and any source beyond ISP.
2. Allow only established TCP sessions from ISP and any source beyond ISP.
3. Explicitly block all other inbound access from ISP and any source beyond ISP. Although this is not needed because of the implicit deny, having an explicit deny helps remind administrators that all other traffic is denied.

- Use a standard or extended ACL? _______________
- Configure the ACL on which router? _______________
- Apply the ACL to which interface? _______________
- Apply the ACL in which direction? _______________

Step 13. Verify that security policy number 5 is implemented.

To test this policy, any PC should be able to ping ISP or Web Server. However, neither ISP nor Web Server should be able to ping HQ or any other device behind the ACL.

Step 14. Check the results.

Your completion percentage should be 100%. If not, click **Check Results** to see which required components are not yet completed.

CHAPTER 6

Teleworker Services

The Study Guide portion of this chapter uses a combination of matching, fill-in-the-blank, multiple-choice, and open-ended question exercises to test your knowledge of teleworker requirements and services. This will include knowledge in broadband services such as cable, digital subscriber line (DSL), and wireless technologies. Your knowledge in virtual private networks (VPN) is also tested.

There are no curriculum labs or activities in this chapter. Packet Tracer labs in wireless and cable have been added to assist in learning how to configure these new technologies.

As you work through this chapter, use Chapter 6 in the *Accessing the WAN, CCNA Exploration Companion Guide* or use the corresponding Chapter 6 in the Accessing the WAN, CCNA Exploration online curriculum for assistance.

Study Guide

Business Requirements for Teleworker Services

In today's world, many businesses have employees who not only work on the road, but also work from home. Even though they are not directly connected to the network, it is important for them to have access to files and information in order to perform their jobs from abroad. Therefore, it is important for the network administrator to provide a secure means for these workers to access the network. Home office workers need an Internet connection, a router, and, of course, a PC. A secure connection can be established using VPN client software. Depending on the area that the employees live in, various connection types and speeds can be used to connect to the office. Connection types can include cable, DSL, wireless, and, of course, basic dial-up service.

Review Questions

1. More and more companies (including Cisco) are having their employees work from home as opposed to commuting to the office on a daily basis. Briefly describe some of the organizational, social, and environmental benefits to having employees work from home.

____

____

____

____

____

____

____

2. We have just mentioned some of the benefits from working at home. Now list some of the disadvantages that individuals may suffer from while working at home.

____

____

____

____

____

3. List and briefly describe some of the technologies available to allow teleworkers to connect to resources located at the organization's offices.

____

____

____

____

____

Broadband Services: Fill-in-the-Blank Exercise

Fill in the blanks for the following sentences based on broadband services.

________________, ______, and __________________ are three options that provide high bandwidth to teleworkers. Dialup and DSL use existing ____________, but dialup requires a _________ to convert the signal from __________ to ________. Satellite connections use _____________ to transport data and require an antenna to be installed at the location.

CATV originally meant ____________________________. In a classic cable system called a ________________________ cable system, the distribution network consists of _______ and ________ cables. The _________ is the ___________ that distributes signals throughout the community. The __________ branches reach all the subscribers via ________ cable. Modern cable systems use __________ and coaxial cable for signal transmission. Carriers use different frequencies to send voice, video, and data simultaneously across a coaxial cable without interfering with one another. Frequency is the rate at which ________________ cycles occur computed as the number of waves per second. ________________ is the speed of propagation of the electromagnetic signal divided by its frequency in cycles per second. Cable networks can transmit in either direction, called downstream and upstream. ________________ is from headend to subscriber, with frequencies in the range of 50 to 860 MHz. ________________ is from subscriber to headend, with frequencies in the range of 5 to 42 MHz. ____________ is an international standard that specifies Layers 1 and 2 requirements. The _____________ layer specifies the bandwidth of each channel. The ________ layer defines the deterministic access method per various communications technology. Cable Modem Termination System (CMTS) and a cable modem are the two types of equipment required to send digital modem signals on a cable system. A headend ____________ communicates with ____________ located at subscriber homes. DSL delivers high-speed data services from 3 kHz up to 1 MHz over ordinary ________ lines.

The two types of DSL are ADSL and SDSL. ____________ DSL provides higher ___________ bandwidth to the user than upload bandwidth. _____________ DSL provides the same speeds in both directions. A _____________ connects the teleworker's PC to the DSL network. A _________ combines individual DSL connections into a high-capacity link to an ISP. The advantage of DSL over cable is that DSL provides each subscriber a dedicated connection to the DSLAM where cable uses a _________ medium. ______________ and _____________ allow the consumer to use the phone line for calls and the ADSL for data services ________________ without adverse effects on either service. Wall-mounted microfilters can be installed inline or can be used in place of regular telephone ___________. A _____________ requires a technician to go to the customer's house to do the install.

Broadband __________ uses 802.11 standards. Wireless uses ___________ radio spectrum that is not regulated by the government the way most radio and TV transmissions are, making wireless easy to deploy. _____________, the areas covered by one or more interconnected access points, have allowed wireless users more mobility. With the idea of increasing business, coffee shops, parks, and libraries have created ________ hotspots. ________________, ___________, and ______________ are some of the new developments in broadband wireless that are increasing wireless availability. Most municipal wireless networks use a ______ topology rather that a hub-and-spoke model. It is more reliable than ___________________ because if one access point fails, others can compensate for it. ________ is capable of providing wireless connectivity over long distances. It operates at _________ speeds, over ________ distances, and for a greater number of ________ than WiFi. A WiMAX network consists of a ________ and __________. The _________ provides coverage for distances of up to 3000 miles. A _________ allows connectivity to the WiMAX network. ______________ allows a small antenna on your PC to connect to a tower using _________ frequencies, which are not easily interrupted by physical obstructions. _____________ is stronger and more stable and uses __________ frequencies to send a lot of data with fewer errors.

______________ Internet services are used for temporary installations that are continually on the move. This type of Internet access is available everywhere, including at sea and on airplanes. There are three ways to connect to the Internet using satellites: one-way multicast, one-way terrestrial return, and two-way. _______________ is used for IP multicast-based data. ____________ sends data from remote sites via satellite to hub, which then sends the data to the Internet. ____________________ uses traditional dialup to send outbound data through a modem, but receives downloads from satellite.

The 802.11 wireless local-area network addresses the 5-GHz and 2.4-GHz unlicensed ___________ bands. The _____________ offers certification for interoperability between vendors of 802.11 products. The __________ standard offers 11 Mbps at 2.4 GHz. The __________ standard offers 54 Mbps at 2.4 GHz. The newest standard, __________, uses MIMO. WiMAX uses the __________ standard and allows transmission speeds of up to 70 Mbps and has a range of 30 miles.

VPN Technology

Vocabulary Exercise: Matching

In the table that follows, match the definition on the right with the term on the left.

Term	Definition
a. Triple DES	__ Uses a public network to carry data for a private network
b. PSK	__ Used by hosts to send and receive data through a VPN tunnel
c. AH	__ Uses 128-, 192-, and 256-bit keys to encrypt data
d. VPN	__ Provides confidentiality and authentication by encrypting the IP packet
e. AES	__ A secret key shared between the two parties using a secure channel
f. VPN tunnel	__ Uses the exchange of digital signatures to authenticate peers
g. Remote-access VPN	__ HMAC algorithm that uses a 128-bit shared secret key
h. VPN gateway	__ Connects two fixed locations
i. MD5	__ Encapsulates an entire packet within another packet and sends it over the network
j. PIX	__ Provides data authentication and integrity when confidentiality is not required or allowed
k. SHA-1	__ Security appliance developed by Cisco
l. ESP	__ Provides a secure connection for teleworkers
m. Site to site	__ Encrypts with one key, decrypts with another, and then encrypts one final time with another different key
n. RSA signature	__ HMAC algorithm that uses a 160-bit secret key

Multiple-Choice Questions

Choose the best answer for each of the questions that follow.

1. Which of the following are benefits of using VPNs? (Choose three.)

A. Cost savings

B. Complexity

C. Security

D. Scalability

E. Adaptability

2. Which of the following is considered an encapsulation protocol? (Choose two.)

A. Frame Relay

B. GRE

C. IPv4

D. IPsec

E. MPLS

F. IPv6

3. As a design feature, which of the following protects the contents of a message from interception? (Choose two.)

A. Encryption

B. Authentication

C. Confidentiality

D. Tunneling

E. Integrity

4. Which of the following can be used to terminate a site-to-site VPN? (Choose three.)

A. A PIX Firewall

B. A router

C. A modem

D. An Adaptive Security Appliance

E. A WAN switch

5. Which of the following is considered a carrier protocol? (Choose two.)

A. Frame Relay

B. GRE

C. IPv4

D. IPsec

E. MPLS

F. IPv6

6. Which of the following are three characteristics of a VPN? (Choose three.)

A. Authentication

B. Authorization

C. Data integrity

D. Data confidentiality

E. Accounting

7. Which of the following are characteristics of asymmetric encryption algorithms? (Choose two.)

A. Public key cryptography

B. Secret key cryptography

C. Encryption and decryption use different keys

D. Encryption and decryption use the same key

8. Which of the following does Encapsulating Security Payload provide? (Choose all that apply.)

A. Encryption

B. Shared secret key

C. Integrity

D. Authentication

E. Digital certificates

9. Which of the following are *not* encryptions algorithms? (Choose two.)

A. Triple DES

B. AES

C. AH

D. SHA-1

E. RSA

10. Which of the following methods guarantee that no tampering or alterations occur to data?

A. Encryption

B. Authentication

C. Confidentiality

D. Tunneling

E. Integrity

Labs and Activities

Packet Tracer
☐ Activity

Packet Tracer Exercise 6-1: DSL/Cable Configuration

This Packet Tracer exercise tests your ability to configure DSL and cable. Open the file lsg04-0601.pka on the CD-ROM that accompanies this book to do this exericse. Detailed instructions are provided within the activity file.

Packet Tracer
☐ Activity

Packet Tracer Exercise 6-2: Wireless Configuration

This Packet Tracer exercise tests your ability to configure wireless. Open the file lsg04-0602.pka on the CD-ROM that accompanies this book to do this exercise. Detailed instructions are provided within the activity file.

Packet Tracer
☐ Challenge

Packet Tracer Skills Integration Challenge

Open file LSG04-PTSkills6.pka on the CD-ROM that accompanies this book to perform this exercise using Packet Tracer. In this culminating activity, you will to configure a default route as well as dynamic routing using RIP version 2. You will also add broadband devices to the network. Finally, you will set up ACLs on two routers to control network traffic. Because Packet Tracer is very specific in how it grades ACLs, you will need to configure the ACL rules in the order given.

Upon completion of this skills integration challenge, you will be able to

- Apply basic router configurations
- Configure dynamic and default routing
- Establish teleworker services
- Test connectivity before ACL configuration
- Apply ACL policies
- Test connectivity after ACL configuration

Figure 6-1 shows the network topology for this skills integration challenge and Table 6-1 provides the IP addresses and subnet masks for all device interfaces in the topology.

Figure 6-1 Network Topology for Lab 6-3: Skills Integration Challenge

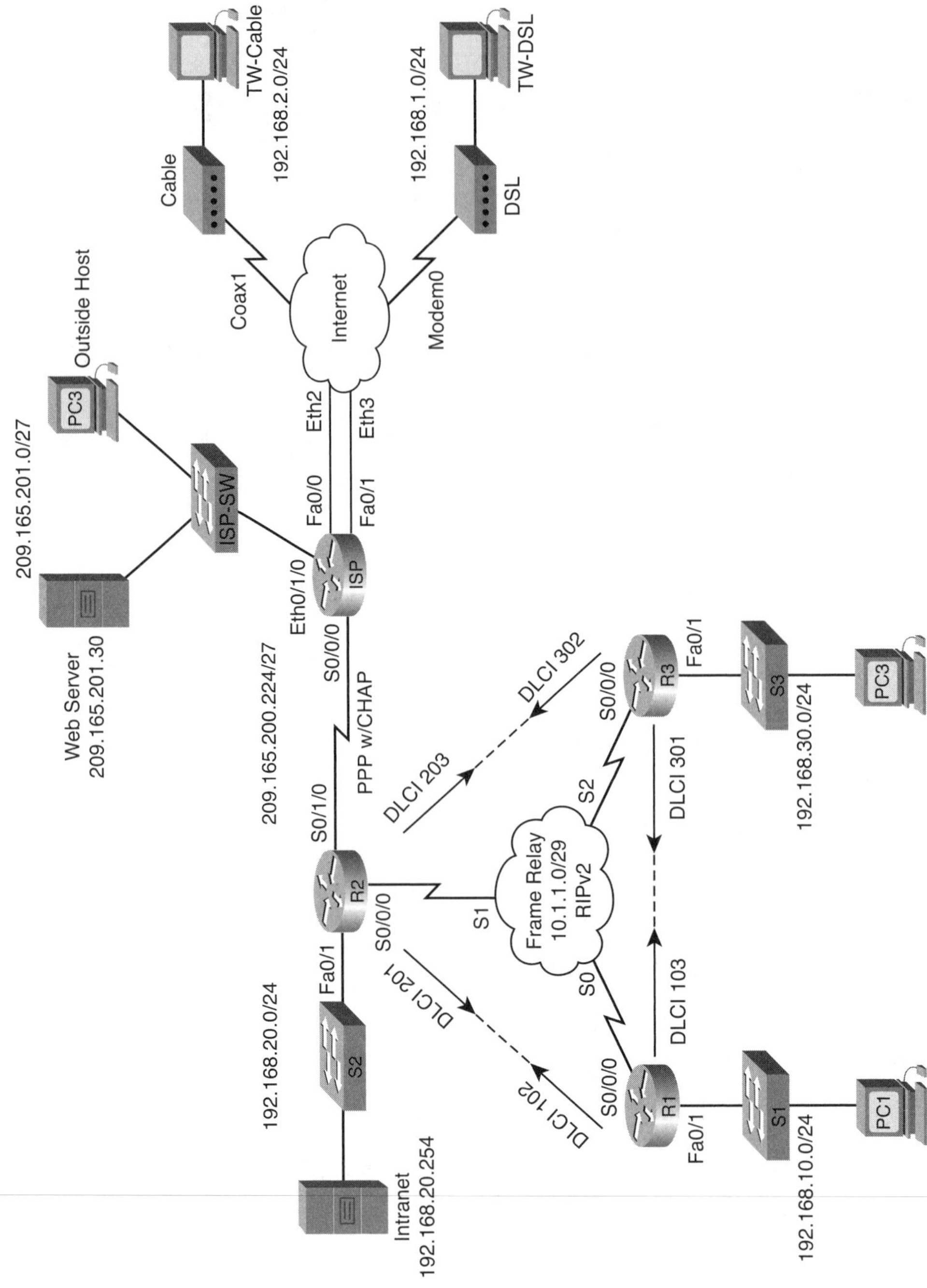

Table 6-1 Addressing Table for Skills Integration Challenge

Device	Interface	IP Address	Subnet Mask
R1	Fa0/1	192.168.10.1	255.255.255.0
	S0/0/0	10.1.1.1	255.255.255.248
R2	Fa0/1	192.168.20.1	255.255.255.0
	S0/0/0	10.1.1.2	255.255.255.248
	S0/1/0	209.165.200.225	255.255.255.224

Device	Interface	IP Address	Subnet Mask
R3	Fa0/1	192.168.30.1	255.255.255.0
	S0/0/0	10.1.1.3	255.255.255.248
ISP	S0/0/0	209.165.200.226	255.255.255.224
	Eth0/1/0	209.165.201.1	255.255.255.224
	Fa0/0	192.168.1.1	255.255.255.0
	Fa0/1	192.168.2.1	255.255.255.0
PC1	NIC	192.168.10.10	255.255.255.0
PC3	NIC	192.168.30.10	255.255.255.0
Intranet	NIC	192.168.20.254	255.255.255.0
TW-DSL	NIC	192.168.1.10	255.255.255.0
TW-Cable	NIC	192.168.2.10	255.255.255.0
Web Server	NIC	209.165.201.30	255.255.255.224
Outside Host	NIC	209.165.201.10	255.255.255.224

Task 1: Apply Basic Router Configurations

Using the information in the topology diagram and addressing table, configure the basic device configurations on R1, R2, and R3. Hostnames are configured for you.

Include the following:

- Console and vty lines
- Banners
- Disable domain name lookup
- Interface descriptions

Task 2: Configure Dynamic and Default Routing

Step 1. **Configure default routing**: R2 needs a default route. Use the **exit-interface** argument in the default route configuration.

Step 2. **Configure dynamic routing**: Configure RIPv2 on R1, R2, and R3 for all available networks. R2 needs to pass its default network configuration to the other routers. Also, be sure to use the **passive-interface** command on all active interfaces not used for routing.

Step 3. **Check results**: Your completion percentage should be 59%. If not, click Check Results to see which required components are not yet completed.

Task 3: Establish Teleworker Services

Step 1. **Add WAN devices**: Add one DSL and one cable modem according to the topology diagram.

Step 2. **Name the WAN devices**: Use the Config tab to change the display name of each WAN device to Cable and DSL, respectively.

Step 3. **Connect the WAN devices**: Connect the WAN devices to their PCs and the Internet using the appropriate cables and interfaces.

Step 4. **Check results**: Your completion percentage should be 86%. If not, click Check Results to see which required components are not yet completed.

Task 4: Test Connectivity Before ACL Configuration

At this point, all branches of the topology should have connectivity. Switching between Simulation mode and Realtime mode can speed up convergence.

Task 5: Apply ACL Policies

Step 1. **Create and apply security policy number 1**: Implement the following ACL rules using ACL number 101:

- Allow hosts on the 192.168.30.0/24 network web access to any destination.
- Allow hosts on the 192.168.30.0/24 network ping access to any destination.
- Deny any other access originating from the network.

Step 2. **Create and apply security policy number 2**: Because ISP represents connectivity to the Internet, configure a named ACL called FIREWALL in the following order:

a. Allow TW-DSL web access to the Intranet server.

b. Allow TW-Cable web access to the Intranet server.

c. Allow only inbound ping replies from ISP and any source beyond ISP.

d. Allow only established TCP sessions from ISP and any source beyond ISP.

e. Explicitly block all other inbound access from ISP and any source beyond ISP.

Step 3. **Check results**: Your completion percentage should be 100%. If not, click Check Results to see which required components are not yet completed.

Task 6: Test Connectivity After ACL Configuration

Teleworkers should not be able to ping the Intranet Server, but should be able to access its HTTP server via the web browser. Included in the activity are three PDUs, two of which should fail and one should succeed. Check the Connectivity Tests in the Check Results menu to be sure that the completion results are 100%.

CHAPTER 7

IP Addressing Services

The Study Guide portion of this chapter uses a combination of matching, fill-in-the-blank, multiple-choice, and open-ended question exercises to test your knowledge of and skills in DHCP, NAT/PAT, and IPv6.

The Labs and Activities portion of this chapter includes all the online curriculum labs as well as Challenge and Comprehensive labs and Packet Tracer Activities to ensure that you have mastered the practical, hands-on skills needed to understand, configure, and troubleshoot DHCP, NAT/PAT, and IPv6.

As you work through this chapter, use Chapter 7 in the *Accessing the WAN, CCNA Exploration Companion Guide*, or use the corresponding Chapter 7 in the Accessing the WAN, CCNA Exploration online curriculum, for assistance.

Study Guide

DHCP

DHCP allows a device to dynamically receive an IP address at bootup. The network administrator allocates a pool of addresses for the devices to use, and they are automatically distributed as the devices are turned on. When multiple subnets or VLANs exist on the network, a separate DHCP pool is required for each. A dedicated server is used in enterprise networks to handle this task, but with a small office/home office (SOHO), this expense can be spared, because Cisco's routers can be configured to operate as DHCP servers. Simply create the DHCP pool and assign the addresses with the correct subnet mask, and you're all set. The basic configurations needed are the IP address, subnet mask, and default gateway. If the wrong default gateway is configured, the host can communicate with hosts on the same network, but not with those on other networks.

Vocabulary Exercise: Matching

Match each term on the left with its definition on the right.

Terms

- **a.** Manual allocation
- **b.** DHCP relay
- **c.** **show ip dhcp binding** command
- **d.** Excluded address
- **e.** DHCP discover
- **f.** Lease
- **g.** Default router
- **h.** CHADDR
- **i.** Automatic allocation
- **j.** **show ip dhcp conflict** command
- **k.** **ip forward-protocol** command
- **l.** DHCP offer
- **m.** DHCP pool
- **n.** Diskless workstation
- **o.** Dynamic allocation
- **p.** Helper address
- **q.** Service DHCP
- **r.** DHCP request
- **s.** **show ip dhcp server** command
- **t.** BOOTP

Definitions

__ Locates DHCP servers on the network.

__ Enables routers to forward DHCP broadcasts to DHCP servers located on a different network or subnet.

__ A permanently assigned address.

__ Verifies that the router sends or receives DHCP messages.

__ Enables the DHCP server process.

__ A statically assigned address without the use of DHCP.

__ A troubleshooting command that checks whether DHCP assigned one address to multiple devices.

__ A way to download addresses and boot configurations for diskless workstations.

__ How long a device is given an IP address.

__ Specifies which broadcast packets to forward.

__ IP address and lease time tendered to the client.

__ A device that listens for DHCP broadcasts and forwards them to the DHCP server, which is located on another network or subnet.

__ A client hardware address.

__ The client asks for verification of an IP just recently assigned.

__ Addresses within the DHCP scope that should not be offered to DHCP clients.

__ An IP address assigned from a pool for a determined period of time.

__ Available addresses to be dynamically assigned to a device on a subnet or network.

__ Displays the IP-to-MAC address list.

__ Default gateway.

__ Does not have a hard drive or operating system.

Scaling Networks with NAT

DHCP is used to dynamically assign IP addresses to hosts on the inside of your network. These addresses could be public, global addresses allocated to a company from its ISP, or they could be private addresses set aside in RFC 1918. But when accessing the Internet, only registered global addresses are permitted. Because the Internet has grown beyond anyone's expectations, the number of available IP addresses will be exhausted. If something isn't done soon, it's possible that we might no longer be able to accommodate additional networks with globally unique address space.

One solution is to use private address on the inside of your network, which is "private" to the outside world. This requires devices that need Internet access to use public registered addresses. If this doesn't make sense, keep in mind that not all devices on a network need access to the outside world. Printers, servers, and switches are such devices. Also remember that not everyone on the network needs access to the Internet. This keeps traffic on the outside connection to a minimum. If an employee's job description does not require him or her to access the Internet, access does not need to be granted. Therefore, only those who need access to perform their day-to-day jobs will be allowed, and all others will be denied. In this case, Network Address Translation (NAT) is adequate.

When networks grow, the number of available addresses may not be enough. To accommodate these devices without having to purchase additional addresses, you can use Port Address Translation (PAT). This allows multiple devices to access the outside world using a single registered global address. PAT uses unique source port numbers on the inside global IP address to distinguish between translations. Because there are 65,535 ports, theoretically, there could be this many translations. Either way, thousands of devices could be translated using only a single IP address. PAT is something that most people use without even knowing. Have you ever wondered how adding a Linksys router at home gives more than one computer access to the Internet, whereas before, only one computer at a time had Internet access?

Fill-in-the-Blank Exercise

Fill in the blanks in the following sentences based on your knowledge of scaling networks with NAT:

The purpose of _______________ is to provide functionality as if the private network has globally unique addresses to access the _______________. When a router receives a packet on the inside _______________ network, it saves the address in an address translation _____________ and replaces it with a _______________ global address. When a packet returns, the router translates the address in the ______________ order. Therefore, NAT allows nonroutable addresses set aside by ____________ to access the Internet using global registered numbers. Routers are used to _______________ the public and private addresses at the edge of networks. NAT has four different types of addresses. The _______________ address is the IP address configured to a host on the inside of your network. This address can be ____________ unique or assigned from the private address space. An _____________ address is the translated address that a host on the inside is given as it exits the router. The _____________ address is the address of an outside host as it appears to the ___________ network. The ____________ address is allocated from a globally __________ address space and is assigned to a host on the outside network. The two types of NAT translation are static and dynamic. ___________ NAT uses a pool of addresses and assigns them as hosts attempt to leave the private network to enter the _______________ domain. _______________ NAT uses a one-to-one mapping between local and global addresses. Static NAT is particularly useful when a device needs to be accessible from _______________ the network. ______ extends NAT from one-to-one to one-to-many. It uses unique source port numbers to distinguish between _______________. This allows a _______________ global IP address to be used by many to access the outside. This is also called NAT _______________. The _______________ keeps track of each conversation based on the original source port. A benefit of using NAT and PAT is that it _______________ legally registered addresses. A drawback of this is that the translation process _______________ delay, and end-to-end _______________ is lost.

Vocabulary Exercise: Matching

The following lists the commands and methods used to configure NAT on a router. Match the command or method on the left with its definition.

Command or Method

a. **ip nat inside**
b. **overload** keyword
c. **ip nat pool**
d. Port forwarding
e. **ip nat inside source list 1**
f. **show ip nat translations**
g. **ip nat inside source static**
h. **show ip nat statistics**

Definition

__ Establishes a one-to-one mapping between a local and global address pair.

__ Packets arriving on this interface are marked for translation.

__ Enables dynamic translation when packets match a standard ACL.

__ Displays information about the total number of translations.

__ Equivalent to Port Address Translation (PAT).

__ Allows an external user to reach a port on a private IP address common with game servers.

__ Defines a start and end address to be allocated when needed.

__ Displays details of NAT assignments.

Reasons for Using IPv6

The primary motivation for creating IPv6 was to remedy the addressing problems of IPv4. More addresses were required, but more than this, the IPv6 designers needed a way to interpret, assign, and use addresses that was more consonant with modern internetworking.

The IPv6 addressing scheme is similar in concept to IPv4 addressing, but it has been completely overhauled to create an addressing system that can support continued Internet development and new applications for the foreseeable future. IPv6, formerly known as IPng (IP next generation), is a 128-bit address represented by 32 hexadecimal characters. The 128 bits were chosen to allow multiple levels of hierarchy and flexibility in designing hierarchical addressing and routing. The addressing format is represented in 16-bit hexadecimal addresses with hex characters separated by a colon (:). Leading 0s in a contiguous block can be represented with a double colon (::), which can be used anywhere within the address.

IPv6 uses unicast, multicast, and anycast addresses. Unicast is one-to-one delivery to an interface address. Multicast is a set of interfaces, and delivery is to each interface. An anycast address is similar to a multicast address in that it is a group of interfaces, but delivery is to the nearest interface of the bunch. A typical unicast address uses 64 bits for the subnet ID and 64 bits for the interface ID. The subnet ID is broken into multiple parts, consisting of the registry, which is /23; the ISP prefix, /32; the site prefix, /48; and the subnet prefix, /64. The interface ID is made up of the MAC address (48 bits). An additional 16 bits, FFFE, are inserted into the middle of the MAC address. Dual stack allows IPv4 and IPv6 to coexist.

Tunneling allows IPv6 networks to connect using an IPv4 network. Translation works like NAT in that it converts one set of IP addresses into another.

Multiple-Choice Questions

Choose the best answer for each question.

1. What does the term multihoming refer to?

   A. When you work from multiple homes

   B. When you have more than one connection to an ISP

   C. When you connect to multiple ISPs through a single physical connection

   D. When you have one link per ISP

2. Which of the following are frame fields found in both IPv4 and IPv6? (Choose three.)

   A. Version

   B. Time to live

   C. Source address

   D. Destination address

   E. Protocol

   F. Checksum

3. Which of the following are advanced IP addressing features when using IPv6? (Choose all that apply.)

   A. Routing efficiency

   B. Aggregation

   C. No broadcasts

   D. Autoconfiguration

   E. Multihoming

   F. IPsec mandatory for IPv6

4. How can you use colons to shorten the address 2031:130F:0000:0000:876A:0000:130B?

   A. 2031:130F:876A:0000:130B

   B. 2031:130F::876A:0000:130B

   C. 2031:130F::876A::130B

   D. 2031:130F::876A:0:130B

5. How many bits does an EUI-64 address have?

   A. 16

   B. 32

   C. 48

   D. 64

   E. 128

6. Which IPv6 private address type is similar to the ones used in RFC 1918?

   A. Inside local address

   B. Site-local address

   C. Outside global address

   D. Link-local address

7. Which IP address management feature allows a device to connect to the network without any configuration?

   A. Static assignment using a manual interface ID
   B. Static assignment using an EUI-64 interface ID
   C. Stateless autoconfiguration
   D. DHCP for IPv6

8. How does an EUI-64 address stretch a MAC address from 48 to 64 bits?

   A. It adds padding bits.
   B. It adds FFFE in the middle of the MAC address.
   C. It adds 16 bits to the end of the address, represented in a / notation.
   D. IPv6 uses 64-bit MAC addresses.

9. Which of the following are mechanisms to enable a smooth transition from IPv4 to IPv6? (Choose three.)

   A. ISATAP stack
   B. 6to4 tunnel
   C. NAT-PT
   D. Teredo tunnel

10. What allows IPv4 and IPv6 to coexist?

    A. ISATAP stack
    B. 6to4 tunnel
    C. Dual stack
    D. Teredo tunnel

11. What allows IPv6 to be encapsulated by another protocol, such as IPv4?

    A. Tunneling
    B. Dual stack
    C. NAT-PT
    D. Unicast routing

12. What two issues does tunneling present?

    A. MTU.
    B. It raises scaling concerns.
    C. It adds complexity.
    D. It's difficult to troubleshoot.

13. Enabling IPv6 on a router starts which operating process and the resources necessary to operate it?

    A. Forwarding plane
    B. Control plane
    C. Data plane
    D. Protocol plane

14. Which of the following are data plane considerations? (Choose two.)

A. IPv6 address size

B. IPv6 routing protocols

C. Parsing IPv6 extension

D. IPv6 address lookup

15. Which of the following are features of RIPng? (Choose two.)

A. Poison reverse.

B. It uses IPv6 for transport.

C. It has a 15-hop-count limit.

D. It sends updates on UDP port 520.

E. It sends updates on UDP port 521.

16. Which command enables IPv6 on a Cisco router?

A. **ipv6 address** [*IPv6 address/prefix*]

B. **ipv6 hostname** [*port*] [*IPv6 address*]

C. **ipv6 router rip**

D. **ipv6 unicast-routing**

17. Which command displays real-time messages for IPv6 RIP routing transactions?

A. **show ip route**

B. **show ip protocol**

C. **debug ipv6 rip**

D. **debug ipv6 routing**

18. Which command displays the contents of the current IPv6 routing table?

A. **show ip route**

B. **show ipv6 route**

C. **show ipv6 route summary**

D. **show ipv6 routers**

19. Which command identifies the interfaces that should run RIPng?

A. **router rip**

B. **ipv6 router rip**

C. **ipv6 rip** [*name*] **enable**

D. **network**

20. Which command specifies a DNS server for IPv4 or IPv6?

A. **ipv6** *host name* [*port*][*ipv6 address*]

B. **ip name-server** [*address*]

C. **ip host** [*host name*]

D. **ip** *dns-name-server*

Concept Questions

1. Compare and contrast IPv4 addresses with IPv6 addresses.

____

____

____

____

____

____

2. Compare and contrast RIP with RIPng.

____

____

____

____

Labs and Activities

Lab 7-1: Basic DHCP and NAT Configuration (7.4.1)

Upon completion of this lab, you will be able to

- Prepare the network
- Perform basic router configurations
- Configure a Cisco IOS DHCP server
- Configure static and default routing
- Configure static NAT
- Configure dynamic NAT with a pool of addresses
- Configure NAT overload

Figure 7-1 shows the network topology for this lab. Table 7-1 provides the IP addresses, subnet masks, and default gateways (where applicable) for all devices in the topology.

Figure 7-1 Network Topology for Lab 7-1

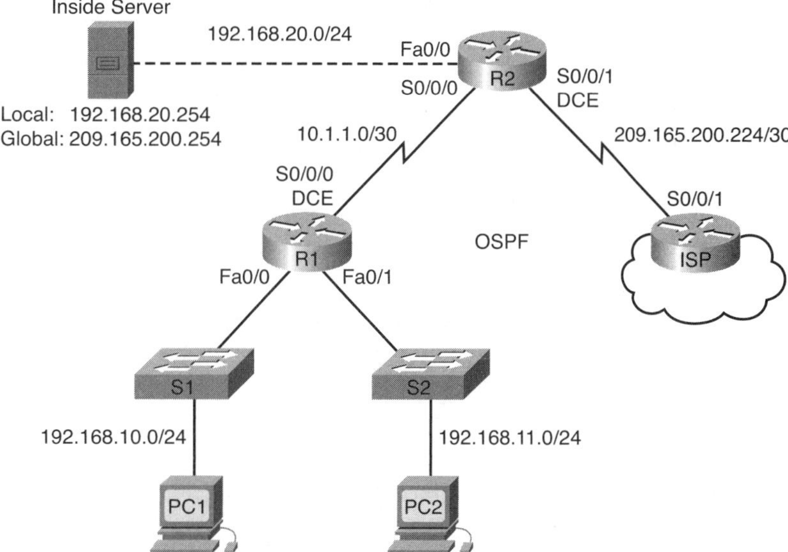

Table 7-1 Lab 7-1 Addressing Table

Device	Interface	IP Address	Subnet Mask
R1	S0/0/0	10.1.1.1	255.255.255.252
	Fa0/0	192.168.10.1	255.255.255.0
	Fa0/1	192.168.11.1	255.255.255.0
R2	S0/0/0	10.1.1.2	255.255.255.252
	S0/0/1	209.165.200.225	255.255.255.252
	Fa0/0	192.168.20.254	255.255.255.0
ISP	S0/0/1	209.165.200.226	255.255.255.252

Scenario

In this lab, you will configure DHCP and NAT IP services. One router is the DHCP server. The other router forwards DHCP requests to the server. You will also configure both static and dynamic NAT configurations, including NAT overload. When you have completed the configurations, verify connectivity between the inside and outside addresses.

Task 1: Prepare the Network

Step 1. Cable a network that is similar to the one shown in Figure 7-1.

You can use any current router in your lab as long as it has the required interfaces shown in the topology.

Note: If you use a 1700, 2500, or 2600 series router, the router outputs and interface descriptions may look different. On older routers some commands may be different or nonexistent.

Step 2. Clear all existing configurations on the routers.

Task 2: Perform Basic Router Configurations

Configure the R1, R2, and ISP routers according to the following guidelines:

- Configure the device hostname.
- Disable DNS lookup.
- Configure a privileged EXEC mode password.
- Configure a message-of-the-day banner.
- Configure a password for the console connections.
- Configure a password for all vty connections.
- Configure IP addresses on all routers. The PCs will receive IP addressing from DHCP later in the lab.
- Enable OSPF with process ID 1 on R1 and R2. Do not advertise the 209.165.200.224/27 network.

Note: Instead of attaching a server to R2, you can configure a loopback interface on R2 to use the IP address 192.168.20.254/24. If you do this, you do not need to configure the Fast Ethernet interface.

Task 3: Configure PC1 and PC2 to Receive an IP Address Through DHCP

On a Windows PC, choose **Start > Control Panel > Network Connections > Local Area Connection**. Right-click the Local Area Connection, and choose Properties, as shown in Figure 7-2.

Scroll down and highlight **Internet Protocol (TCP/IP)**. Click the **Properties** button, as shown in Figure 7-3.

Figure 7-2 Selecting Local Area Connection Properties

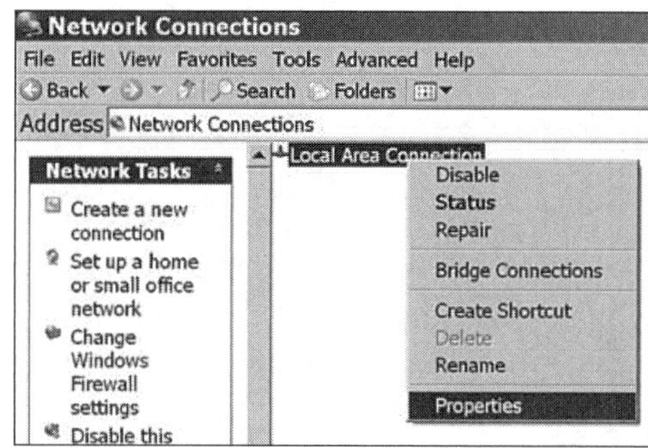

Figure 7-3 Selecting TCP/IP Properties

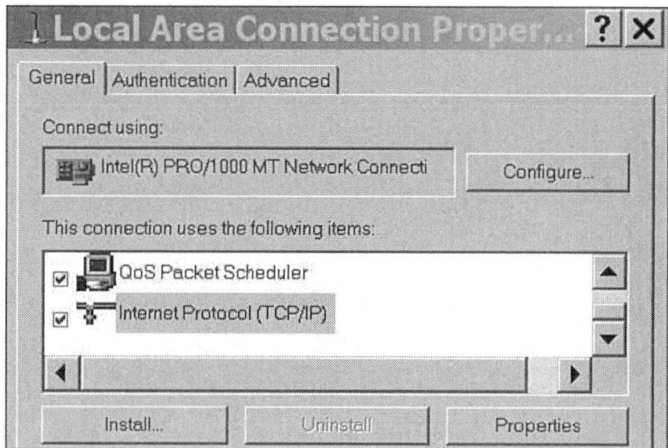

Make sure that the button is selected that says **Obtain an IP address automatically**, as shown in Figure 7-4.

Figure 7-4 Obtaining an IP Address Automatically

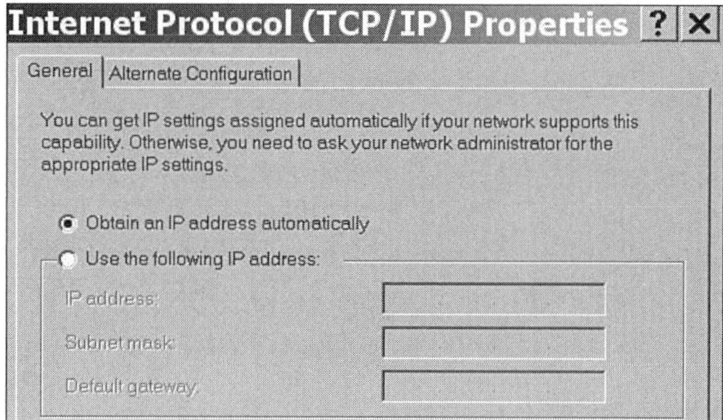

After this has been done on both PC1 and PC2, they are ready to receive an IP address from a DHCP server.

Task 4: Configure a Cisco IOS DHCP Server

Cisco IOS software supports a DHCP server configuration called Easy IP. The goal of this lab is to have devices on networks 192.168.10.0/24 and 192.168.11.0/24 request IP addresses via DHCP from R2.

Step 1. Exclude statically assigned addresses.

The DHCP server assumes that all IP addresses in a DHCP address pool subnet are available for assigning to DHCP clients. You must specify the IP addresses that the DHCP server should not assign to clients. These IP addresses usually are static addresses reserved for the router interface, switch management IP address, servers, and the local network printer. The **ip dhcp excluded-address** command prevents the router from assigning IP addresses within the configured range. The following commands exclude the first ten IP addresses from each pool for the LANs attached to R1. These addresses will not be assigned to any DHCP clients.

```
R2(config)# ip dhcp excluded-address 192.168.10.1 192.168.10.10
R2(config)# ip dhcp excluded-address 192.168.11.1 192.168.11.10
```

Step 2. Configure the pool.

Create the DHCP pool using the **ip dhcp pool** command, and name it R1Fa0:

```
R2(config)# ip dhcp pool R1Fa0
```

Specify the subnet to use when assigning IP addresses. DHCP pools automatically associate with an interface based on the **network** statement. The router now acts as a DHCP server, handing out addresses in the 192.168.10.0/24 subnet, starting with 192.168.10.1.

```
R2(dhcp-config)# network 192.168.10.0 255.255.255.0
```

Configure the default router and domain name server for the network. Clients receive these settings via DHCP, along with an IP address.

```
R2(dhcp-config)# dns-server 192.168.11.5
R2(dhcp-config)# default-router 192.168.10.1
```

Note: There is no DNS server at 192.168.11.5. You are configuring the command for practice only.

Because devices from the network 192.168.11.0/24 also request addresses from R2, a separate pool must be created to serve devices on that network. The commands are similar to the commands just shown:

```
R2(config)# ip dhcp pool R1Fa1
R2(dhcp-config)# network 192.168.11.0 255.255.255.0
R2(dhcp-config)# dns-server 192.168.11.5
R2(dhcp-config)# default-router 192.168.11.1
```

Step 3. Test DHCP.

On PC1 and PC2, test whether each has received an IP address automatically. On each PC, choose **Start > Run > cmd** and enter **ipconfig**, as shown in Figure 7-5.

Figure 7-5 Testing for Automatic IP Address Assignment

What is the result of your test? ______________________________

Why is this the result? ______________________________

Step 4. Configure a helper address.

Network services such as DHCP rely on Layer 2 broadcasts to function. When the devices providing these services exist on a different subnet than the clients, they cannot receive the broadcast packets. Because the DHCP server and the DHCP clients are not on the same subnet, configure R1 to forward DHCP broadcasts to R2, which is the DHCP server, using the **ip helper-address** interface configuration command.

Notice that **ip helper-address** must be configured on each interface involved.

```
R1(config)# interface fa0/0
R1(config-if)# ip helper-address 10.1.1.2
R1(config)# interface fa0/1
R1(config-if)# ip helper-address 10.1.1.2
```

Step 5. Release and renew the IP addresses on PC1 and PC2.

Depending on whether your PCs have been used in a different lab, or connected to the Internet, they may already have learned an IP address automatically from a different DHCP server. You need to clear this IP address using the **ipconfig /release** and **ipconfig /renew** commands, as shown in Figure 7-6.

Figure 7-6 Clearing and Renewing IP Addressing

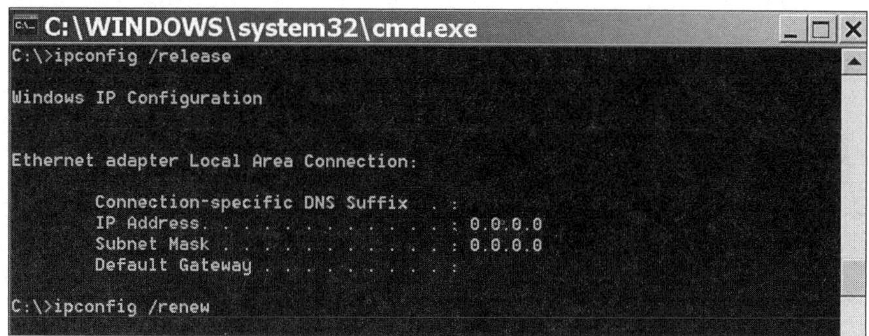

Step 6. Verify the DHCP configuration.

You can verify the DHCP server configuration in several different ways. Issue the command **ipconfig** on PC1 and PC2 to verify that they have received an IP address dynamically. You can then issue commands on the router to get more information. The **show ip dhcp binding** command provides information on all currently assigned DHCP addresses. For instance, the following output shows that the IP address 192.168.10.11 has been assigned to MAC address 3031.632e.3537.6563. The IP lease expires on September 14, 2007 at 7:33 p.m.

```
R1# show ip dhcp binding
Bindings from all pools not associated with VRF:
IP address          Client-ID/              Lease expiration          Type
                    Hardware address/
                    User name
192.168.10.11       0063.6973.636f.2d30.    Sep 14 2007 07:33 PM      Automatic
```

```
                 3031.632e.3537.6563.
                 2e30.3634.302d.566c.
                 31
```

The **show ip dhcp pool** command displays information on all currently configured DHCP pools on the router. In the following output, the pool **R1Fa0** is configured on R1. One address has been leased from this pool. The next client to request an address will receive 192.168.10.12.

```
R2# show ip dhcp pool
Pool R1Fa0 :
 Utilization mark (high/low)    : 100 / 0
 Subnet size (first/next)       : 0 / 0
 Total addresses                : 254
 Leased addresses               : 1
 Pending event                  : none
 1 subnet is currently in the pool :
 Current index        IP address range                    Leased addresses
 192.168.10.12        192.168.10.1     - 192.168.10.254    1
```

The **debug ip dhcp server events** command can be extremely useful when you troubleshoot DHCP leases with a Cisco IOS DHCP server. The following is the debug output on R1 after connecting a host. Notice that the highlighted portion shows DHCP giving the client an address of 192.168.10.12 and a mask of 255.255.255.0.

```
*Sep 13 21:04:18.072: DHCPD: Sending notification of DISCOVER:
*Sep 13 21:04:18.072:   DHCPD: htype 1 chaddr 001c.57ec.0640
*Sep 13 21:04:18.072:   DHCPD: remote id 020a0000c0a80b01010000000000
*Sep 13 21:04:18.072:   DHCPD: circuit id 00000000
*Sep 13 21:04:18.072: DHCPD: Seeing if there is an internally specified pool
  class:
*Sep 13 21:04:18.072:   DHCPD: htype 1 chaddr 001c.57ec.0640
*Sep 13 21:04:18.072:   DHCPD: remote id 020a0000c0a80b01010000000000
*Sep 13 21:04:18.072:   DHCPD: circuit id 00000000
*Sep 13 21:04:18.072: DHCPD: there is no address pool for 192.168.11.1.
*Sep 13 21:04:18.072: DHCPD: Sending notification of DISCOVER:
R1#
*Sep 13 21:04:18.072:   DHCPD: htype 1 chaddr 001c.57ec.0640
*Sep 13 21:04:18.072:   DHCPD: remote id 020a0000c0a80a01000000000000
*Sep 13 21:04:18.072:   DHCPD: circuit id 00000000
*Sep 13 21:04:18.072: DHCPD: Seeing if there is an internally specified pool
  class:
*Sep 13 21:04:18.072:   DHCPD: htype 1 chaddr 001c.57ec.0640
*Sep 13 21:04:18.072:   DHCPD: remote id 020a0000c0a80a01000000000000
*Sep 13 21:04:18.072:   DHCPD: circuit id 00000000
R1#
```

```
*Sep 13 21:04:20.072: DHCPD: Adding binding to radix tree (192.168.10.12)
*Sep 13 21:04:20.072: DHCPD: Adding binding to hash tree
*Sep 13 21:04:20.072: DHCPD: assigned IP address 192.168.10.12 to client
0063.6973.636f.2d30.3031.632e.3537.6563.2e30.3634.302d.566c.31.
*Sep 13 21:04:20.072: DHCPD: Sending notification of ASSIGNMENT:
*Sep 13 21:04:20.072:  DHCPD: address 192.168.10.12 mask 255.255.255.0
*Sep 13 21:04:20.072:   DHCPD: htype 1 chaddr 001c.57ec.0640
*Sep 13 21:04:20.072:   DHCPD: lease time remaining (secs) = 86400
*Sep 13 21:04:20.076: DHCPD: Sending notification of ASSIGNMENT:
*Sep 13 21:04:20.076:  DHCPD: address 192.168.10.12 mask 255.255.255.0
R1#
*Sep 13 21:04:20.076:   DHCPD: htype 1 chaddr 001c.57ec.0640
*Sep 13 21:04:20.076:   DHCPD: lease time remaining (secs) = 86400
```

Task 5: Configure Static and Default Routing

ISP uses static routing to reach all networks beyond R2. However, R2 translates private addresses into public addresses before sending traffic to ISP. Therefore, ISP must be configured with the public addresses that are part of the NAT configuration on R2. Enter the following static route on ISP:

```
ISP(config)# ip route 209.165.200.240 255.255.255.240 serial 0/0/1
```

This static route includes all addresses assigned to R2 for public use.

Configure a default route on R2, and propagate the route in OSPF:

```
R2(config)# ip route 0.0.0.0 0.0.0.0 209.165.200.226
R2(config)# router ospf 1
R2(config-router)# default-information originate
```

Allow a few seconds for R1 to learn the default route from R2, and then check the R1 routing table. Alternatively, you can clear the routing table with the **clear ip route** * command. A default route pointing to R2 should appear in the R1 routing table. From R1, ping the serial 0/0/1 interface on ISP (209.165.200.226). The pings should be successful. Troubleshoot if the pings fail.

Task 6: Configure Static NAT

Step 1. Statically map a public IP address to a private IP address.

The inside server attached to R2 is accessible by outside hosts beyond ISP. Statically assign the public IP address 209.165.200.254 as the address for NAT to use to map packets to the private IP address of the inside server at 192.168.20.254:

```
R2(config)# ip nat inside source static 192.168.20.254 209.165.200.254
```

Step 2. Specify inside and outside NAT interfaces.

Before NAT can work, you must specify which interfaces are inside and which interfaces are outside:

```
R2(config)# interface serial 0/0/1
R2(config-if)# ip nat outside
R2(config-if)# interface fa0/0
R2(config-if)# ip nat inside
```

Note: If you're using a simulated inside server, assign the **ip nat inside** command to the loopback interface.

Step 3. Verify the static NAT configuration.

From ISP, ping the public IP address 209.165.200.254.

Task 7: Configure Dynamic NAT with a Pool of Addresses

Whereas static NAT provides a permanent mapping between an internal address and a specific public address, dynamic NAT maps private IP addresses to public addresses. These public IP addresses come from a NAT pool.

Step 1. Define a pool of global addresses.

Create a pool of addresses to which matched source addresses are translated. The following command creates a pool named MY-NAT-POOL that translates matched addresses to an available IP address in the 209.165.200.241 to 209.165.200.246 range.

```
R2(config)# ip nat pool MY-NAT-POOL 209.165.200.241 209.165.200.246 netmask
  255.255.255.248
```

Step 2. Create an extended access control list to identify which inside addresses are translated:

```
R2(config)# ip access-list extended NAT
R2(config-ext-nacl)# permit ip 192.168.10.0 0.0.0.255 any
R2(config-ext-nacl)# permit ip 192.168.11.0 0.0.0.255 any
```

Step 3. Establish dynamic source translation by binding the pool with the access control list.

A router can have more than one NAT pool and more than one ACL. The following command tells the router which address pool to use to translate hosts that are allowed by the ACL:

```
R2(config)# ip nat inside source list NAT pool MY-NAT-POOL
```

Step 4. Specify inside and outside NAT interfaces.

You have already specified the inside and outside interfaces for your static NAT configuration. Now add the serial interface linked to R1 as an inside interface:

```
R2(config)# interface serial 0/0/0
R2(config-if)# ip nat inside
```

Step 5. Verify the configuration.

Ping ISP from PC1 or the Fast Ethernet interface on R1 using extended **ping**. Then use the **show ip nat translations** and **show ip nat statistics** commands on R2 to verify NAT.

```
R2# show ip nat translations

Pro Inside global        Inside local       Outside local        Outside global
icmp 209.165.200.241:4 192.168.10.1:4     209.165.200.226:4  209.165.200.226:4
--- 209.165.200.241      192.168.10.1       ---                  ---
--- 209.165.200.254      192.168.20.254     ---                  ---
R2# show ip nat statistics

Total active translations: 2 (1 static, 1 dynamic; 0 extended)
Outside interfaces:
  Serial0/0/1
Inside interfaces:
  Serial0/0/0, Loopback0
Hits: 23  Misses: 3
CEF Translated packets: 18, CEF Punted packets: 0
Expired translations: 3
Dynamic mappings:
-- Inside Source
[Id: 1] access-list NAT pool MY-NAT-POOL refcount 1
 pool MY-NAT-POOL: netmask 255.255.255.248
        start 209.165.200.241 end 209.165.200.246
        type generic, total addresses 6, allocated 1 (16%), misses 0
Queued Packets: 0
```

To troubleshoot issues with NAT, you can use the **debug ip nat** command. Turn on NAT debugging, and repeat the ping from PC1:

```
R2# debug ip nat

IP NAT debugging is on
R2#
*Sep 13 21:15:02.215: NAT*: s=192.168.10.11->209.165.200.241,
  d=209.165.200.226 [25]
*Sep 13 21:15:02.231: NAT*: s=209.165.200.226, d=209.165.200.241-
  >192.168.10.11 [25]
*Sep 13 21:15:02.247: NAT*: s=192.168.10.11->209.165.200.241,
  d=209.165.200.226 [26]
*Sep 13 21:15:02.263: NAT*: s=209.165.200.226, d=209.165.200.241-
  >192.168.10.11 [26]
*Sep 13 21:15:02.275: NAT*: s=192.168.10.11->209.165.200.241,
  d=209.165.200.226 [27]
```

```
*Sep 13 21:15:02.291: NAT*: s=209.165.200.226, d=209.165.200.241-
  >192.168.10.11 [27]
*Sep 13 21:15:02.307: NAT*: s=192.168.10.11->209.165.200.241,
  d=209.165.200.226 [28]
*Sep 13 21:15:02.323: NAT*: s=209.165.200.226, d=209.165.200.241-
  >192.168.10.11 [28]
*Sep 13 21:15:02.335: NAT*: s=192.168.10.11->209.165.200.241,
  d=209.165.200.226 [29]
*Sep 13 21:15:02.351: NAT*: s=209.165.200.226, d=209.165.200.241-
  >192.168.10.11 [29]
R2#
```

Task 8: Configure NAT Overload

In the previous example, what would happen if you needed more than the six public IP addresses that the pool allows?

____

____

By tracking port numbers, NAT overloading allows multiple inside users to reuse a public IP address.

In this task, you will remove the pool and mapping statement configured in the previous task. Then you will configure NAT overload on R2 so that all internal IP addresses are translated to the R2 S0/0/1 address when connecting to any outside device.

Step 1. Remove the NAT pool and mapping statement.

Use the following commands to remove the NAT pool and the map to the NAT ACL:

```
R2(config)# no ip nat inside source list NAT pool MY-NAT-POOL
R2(config)# no ip nat pool MY-NAT-POOL 209.165.200.241 209.165.200.246
  netmask 255.255.255.248
```

If you receive the following message, clear your NAT translations:

```
%Pool MY-NAT-POOL in use, cannot destroy
R2# clear ip nat translation *
```

Step 2. Configure PAT on R2 using the serial 0/0/1 interface public IP address.

The configuration is similar to dynamic NAT, except that instead of a pool of addresses, the **interface** keyword is used to identify the outside IP address. Therefore, no NAT pool is defined. The **overload** keyword enables the addition of the port number to the translation.

Because you already configured an ACL to identify which inside IP addresses to translate, as well as which interfaces are inside and outside, you only need to configure the following:

```
R2(config)# ip nat inside source list NAT interface S0/0/1 overload
```

Step 3. Verify the configuration.

Ping ISP from PC1 or the Fast Ethernet interface on R1 using an extended ping. Then use the **show ip nat translations** and **show ip nat statistics** commands on R2 to verify NAT:

```
R2# show ip nat translations

Pro Inside global      Inside local      Outside local      Outside global
icmp 209.165.200.225:6 192.168.10.11:6   209.165.200.226:6
209.165.200.226:6
--- 209.165.200.254    192.168.20.254    ---                ---
R2# show ip nat statistics

Total active translations: 2 (1 static, 1 dynamic; 1 extended)
Outside interfaces:
  Serial0/0/1
Inside interfaces:
  Serial0/0/0, Loopback0
Hits: 48  Misses: 6
CEF Translated packets: 46, CEF Punted packets: 0
Expired translations: 5
Dynamic mappings:
-- Inside Source
[Id: 2] access-list NAT interface Serial0/0/1 refcount 1
Queued Packets: 0
```

Note: In this task, you could have added the keyword **overload** to the **ip nat inside source list NAT pool MY-NAT-POOL** command to allow for more than six concurrent users.

Task 9: Document the Network

On each router, issue the **show run** command, and capture the configurations:

Task 10: Clean Up

Erase the configurations and reload the routers. Disconnect and store the cabling. For PC hosts that normally are connected to other networks, such as the school LAN or the Internet, reconnect the appropriate cabling and restore the TCP/IP settings.

Packet Tracer Companion: Basic DHCP and NAT Configuration (7.4.1)

You can now open the file LSG04-Lab0701.pka on the CD-ROM that accompanies this book to repeat this hands-on lab using Packet Tracer. Remember, however, that Packet Tracer is not a substitute for hands-on lab experience with real equipment.

Lab 7-2: Challenge DHCP and NAT Configuration (7.4.2)

Upon completion of this lab, you will be able to

- Prepare the network
- Perform basic router configurations
- Configure a Cisco IOS DHCP server
- Configure static and default routing
- Configure static NAT
- Configure dynamic NAT with a pool of addresses
- Configure NAT overload

Figure 7-7 shows the network topology for this lab. Table 7-2 provides the IP addresses, subnet masks, and default gateways (where applicable) for all devices in the topology.

Figure 7-7 Network Topology for Lab 7-2

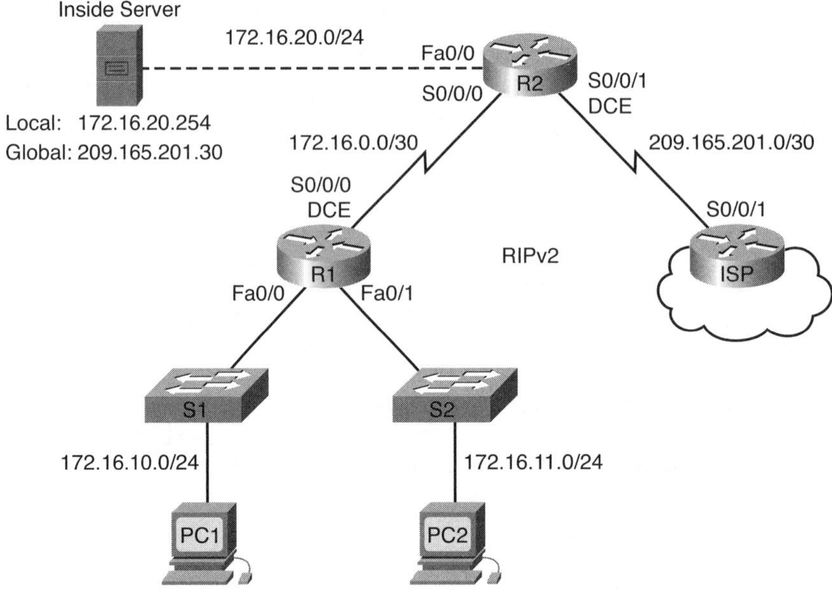

Table 7-2 Lab 7-2 Addressing Table

Device	Interface	IP Address	Subnet Mask
R1	S0/0/0	172.16.0.1	255.255.255.252
	Fa0/0	172.16.10.1	255.255.255.0
	Fa0/1	172.16.11.1	255.255.255.0
R2	S0/0/0	172.16.0.2	255.255.255.252
	S0/0/1	209.165.201.1	255.255.255.252
	Fa0/0	172.16.20.1	255.255.255.0
ISP	S0/0/1	209.165.201.2	255.255.255.252

Scenario

In this lab, configure the IP address services using the network shown in Figure 7-7. If you need assistance, refer to the basic DHCP and NAT configuration lab. However, try to do as much on your own as possible.

Task 1: Prepare the Network

Step 1. Cable a network that is similar to the one shown in Figure 7-7.

You can use any current router in your lab as long as it has the required interfaces shown in the topology.

Note: If you use a 1700, 2500, or 2600 series router, the router outputs and interface descriptions may look different.

Step 2. Clear all existing configurations on the routers.

Task 2: Perform Basic Router Configurations

Configure the R1, R2, and ISP routers according to the following guidelines:

- Configure the device hostname.
- Disable DNS lookup.
- Configure a privileged EXEC mode password.
- Configure a message-of-the-day banner.
- Configure a password for the console connections.
- Configure a password for all vty connections.
- Configure IP addresses on all routers. The PCs will receive IP addressing from DHCP later in the lab.
- Enable OSPF with process ID 1 on R1 and R2. Do not advertise the 209.165.200.224/27 network.

Note: Instead of attaching a server to R2, you can configure a loopback interface on R2 to use the IP address 192.168.20.254/24. If you do this, you do not need to configure the Fast Ethernet interface.

Task 3: Configure a Cisco IOS DHCP Server

Configure R2 as the DHCP server for the two R1 LANs.

Step 1. Exclude statically assigned addresses.

Exclude the first three addresses from each pool.

____

____

Step 2. Configure the DHCP pool.

Create two DHCP pools. Name one of them R1_LAN10 for the 172.16.10.0/24 network, and name the other R1_LAN11 for the 172.16.11.0/24 network.

Configure each pool with a default gateway and a simulated DNS at 172.16.20.254.

Step 3. Configure a helper address.

Configure helper addresses so that broadcasts from clients are forwarded to the DHCP server.

Step 4. Verify the DHCP configuration.

Task 4: Configure Static and Default Routing

Configure ISP with a static route for the 209.165.201.0/27 network. Use the **exit** interface as an argument.

Configure a default route on R2, and propagate the route in OSPF. Use the next-hop IP address as an argument.

Task 5: Configure Static NAT

Step 1. Statically map a public IP address to a private IP address.

Statically map the inside server IP address to the public address 209.165.201.30.

____

Step 2. Specify inside and outside NAT interfaces.

____

____

____

____

Step 3. Verify the static NAT configuration.

Task 6: Configure Dynamic NAT with a Pool of Addresses

Step 1. Define a pool of global addresses.

Create a pool named NAT_POOL for the IP addresses 209.165.201.9 through 209.165.201.14 using a /29 subnet mask.

____

____

Step 2. Create a standard named access control list to identify which inside addresses are translated.

Use the name NAT_ACL, and allow all hosts attached to the two LANs on R1.

____

____

____

Step 3. Establish dynamic source translation.

Bind the NAT pool to the ACL, and allow NAT overloading.

____

Step 4. Specify the inside and outside NAT interfaces.

Verify that the inside and outside interfaces are all correctly specified.

____

____

Step 5. Verify the configuration.

Task 7: Document the Network

On each router, issue the **show run** command, and capture the configurations.

Task 8: Clean Up

Erase the configurations and reload the routers. Disconnect and store the cabling. For PC hosts that normally are connected to other networks, such as the school LAN or the Internet, reconnect the appropriate cabling and restore the TCP/IP settings.

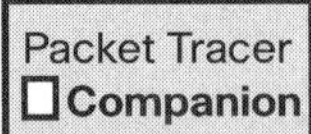

Packet Tracer Companion: Challenge DHCP and NAT Configuration (7.4.2)

You can now open the file LSG04-Lab0702.pka on the CD-ROM that accompanies this book to repeat this hands-on lab using Packet Tracer. Remember, however, that Packet Tracer is not a substitute for hands-on lab experience with real equipment.

Lab 7-3: Troubleshooting DHCP and NAT (7.4.3)

Upon completion of this lab, you will be able to

- Prepare the network
- Load routers with scripts
- Find and correct network errors
- Document the corrected network

Figure 7-8 shows the network topology for this lab. Table 7-3 provides the IP addresses, subnet masks, and default gateways (where applicable) for all devices in the topology.

Figure 7-8 Network Topology for Lab 7-3

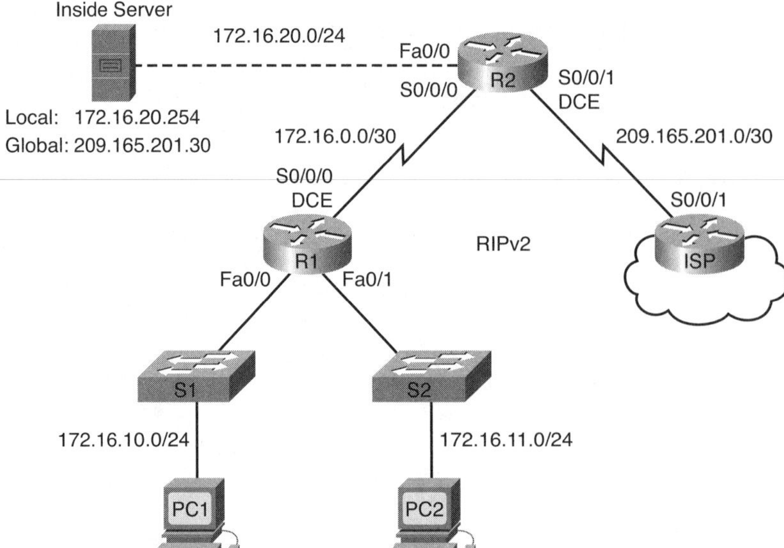

Table 7-3 Lab 7-3 Addressing Table

Device	Interface	IP Address	Subnet Mask
R1	S0/0/0	172.16.0.1	255.255.255.252
	Fa0/0	172.16.10.1	255.255.255.0
	Fa0/1	172.16.11.1	255.255.255.0
R2	S0/0/0	172.16.0.2	255.255.255.252
	S0/0/1	209.165.201.1	255.255.255.252
	Fa0/0	172.16.20.1	255.255.255.0
ISP	S0/0/1	209.165.201.2	255.255.255.252

Scenario

The routers at your company, R1 and R2, were configured by an inexperienced network engineer. Several errors in the configuration have resulted in connectivity issues. Your boss has asked you to troubleshoot and correct the configuration errors and document your work. Using your knowledge of DHCP, NAT, and standard testing methods, find and correct the errors. Make sure that all clients have full connectivity. The ISP has been configured correctly.

Ensure that the network supports the following:

- The router R2 should serve as the DHCP server for the 172.16.10.0/24 and 172.16.11.0/24 networks connected to R1.
- All PCs connected to R1 should receive an IP address in the correct network via DHCP.
- Traffic from the R1 LANs entering the Serial 0/0/0 interface on R2 and exiting the Serial 0/0/1 interface on R2 should receive NAT translation with a pool of addresses provided by the ISP.
- The Inside Server should be reachable from outside networks using IP address 209.165.201.30, and to inside networks using IP address 172.16.20.254.

Task 1: Prepare the Network

Step 1. Cable a network that is similar to the one shown in Figure 7-8.

Step 2. Clear all existing configurations on the routers.

Step 3. Import the following configurations.

```
R1
hostname R1
!
enable secret class
!
no ip domain lookup
```

```
!
interface FastEthernet0/0
 ip address 172.16.10.1 255.255.255.0
 ip helper-address 172.16.0.2
 no shutdown
!
interface FastEthernet0/1
 ip address 172.16.11.1 255.255.255.0
 no shutdown
!
interface Serial0/0/0
 ip address 172.16.0.1 255.255.255.252
 clock rate 125000
 no shutdown
!
router rip
 version 2
 network 172.16.0.0
 no auto-summary
!
banner motd $AUTHORIZED ACCESS ONLY$
!
line con 0
password cisco
 logging synchronous
 login
line vty 0 4
 password cisco
 logging synchronous
 login
!
end
```

R2

```
hostname R2
!
enable secret class
!
ip dhcp excluded-address 172.16.10.1 172.16.10.3
ip dhcp excluded-address 172.16.11.1 172.16.11.3
!
ip dhcp pool R1_LAN10
   network 172.16.10.0 255.255.255.0
   dns-server 172.16.20.254
!
```

```
ip dhcp pool R1_LAN11
   network 172.16.11.0 255.255.255.0
   dns-server 172.16.20.254
!
no ip domain lookup
!
interface FastEthernet0/0
 ip address 172.16.20.1 255.255.255.0
 ip nat inside
 no shutdown
!
interface Serial0/0/0
 ip address 172.16.0.2 255.255.255.252
 no shutdown
!
interface Serial0/0/1
 ip address 209.165.201.1 255.255.255.252
 ip nat outside
 clock rate 125000
 no shutdown
!
router rip
 version 2
 network 172.16.0.0
 default-information originate
 no auto-summary
!
ip route 0.0.0.0 0.0.0.0 209.165.201.2
!
ip nat pool NAT_POOL 209.165.201.9 209.165.201.14 netmask 255.255.255.248
ip nat inside source list NAT_ACL pool NATPOOL overload
!
ip access-list standard NAT_ACL
 permit 172.16.10.0 0.0.0.255
!
banner motd $AUTHORIZED ACCESS ONLY$
!
line con 0
 password cisco
 logging synchronous
 login
line vty 0 4
 password cisco
 logging synchronous
```

```
 login
!
end
```

```
ISP
hostname ISP
!
enable secret class
!
interface Serial0/0/1
 ip address 209.165.201.2 255.255.255.252
 no shutdown
!
ip route 0.0.0.0 0.0.0.0 Serial0/0/1
!
banner motd $AUTHORIZED ACCESS ONLY$
!
line con 0
 password cisco
 logging synchronous
 login
line vty 0 4
 password cisco
 logging synchronous
 login
!
end
```

Task 2: Find and Correct Network Errors

When the network is configured correctly:

- PC1 and PC2 should be able to receive IP addresses from the correct DHCP pool, as evidenced by an **ipconfig** on the PCs. Additionally, a **show ip dhcp bindings** command on R2 should show that both PCs have received IP addresses.
- Test pings from PC1 and PC2 to the ISP should receive NAT overload translation, as evidenced by a **show ip nat translations** command on R2.
- Test pings from the Inside Server to ISP should receive the static NAT translation indicated on the topology. Use the **show ip nat translations** command to verify this.
- A ping from ISP to the global address of the Inside Server should be successful.
- Test pings from ISP to R1 should not receive NAT translation, as evidenced by a **show ip nat translations** or **debug ip nat** command on R2.

Task 3: Document the Router Configurations

On each router, issue the **show run** command, and capture the configurations.

Task 4: Clean Up

Erase the configurations and reload the routers. Disconnect and store the cabling. For PC hosts that normally are connected to other networks, such as the school LAN or the Internet, reconnect the appropriate cabling and restore the TCP/IP settings.

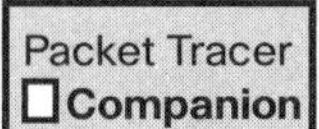

Packet Tracer Companion: Troubleshooting DHCP and NAT Configuration (7.4.3)

You can now open the file LSG04-Lab0703.pka on the CD-ROM that accompanies this book to repeat this hands-on lab using Packet Tracer. Remember, however, that Packet Tracer is not a substitute for hands-on lab experience with real equipment.

Lab 7-4: IPv6 Basic Configuration Using an Adtran

Upon completion of this bonus lab, you will be able to

- Find and install an IOS image that will support IPv6 on your hardware
- Enable IPv6 unicast routing throughout the network
- Enable the IPv6 protocol on each participating interface, and assign an appropriate IPv6 address
- Configure RIPng to route traffic across the network

Figure 7-9 shows the network topology for this lab.

Figure 7-9 Network Topology for Lab 7-4

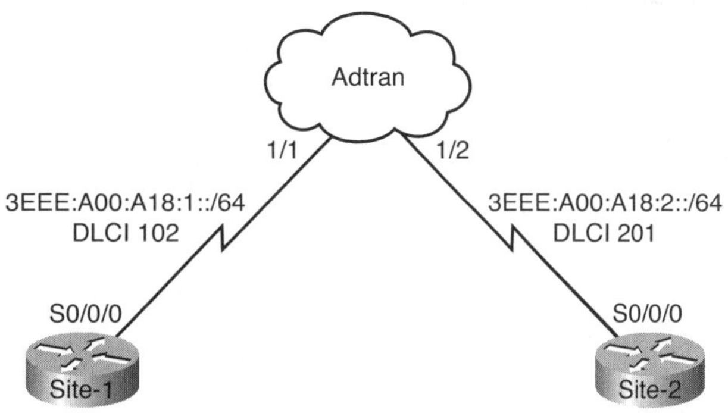

Scenario

You are the network administrator for the topology shown in Figure 7-9. Due to the growth and availability of IPv6 Internet sites, management has asked you to upgrade all the routers in your organization to support IPv6.

Your network is connected to the IPv6 Internet via the Adtran, as shown in Figure 7-9. You will configure the two remote site routers to support IPv6. All routers will participate in RIPng routing to allow full communication between remote sites as well as from each remote site to the Internet cloud.

Task 1: Upgrade IOS to Support IPv6

Most Cisco hardware can be upgraded to an IOS image that supports IPv6. You can use the Cisco Feature Navigator to find an image for your hardware that supports IPv6.

Note: This lab was completed using Cisco 2811 routers with the c2800nm-adventerprisek9-mz.123-11.YZ2.bin image, which requires 256 Mbps of RAM and 64 Mbps of flash. Before downloading an IOS image, use the **show version** command to make sure that the routers have enough memory to support the new image. Also, it is good practice to save your IOS images to a TFTP server for future use. If you are using 1700 or 2600 routers, the interface configurations may differ (S0/0/0 to S0/0).

After upgrading the hardware to support IPv6, issue the **ipv6 ?** command from global configuration mode. The output should look similar to the following:

```
router(config)# ipv6 ?

  access-list      Configure access lists
  cef              Cisco Express Forwarding for IPv6
  hop-limit        Configure hop count limit
  host             Configure static hostnames
  icmp             Configure ICMP parameters
  local            Specify local options
  neighbor         Neighbor
  ospf             OSPF
  prefix-list      Build a prefix list
  route            Configure static routes
  router           Enable an IPV6 routing process
  source-route     Process packets with source routing header options
  unicast-routing  Enable unicast routing
```

Task 2: Enter Basic Configuration for Each Device

The basic settings for each device should be configured before you perform IPv6 configuration tasks. In this lab, Frame Relay is used for site-to-site connectivity, and loopback interfaces are used to simulate hosts. Other suitable WAN protocols may also be used. PCs running IPv6 protocol stacks can be used rather than loopback interfaces.

```
hostname site-1
!
interface Serial0/0/0.1
 no ip address
 encapsulation frame-relay
 no keepalive

 no shutdown
```

```
!
interface Serial0/0/0.1 point-to-point
 frame-relay interface-dlci 102
 no shutdown
!
end
```

```
hostname site-2
!
interface Serial0/0/0.1
 no ip address
 encapsulation frame-relay
 no keepalive
no shutdown
!
interface Serial0/0/0.1 point-to-point
 frame-relay interface-dlci 201
 no shutdown
!
end
```

Task 3: Enable IPv6 Forwarding

Two basic steps activate IPv6 on a router. First, IPv6 traffic forwarding must be enabled in both global configuration mode and for each interface participating in the IPv6 network. Then, each interface where IPv6 is required must be configured with an appropriate Internet Assigned Numbers Authority (IANA) IPv6 registered address.

Step 1. Enable forwarding of IPv6 traffic on all routers. Forwarding of IPv6 unicast datagrams is disabled by default on Cisco routers.

```
Site-1(config)# ipv6 unicast-routing
Site-2(config)# ipv6 unicast-routing
```

Step 2. Enable IPv6 on each active interface. For subinterfaces, be sure to enter the command from subinterface configuration mode.

On the Site-1 router:

```
Site-1(config)# interface Serial0/0/0.1 point-to-point
Site-1(config-subif)# ipv6 enable
```

On the Site-2 router:

```
Site-2(config)# interface Serial0/0/0.1 point-to-point
Site-2(config-subif)# ipv6 enable
```

With IPv6 enabled on each active interface, the software automatically configures an IPv6 link-local address. However, if no other address is configured, the interface can communicate only with nodes on the same network link.

Step 3. To view the link-local addresses, use the **show ipv6 interface brief** command.

On the Site-1 router:

```
site-1# show ipv6 interface brief
FastEthernet0/0              [up/down]
    unassigned
FastEthernet0/1              [administratively down/down]
    unassigned
Serial0/0/0                  [up/up]
    unassigned
Serial0/0/0.1                [up/up]
    FE80::218:B9FF:FE22:4DB8
! output omitted
```

Task 4: Configure IPv6 Addresses

Configure aggregatable global unicast addresses on all active interfaces using the command with a keyword that specifies an EUI-64 interface ID in the low-order 64 bits of the address. This combined with the prefix ensures unique global addresses for each interface.

On the Site-1 router:

```
Site-1(config)# interface Serial0/0/0.1 point-to-point
Site-1(config-subif)# ipv6 address 3EEE:A00:A18:1::/64 eui-64
```

On the Site-2 router:

```
Site-2(config)# interface Serial0/0/0.1 point-to-point
Site-2(config-subif)# ipv6 address 3EEE:A00:A18:2::/64 eui-64
```

The software creates valid IPv6 addresses using the device's prefix and MAC address. To view the status of these addresses, use the **show ipv6 interface brief** command. Notice that each configured link displays two IPv6 addresses:

```
Site-1# show ipv6 interface brief
FastEthernet0/0              [up/down]
unassigned
FastEthernet0/1              [administratively down/down]
unassigned
Serial0/0/0                  [up/up]
unassigned
Serial0/0/0.1                [up/up]
FE80::218:B9FF:FE22:4DB8
3EEE:A00:A18:1:218:B9FF:FE22:4DB8
! output omitted
```

What is the first address listed for each IPv6 interface, and how is it used?

____

How many bits are used to identify the prefix in this example?

____

How many bits are used to identify the node in this example?

____

Task 5: Create and Address Loopbacks

To avoid having to configure hosts for the topology, this lab uses loopback interfaces to simulate these hosts. The loopback interfaces will be configured with IPv6 addresses and will also participate in RIPng routing in a later step.

Step 1. Configure the loopback interface on the Site-1 router:

```
Site-1(config)# interface Loopback0
Site-1(config-if)# ipv6 address 2FFF:B00:C18:1::AAAA/64
```

Step 2. Configure the loopback interface on the Site-2 router:

```
Site-2(config)# interface Loopback0
Site-2(config-if)# ipv6 address 2FFF:B00:C18:2::AAAA/64
```

With all the interfaces addressed, you can see routes using the **show ipv6 route** command. Only networks directly connected and local to the router are present before RIPng routing is configured.

Step 3. View the routes on Site-1:

```
Site-1# show ipv6 route

IPv6 Routing Table - 6 entries
Codes: C - Connected, L - Local, S - Static, R - RIP, B - BGP
       U - Per-user Static route
       I1 - ISIS L1, I2 - ISIS L2, IA - ISIS interarea, IS - ISIS summary
       O - OSPF intra, OI - OSPF inter, OE1 - OSPF ext 1, OE2 - OSPF ext 2
       ON1 - OSPF NSSA ext 1, ON2 - OSPF NSSA ext 2
C   2FFF:B00:C18:1::/64 [0/0]
     via ::, Loopback0
L   2FFF:B00:C18:1::AAAA/128 [0/0]
     via ::, Loopback0
C   3EEE:A00:A18:1::/64 [0/0]
     via ::, Serial0/0/0.1
L   3EEE:A00:A18:1:218:B9FF:FE22:4DB8/128 [0/0]
     via ::, Serial0/0/0.1
L   FE80::/10 [0/0]
     via ::, Null0
L   FF00::/8 [0/0]
     via ::, Null0
```

Step 4. View the routes on Site-2:

```
Site-2# show ipv6 route

IPv6 Routing Table - 6 entries
Codes: C - Connected, L - Local, S - Static, R - RIP, B - BGP
       U - Per-user Static route
       I1 - ISIS L1, I2 - ISIS L2, IA - ISIS interarea, IS - ISIS summary
       O - OSPF intra, OI - OSPF inter, OE1 - OSPF ext 1, OE2 - OSPF ext 2
       ON1 - OSPF NSSA ext 1, ON2 - OSPF NSSA ext 2
C   2FFF:B00:C18:2::/64 [0/0]
     via ::, Loopback0
L   2FFF:B00:C18:2::AAAA/128 [0/0]
     via ::, Loopback0
C   3EEE:A00:A18:2::/64 [0/0]
     via ::, Serial0/0/0.1
L   3EEE:A00:A18:2:218:B9FF:FEBF:CC88/128 [0/0]
     via ::, Serial0/0/0.1
L   FE80::/10 [0/0]
     via ::, Null0
L   FF00::/8 [0/0]
     via ::, Null0
```

Task 6: Configure RIPng Routing

Dynamic routing will be configured using RIPng (ng stands for "next generation"). Internet connectivity is provided using Frame Relay through the Adtran.

Step 1. Configure a RIPng routing process on each router. The tag MYRIP will be used during the lab exercise.

```
Site-1(config)# ipv6 router rip MYRIP
Site-2(config)# ipv6 router rip MYRIP
```

There is no need to use the **network** command under RIPng. In IPv4, the **network** *network-number* router configuration command is used to explicitly specify the interfaces on which to run IPv4 RIP. In IPv6, you just need to enable RIPng on the desired interface.

Step 2. Enable RIPng on all interfaces with IPv6 addresses on the Site-1 router:

```
Site-1(config)# interface Serial0/0/0.1 point-to-point
Site-1(config-subif)# ipv6 rip MYRIP enable
Site-1(config)# interface Loopback0
Site-1(config-subif)# ipv6 rip MYRIP enable
```

Step 3. Enable RIPng on all interfaces with IPv6 addresses on the Site-2 router:

```
Site-2(config)# interface Serial0/0/0.1 point-to-point
Site-2(config-subif)# ipv6 rip MYRIP enable
Site-2(config)# interface Loopback0
Site-2(config-subif)# ipv6 rip MYRIP enable
```

Step 4. On each router, confirm that the MYRIP routing process is configured correctly. Make sure that each interface that should be participating in RIP is listed under Interfaces.

Site-1 router:

```
Site-1# show ipv6 rip MYRIP

RIP process "MYRIP", port 521, multicast-group FF02::9, pid 166
     Administrative distance is 120. Maximum paths is 16
     Updates every 30 seconds, expire after 180
     Holddown lasts 0 seconds, garbage collect after 120
     Split horizon is on; poison reverse is off
     Default routes are not generated
     Periodic updates 3, trigger updates 3
  Interfaces:
    Loopback0
    Serial0/0/0.1
  Redistribution:
    None
```

Site-2 router:

```
site-2# show ipv6 rip MYRIP

   RIP process "MYRIP", port 521, multicast-group FF02::9, pid 212
     Administrative distance is 120. Maximum paths is 16
     Updates every 30 seconds, expire after 180
     Holddown lasts 0 seconds, garbage collect after 120
     Split horizon is on; poison reverse is off
     Default routes are not generated
     Periodic updates 3, trigger updates 4
  Interfaces:
    Loopback0
    Serial0/0/0.1
  Redistribution: None
```

Step 5. On each router, view the routing table to confirm that the router has a route to each IPv6 network. Because the default route to the Internet has not been shared, Site-1 and Site-2 do not know about this route.

```
Site-2# show ipv6 route

IPv6 Routing Table - 8 entries
Codes: C - Connected, L - Local, S - Static, R - RIP, B - BGP
       U - Per-user Static route
       I1 - ISIS L1, I2 - ISIS L2, IA - ISIS interarea, IS - ISIS summary
       O - OSPF intra, OI - OSPF inter, OE1 - OSPF ext 1, OE2 - OSPF ext 2
       ON1 - OSPF NSSA ext 1, ON2 - OSPF NSSA ext 2
```

```
R    2FFF:B00:C18:1::/64 [120/2]
      via FE80::218:B9FF:FE22:4DB8, Serial0/0/0.1
C    2FFF:B00:C18:2::/64 [0/0]
      via ::, Loopback0
L    2FFF:B00:C18:2::AAAA/128 [0/0]
      via ::, Loopback0
R    3EEE:A00:A18:1::/64 [120/2]
      via FE80::218:B9FF:FE22:4DB8, Serial0/0/0.1
C    3EEE:A00:A18:2::/64 [0/0]
      via ::, Serial0/0/0.1
L    3EEE:A00:A18:2:218:B9FF:FEBF:CC88/128 [0/0]
      via ::, Serial0/0/0.1
L    FE80::/10 [0/0]
      via ::, Null0
L    FF00::/8 [0/0]
      via ::, Null0
```

Or, to view a summary of the routing table, use this command:

```
Site-1# show ipv6 route summary

IPv6 Routing Table Summary - 8 entries
  4 local, 2 connected, 0 static, 2 RIP, 0 BGP 0 IS-IS, 0 OSPF
  Number of prefixes:
    /8: 1, /10: 1, /64: 4, /128: 2
```

The output contains the number of entries in the IPv6 routing table, a route source (which can be local routes, connected routes, static routes, or a routing protocol), and the number of routing table entries for a given prefix length.

Task 7: Test Connectivity

The loopback on Site-1 should be able to ping the loopback on Site-2. Confirm this by using the **ping** command:

```
Site-1# ping ipv6 2FFF:B00:C18:2::AAAA

Type escape sequence to abort.
Sending 5, 100-byte ICMP Echos to 2FFF:B00:C18:2::AAAA, timeout is 2 seconds:
!!!!!
Success rate is 100 percent (5/5), round-trip min/avg/max = 56/58/60 ms
```

Lab 7-5: IPv6 Basic Configuration Using a Frame Switch

Upon completion of this bonus lab, you will be able to

- Find and install an IOS image that will support IPv6 on your hardware
- Enable IPv6 unicast routing throughout the network
- Enable the IPv6 protocol on each participating interface, and assign an appropriate IPv6 address
- Configure RIPng to route traffic across the network

Figure 7-10 shows the network topology for this lab.

Figure 7-10 Network Topology for Lab 7-5

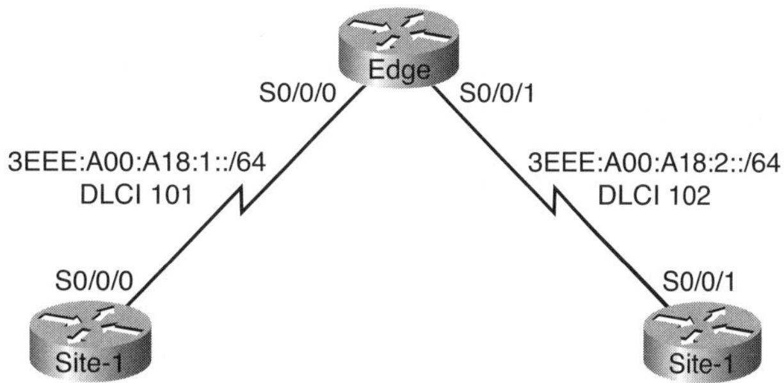

Scenario

You are the network administrator for the topology shown in Figure 7-10. Due to the growth and availability of IPv6 Internet sites, management has asked you to upgrade the three routers in your organization to support IPv6.

Your network is connected to the IPv6 Internet via the Edge router, as shown in the topology. You will configure the two remote site routers to support IPv6. All routers will participate in RIPng routing to allow full communication between remote sites as well as from each remote site to the Internet cloud.

Task 1: Upgrade IOS to Support IPv6

Most Cisco hardware can be upgraded to an IOS image that supports IPv6. You can use the Cisco Feature Navigator to find an image for your hardware that supports IPv6.

Note: This lab was completed using Cisco 2811 routers with the c2800nm-adventerprisek9-mz.123-11.YZ2.bin image, which requires 256 Mbps of RAM and 64 Mbps of flash. Before downloading an IOS image, use the **show version** command to make sure that the routers have enough memory to support the new image. Also, it is good practice to save your IOS images to a TFTP server for future use. If you are using 1700 or 2600 routers, the interface configurations may differ (S0/0/0 to S0/0).

After upgrading the hardware to support IPv6, issue the **ipv6 ?** command from global configuration mode. The output should look similar to the following:

```
router(config)# ipv6 ?

  access-list      Configure access lists
  cef              Cisco Express Forwarding for IPv6
  hop-limit        Configure hop count limit
  host             Configure static hostnames
  icmp             Configure ICMP parameters
  local            Specify local options
  neighbor         Neighbor
  ospf             OSPF
  prefix-list      Build a prefix list
  route            Configure static routes
  router           Enable an IPV6 routing process
  source-route     Process packets with source routing header options
  unicast-routing  Enable unicast routing
```

Task 2: Enter the Basic Configuration for Each Device

The basic settings for each device should be configured before IPv6 configuration tasks are performed. In this lab, Frame Relay is used for site-to-site connectivity, and loopback interfaces are used to simulate hosts. Other suitable WAN protocols may also be used. PCs running IPv6 protocol stacks can be used rather than loopback interfaces.

```
hostname edge
!
interface Serial0/0/0
 no ip address
 encapsulation frame-relay
 no keepalive
 no shutdown
!
interface Serial0/0/0.1 point-to-point
 frame-relay interface-dlci 101
 no shutdown
!
interface Serial0/0/1
 no ip address
 encapsulation frame-relay
 no keepalive
 clockrate 64000
 no shutdown
!
interface Serial0/0/1.1 point-to-point
 frame-relay interface-dlci 102
```

```
 no shutdown
!
end
```

```
hostname site-1
!
interface Serial0/0/0
 no ip address
 encapsulation frame-relay
 no keepalive
 clockrate 64000
 no shutdown
!
interface Serial0/0/0.1 point-to-point
 frame-relay interface-dlci 101
 no shutdown
!
end
```

```
hostname site-2
!
interface Serial0/0/1
 no ip address
 encapsulation frame-relay
 no keepalive
no shutdown
!
interface Serial0/0/1.1 point-to-point
 frame-relay interface-dlci 102
 no shutdown
!
end
```

Task 3: Enable IPv6 Forwarding

Two basic steps activate IPv6 on a router. First, IPv6 traffic forwarding must be enabled in both global configuration mode and for each interface participating in the IPv6 network. Then, each interface where IPv6 is required must be configured with an appropriate IANA IPv6 registered address.

Step 1. Enable forwarding of IPv6 traffic on all routers. Forwarding of IPv6 unicast datagrams is disabled by default on Cisco routers.

```
Edge(config)# ipv6 unicast-routing
Site-1(config)# ipv6 unicast-routing
Site-2(config)# ipv6 unicast-routing
```

Step 2. Enable IPv6 on each active interface. For subinterfaces, be sure to enter the command from subinterface configuration mode.

On the Edge router:

```
Edge(config)# interface Serial0/0/0.1 point-to-point
Edge(config-subif)# ipv6 enable
Edge(config)# interface Serial0/0/1.1 point-to-point
Edge(config-subif)# ipv6 enable
```

On the Site-1 router:

```
Site-1(config)# interface Serial0/0/0.1 point-to-point
Site-1(config-subif)# ipv6 enable
```

On the Site-2 router:

```
Site-2(config)# interface Serial0/0/1.1 point-to-point
Site-2(config-subif)# ipv6 enable
```

With IPv6 enabled on each active interface, the software automatically configures an IPv6 link-local address. However, if no other address is configured, the interface can communicate only with nodes on the same network link.

Step 3. To view the link-local addresses, use the **show ipv6 interface brief** command.

On the Site-1 router:

```
site-1# show ipv6 interface brief

FastEthernet0/0            [administratively down/down]
    unassigned
Serial0/0/0                  [up/up]
    unassigned
Serial0/0/0.1                [up/up]
    FE80::202:FDFF:FE4B:4FA0
! output omitted
```

Task 4: Configure IPv6 Addresses

Configure aggregatable global unicast addresses on all active interfaces using the command with a keyword that specifies an EUI-64 interface ID in the low-order 64 bits of the address. This combined with the prefix ensures unique global addresses for each interface.

On the Edge router:

```
Edge(config)# interface Serial0/0/0.1 point-to-point
Edge(config-subif)# ipv6 address 3EEE:A00:A18:1::/64 eui-64
Edge(config)# interface Serial0/0/1.1 point-to-point
Edge(config-subif)# ipv6 address 3EEE:A00:A18:2::/64 eui-64
```

On the Site-1 router:

```
Site-1(config)# interface Serial0/0/0.1 point-to-point
Site-1(config-subif)# ipv6 address 3EEE:A00:A18:1::/64 eui-64
```

On the Site-2 router:

```
Site-2(config)# interface Serial0/0/1.1 point-to-point
Site-2(config-subif)# ipv6 address 3EEE:A00:A18:2::/64 eui-64
```

The software creates valid IPv6 addresses using the device's prefix and MAC address. To view the status of these addresses, use the **show ipv6 interface brief** command. Notice that each configured link displays two IPv6 addresses:

```
Edge# show ipv6 interface brief

Serial0/0/0.1           [up/up]
FE80::20E:38FF:FE2F:4B00
3EEE:A00:A18:1:20E:38FF:FE2F:4B00
Serial0/0/1.1          [up/up]
FE80::20E:38FF:FE2F:4B00
3EEE:A00:A18:2:20E:38FF:FE2F:4B00
! output omitted
```

What is the first address listed for each IPv6 interface, and how is it used?

____

How many bits are used to identify the prefix in this example?

____

How many bits are used to identify the node in this example?

____

Task 5: Create and Address Loopbacks

To avoid having to configure hosts for the topology, this lab uses loopback interfaces to simulate those hosts. The loopback interfaces will be configured with IPv6 addresses and will also participate in RIPng routing in a later step.

Step 1. Configure the loopback interface on the Edge router:

```
Edge(config)# interface Loopback0
Edge(config-if)# ipv6 address 2FFF:B00:C18:3::AAAA/64
```

Step 2. Configure the loopback interface on the Site-1 router:

```
Site-1(config)# interface Loopback0
Site-1(config-if)# ipv6 address 2FFF:B00:C18:1::AAAA/64
```

Step 3. Configure the loopback interface on the Site-2 router:

```
Site-2(config)# interface Loopback0
Site-2(config-if)# ipv6 address 2FFF:B00:C18:2::AAAA/64
```

With all interfaces addressed, you can see routes using the **show ipv6 route** command. Only networks directly connected and local to the router are present before RIPng routing is configured.

Step 6. View the routes on Edge:

```
Edge# show ipv6 route

IPv6 Routing Table - 8 entries
Codes: C - Connected, L - Local, S - Static, R - RIP, B - BGP
       U - Per-user Static route
       I1 - ISIS L1, I2 - ISIS L2, IA - ISIS interarea, IS - ISIS summary
       O - OSPF intra, OI - OSPF inter, OE1 - OSPF ext 1, OE2 - OSPF ext 2
       ON1 - OSPF NSSA ext 1, ON2 - OSPF NSSA ext 2
C   2FFF:B00:C18:1::/64 [0/0]
     via ::, Loopback0
L   2FFF:B00:C18:1::AAAA/128 [0/0]
     via ::, Loopback0
C   3EEE:A00:A18:1::/64 [0/0]
     via ::, Serial0/0/0.1
L   3EEE:A00:A18:1:20E:38FF:FE2F:4B00/128 [0/0]
     via ::, Serial0/0/0.1
C   3EEE:A00:A18:2::/64 [0/0]
     via ::, Serial0/0/1.1
L   3EEE:A00:A18:2:20E:38FF:FE2F:4B00/128 [0/0]
     via ::, Serial0/0/1.1
L   FE80::/10 [0/0]
     via ::, Null0
L   FF00::/8 [0/0]
     via ::, Null0
```

Task 6: Configure RIPng Routing

Routing will be configured using a combination of static and dynamic routing. Default routing is used on the Edge router to provide Internet connectivity. The Internet connection will be emulated by the Edge router's Loopback 0 interface, and a default static route to that interface will be used. All other network segments will use RIPng to share routing information.

Step 1. Configure the static route on the Edge router:

```
Edge(config)# ipv6 route ::/0 Loopback0
```

Step 2. Configure a RIPng routing process on each router. The tag MYRIP will be used during the lab exercise.

```
Edge(config)# ipv6 router rip MYRIP
Site-1(config)# ipv6 router rip MYRIP
Site-2(config)# ipv6 router rip MYRIP
```

There is no need to use the **network** command under RIPng. In IPv4, the **network** *network-number* router configuration command is used to explicitly specify the interfaces on which to run IPv4 RIP. In IPv6, you just need to enable RIPng on the desired interface.

Step 3. Enable RIPng on all interfaces with IPv6 addresses on the Edge router:

```
Edge(config)# interface Serial0/0/0.1 point-to-point
Edge(config-subif)# ipv6 rip MYRIP enable
Edge(config)# interface Serial0/0/1.1 point-to-point
Edge(config-subif)# ipv6 rip MYRIP enable
```

Step 4. Enable RIPng on all interfaces with IPv6 addresses on the Site-1 router:

```
Site-1(config)# interface Serial0/0/0.1 point-to-point
Site-1(config-subif)# ipv6 rip MYRIP enable
Site-1(config)# interface Loopback0
Site-1(config-subif)# ipv6 rip MYRIP enable
```

Step 5. Enable RIPng on all interfaces with IPv6 addresses on the Site-2 router:

```
Site-2(config)# interface Serial0/0/1.1 point-to-point
Site-2(config-subif)# ipv6 rip MYRIP enable
Site-2(config)# interface Loopback0
Site-2(config-subif)# ipv6 rip MYRIP enable
```

Step 6. On each router, confirm that the MYRIP routing process is configured correctly. Make sure that each interface that should be participating in RIP is listed under Interfaces.

Edge router:

```
Edge# show ipv6 rip MYRIP

RIP process "MYRIP", port 521, multicast-group FF02::9, pid 116
     Administrative distance is 120. Maximum paths is 16
     Updates every 30 seconds, expire after 180
     Holddown lasts 0 seconds, garbage collect after 120
     Split horizon is on; poison reverse is off
     Default routes are not generated
     Periodic updates 137, trigger updates 4
  Interfaces:
    Serial0/0/1.1
    Serial0/0/0.1
  Redistribution:
    None
```

Site-1 router:

```
Site-1# show ipv6 rip MYRIP

RIP process "MYRIP", port 521, multicast-group FF02::9, pid 105
     Administrative distance is 120. Maximum paths is 16
     Updates every 30 seconds, expire after 180
     Holddown lasts 0 seconds, garbage collect after 120
     Split horizon is on; poison reverse is off
     Default routes are not generated
     Periodic updates 143, trigger updates 5
```

```
  Interfaces:
    Serial0/0/0.1
    Loopback0
  Redistribution:
    None
```

Site-2 router:

```
site-2# show ipv6 rip MYRIP

RIP process "MYRIP", port 521, multicast-group FF02::9, pid 105
     Administrative distance is 120. Maximum paths is 16
     Updates every 30 seconds, expire after 180
     Holddown lasts 0 seconds, garbage collect after 120
     Split horizon is on; poison reverse is off
     Default routes are not generated
     Periodic updates 132, trigger updates 2
  Interfaces:
    Serial0/0/1.1
    Loopback0
  Redistribution:
    None
```

Step 7. On each router, view the routing table to confirm that the router has a route to each of the IPv6 networks. Because the default route to the Internet has not been shared, Site-1 and Site-2 do not know about this route.

```
Edge# show ipv6 route

IPv6 Routing Table - 11 entries
Codes: C - Connected, L - Local, S - Static, R - RIP, B - BGP
       U - Per-user Static route
       I1 - ISIS L1, I2 - ISIS L2, IA - ISIS interarea, IS - ISIS summary
       O - OSPF intra, OI - OSPF inter, OE1 - OSPF ext 1, OE2 - OSPF ext 2
       ON1 - OSPF NSSA ext 1, ON2 - OSPF NSSA ext 2
S   ::/0 [1/0]
     via ::, Loopback0
C   2FFF:B00:C18:1::/64 [0/0]
     via ::, Loopback0
L   2FFF:B00:C18:1::AAAA/128 [0/0]
     via ::, Loopback0
R   2FFF:B00:C18:2::/64 [120/2]
     via FE80::20E:83FF:FE4C:FE40, Serial0/0/1.1
R   2FFF:B00:C18:3::/64 [120/2]
     via FE80::202:FDFF:FE4B:4FA0, Serial0/0/0.1
C   3EEE:A00:A18:1::/64 [0/0]
     via ::, Serial0/0/0.1
```

```
L    3EEE:A00:A18:1:20E:38FF:FE2F:4B00/128 [0/0]
      via ::, Serial0/0/0.1
C    3EEE:A00:A18:2::/64 [0/0]
      via ::, Serial0/0/1.1
L    3EEE:A00:A18:2:20E:38FF:FE2F:4B00/128 [0/0]
      via ::, Serial0/0/1.1
L    FE80::/10 [0/0]
      via ::, Null0
L    FF00::/8 [0/0]
      via ::, Null0
```

```
Site-2# show ipv6 route

IPv6 Routing Table - 8 entries
Codes: C - Connected, L - Local, S - Static, R - RIP, B - BGP
       U - Per-user Static route
       I1 - ISIS L1, I2 - ISIS L2, IA - ISIS interarea, IS - ISIS summary
       O - OSPF intra, OI - OSPF inter, OE1 - OSPF ext 1, OE2 - OSPF ext 2
       ON1 - OSPF NSSA ext 1, ON2 - OSPF NSSA ext 2
C    2FFF:B00:C18:2::/64 [0/0]
      via ::, Loopback0
L    2FFF:B00:C18:2::AAAA/128 [0/0]
      via ::, Loopback0
R    2FFF:B00:C18:3::/64 [120/3]
      via FE80::20E:38FF:FE2F:4B00, Serial0/0/1.1
R    3EEE:A00:A18:1::/64 [120/2]
      via FE80::20E:38FF:FE2F:4B00, Serial0/0/1.1
C    3EEE:A00:A18:2::/64 [0/0]
      via ::, Serial0/0/1.1
L    3EEE:A00:A18:2:20E:83FF:FE4C:FE40/128 [0/0]
      via ::, Serial0/0/1.1
L    FE80::/10 [0/0]
      via ::, Null0
L    FF00::/8 [0/0]
      via ::, Null0
```

Or, to view a summary of the routing table, use this command:

```
Site-1# show ipv6 route summary

IPv6 Routing Table Summary - 8 entries
  4 local, 2 connected, 0 static, 2 RIP, 0 BGP 0 IS-IS, 0 OSPF
  Number of prefixes:
    /8: 1, /10: 1, /64: 4, /128: 2
```

The output contains the number of entries in the IPv6 routing table, a route source (which can be local routes, connected routes, static routes, or a routing protocol), and the number of routing table entries for a given prefix length.

Task 7: Test Connectivity

The loopback on Site-1 should be able to ping the loopback on Site-2. Confirm this by using the **ping** command:

```
Site-1# ping ipv6 2FFF:B00:C18:2::AAAA

Type escape sequence to abort.
Sending 5, 100-byte ICMP Echos to 2FFF:B00:C18:2::AAAA, timeout is 2 seconds:
!!!!!
Success rate is 100 percent (5/5), round-trip min/avg/max = 56/58/60 ms
site-1#
```

Task 8: Advertise the Default Route

The router Edge is providing Internet access for your network. Announcing a default route into RIPng at Edge is the preferred way to inform the rest of the network about the Internet connectivity. The default route in IPv6 is not originated by default.

Step 1. Use the **ipv6 rip MYRIP default-information originate** command on each of the serial interfaces on the Edge router. This will allow Site-1 and Site-2 to learn about the static route to the Internet.

```
Edge(config)# interface Serial0/0/0.1 point-to-point
Edge(config-subif)# ipv6 rip MYRIP default-information originate
Edge(config)# interface Serial0/0/1.1 point-to-point
Edge(config-subif)# ipv6 rip MYRIP default-information originate
```

Step 2. Now that the default route is being advertised to the remote sites, each of them should see a new RIP route. Use the **show ipv6 route** command at Site-1 and Site-2 to confirm that the default route has been learned:

```
Site-1# show ipv6 route

IPv6 Routing Table - 9 entries
Codes: C - Connected, L - Local, S - Static, R - RIP, B - BGP
       U - Per-user Static route
       I1 - ISIS L1, I2 - ISIS L2, IA - ISIS interarea, IS - ISIS summary
       O - OSPF intra, OI - OSPF inter, OE1 - OSPF ext 1, OE2 - OSPF ext 2
       ON1 - OSPF NSSA ext 1, ON2 - OSPF NSSA ext 2
R   ::/0 [120/2]
     via FE80::20E:38FF:FE2F:4B00, Serial0/0/0.1
! output omitted
```

```
Site-2# show ipv6 route

IPv6 Routing Table - 9 entries
Codes: C - Connected, L - Local, S - Static, R - RIP, B - BGP
```

```
           U - Per-user Static route
           I1 - ISIS L1, I2 - ISIS L2, IA - ISIS interarea, IS - ISIS summary
           O - OSPF intra, OI - OSPF inter, OE1 - OSPF ext 1, OE2 - OSPF ext 2
           ON1 - OSPF NSSA ext 1, ON2 - OSPF NSSA ext 2
R   ::/0 [120/2]
     via FE80::20E:38FF:FE2F:4B00, Serial0/0/1.1
! output omitted
```

Packet Tracer Exercise 7-1: DHCP

This Packet Tracer activity tests your knowledge of DHCP. Open the file lsg04-0706.pka on the CD-ROM that accompanies this book to do this activity. Detailed instructions are provided within the activity file.

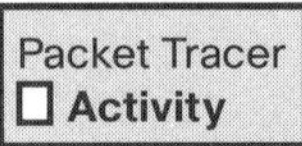

Packet Tracer Exercise 7-2: DHCP Troubleshooting

This Packet Tracer activity tests your ability to troubleshoot DHCP. Open the file lsg04-0707.pka on the CD-ROM that accompanies this book to do this activity. Detailed instructions are provided within the activity file.

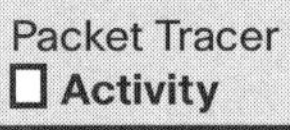

Packet Tracer Exercise 7-3: Configuring NAT, PAT, and Static NAT

This Packet Tracer activity tests your ability to configure NAT, PAT, and static NAT. Open the file lsg04-0708.pka on the CD-ROM that accompanies this book to do this activity. Detailed instructions are provided within the activity file.

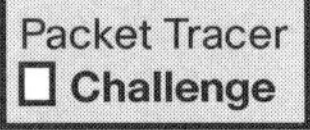

Packet Tracer Exercise 7-4: Double NAT with DHCP

This Packet Tracer activity tests your ability to configure NAT with DHCP. Open the file lsg04-0709.pka on the CD-ROM that accompanies this book to do this activity. Detailed instructions are provided within the activity file.

Packet Tracer
☐ Challenge

Packet Tracer Skills Integration Challenge

Open file LSG04-PTSkills7.pka on the CD-ROM that accompanies this book to perform this exercise using Packet Tracer. In this culminating activity, you will configure PPP, OSPF, DHCP, NAT, and default routing to ISP. You will then verify your configuration.

Upon completion of this skills integration challenge, you will be able to

- Apply basic configurations
- Configure PPP encapsulation with CHAP
- Configure dynamic and default routing

- Configure routers with Easy IP
- Verify that PCs are automatically configured with addressing details
- Configure a DNS server with DNS entries
- Configure an ACL to permit NAT
- Configure static NAT
- Configure dynamic NAT with overload
- Configure the ISP router with a static route
- Test connectivity

Figure 7-11 shows the network topology for this skills integration challenge. Table 7-4 provides the IP addresses and subnet masks for all device interfaces in the topology.

Figure 7-11 Network Topology for Lab 7-10: Skills Integration Challenge

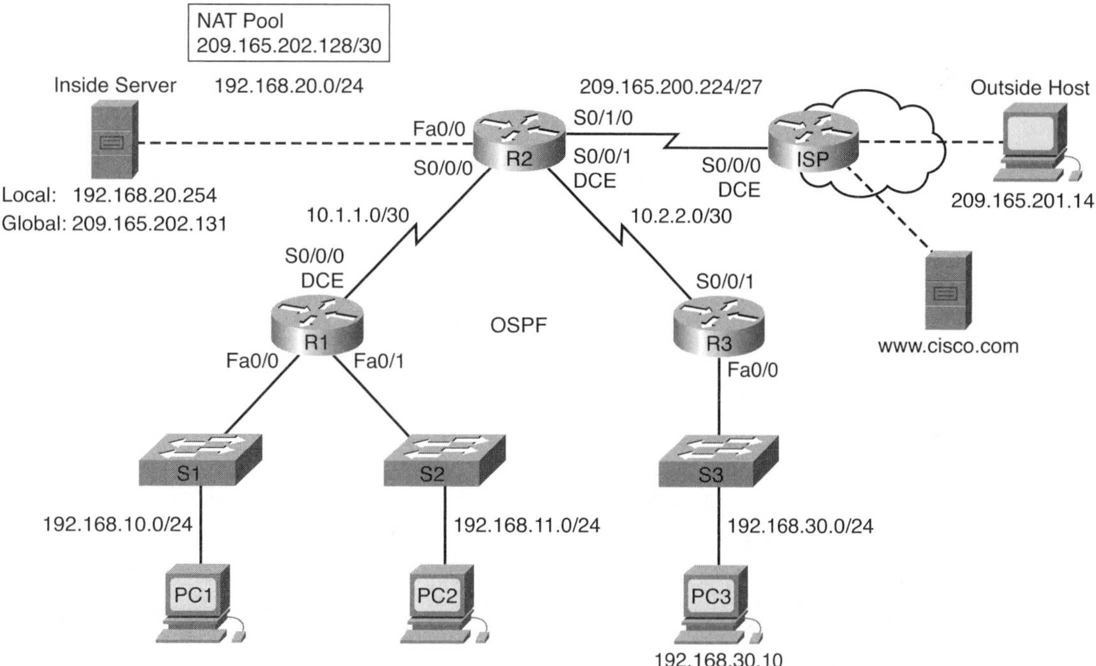

Table 7-4 Addressing Table for Lab 7-10: Skills Integration Challenge

Device	Interface	IP Address	Subnet Mask
R1	Fa0/0	192.168.10.1	255.255.255.0
	Fa0/1	192.168.11.1	255.255.255.0
	S0/0/0	10.1.1.1	255.255.255.252
R2	Fa0/0	192.168.20.1	255.255.255.0
	S0/0/0	10.1.1.2	255.255.255.252
	S0/0/1	10.2.2.1	255.255.255.252
	S0/1/0	209.165.200.225	225.255.255.224

continued

Table 7-4 Addressing Table for Lab 7-10: Skills Integration Challenge continued

Device	Interface	IP Address	Subnet Mask
R3	Fa0/1	192.168.30.1	255.255.255.0
	S0/0/1	10.2.2.2	255.255.255.252
Inside Server	NIC	Local: 192.168.20.254	255.255.255.0
	NIC	Global: 209.165.202.131	255.255.255.252
Outside Host	NIC	209.165.201.14	255.255.255.240

Task 1: Apply Basic Configurations

Step 1. Configure R1, R2, and R3 with this basic global configuration:

- Hostname as listed in the addressing table
- Console line for login with password **cisco**
- vtys 0 to 4 for login with password **cisco**
- Secret password **class**
- Banner of "AUTHORIZED ACCESS ONLY!"

Only the hostname and banner are graded.

Step 2. Configure the interfaces on R1, R2, and R3.

Use the addressing table to determine the interface addresses. Use the topology diagram to determine which interfaces are DCE interfaces. Configure the DCE interfaces for a clock rate of 64000.

Step 3. Check the results.

Your completion percentage should be 38%. If not, click **Check Results** to see which required components are not yet completed.

Task 2: Configure PPP Encapsulation with CHAP

Step 1. Configure the link between R1 and R2 to use PPP encapsulation with CHAP authentication.

The password for CHAP authentication is **cisco123**.

Step 2. Configure the link between R2 and R3 to use PPP encapsulation with CHAP authentication.

The password for CHAP authentication is **cisco123**.

Step 3. Verify that connectivity is restored between the routers.

R2 should be able to ping both R1 and R3. The interfaces may take a few minutes to come back up. You can switch between Realtime and Simulation modes to speed up the process.

Another possible workaround to this Packet Tracer behavior is to use the **shutdown** and **no shutdown** commands on the interfaces.

Note: The interfaces may go down at random points during the activity because of a Packet Tracer bug. The interface normally comes back up on its own if you wait a few seconds.

Step 4. Check the results.

Your completion percentage should be 51%. If not, click **Check Results** to see which required components are not yet completed.

Task 3: Configure Dynamic and Default Routing

Step 1. Configure R1, R2, and R3 to use the OSPF routing protocol.

- Use a process ID of 1 when configuring OSPF on the routers.
- Advertise all networks connected to R1 and R3, but do not send routing updates out the LAN interfaces.
- On R2, do not advertise the 209.165.200.224 network, and do not send routing updates out the Fa0/0 or the Serial0/1/0 interfaces.

Step 2. Configure a default route on R2.

Configure a default route to ISP, specifying the outgoing interface on R2 as the next-hop address.

Step 3. Configure OSPF to advertise the default route.

On R2, enter the command to advertise the default route to R1 and R3 via OSPF.

Step 4. Check the results.

Your completion percentage should be 66%. If not, click **Check Results** to see which required components are not yet completed.

Task 4: Configure Routers Using DHCP

Step 1. Configure R1 to act as a DHCP server for the 192.168.10.0 and 192.68.11.0 networks:

- Name the DHCP pool for the 192.168.10.0 network R1LAN1. For the 192.168.11.0 network, use the name R1LAN2.
- Exclude the first nine addresses on each network from dynamic assignment.
- In addition to the IP address and subnet mask, assign the default gateway and DNS server addresses.

Step 2. Configure R3 to act as a DHCP server for the 192.168.30.0 network:

- Name the DHCP pool for the 192.168.30.0 network R3LAN.
- Exclude the first nine addresses on each network from dynamic assignment.
- In addition to the IP address and subnet mask, assign the default gateway and DNS server addresses.

Step 3. Check the results.

Your completion percentage should be 75%. If not, click **Check Results** to see which required components are not yet completed.

Task 5: Verify That PCs Are Automatically Configured with Addressing Details

Step 1. Configure PC1, PC2, and PC3 for automatic IP configuration using DHCP.

Step 2. Verify that each PC has an address assigned from the correct DHCP pool.

Step 3. Check the results.

Your completion percentage should be 88%. If not, click **Check Results** to see which required components are not yet completed.

Task 6: Configure a DNS Server with DNS Entries

Step 1. Configure the DNS server.

To configure DNS on the Inside Server, click the **DNS** button on the **Config** tab.

Make sure that DNS is turned on, and enter the following DNS entry:

www.cisco.com: 209.165.201.30

Step 2. Check the results.

You cannot ping the www.cisco.com server by domain name until you configure the static route in Task 10. Your completion percentage should be 90%. If not, click **Check Results** to see which required components are not yet completed.

Task 7: Configure an ACL to Permit NAT

Step 1. Create a standard named ACL.

Create the standard named ACL, R2NAT, which permits all the internal networks to be mapped by NAT.

Note: For Packet Tracer to grade this task correctly, you must enter the permitted networks in the following order:

- 192.168.10.0
- 192.168.20.0
- 192.168.30.0
- 192.168.11.0

Step 2. Check the results.

Your completion percentage should be 91%. If not, click **Check Results** to see which required components are not yet completed.

Task 8: Configure Static NAT

Step 1. Configure static NAT for an inside web server.

Configure static NAT to map the local IP address and global IP addresses for Inside Server. Use the addresses listed in the addressing table.

Step 2. Check the results.

Your completion percentage should be 92%. If not, click **Check Results** to see which required components are not yet completed.

Task 9: Configure Dynamic NAT with Overload

Step 1. Configure the dynamic NAT pool.

Configure a dynamic NAT address pool using the NAT Pool specified in Figure 7-11. Name the address pool R2POOL.

Step 2. Configure the dynamic NAT mapping.

Map the addresses in R2POOL to the networks you defined in R2NAT.

Step 3. Apply NAT to the internal and external interfaces of R2.

Step 4. Check the results.

Your completion percentage should be 99%. If not, click **Check Results** to see which required components are not yet completed.

Task 10: Configure the ISP Router with a Static Route

Step 1. Configure a static route to the global IP addresses of R2.

This is the 209.165.202.128/27 network. Use the serial interface of ISP as the next-hop address.

Step 2. Check the results.

Your completion percentage should be 100%. If not, click **Check Results** to see which required components are not yet completed.

Task 11: Test Connectivity

Inside hosts should be able to ping Outside Host.

Inside hosts should be able to ping www.cisco.com.

Outside Host should be able to ping Inside Server using its global IP address.

CHAPTER 8

Network Troubleshooting

The Study Guide portion of this chapter uses a combination of matching, fill-in-the-blank, multiple-choice, and open-ended question exercises to test your knowledge and skills of network documentation, WAN implementation issues, and troubleshooting.

The Labs and Activities portion of this chapter includes all the online curriculum labs to ensure that you have mastered the practical, hands-on skills needed to understand how to properly document and troubleshoot networks.

As you work through this chapter, use Chapter 8 in the *Accessing the WAN, CCNA Exploration Companion Guide* or use the corresponding Chapter 8 in the Accessing the WAN, CCNA Exploration online curriculum for assistance.

Study Guide

Documenting Your Network

Documentation is essential to troubleshooting networks in an efficient and effective manner. It is also one of the most overlooked components of network design and administration. Network documentation should be a working document that consists of everything connected, configured, and functioning that allows users to communicate and share information. This will include cable drops, speeds, and locations. The amount of memory, storage capacity, operating system, and programs that PCs have should also be documented. Wiring closets, device location, and configurations should be noted and backed up. The addressing scheme of each device and interface and remaining address space should be documented, which will tell an administrator how scalable the network is for future growth and the implementation of new devices and technologies. Establishing a network baseline is an essential tool that should be documented, too. It should consist of the initial performance and availability of network devices and services on the network. This will allow a network technician to notice abnormal traffic patterns against baseline standards as the network grows. A protocol analyzer is one such tool that enables you to analyze packets sent through different protocols. Some can generate statistical analysis of data traffic, whereas others enable you to generate traffic to test and determine network baselines. All this will assist a network administrator when implementing new technologies or troubleshooting if something fails.

Concept Questions

1. Network documentation includes end-device capabilities, memory, peripherals, operating system, and address. Why is a host device's information critical to network documentation?

   ____

   ____

   ____

   ____

2. Device configurations and IOS should be documented and stored in case of a network or device failure. Which commands enable you to store configuration files to a backup server? Also, list the command that tells a router to boot to the location where the configuration is stored.

   ____

   ____

   ____

   ____

3. Which commands enable you to gather information from remote devices that you can use to document the network topology? List the appropriate commands and the information they display.

____

____

____

____

____

____

____

____

4. Software applications such as protocol analyzers enable you to establish baselines and test network performance. List the types of data that protocol analyzers can find that will determine performance abnormalities within the network.

____

Troubleshooting Methodologies and Tools

A good troubleshooting methodology will save an organization time and money. Before a technician can troubleshoot a network, proper documentation should exist, which will assist with finding the problem expeditiously. A layered approach can be used when troubleshooting a logical network model such as the OSI reference model. The upper layers (5–7) deal with software application issues, and the lower layers (1–4) deal with data transport issues. In Layers 1 and 2, data is placed on the physical medium. Layers 3 and 4 are implemented within software configuration.

A general troubleshooting procedure requires you to gather information from symptoms, isolate the problem, and then correct the problem. Troubleshooting methods include the following:

- **The bottom-up troubleshooting method**: Requires you to start at the physical layer and work your way up. This approach works well because most network problems, such as bad cabling and connections, reside on the bottom layers.
- **The top-down troubleshooting method**: Starts with end-user applications at Layer 7 and works its way down.
- **The divide-and-conquer troubleshooting method**: Requires you to collect user experience on the problem, document it, and predict which layer might have the problem. If that layer is functioning properly, work your way up the layers. If the layer is not functioning properly, work your way down.

Gathering symptoms allows a network administrator to analyze network functionality, which will allow him to properly diagnose network failures/abnormalities. Tools that enable you to troubleshoot and analyze symptoms on a network include baseline tools, protocol analyzers, network management tools such as What's Up Gold NMS software, and online knowledge-based websites such as Google.

Multiple-Choice Questions

Choose the best answer for each of the questions that follow.

1. Which troubleshooting approach minimizes confusion and cuts down on time wasted?

   A. Rocket scientist approach

   B. Caveman approach

   C. Systematic approach

   D. Modern-day approach

2. In a layered approach to troubleshooting networks, which layers deal with application issues?

   A. 4–7

   B. 5–7

   C. 1–4

   D. 1–3

3. Which device found on a network operates on all seven layers of the OSI reference model?

   A. End system

   B. Firewall

   C. Multilayer switch

   D. Router

4. On the TCP/IP model, which layer provides communication between applications such as FTP, HTTP, and SMTP?

   A. Transport

   B. Session

   C. Presentation

   D. Application

5. What are the three stages of the general troubleshooting process?

   A. Gather symptoms

   B. Divide and conquer

   C. Isolate the problem

   D. Verify the problem

   E. Correct the problem

6. Which troubleshooting method requires that you check every device and interface on the network until you find the possible cause of the problem?

   A. Bottom-up method

   B. Top-down method

   C. Divide-and-conquer method

   D. Process-of-elimination method

7. When gathering symptoms, which step determines whether the problem is at the core, distribution, or access layer of the network?

   A. Step 1: Analyze existing symptoms.
   B. Step 2: Determine ownership.
   C. Step 3: Narrow the scope.
   D. Step 4: Gather symptoms from suspected devices.

8. Which software troubleshooting tool enables network managers to monitor remote devices without actually physically checking them?

   A. NMS tools
   B. Knowledge based
   C. Baselining tools
   D. Protocol analyzers

9. Which software troubleshooting tool displays the physical, data link, protocol, and description of each frame?

   A. NMS tools
   B. Knowledge based
   C. Baselining tools
   D. Protocol analyzers

10. Which hardware troubleshooting tool is used to test and certify copper and fiber cables for different services and standards?

   A. Digital meter
   B. Cable tester
   C. Cable analyzer
   D. Portable network analyzer

WAN Communications

WAN communications consist of a relatively slow connection that all users on a network use to access the Internet. It is also used to connect remote locations and telecommuters. WAN traffic, which consists of voice, video, and data, is forwarded to remote destinations by routers. WAN design is built around connection speeds, number of remote locations, and the type of data sent. WAN traffic characteristics should be analyzed to determine traffic flow conditions and WAN connection speeds. WAN topology is based on the number of remote locations and the way they are connected.

Step 4. View the routes on Site-1:

```
Site-1# show ipv6 route

IPv6 Routing Table - 6 entries
Codes: C - Connected, L - Local, S - Static, R - RIP, B - BGP
       U - Per-user Static route
       I1 - ISIS L1, I2 - ISIS L2, IA - ISIS interarea, IS - ISIS summary
       O - OSPF intra, OI - OSPF inter, OE1 - OSPF ext 1, OE2 - OSPF ext 2
       ON1 - OSPF NSSA ext 1, ON2 - OSPF NSSA ext 2
C   2FFF:B00:C18:3::/64 [0/0]
     via ::, Loopback0
L   2FFF:B00:C18:3::AAAA/128 [0/0]
     via ::, Loopback0
C   3EEE:A00:A18:1::/64 [0/0]
     via ::, Serial0/0/0.1
L   3EEE:A00:A18:1:202:FDFF:FE4B:4FA0/128 [0/0]
     via ::, Serial0/0/0.1
L   FE80::/10 [0/0]
     via ::, Null0
L   FF00::/8 [0/0]
     via ::, Null0
```

Step 5. View the routes on Site-2:

```
Site-2# show ipv6 route

IPv6 Routing Table - 6 entries
Codes: C - Connected, L - Local, S - Static, R - RIP, B - BGP
       U - Per-user Static route
       I1 - ISIS L1, I2 - ISIS L2, IA - ISIS interarea, IS - ISIS summary
       O - OSPF intra, OI - OSPF inter, OE1 - OSPF ext 1, OE2 - OSPF ext 2
       ON1 - OSPF NSSA ext 1, ON2 - OSPF NSSA ext 2
C   2FFF:B00:C18:2::/64 [0/0]
     via ::, Loopback0
L   2FFF:B00:C18:2::AAAA/128 [0/0]
     via ::, Loopback0
C   3EEE:A00:A18:2::/64 [0/0]
     via ::, Serial0/0/1.1
L   3EEE:A00:A18:2:20E:83FF:FE4C:FE40/128 [0/0]
     via ::, Serial0/0/1.1
L   FE80::/10 [0/0]
     via ::, Null0
L   FF00::/8 [0/0]
     via ::, Null0
```

Fill-in-the-Blank Exercise

Fill in the correct answer for each blank with words located in the word bank that follows. Some words may be used multiple times.

Word Bank

voice	partial mesh	traffic	implementation	routers
WAN	latency	traffic type	ISDN	costs
bandwidth	video	star	full mesh	hierarchical
hierarchy	jitter	volume	connection	DSL
data	high-speed			

WANs carry a variety of traffic types such as __________, __________, and __________. __________ determine the most appropriate path to the destination for delivery across the physical WAN connections. When designing a __________, a network technician should know what data traffic must be carried, its origin, and its destination. WANs carry a variety of traffic types with varying requirements for __________, __________, and __________. When all the requirements are established, installation and operational __________ should be determined and compared with business needs. To determine traffic flow conditions, you must analyze the __________ characteristics specific to each LAN that is connected to the WAN. WAN topology considerations include _____, ______________, ______________, and __________. A three-layer __________ is often useful when the network is divided into regions, areas, and branches. WAN connection technologies are usually chosen based on ________________ and __________. Typical __________ types include ISDN, Frame Relay, and leased lines. ______ is an always-on connection, whereas ______ requires the connection to be established before data can be transmitted. Many companies rely on ______________ transfer of data between remote locations. When __________ isn't adequate, competition between different types of ________ causes response times to increase, which reduces employee productivity. Common WAN ______________ issues include reliability, confidentiality, and security.

Network Troubleshooting

A network diagram along with documentation is the only way to properly troubleshoot and diagnose issues within your network. A physical diagram of the network should include device type, make and model, and operating system, just to name a few. A logical diagram of the network should include interface identifiers, connection types, routing protocols, and connection speeds.

When troubleshooting Layer 1 (physical layer), symptoms may include loss of connectivity, high collision rates, and performance lower than the baseline. Possible physical layer problems can be related to hardware, cabling, attenuation, and interface configuration errors.

Isolating problems at the physical layer should include the following steps:

- Checking for bad cables or connections
- Checking that cabling standards are adhered to
- Verifying proper interface configuration

Symptoms of Layer 2 (data link layer) problems include no connectivity at the network layer or above, network performance operating below the baseline, and excessive broadcast and console error messages. Causes of data link layer problems include encapsulation, address mapping, and framing errors and STP failures or loops.

Troubleshooting at Layer 2 involves verifying proper WAN encapsulation and maps. Debugging enables you to troubleshoot association and authentication of WAN links. Frame Relay should be checked for proper encapsulation options, Local Management Interface (LMI) type, and map and permanent virtual circuit (PVC) statements. Spanning Tree Protocol (STP) is an overlooked protocol that operates at the data link layer. STP should be running on all switches and should be disabled only if it is not a part of the physically looped topology. High link utilization and high switch backbone utilization as compared to the baseline indicates that a loop has occurred. After you have determined there is a loop, the next task is to determine what caused it and repair it as quickly as possible.

When troubleshooting Layer 3 (network layer), symptoms may include network failure and performance below the baseline. Troubleshooting Layer 3 problems includes checking for topology changes and routing issues, which may include network relationships and topology database issues.

Layer 4 (transport layer) errors and symptoms may include intermittent network problems, security, and address translation problems. Translation issues could be related to improper Dynamic Host Control Protocol (DHCP) configurations and errors with encryption and tunneling protocols.

Layer 7 (application layer) is the layer closest to the user and includes protocols such as Telnet, HTTP, FTP, and TFTP. Problems with the application layer include complaints about slow application performance and application and console error messages. When troubleshooting the application layer, verify connectivity to the default gateway and verify Network Address Translation (NAT) and access control list (ACL) operation.

Vocabulary Exercise: Define

The following is a list of terms associated with network troubleshooting. Match the concept on the left with the symptoms or processes on the right.

Troubleshooting Concept

- **a.** Troubleshooting Frame Relay
- **b.** Telnet, HTTP, FTP, and TFTP
- **c.** STP symptoms
- **d.** Physical layer symptoms
- **e.** Data link layer problems
- **f.** Troubleshooting PPP
- **g.** Baseline
- **h.** Network layer problems
- **i.** Common ACL issues
- **j.** Common NAT issues

Symptom or Process

__ High link utilization and loss of connectivity to and from affected regions.

__ Authentication and LCP negotiations.

__ Topology changes and neighbor relationships.

__ Tunneling and encryption protocols do not support translations.

__ PVC and map statements.

__ Performance standards of a network.

__ Incorrect port numbers and address and wildcard masks.

__ Application layer protocols.

__ Encapsulation and address mapping errors.

__ High collisions, bottlenecks, or congestion.

Labs and Activities

Activity 8-1: Troubleshooting Role Play (8.3.7)

Upon completion of this activity, you will be able to

- Build a network.
- Test a network.
- Break a network.
- Troubleshoot a problem.
- Gather symptoms.
- Correct the problem.
- Document the problem and solution.

Figure 8-1 shows the network topology for this activity.

Figure 8-1 Network Topology for Activity 8-1

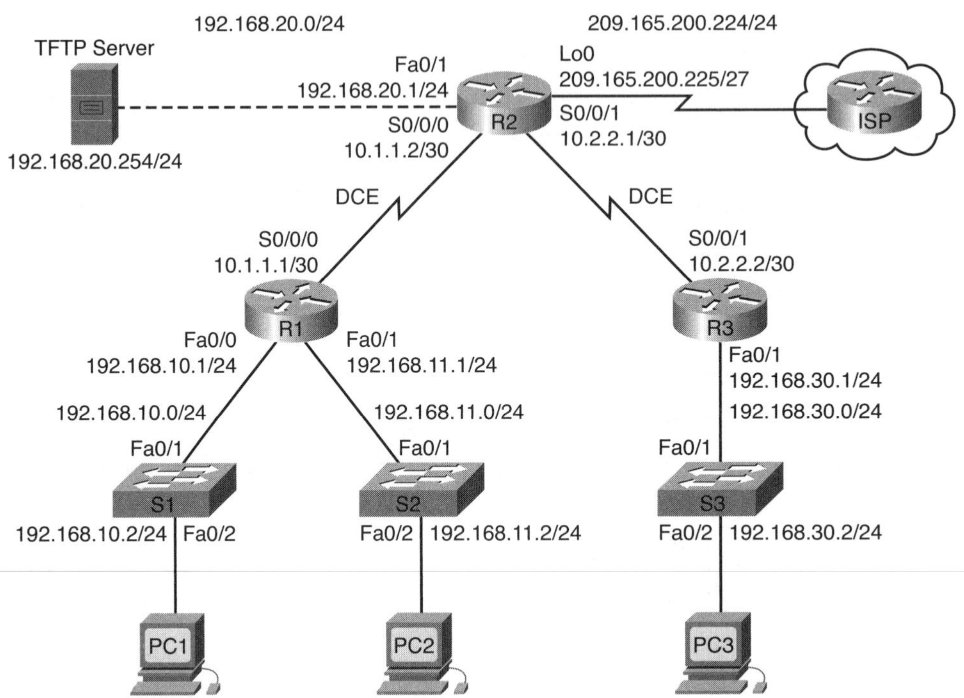

Scenario

In this activity, you and another student build the network displayed in the topology diagram. You configure NAT, DHCP, and OSPF, and then verify connectivity. When the network is fully operational, one student introduces several errors. Then, the other student uses troubleshooting skills to isolate and solve the problem. Then, the students reverse roles and repeat the process. This activity can be done on real equipment or with Packet Tracer.

Task 1: Build the Network

Step 1. Cable and configure devices according to the topology diagram.

Step 2. Configure NAT, DHCP, and OSPF.

Task 2: Test the Network

Step 1. Ensure that you have connectivity from end to end.

Step 2. Verify that DHCP and NAT are working correctly.

Step 3. Become familiar with every device using **show** and **debug** commands.

Task 3: Break the Network

One student leaves the room, if necessary, while the other student breaks the configuration. The break should be the only problem. The idea is to help each other develop troubleshooting skills. Creating multiple problems magnifies the scope of the work, which is not the goal of the lab. The goal is to help you become aware of the various changes that can occur in the network from just one problem.

Task 4: Troubleshoot the Problem

The student returns and questions the other student about the symptoms of the problem. Begin with general questions and attempt to narrow the scope of the problem. When the student being questioned thinks that enough information has been provided, the questioning can stop.

Task 5: Gather Symptoms from Suspect Devices

Begins gathering symptoms using various **show** and **debug** commands. Use the **show running-config** command as the last option.

Task 6: Correct the Problem

Correct the configuration and test the solution.

Task 7: Document the Problem and Solution

Both students should enter the problem in their journal and document the solution.

Task 8: Reverse the Roles and Start Over

The students should now switch roles and start the process over.

Task 9: Clean Up

Erase the configurations and reload the routers. Disconnect and store the cabling. For PC hosts normally connected to other networks, such as the school LAN or to the Internet, reconnect the appropriate cabling and restore the TCP/IP settings.

Lab 8-1: Troubleshooting Enterprise Networks 1 (8.5.1)

Upon completion of this lab, you will be able to

- Cable a network according to the topology diagram in Figure 8-2.
- Erase the startup configuration and reload a router to the default state.
- Load the routers and switches with supplied scripts.
- Find and correct all network errors.
- Document the corrected network.

Figure 8-2 shows the network topology for this lab, and Table 8-1 provides the IP addresses, subnet masks, and default gateways (where applicable) for all devices in the topology.

Figure 8-2 Network Topology for Lab 8-1

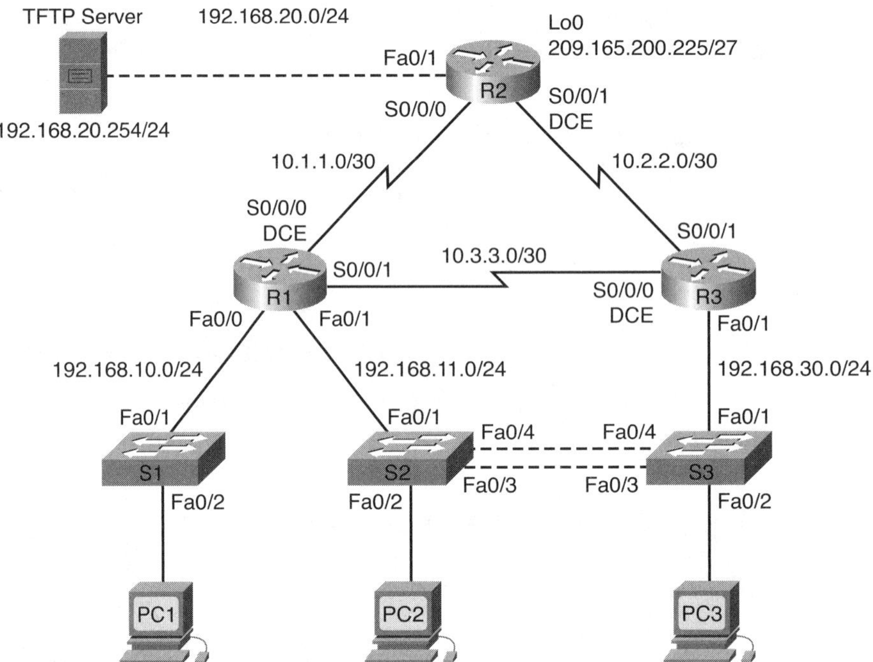

Table 8-1 Lab 8-1 Addressing Table

Device	Interface	IP Address	Subnet Mask	Default Gateway
R1	Fa0/0	192.168.10.1	255.255.255.0	N/A
	Fa0/1	192.168.11.1	255.255.255.0	N/A
	S0/0/0	10.1.1.1	255.255.255.252	N/A
	S0/0/1	10.3.3.1	255.255.255.252	N/A

Device	Interface	IP Address	Subnet Mask	Default Gateway
R2	Fa0/1	192.168.20.1	255.255.255.0	N/A
	S0/0/0	10.1.1.2	255.255.255.252	N/A
	S0/0/1	10.2.2.1	255.255.255.252	N/A
	Lo0	209.165.200.225	255.255.255.224	209.165.200.226
R3	Fa0/1	N/A	N/A	N/A
	Fa0/1.11	192.168.11.3	255.255.255.0	N/A
	Fa0/1.30	192.168.30.1	255.255.255.0	N/A
	S0/0/0	10.3.3.2	255.255.255.252	N/A
	S0/0/1	10.2.2.2	255.255.255.252	N/A
S1	VLAN10	DHCP	255.255.255.0	N/A
S2	VLAN11	192.168.11.2	255.255.255.0	N/A
S3	VLAN30	192.168.30.2	255.255.255.0	N/A
PC1	NIC	192.168.10.10	255.255.255.0	192.168.10.1
PC2	NIC	192.168.11.10	255.255.255.0	192.168.11.1
PC3	NIC	192.168.30.10	255.255.255.0	192.168.30.1
TFTP Server	NIC	192.168.20.254	255.255.255.0	192.168.20.1

Scenario

You have been asked to correct configuration errors in the company network. For this lab, do not use login or password protection on any console lines to prevent accidental lockout. Use **ciscoccna** for all passwords in this scenario.

Note: Because this lab is cumulative, you use all the knowledge and troubleshooting techniques that you have acquired from the previous material to successfully complete this lab.

The requirements for this lab are as follows:

- S2 is the spanning-tree root for VLAN 11, and S3 is the spanning-tree root for VLAN 30.
- S3 is a VTP server with S2 as a client.
- The serial link between R1 and R2 is Frame Relay. Make sure that each router can ping its own Frame Relay interface.
- The serial link between R2 and R3 uses HDLC encapsulation.
- The serial link between R1 and R3 uses PPP.
- The serial link between R1 and R3 is authenticated using CHAP.
- R2 must have secure login procedures because it is the Internet edge router.
- All vty lines, except those belonging to R2, allow connections only from the subnets shown in the topology diagram, excluding the public address.

Hint:

```
R2# telnet 10.1.1.1 /source-interface loopback 0
Trying 10.1.1.1 ...
% Connection refused by remote host
```

- Source IP address spoofing should be prevented on all links that do not connect to other routers.
- Routing protocols must be secured. All RIP routers must use MD5 authentication.
- R3 must not be able to telnet to R2 through the directly connected serial link.
- R3 has access to both VLAN 11 and 30 via its Fast Ethernet port 0/0.
- The TFTP server should not get any traffic that has a source address outside the subnet. All devices have access to the TFTP Server.
- All devices on the 192.168.10.0 subnet must be able to get their IP addresses from DHCP on R1. This includes S1.
- R1 must be accessible via SDM.
- All addresses shown in the diagram must be reachable from every device.

Task 1: Load Routers with the Supplied Scripts

```
!-------------------------------------------
!                   R1
!-------------------------------------------
no service password-encryption
!
hostname R1
!
boot-start-marker
boot-end-marker
!
security passwords min-length 6
enable secret 5 ciscoccna
!
ip cef
!
ip dhcp pool Access1
   network 192.168.10.0 255.255.255.0
   default-router 192.168.10.1
!
no ip domain lookup
!
!
```

```
username R3 password 0 ciscoccna
username ccna password 0 ciscoccna
!
interface FastEthernet0/0
 ip address 192.168.10.1 255.255.255.0
 ip rip authentication mode md5
 ip rip authentication key-chain RIP_KEY
 no shutdown
!
interface FastEthernet0/1
 ip address 192.168.11.1 255.255.255.0
 ip rip authentication mode md5
 ip rip authentication key-chain RIP_KEY
 no shutdown
!
interface Serial0/0/0
 ip address 10.1.1.1 255.255.255.252
 ip rip authentication mode md5
 ip rip authentication key-chain RIP_KEY
 encapsulation frame-relay

 clockrate 128000
 frame-relay map ip 10.1.1.1 201
 frame-relay map ip 10.1.1.2 201 broadcast
 no frame-relay inverse-arp
 no shutdown
!
interface Serial0/0/1
 ip address 10.3.3.1 255.255.255.252
 ip rip authentication mode md5
 ip rip authentication key-chain RIP_KEY
 encapsulation ppp
 ppp authentication chap
 no shutdown
!
!
router rip
 version 2
 passive-interface default
  network 10.1.1.0
 network 192.168.10.0
```

```
 network 192.168.11.0
 no auto-summary
!
ip classless
!
no ip http server
!
ip access-list standard Anti-spoofing
 permit 192.168.10.0 0.0.0.255
 deny  any
ip access-list standard VTY
 permit 10.0.0.0 0.255.255.255
 permit 192.168.10.0 0.0.0.255
 permit 192.168.11.0 0.0.0.255
 permit 192.168.20.0 0.0.0.255
 permit 192.168.30.0 0.0.0.255
!
line con 0
 exec-timeout 0 0
 logging synchronous
line aux 0
line vty 0 4
 access-class VTY in
 login local
!
end
```

```
!-----------------------------------------
!                  R2
!-----------------------------------------
no service password-encryption
!
hostname R2
!
security passwords min-length 6
enable secret ciscoccna
!
aaa new-model
!
aaa authentication login LOCAL_AUTH local
aaa session-id common
!
```

```
ip cef
!
no ip domain lookup
!
key chain RIP_KEY
 key 1
  key-string cisco
username ccna password 0 ciscoccna
!
interface Loopback0
 description Simulated ISP Connection
 ip address 209.165.200.245 255.255.255.224
!
interface FastEthernet0/0
 no ip address
 shutdown
 duplex auto
 speed auto
!
interface FastEthernet0/1
 ip address 192.168.20.1 255.255.255.0
 ip access-group TFTP out
 ip access-group Anti-spoofing in
 ip nat outside
 duplex auto
 speed auto
!
!
interface Serial0/0/0
 ip address 10.1.1.2 255.255.255.0
 ip nat inside
 encapsulation frame-relay
 no keepalive
 frame-relay map ip 10.1.1.1 201 broadcast
 no frame-relay inverse-arp
!
interface Serial0/0/1
 ip address 10.2.2.1 255.255.255.0
 ip access-group R3-telnet in
 ip nat inside
 ip rip authentication mode md5
```

```
 ip rip authentication key-chain RIP_KEY
 clockrate 128000
!
!
router rip
 version 2
 passive-interface default
 no passive-interface Serial0/0/0
 no passive-interface Serial0/0/1
 network 10.0.0.0
 network 192.168.20.0
 default-information originate
 no auto-summary
!
ip classless
ip route 0.0.0.0 0.0.0.0 209.165.200.226
!
no ip http server
ip nat inside source list NAT interface FastEthernet0/0 overload
!
ip access-list standard Anti-spoofing
 permit 192.168.20.0 0.0.0.255
 deny   any
ip access-list standard NAT
 permit 10.0.0.0 0.255.255.255
 permit 192.168.0.0 0.0.255.255
!
ip access-list extended R3-telnet
 deny   tcp host 10.2.2.2 host 10.2.2.1 eq telnet
 deny   tcp host 10.3.3.2 host 10.2.2.1 eq telnet
 deny   tcp host 192.168.11.3 host 10.2.2.1 eq telnet
 deny   tcp host 192.168.30.1 host 10.2.2.1 eq telnet
 permit ip any any
!
ip access-list standard TFTP
 permit 192.168.20.0 0.0.0.255
!
control-plane
!
line con 0
 exec-timeout 0 0
```

```
 logging synchronous
line aux 0
 exec-timeout 15 0
 logging synchronous
 login authentication local_auth
 transport output telnet
line vty 0 4
 exec-timeout 15 0
 logging synchronous
 login authentication local_auth
 transport input telnet
!
end
```

```
!----------------------------------------
!                  R3
!----------------------------------------
no service password-encryption
!
hostname R3
!
security passwords min-length 6
enable secret ciscoccna
!
no aaa new-model
!
ip cef
!
no ip domain lookup
!
key chain RIP_KEY
 key 1
  key-string cisco
username R1 password 0 ciscoccna
username ccna password 0 ciscoccna
!
interface FastEthernet0/1
 no shutdown
!
interface FastEthernet0/1.11
 encapsulation dot1Q 11
ip address 192.168.11.3 255.255.255.0
```

```
 no snmp trap link-status
!
interface FastEthernet0/1.30
 encapsulation dot1Q 30
 ip address 192.168.30.1 255.255.255.0
 ip access-group Anti-spoofing in
 no snmp trap link-status
!
!
interface Serial0/0/0
 ip address 10.3.3.2 255.255.255.252
 encapsulation ppp
 clockrate 125000
 ppp authentication chap
!
interface Serial0/0/1
 ip address 10.2.2.2 255.255.255.252
!
router rip
 version 2
 passive-interface default
 no passive-interface FastEthernet0/1.11
 no passive-interface FastEthernet0/1.30
 no passive-interface Serial0/0/0
 no passive-interface Serial0/0/1
 network 10.0.0.0
 network 192.168.11.0
 network 192.168.30.0
 no auto-summary
!
ip classless
!
ip http server
!
ip access-list standard Anti-spoofing
 permit 192.168.30.0 0.0.0.255
 deny  any
ip access-list standard VTY
 permit 10.0.0.0 0.255.255.255
 permit 192.168.10.0 0.0.0.255
 permit 192.168.11.0 0.0.0.255
```

```
 permit 192.168.20.0 0.0.0.255
 permit 192.168.30.0 0.0.0.255
!
control-plane
!
line con 0
 exec-timeout 0 0
 logging synchronous
line aux 0
 exec-timeout 15 0
 logging synchronous
line vty 0 4
 access-class VTY in
 exec-timeout 15 0
 logging synchronous
 login local
!
end
```

```
!-----------------------------------------
!                 S1
!-----------------------------------------
no service password-encryption
!
hostname S1
!
security passwords min-length 6
enable secret ciscoccna
!
no aaa new-model
vtp domain CCNA_Troubleshooting
vtp mode transparent
vtp password ciscoccna
ip subnet-zero
!
no ip domain-lookup
!
no file verify auto
spanning-tree mode pvst
spanning-tree extend system-id
!
vlan internal allocation policy ascending
!
vlan 10
!
```

```
interface FastEthernet0/1
 switchport access vlan 10
 switchport mode access
!
interface FastEthernet0/2
 switchport access vlan 10
 switchport mode access
!
interface range FastEthernet0/3-24
!
interface GigabitEthernet0/1
 shutdown
!
interface GigabitEthernet0/2
 shutdown
!
interface Vlan1
 no ip address
 no ip route-cache
!
interface Vlan10
 ip address dhcp
 no ip route-cache
!
ip default-gateway 192.168.10.1
ip http server
!
control-plane
!
line con 0
 exec-timeout 0 0
 logging synchronous
line vty 0 4
 password ciscoccna
 login
line vty 5 15
 no login
!
end
```

```
!-----------------------------------------
!                S2
!-----------------------------------------
no service password-encryption
```

```
!
hostname S2
!
security passwords min-length 6
enable secret ciscoccna
!
no aaa new-model
vtp domain CCNA_Troubleshooting
vtp mode transparent
vtp password ciscoccna
ip subnet-zero
!
no ip domain-lookup
!
no file verify auto
!
spanning-tree mode rapid-pvst
spanning-tree extend system-id
spanning-tree vlan 11 priority 24576
spanning-tree vlan 30 priority 28672
!
vlan internal allocation policy ascending
!
interface FastEthernet0/1
 switchport access vlan 11
 switchport mode access
!
interface FastEthernet0/2
 switchport access vlan 11
 switchport mode access
!
interface FastEthernet0/3
 switchport trunk native vlan 99
 switchport trunk allowed vlan 11,30
 switchport mode trunk
!
interface FastEthernet0/4
 switchport trunk native vlan 99
 switchport trunk allowed vlan 11,30
 switchport mode trunk
!
interface range FastEthernet0/5-24
```

```
 shutdown
!
interface GigabitEthernet0/1
 shutdown
!
interface GigabitEthernet0/2
 shutdown
!
interface Vlan1
 no ip address
 no ip route-cache
!
interface Vlan11
 ip address 192.168.11.2 255.255.255.0
 no ip route-cache
!
ip http server
!
control-plane
!
line con 0
 exec-timeout 0 0
 logging synchronous
line vty 0 4
 password ciscoccna
 login
line vty 5 15
 no login
!
end
```

```
!----------------------------------------
!                S3
!----------------------------------------
no service password-encryption
!
hostname S3
!
security passwords min-length 6
enable secret ciscoccna
!
no aaa new-model
vtp domain CCNA_troubleshooting
vtp mode server
vtp password ciscoccna
```

```
ip subnet-zero
!
no ip domain-lookup
!
no file verify auto
!
spanning-tree mode rapid-pvst
spanning-tree extend system-id
spanning-tree vlan 11 priority 28672
spanning-tree vlan 30 priority 24576
!
vlan internal allocation policy ascending
!
!
interface FastEthernet0/1
 switchport trunk allowed vlan 30
 switchport mode trunk
!
interface FastEthernet0/2
 switchport access vlan 30
 switchport mode access
!
interface FastEthernet0/3
 switchport trunk native vlan 99
 switchport trunk allowed vlan 11,30
 switchport mode trunk
!
interface FastEthernet0/4
 switchport trunk native vlan 99
 switchport trunk allowed vlan 11,30
 switchport mode trunk
!
interface range FastEthernet0/5-24
 shutdown
!
interface GigabitEthernet0/1
 shutdown
!
interface GigabitEthernet0/2
 shutdown
!
interface Vlan1
 no ip address
 no ip route-cache
```

```
!
interface Vlan30
 ip address 192.168.30.2 255.255.255.0
 no ip route-cache
!
ip default-gateway 192.168.30.1
ip http server
!
control-plane
!
line con 0
 exec-timeout 5 0
 logging synchronous
line vty 0 4
 password ciscoccna
 login
line vty 5 15
 no login
!
end
```

Task 2: Find and Correct All Network Errors

Task 3: Verify That Requirements Are Fully Met

Because time constraints prevent troubleshooting a problem on each topic, only a select number of topics have problems. However, to reinforce and strengthen troubleshooting skills, you should verify that each requirement is met. To do this, present an example of each requirement (for example, a **show** or **debug** command).

Task 4: Document the Corrected Network

Task 5: Clean Up

Erase the configurations and reload the routers. Disconnect and store the cabling. For PC hosts normally connected to other networks (such as the school LAN or to the Internet), reconnect the appropriate cabling and restore the TCP/IP settings.

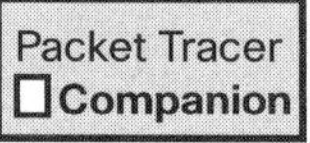

Packet Tracer Companion: Troubleshooting Enterprise Networks 1 (8.5.1)

You can now open the file LSG04-Lab0801.pka on the CD-ROM that accompanies this book to repeat this hands-on lab using Packet Tracer. Remember, however, that Packet Tracer is not a substitute for a hands-on lab experience with real equipment. A summary of the instructions is provided within the activity.

Lab 8-2: Troubleshooting Enterprise Networks 2 (8.5.2)

Upon completion of this lab, you will be able to

- Cable a network according to the topology diagram.
- Erase the startup configuration and reload a router to the default state.
- Load the routers and switches with supplied scripts.
- Find and correct all network errors.
- Document the corrected network.

Figure 8-3 shows the network topology for this lab, and Table 8-2 provides the IP addresses, subnet masks, and default gateways (where applicable) for all devices in the topology.

Figure 8-3 Network Topology for Lab 8-2

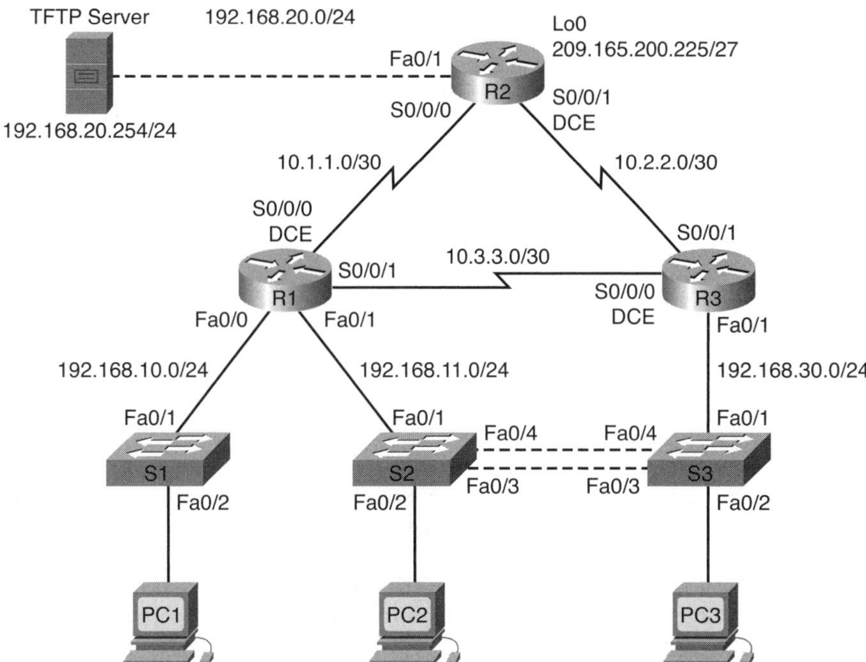

Table 8-2 Lab 8-2 Addressing Table

Device	Interface	IP Address	Subnet Mask	Default Gateway
R1	Fa0/0	192.168.10.1	255.255.255.0	N/A
	Fa0/1	192.168.11.1	255.255.255.0	N/A
	S0/0/0	10.1.1.1	255.255.255.252	N/A
	S0/0/1	10.3.3.1	255.255.255.252	N/A

continues

Table 8-2 Lab 8-2 Addressing Table *continued*

Device	Interface	IP Address	Subnet Mask	Default Gateway
R2	Fa0/1	192.168.20.1	255.255.255.0	N/A
	S0/0/0	10.1.1.2	255.255.255.252	N/A
	S0/0/1	10.2.2.1	255.255.255.252	N/A
	Lo0	209.165.200.225	255.255.255.224	209.165.200.226
R3	Fa0/1	N/A	N/A	N/A
	Fa0/1.11	192.168.11.3	255.255.255.0	N/A
	Fa0/1.30	192.168.30.1	255.255.255.0	N/A
	S0/0/0	10.3.3.2	255.255.255.252	N/A
	S0/0/1	10.2.2.2	255.255.255.252	N/A
S1	VLAN10	DHCP	N/A	N/A
S2	VLAN11	192.168.11.2	255.255.255.0	N/A
S3	VLAN30	192.168.30.2	255.255.255.0	N/A
PC1	NIC	DHCP	N/A	N/A
PC2	NIC	192.168.11.10	255.255.255.0	192.168.11.1
PC3	NIC	192.168.30.10	255.255.255.0	192.168.30.1
TFTP Server	NIC	192.168.20.254	255.255.255.0	192.168.20.1

Scenario

For this lab, do not use login or password protection on any console lines to prevent accidental lock-out. Use **ciscoccna** for all passwords in this lab.

Because this lab is cumulative, you use all the knowledge and troubleshooting techniques that you have acquired from the previous material to successfully complete this lab.

The requirements for this lab are as follows:

- S2 is the spanning-tree root for VLAN 11, and S3 is the spanning-tree root for VLAN 30.
- S3 is a VTP server with S2 as a client.
- The serial link between R1 and R2 is Frame Relay.
- The serial link between R2 and R3 uses HDLC encapsulation.
- The serial link between R1 and R3 is authenticated using CHAP.
- R2 must have secure login procedures because it is the Internet edge router.
- All vty lines, except those belonging to R2, allow connections only from the subnets shown in the topology diagram, excluding the public address.
- Source IP address spoofing should be prevented on all links that do not connect to other routers.
- Routing protocols must be used securely. EIGRP is used in this scenario.

- R3 must not be able to telnet to R2 through the directly connected serial link.
- R3 has access to both VLAN 11 and 30 via its Fast Ethernet port 0/1.
- The TFTP Server should not get any traffic that has a source address outside the subnet. All devices have access to the TFTP Server.
- All devices on the 192.168.10.0 subnet must be able to get their IP addresses from DHCP on R1. This includes S1.
- All addresses shown in diagram must be reachable from every device.

Task 1: Load Routers with the Supplied Scripts

```
!----------------------------------------
!                  R1
!----------------------------------------
no service password-encryption
!
hostname R1
!
boot-start-marker
boot-end-marker
!
security passwords min-length 6
enable secret ciscoccna
!
ip cef
!
ip dhcp pool Access1
   network 192.168.10.0 255.255.255.0
   default-router 192.168.10.1
!
no ip domain lookup
frame-relay switching
!
username R2 password ciscoccna
username ccna password ciscoccna
!
interface FastEthernet0/0
 ip address 192.168.10.1 255.255.255.0
 ip access-group Anti-spoofing out
 duplex auto
 speed auto
 no shutdown
!
interface FastEthernet0/1
 ip address 192.168.11.1 255.255.255.0
```

```
 duplex auto
 speed auto
 no shutdown
!
interface Serial0/0/0
 ip address 10.1.1.1 255.255.255.252
 encapsulation frame-relay
 no keepalive
 clockrate 128000
 frame-relay map ip 10.1.1.1 201
 frame-relay map ip 10.1.1.2 201 broadcast
 no frame-relay inverse-arp
 frame-relay intf-type dce
 no shutdown
!
interface Serial0/0/1
 ip address 10.3.3.1 255.255.255.0
 encapsulation ppp
 ppp authentication chap
 no shutdown
!
interface Serial0/1/0
 no ip address
 shutdown
 clockrate 2000000
!
interface Serial0/1/1
 no ip address
 shutdown
!
router eigrp 10
 passive-interface default
 no passive-interface FastEthernet0/0
 no passive-interface FastEthernet0/1
 no passive-interface Serial0/0/0
 no passive-interface Serial0/0/1
 network 10.1.1.0 0.0.0.255
 network 10.2.2.0 0.0.0.255
 network 192.168.10.0 0.0.0.255
 network 192.168.11.0 0.0.0.255
 no auto-summary
!
ip route 0.0.0.0 0.0.0.0 10.1.1.2
!
```

```
ip http server
!
ip access-list standard Anti-spoofing
 permit 192.168.10.0 0.0.0.255
 deny   any
ip access-list standard VTY
 permit 10.0.0.0 0.255.255.255
 permit 192.168.10.0 0.0.0.255
 permit 192.168.11.0 0.0.0.255
 permit 192.168.20.0 0.0.0.255
 permit 192.168.30.0 0.0.0.255
!
line con 0
 exec-timeout 5 0
 logging synchronous
line aux 0
line vty 0 4
 access-class VTY in
 login local
!
end
```

```
!-----------------------------------------
!                   R2
!-----------------------------------------
no service password-encryption
!
hostname R2
!
security passwords min-length 6
enable secret ciscoccna
!
aaa new-model
!
aaa authentication login local_auth local
aaa session-id common
!
ip cef
!
no ip domain lookup
!
username ccna password 0 ciscoccna
!
interface Loopback0
 ip address 209.165.200.225 255.255.255.224
```

```
 ip access-group private in
!
interface FastEthernet0/1
 ip address 192.168.20.1 255.255.255.0
 ip access-group TFTP out
 ip access-group Anti-spoofing in
 ip nat outside
 no shutdown
!
!
interface Serial0/0/0
 ip address 10.1.1.2 255.255.255.252
 ip nat inside
 encapsulation frame-relay
 no keepalive
 frame-relay map ip 10.1.1.1 201 broadcast
 frame-relay map ip 10.1.1.2 201
 no frame-relay inverse-arp
 no shutdown
!
interface Serial0/0/1
 ip address 10.2.2.1 255.255.255.252
 ip nat inside
 clockrate 128000
 no shutdown
!
!
router eigrp 100
 passive-interface default
 no passive-interface FastEthernet0/1
 no passive-interface Serial0/0/0
 no passive-interface Serial0/0/1
 no passive interface lo0
 network 10.1.1.0 0.0.0.3
 network 10.2.2.0 0.0.0.3
 network 192.168.20.0 0.0.0.255
network 209.165.200.0 0.0.0.7
 no auto-summary
!
ip route 0.0.0.0 0.0.0.0 209.165.200.226
!
no ip http server
ip nat inside source list NAT interface FastEthernet0/0 overload
!
```

```
ip access-list standard Anti-spoofing
 permit 192.168.20.0 0.0.0.255
 deny   any
ip access-list standard NAT
 permit 10.0.0.0 0.255.255.255
 permit 192.168.0.0 0.0.255.255
ip access-list standard private
 deny   127.0.0.1
 deny   10.0.0.0 0.255.255.255
 deny   172.16.0.0 0.15.255.255
 deny   192.168.0.0 0.0.255.255
 permit any
!
ip access-list extended R3-telnet
 deny   tcp host 10.2.2.2 host 10.2.2.1 eq telnet
 deny   tcp host 10.3.3.2 host 10.2.2.1 eq telnet
 deny   tcp host 192.168.11.3 host 10.2.2.1 eq telnet
 deny   tcp host 192.168.30.1 host 10.2.2.1 eq telnet
!
ip access-list standard TFTP
 permit 192.168.20.0 0.0.0.255
!
control-plane
!
line con 0
 exec-timeout 5 0
 logging synchronous
line aux 0
 exec-timeout 15 0
 logging synchronous
 login authentication local_auth
 transport output telnet
line vty 0 4
 exec-timeout 15 0
 logging synchronous
 login authentication local_auth
 transport input telnet
!
end
```

```
!-----------------------------------------
!                  R3
!-----------------------------------------
no service password-encryption
!
```

```
hostname R3
!
security passwords min-length 6
!
no aaa new-model
!
ip cef
!
no ip domain lookup
!
username R1 password ciscoccna
username ccna password  ciscoccna
!
interface FastEthernet0/1
 no shutdown
!
interface FastEthernet0/1.11
 encapsulation dot1Q 11
 ip address 192.168.11.3 255.255.255.0
 no snmp trap link-status
!
interface FastEthernet0/1.30
 encapsulation dot1Q 30
 ip address 192.168.30.1 255.255.255.0
 ip access-group Anti-Spoofin in
  no shutdown
!
!
interface Serial0/0/0
 ip address 10.3.3.2 255.255.255.252
 encapsulation ppp
 ppp authentication pap
!
interface Serial0/0/1
 ip address 10.2.2.2 255.255.255.252
 no shutdown
!
router eigrp 10
 network 10.3.3.0 0.0.0.3
 network 10.2.2.0 0.0.0.3
 network 192.168.11.0 0.0.0.255
 network 192.168.30.0 0.0.0.255
 no auto-summary
!
```

```
ip classless
!
ip http server
!
ip access-list standard Anti-spoofing
 permit 192.168.30.0 0.0.0.255
 deny   any
ip access-list standard VTY
 permit 10.0.0.0 0.255.255.255
 permit 192.168.10.0 0.0.0.255
 permit 192.168.11.0 0.0.0.255
 permit 192.168.20.0 0.0.0.255
 permit 192.168.30.0 0.0.0.255
!
!
line con 0
 exec-timeout 5 0
 logging synchronous
line aux 0
 exec-timeout 15 0
 logging synchronous
line vty 0 4
 access-class VTY out
 exec-timeout 15 0
 logging synchronous
 login local
!
end
```

```
!-----------------------------------------
!                S1
!-----------------------------------------
no service password-encryption
!
hostname S1
!
security passwords min-length 6
enable secret ciscoccna
!
no aaa new-model
vtp domain CCNA_Troubleshooting
vtp mode transparent
vtp password ciscoccna
ip subnet-zero
!
```

```
no ip domain-lookup
!
no file verify auto
spanning-tree mode pvst
spanning-tree extend system-id
!
vlan internal allocation policy ascending
!
vlan 10
!
interface FastEthernet0/1
 switchport access vlan 10
 switchport mode access
!
interface FastEthernet0/2
 switchport access vlan 10
 switchport mode access
!
interface range FastEthernet0/3-24
!
interface GigabitEthernet0/1
 shutdown
!
interface GigabitEthernet0/2
 shutdown
!
interface Vlan1
 no ip address
 no ip route-cache
!
interface Vlan10
 ip address dhcp
 no ip route-cache
!
ip default-gateway 192.168.10.1
ip http server
!
line con 0
 exec-timeout 5 0
 logging synchronous
line vty 0 4
 password ciscoccna
 login
line vty 5 15
```

```
 no login
!
end
```

```
!----------------------------------------
!                S2
!----------------------------------------
no service pad
service timestamps debug uptime
service timestamps log uptime
no service password-encryption
!
hostname S2
!
security passwords min-length 6
enable secret ciscoccna
!
no aaa new-model
vtp domain CCNA_Troubleshooting
vtp mode Client
vtp password ciscoccna
ip subnet-zero
!
no ip domain-lookup
!
no file verify auto
!
spanning-tree mode mst
spanning-tree extend system-id
spanning-tree vlan 30 priority 4096
!
vlan internal allocation policy ascending
!
interface FastEthernet0/1
 switchport access vlan 11
 switchport mode access
!
interface FastEthernet0/2
 switchport access vlan 11
 switchport mode access
!
interface FastEthernet0/3
 switchport trunk allowed vlan 11,30
 switchport mode trunk
!
```

```
interface FastEthernet0/4
 switchport trunk allowed vlan 11,30
 switchport mode trunk
!
interface range FastEthernet0/5-24
 shutdown
!
interface GigabitEthernet0/1
 shutdown
!
interface GigabitEthernet0/2
 shutdown
!
interface Vlan1
 no ip address
 no ip route-cache
!
interface Vlan11
 ip address 192.168.11.2 255.255.255.0
 no ip route-cache
!
ip http server
!
control-plane
!
line con 0
 exec-timeout 5 0
 logging synchronous
line vty 0 4
 password ciscoccna
 login
line vty 5 15
 no login
!
end
```

```
!-----------------------------------------
!                 S3
!-----------------------------------------
no service password-encryption
!
hostname S3
!
security passwords min-length 6
enable secret ciscoccna
```

```
!
no aaa new-model
vtp domain CCNA_Troubleshooting
vtp mode Server
vtp password ciscoccna
ip subnet-zero
!
no ip domain-lookup
!
no file verify auto
!
spanning-tree mode rapid-pvst
spanning-tree extend system-id
spanning-tree vlan 11 priority 4096
vlan internal allocation policy ascending
!
Vlan 11,30
!
interface FastEthernet0/1
 switchport trunk allowed vlan 11,30
 switchport mode trunk
!
interface FastEthernet0/2
 switchport access vlan 30
 switchport mode access
!
interface FastEthernet0/3

 switchport trunk allowed vlan 11,30
 switchport mode trunk
!
interface FastEthernet0/4
 switchport trunk allowed vlan 11,30
 switchport mode trunk
!
interface range FastEthernet0/5-24
 shutdown
!
interface GigabitEthernet0/1
 shutdown
!
interface GigabitEthernet0/2
 shutdown
!
```

```
interface Vlan1
 no ip address
 no ip route-cache
!
interface Vlan30
 ip address 192.168.30.2 255.255.255.0
 no ip route-cache
!
ip default-gateway 192.168.30.1
ip http server
!
line con 0
 exec-timeout 5 0
 logging synchronous
line vty 0 4
 password ciscoccna
 login
line vty 5 15
 no login
!
end
```

Task 2: Find and Correct All Network Errors

Task 3: Verify That Requirements Are Fully Met

Because time constraints prevent troubleshooting a problem on each topic, only a select number of topics have problems. However, to reinforce and strengthen troubleshooting skills, you should verify that each requirement is met. To do this, present an example of each requirement (for example, a **show** or **debug** command).

Task 4: Document the Corrected Network

Task 5: Clean Up

Erase the configurations and reload the routers. Disconnect and store the cabling. For PC hosts normally connected to other networks (such as the school LAN or to the Internet), reconnect the appropriate cabling and restore the TCP/IP settings.

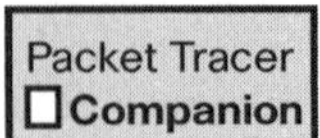

Packet Tracer Companion: Troubleshooting Enterprise Networks 2 (8.5.2)

You can now open the file LSG04-Lab0802.pka on the CD-ROM that accompanies this book to repeat this hands-on lab using Packet Tracer. Remember, however, that Packet Tracer is not a substitute for a hands-on lab experience with real equipment. A summary of the instructions is provided within the activity.

Lab 8-3: Troubleshooting Enterprise Networks 3 (8.5.3)

Upon completion of this lab, you will be able to

- Cable a network according to the topology diagram.
- Erase the startup configuration and reload a router to the default state.
- Load the routers and switches with supplied scripts.
- Find and correct all network errors.
- Document the corrected network.

Figure 8-4 shows the network topology for this lab, and Table 8-3 provides the IP addresses, subnet masks, and default gateways (where applicable) for all devices in the topology.

Figure 8-4 Network Topology for Lab 8-3

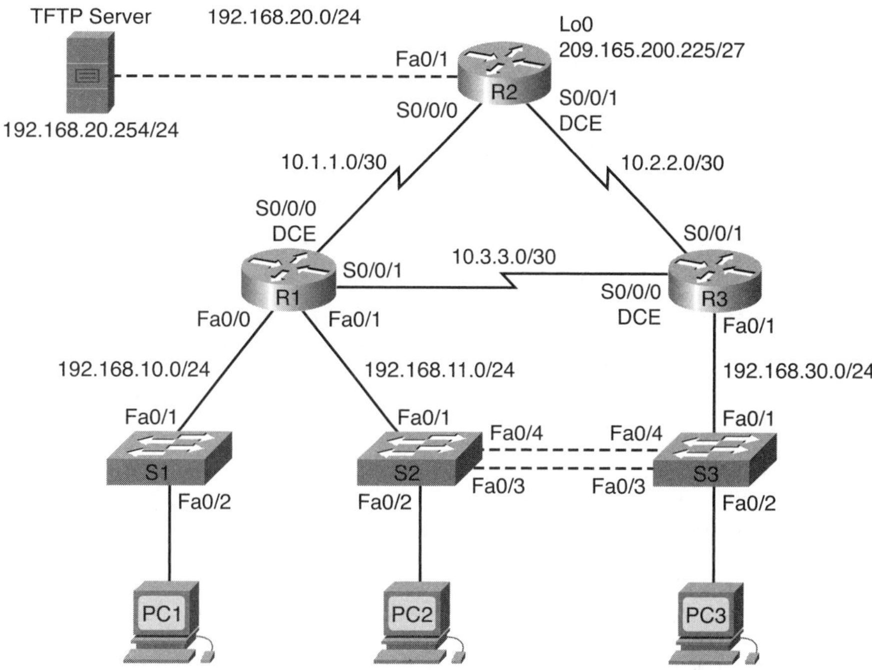

Table 8-3 Lab 8-3 Addressing Table

Device	Interface	IP Address	Subnet Mask	Default Gateway
R1	Fa0/0	192.168.10.1	255.255.255.0	N/A
	Fa0/1	192.168.11.1	255.255.255.0	N/A
	S0/0/0	10.1.1.1	255.255.255.252	N/A
	S0/0/1	10.3.3.1	255.255.255.252	N/A

continues

Table 8-3 Lab 8-3 Addressing Table *continued*

Device	Interface	IP Address	Subnet Mask	Default Gateway
R2	Fa0/1	192.168.20.1	255.255.255.0	N/A
	S0/0/0	10.1.1.2	255.255.255.252	N/A
	S0/0/1	10.2.2.1	255.255.255.252	N/A
	Lo0	209.165.200.225	255.255.255.224	209.165.200.226
R3	Fa0/1	N/A	N/A	N/A
	Fa0/1.11	192.168.11.3	255.255.255.0	N/A
	Fa0/1.30	192.168.30.1	255.255.255.0	N/A
	S0/0/0	10.3.3.2	255.255.255.252	N/A
	S0/0/1	10.2.2.2	255.255.255.252	N/A
S1	VLAN10	DHCP	255.255.255.0	N/A
S2	VLAN11	192.168.11.2	255.255.255.0	N/A
S3	VLAN30	192.168.30.2	255.255.255.0	N/A
PC1	NIC	192.168.10.10	255.255.255.0	192.168.10.1
PC2	NIC	192.168.11.10	255.255.255.0	192.168.11.1
PC3	NIC	192.168.30.10	255.255.255.0	192.168.30.1
TFTP Server	NIC	192.168.20.254	255.255.255.0	192.168.20.1

Scenario

For this lab, do not use login or password protection on any console lines to prevent accidental lockout. Use **ciscoccna** for all passwords in this scenario.

Because this lab is cumulative, you use all the knowledge and troubleshooting techniques that you have acquired from the previous material to successfully complete this lab.

The requirements for this lab are as follows:

- S2 is the spanning-tree root for VLAN 11, and S3 is the spanning-tree root for VLAN 30.
- S3 is a VTP server with S2 as a client.
- The serial link between R1 and R2 is Frame Relay.
- The serial link between R2 and R3 uses HDLC encapsulation.
- The serial link between R1 and R3 is authenticated using CHAP.
- R2 must have secure login procedures because it is the Internet edge router.
- All vty lines, except those belonging to R2, allow connections only from the subnets shown in the topology diagram, excluding the public address.
- Source IP address spoofing should be prevented on all links that do not connect to other routers.
- Routing protocols must be used securely. OSPF is used in this scenario.

- R3 must not be able to telnet to R2 through the directly connected serial link.
- R3 has access to both VLAN 11 and 30 via its Fast Ethernet port 0/1.
- The TFTP Server should not get any traffic that has a source address outside the subnet. All devices have access to the TFTP Server.
- All devices on the 192.168.10.0 subnet must be able to get their IP addresses from DHCP on R1. This includes S1.
- All addresses shown in diagram must be reachable from every device.

Task 1: Load Routers with the Supplied Scripts

```
!-----------------------------------------
!                  R1
!-----------------------------------------
no service password-encryption
!
hostname R1
!
boot-start-marker
boot-end-marker
!
security passwords min-length 6
enable secret ciscoccna
!
ip cef
!
ip dhcp pool Access1
   network 192.168.11.0 255.255.255.0
   default-router 192.168.10.1
!
no ip domain lookup
!
ip dhcp excluded-address 192.168.10.2 192.168.10.254
!
frame-relay switching
!
username R3 password 0 ciscoccna
username ccna password 0 ciscoccna
!
interface FastEthernet0/0
 ip address 192.168.10.1 255.255.255.0
 duplex auto
 speed auto
 no shutdown
!
```

```
interface FastEthernet0/1
 ip address 192.168.11.1 255.255.255.0
 duplex auto
 speed auto
no shutdown
!
interface Serial0/0/0
 ip address 10.1.1.1 255.255.255.252
 encapsulation frame-relay
 no keepalive
 clockrate 128000
 frame-relay map ip 10.1.1.1 201
 frame-relay map ip 10.1.1.2 201 broadcast
 no frame-relay inverse-arp
 frame-relay intf-type dce
 no shutdown
!
interface Serial0/0/1
 ip address 10.3.3.1 255.255.255.252
 encapsulation ppp
 ppp authentication chap
 no shutdown
!
interface Serial0/1/0
 no ip address
 shutdown
 clockrate 2000000
!
interface Serial0/1/1
 no ip address
 shutdown
!
router ospf 1
 log-adjacency-changes
 passive-interface FastEthernet0/0
 network 10.1.1.0 0.0.0.255 area 0
 network 10.2.2.0 0.0.0.255 area 0
 network 192.168.10.0 0.0.0.255 area 0
 network 192.168.11.0 0.0.0.255 area 0
!
ip http server
!
ip access-list standard Anti-spoofing
 permit 192.168.10.0 0.0.0.255
```

```
 deny   any
ip access-list standard VTY
 permit 10.0.0.0 0.255.255.255
 permit 192.168.10.0 0.0.0.255
 permit 192.168.11.0 0.0.0.255
 permit 192.168.20.0 0.0.0.255
 permit 192.168.30.0 0.0.0.255
!
line con 0
 exec-timeout 5 0
 logging synchronous
line aux 0
line vty 0 4
 access-class VTY in
 login local
!
end
```

```
!-----------------------------------------
!                  R2
!-----------------------------------------
no service password-encryption
!
hostname R2
!
security passwords min-length 6
enable secret ciscoccna
!
aaa new-model
!
aaa authentication login local_auth local
aaa session-id common
!
ip cef
!
no ip domain lookup
!
username ccna password 0 ciscoccna
!
interface Loopback0
 ip address 209.165.200.245 255.255.255.224
 ip access-group private in
!
interface FastEthernet0/1
 ip address 192.168.20.1 255.255.255.0
```

```
 ip access-group TFTP out
 ip access-group Anti-spoofing in
 ip nat inside
 duplex auto
 speed auto
!
!
interface Serial0/0/0
 ip address 10.1.1.2 255.255.255.252
 ip nat outside
 encapsulation frame-relay
 no keepalive
 frame-relay map ip 10.1.1.1 201 broadcast
 frame-relay map ip 10.1.1.2 201
 no frame-relay inverse-arp
!
interface Serial0/0/1
 ip address 10.2.2.1 255.255.255.252
 ip access-group R3-telnet in
 ip nat outside
!
!
router ospf 1
 passive-interface FastEthernet0/1
 network 10.1.1.0 0.0.0.3 area 0
 network 10.2.2.0 0.0.0.3 area 0

!
ip classless
ip route 0.0.0.0 0.0.0.0 209.165.200.226
!
no ip http server
ip nat inside source list nat interface FastEthernet0/0
!
ip access-list standard Anti-spoofing
 permit 192.168.20.0 0.0.0.255
 deny   any
ip access-list standard NAT
 permit 10.0.0.0 0.255.255.255
 permit 192.168.0.0 0.0.255.255
ip access-list standard private
 deny   127.0.0.1
 deny   10.0.0.0 0.255.255.255
 deny   172.0.0.0 0.31.255.255
```

```
 deny   192.168.0.0 0.0.255.255
 permit any
!
ip access-list extended R3-telnet
 deny   tcp host 10.2.2.2 host 10.2.2.1 eq telnet
 deny   tcp host 10.3.3.2 host 10.2.2.1 eq telnet
 deny   tcp host 192.168.11.3 host 10.2.2.1 eq telnet
 deny   tcp host 192.168.30.1 host 10.2.2.1 eq telnet
 permit ip any any
!
ip access-list standard TFTP
 permit 192.168.20.0 0.0.0.255
!
line con 0
 exec-timeout 5 0
 logging synchronous
line aux 0
 exec-timeout 15 0
 logging synchronous
 login authentication local_auth
 transport output telnet
line vty 0 4
 exec-timeout 15 0
 logging synchronous
 login authentication local_auth
 transport input telnet
!
end
```

```
!-------------------------------------------
!                  R3
!-------------------------------------------
no service password-encryption
!
hostname R3
!
security passwords min-length 6
enable secret ciscoccna
!
no aaa new-model
!
ip cef
!
no ip domain lookup
!
```

```
username R1 password ciscoccna
username ccna password ciscoccna
!
interface FastEthernet0/1
 no ip address
 duplex auto
 speed auto
 no shutdown
!
interface FastEthernet0/1.11
 encapsulation dot1Q 12
 ip address 192.168.11.3 255.255.255.0
 no snmp trap link-status
!
interface FastEthernet0/1.30
 encapsulation dot1Q 30
 ip address 192.168.30.1 255.255.255.0
 ip access-group Anti-spoofing in
!
!
interface Serial0/0/0
 ip address 10.3.3.2 255.255.255.252
 encapsulation ppp
 clockrate 125000
 ppp authentication chap
 no shutdown
!
interface Serial0/0/1
 ip address 10.2.2.2 255.255.255.252
 encapsulation lapb
 no shutdown
!
router ospf 1
 passive-interface FastEthernet0/1.30
 network 10.2.2.0 0.0.0.3 area 1
 network 10.3.3.0 0.0.0.3 area 1
 network 192.168.11.0 0.0.0.255 area 1
 network 192.168.30.0 0.0.0.255 area 1
!
ip classless
!
ip http server
!
ip access-list standard Anti-spoofing
```

```
 permit 192.168.30.0 0.0.0.255
 deny   any
ip access-list standard VTY
 permit 10.0.0.0 0.255.255.255
 permit 192.168.10.0 0.0.0.255
 permit 192.168.11.0 0.0.0.255
 permit 192.168.20.0 0.0.0.255
 permit 192.168.30.0 0.0.0.255
!
line con 0
 exec-timeout 5 0
 logging synchronous
line aux 0
 exec-timeout 15 0
 logging synchronous
line vty 0 4
 access-class VTY in
 exec-timeout 15 0
 logging synchronous
 login local
!
end
```

```
!----------------------------------------
!                S1
!----------------------------------------
no service password-encryption
!
hostname S1
!
security passwords min-length 6
enable secret ciscoccna
!
no aaa new-model
vtp domain CCNA_Troubleshooting
vtp mode transparent
vtp password ciscoccna
ip subnet-zero
!
no ip domain-lookup
!
no file verify auto
spanning-tree mode pvst
spanning-tree extend system-id
!
```

```
vlan internal allocation policy ascending
!
vlan 10
!
interface FastEthernet0/1
 switchport access vlan 10
 switchport mode access
!
interface FastEthernet0/2
 switchport access vlan 10
 switchport mode access
!
interface range FastEthernet0/3-24
!
interface GigabitEthernet0/1
 shutdown
!
interface GigabitEthernet0/2
 shutdown
!
interface Vlan1
 no ip address
 no ip route-cache
!
interface Vlan10
 ip address dhcp
 no ip route-cache
!
ip default-gateway 192.168.10.1
ip http server
!
line con 0
 exec-timeout 5 0
 logging synchronous
line vty 0 4
 password ciscoccna
 login
line vty 5 15
 no login
!
end
```

```
!----------------------------------------
!                 S2
!----------------------------------------
```

```
no service pad
service timestamps debug uptime
service timestamps log uptime
no service password-encryption
!
hostname S2
!
security passwords min-length 6
enable secret ciscoccna
!
no aaa new-model
vtp domain CCNA_Troubleshooting
vtp mode client
vtp password ciscoccna
ip subnet-zero
!
no ip domain-lookup
!
no file verify auto
!
spanning-tree mode rapid-pvst
spanning-tree extend system-id
spanning-tree vlan 11 priority 24576
spanning-tree vlan 30 priority 28672
!
vlan internal allocation policy ascending
!
interface FastEthernet0/1
 switchport access vlan 11
 switchport mode access
!
interface FastEthernet0/2
 switchport access vlan 11
 switchport mode access
!
interface FastEthernet0/3
 switchport trunk allowed vlan 11,30
 switchport mode trunk
!
interface FastEthernet0/4
 switchport trunk allowed vlan 11,30
 switchport mode trunk
!
interface range FastEthernet0/5-24
```

```
 shutdown
!
interface GigabitEthernet0/1
 shutdown
!
interface GigabitEthernet0/2
 shutdown
!
interface Vlan1
 no ip address
 no ip route-cache
!
interface Vlan11
 ip address 192.168.11.2 255.255.255.0
 no ip route-cache
!
ip http server
!
line con 0
 exec-timeout 5 0
 logging synchronous
line vty 0 4
 password ciscoccna
 login
line vty 5 15
 no login
!
end
```

```
!-----------------------------------------
!                 S3
!-----------------------------------------
no service password-encryption
!
hostname S3
!
security passwords min-length 6
enable secret ciscoccna
!
no aaa new-model
vtp domain CCNA_Troubleshooting
vtp mode Server
vtp password ciscoccna
ip subnet-zero
!
```

```
no ip domain-lookup
!
no file verify auto
!
spanning-tree mode rapid-pvst
spanning-tree extend system-id
spanning-tree vlan 11 priority 28672
spanning-tree vlan 30 priority 24576
!
vlan internal allocation policy ascending
!
vlan 30
!
interface FastEthernet0/1
 switchport trunk allowed vlan 11
 switchport mode trunk
!
interface FastEthernet0/2
 switchport access vlan 30
 switchport mode access
!
interface FastEthernet0/3
 switchport trunk native vlan 99
 switchport trunk allowed vlan 11,30
 switchport mode trunk
!
interface FastEthernet0/4
 switchport trunk native vlan 99
 switchport trunk allowed vlan 11,30
 switchport mode trunk
!
interface range FastEthernet0/5-24
 shutdown
!
interface GigabitEthernet0/1
 shutdown
!
interface GigabitEthernet0/2
 shutdown
!
interface Vlan1
 no ip address
 no ip route-cache
!
```

```
interface Vlan30
 ip address 192.168.30.2 255.255.255.0
 no ip route-cache
!
ip default-gateway 192.168.30.1
ip http server
!
line con 0
 exec-timeout 5 0
 logging synchronous
line vty 0 4
 password ciscoccna
 login
line vty 5 15
 no login
!
end
```

Task 2: Find and Correct All Network Errors

Task 3: Verify That Requirements Are Fully Met

Because time constraints prevent troubleshooting a problem on each topic, only a select number of topics have problems. However, to reinforce and strengthen troubleshooting skills, you should verify that each requirement is met. To do this, present an example of each requirement (for example, a **show** or **debug** command).

Task 4: Document the Corrected Network

Task 5: Clean Up

Erase the configurations and reload the routers. Disconnect and store the cabling. For PC hosts normally connected to other networks (such as the school LAN or to the Internet), reconnect the appropriate cabling and restore the TCP/IP settings.

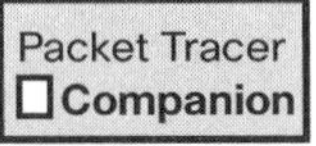

Packet Tracer Companion: Troubleshooting Enterprise Networks 3 (8.5.3)

You can now open the file LSG04-Lab0803.pka on the CD-ROM that accompanies this book to repeat this hands-on lab using Packet Tracer. Remember, however, that Packet Tracer is not a substitute for a hands-on lab experience with real equipment. A summary of the instructions is provided within the activity.

Packet Tracer Exercise 8-1: Comprehensive Network Troubleshooting

Here is an extra activity on documenting and troubleshooting networks to run using Packet Tracer. Open the file lsg04-0804.pka on the CD-ROM that accompanies this book to do this activity. Detailed instructions are provided within the activity file.

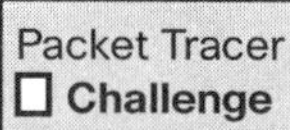

Packet Tracer Skills Integration Challenge

Open file LSG04-PTSkills8.pka on the CD-ROM that accompanies this book to perform this exercise using Packet Tracer. Upon completion of this skills integration challenge, you will be able to

- Configure Frame Relay in a hub-and-spoke topology.
- Configure PPP with CHAP and PAP authentication.
- Configure static and dynamic NAT.
- Configure static and default routing.

In this comprehensive CCNA skills activity, the XYZ Corporation uses a combination of Frame Relay and PPP for WAN connections. The HQ router provides access to the server farm and the Internet through NAT. HQ also uses a basic firewall ACL to filter inbound traffic. Each branch router is configured for inter-VLAN routing and DHCP. Routing is achieved through EIGRP and static and default routes. The VLANs, VTP, and STP are configured on each of the switched networks. Port security is enabled, and wireless access is provided. Your job is to successfully implement all of these technologies, leveraging what you have learned over the four Exploration courses leading up to this culminating activity.

Figure 8-5 shows the network topology for this skills integration challenge.

Table 8-4 provides the IP addresses, subnet masks, and data-link connection identifier (DLCI) mappings for all the HQ router interfaces in the topology. Table 8-5 provides the IP addresses and subnet masks for the branch router interfaces. Table 8-6 provides the VLAN configuration and port mappings for the topology.

Table 8-4 Addressing Table for HQ

HQ Router Interface	IP Address	Subnet Mask	DLCI Mappings
Fa0/0	10.0.1.1	255.255.255.0	N/A
S0/0/0.41	10.255.255.1	255.255.255.252	DLCI 41 to B1
S0/0/0.42	10.255.255.5	255.255.255.252	DLCI 42 to B2
S0/0/0.43	10.255.255.9	255.255.255.252	DLCI 43 to B3
S0/0/1	10.255.255.253	255.255.255.252	N/A
S0/1/0	209.165.201.1	255.255.255.252	N/A

Figure 8-5 Network Topology for the CCNA Skills Integration Challenge

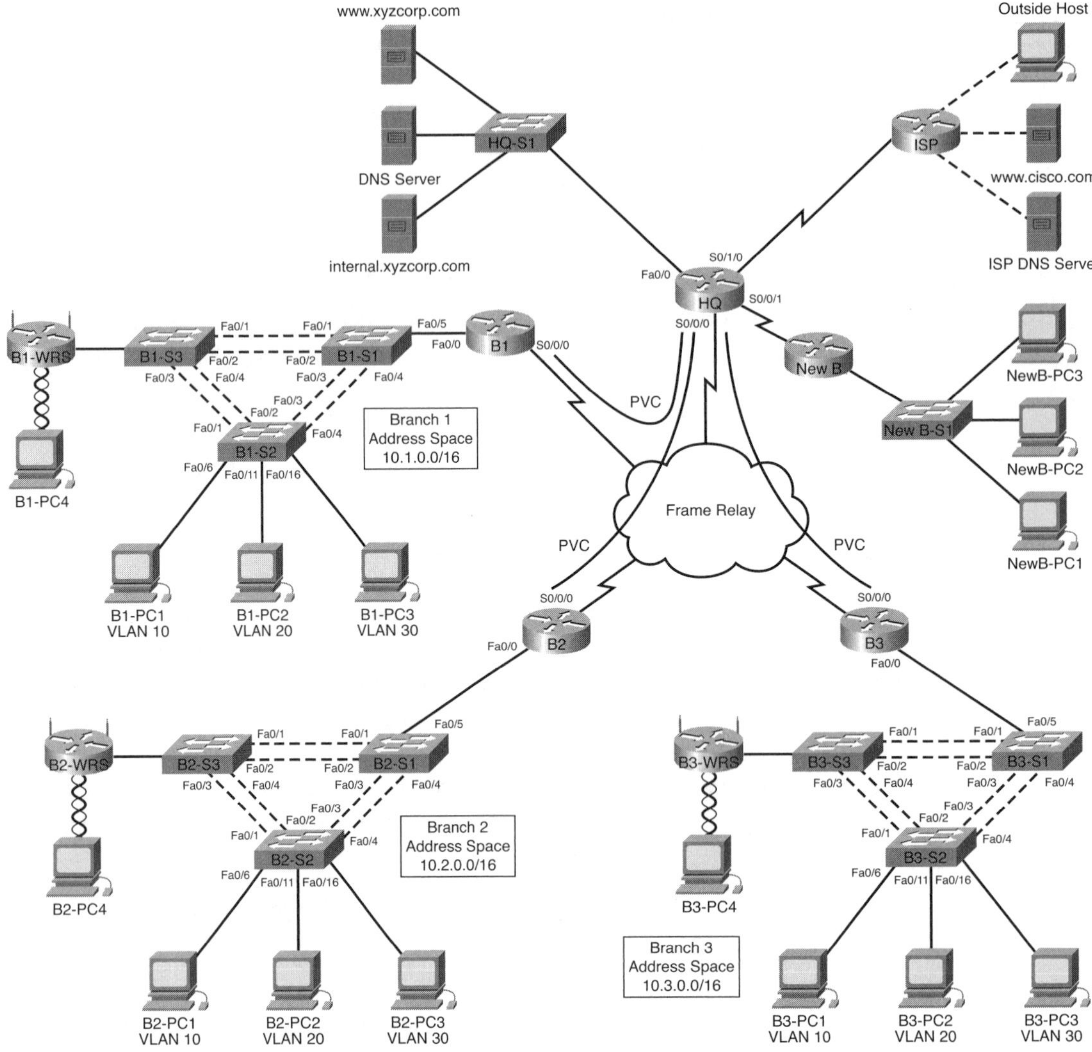

Table 8-5 Addressing Table for Branch Routers

Device	Interface	IP Address	Subnet Mask
BX	Fa0/0.10	10.*x*.10.1	255.255.255.0
	Fa0/0.20	10.*x*.20.1	255.255.255.0
	Fa0/0.30	10.*x*.30.1	255.255.255.0
	Fa0/0.88	10.*x*.88.1	255.255.255.0
	Fa0/0.99	10.*x*.99.1	255.255.255.0
	S0/0/0	2nd address	255.255.255.252
BX-S1	VLAN 99	10.*x*.99.21	255.255.255.0
BX-S2	VLAN 99	10.*x*.99.22	255.255.255.0
BX-S3	VLAN 99	10.*x*.99.23	255.255.255.0
BX-WRS	VLAN 1	10.*x*.40.1	255.255.255.0

Replace *x* with the branch router number (B1, B2, or B3).

The point-to-point PVCs with HQ use the second address in the subnet. HQ is using the first address.

The WRT300N routers get the Internet address through DHCP from the branch router.

Table 8-6 VLAN Configuration and Port Mappings

VLAN Number	Network Address	VLAN Name	Port Mappings
10	10.*x*.10.0/24	Admin	BX-S2, Fa0/6
20	10.*x*.20.0/24	Sales	BX-S2, Fa0/11
30	10.*x*.30.0/24	Production	BX-S2, Fa0/16
88	10.*x*.88.0/24	Wireless	BX-S3, Fa0/7
99	10.*x*.99.0/24	Mgmt&Native	All trunks

You are responsible for configuring HQ and the branch routers, B1, B2, and B3. In addition, you are responsible for configuring every device that attaches to the network through a branch router. The NewB router represents a new branch office acquired through a merger with a smaller company. You do not have access to the NewB router. However, you will establish a link between HQ and NewB to provide this new branch office with access to the internal network and the Internet.

Routers and switches under your administration have no configuration. None of the basic configurations such as hostname, passwords, banners, and other general-maintenance commands are graded by Packet Tracer and will not be part of the task specification. However, you are expected to configure them, and your instructor may choose to grade these commands.

Because this activity uses such a large network with close to 500 required components under the assessment items, you will not necessarily see your completion percentage increase each time you enter a command. In addition, you will not be given a specific percentage that should be complete at the end of each task. Instead, you use connectivity tests to verify each task's configurations. However, at any time, you can click Check Results to see whether a particular component is graded and whether you configured it correctly.

Because the branch routers (B1, B2, and B3) and switches are designed with scalability in mind, you can reuse scripts. For example, your configurations for B1, B1-S1, B1-S2, and B1-S3 can be directly applied to the B2 devices with only minor adjustments.

Note: This CCNA Skills Integration Challenge is also available in an open-ended version where you can choose the addressing scheme and technologies that you want to implement. You verify your configuration by testing end-to-end connectivity.

Task 1: Configure Frame Relay in a Hub-and-Spoke Topology

Step 1. Configure the Frame Relay core.

Use the addressing tables and the following requirements:

- HQ is the hub router. B1, B2, and B3 are the spokes.
- HQ uses a point-to-point subinterface for each of the branch routers.
- B3 must be manually configured to use IETF encapsulation.
- The LMI type must be manually configured as q933a for HQ, B1, and B2. B3 uses ANSI.

Step 2. Configure the LAN interface on HQ.

Step 3. Verify that HQ can ping each of the Branch routers.

Task 2: Configure PPP with CHAP and PAP Authentication

Step 1. Configure the WAN link from HQ to ISP using PPP encapsulation and CHAP authentication.

The CHAP password is **ciscochap**.

Step 2. Configure the WAN link from HQ to NewB using PPP encapsulation and PAP authentication.

You need to connect a cable to the correct interfaces. HQ is the DCE side of the link. You choose the clock rate. The PAP password is **ciscopap**.

Step 3. Verify that HQ can ping ISP and NewB.

Task 3: Configure Static and Dynamic NAT on HQ

Step 1. Configure NAT.

Use the following requirements:

- Allow all addresses for the 10.0.0.0/8 address space to be translated.
- XYZ Corporation owns the 209.165.200.240/29 address space. The pool, XYZCORP, uses addresses .241 through .245 with a /29 mask.
- The www.xyzcorp.com website at 10.0.1.2 is registered with the public DNS system at IP address 209.165.200.246.

Step 2. Verify NAT is operating by using extended ping.

From HQ, ping the Serial 0/0/0 interface on ISP using the HQ LAN interface as the source address. This ping should succeed.

Use the **show ip nat translations** command to verify that NAT translated the ping.

Task 4: Configure Static and Default Routing

Step 1. Configure HQ with a default route to ISP and a static route to the NewB LAN.

Use the exit interface as an argument.

Step 2. Configure the Branch routers with a default route to HQ.

Use the next-hop IP address as an argument.

Step 3. Verify connectivity beyond ISP.

All three NewB PCs and the NetAdmin PC should be able to ping the www.cisco.com web server.

Task 5: Configure Inter-VLAN Routing

Step 1. Configure each branch router for inter-VLAN routing.

Using the addressing table for branch routers, configure and activate the LAN interface for inter-VLAN routing. VLAN 99 is the native VLAN.

Step 2. Verify routing tables.

Each branch router should now have six directly connected networks and one static default route.

Task 6: Configure and Optimize EIGRP Routing

Step 1. Configure HQ, B1, B2, and B3 with EIGRP:

- Use AS 100.
- Disable EIGRP updates on appropriate interfaces.
- Manually summarize EIGRP routes so that each branch router advertises only the 10.*x*.0.0/16 address space to HQ.

Note: Packet Tracer does not accurately simulate the benefit of EIGRP summary routes. Routing tables will still show all subnets, even though you correctly configured the manual summary.

Step 2. Verify routing tables and connectivity.

HQ and the branch routers should now have complete routing tables.

The NetAdmin PC should now be able to ping each VLAN subinterface on each branch router.

Task 7: Configure VTP, Trunking, the VLAN Interface, and VLANs

The following requirements apply to all three branches. Configure one set of three switches. Then use the scripts for those switches on the other two sets of switches.

Step 1. Configure branch switches with VTP.

- BX-S1 is the VTP server. BX-S2 and BX-S3 are VTP clients.
- The domain name is **XYZCORP**.
- The password is **xyzvtp**.

Step 2. Configure trunking on BX-S1, BX-S2, and BX-S3.

Configure the appropriate interfaces in trunking mode and assign VLAN 99 as the native VLAN.

Step 3. Configure the VLAN interface and default gateway on BX-S1, BX-S2, and BX-S3.

Step 4. Create the VLANs on BX-S1.

Create and name the VLANs listed in Table 8-6 (VLAN Configuration and Port Mappings) on BX-S1 only. VTP advertises the new VLANs to BX-S1 and BX-S2.

Step 5. Verify that VLANs have been sent to BX-S2 and BX-S3.

Use the appropriate commands to verify that S2 and S3 now have the VLANs you created on S1. It might take a few minutes for Packet Tracer to simulate the VTP advertisements. A quick way to force the sending of VTP advertisements is to change one of the client switches to transparent mode and then back to client mode.

Task 8: Assign VLANs and Configure Port Security

Step 1. Assign VLANs to access ports.

Use Table 8-6 (VLAN Configuration and Port Mappings) to complete the following requirements:

- Configure access ports.
- Assign VLANs to the access ports.

Step 2. Configure port security.

Use the following policy to establish port security on the BX-S2 access ports:

- Allow only one MAC address.
- Configure the first learned MAC address to "stick" to the configuration.
- Set the port to shut down if there a security violation occurs.

Step 3. Verify VLAN assignments and port security.

Use the appropriate commands to verify that access VLANs are correctly assigned and that the port security policy has been enabled.

Task 9: Configure STP

Step 1. Configure BX-S1 as the root bridge.

Set the priority level to 4096 on BX-S1 so that these switches are always the root bridge for all VLANs.

Step 2. Configure BX-S3 as the backup root bridge.

Set the priority level to 8192 on BX-S3 so that these switches are always the backup root bridge for all VLANs.

Step 3. Verify that BX-S1 is the root bridge.

Task 10: Configure DHCP

Step 1. Configure DHCP pools for each VLAN.

On the branch routers, configure DHCP pools for each VLAN using the following requirements:

- Exclude the first ten IP addresses in each pool for the LANs.
- Exclude the first 24 IP addresses in each pool for the wireless LANs.
- The pool name is **BX_VLAN##,** where **X** is the router number and **##** is the VLAN number.

- Include the DNS server attached to the HQ server farm as part of the DHCP configuration.

Step 2. Configure the PCs to use DHCP.

Currently, the PCs are configured to use static IP addresses. Change this configuration to DHCP.

Step 3. Verify that the PCs and wireless routers have an IP address.

Step 4. Verify connectivity.

All PCs physically attached to the network should be able to ping the www.cisco.com web server.

Task 11: Configure a Firewall ACL

Step 1. Verify connectivity from Outside Host.

The Outside Host PC should be able to ping the server at www.xyzcorp.com.

Step 2. Implement a basic firewall ACL.

Because ISP represents connectivity to the Internet, configure a named ACL called **FIREWALL** in the following order:

a. Allow inbound HTTP requests to the www.xyzcorp.com server.

b. Allow only established TCP sessions from ISP and any source beyond ISP.

c. Allow only inbound ping replies from ISP and any source beyond ISP.

d. Explicitly block all other inbound access from ISP and any source beyond ISP.

Step 3. Verify connectivity from Outside Host.

The Outside Host PC should not be able to ping the server at www.xyzcorp.com. However, the Outside Host PC should be able to request a web page.

Task 12: Configure Wireless Connectivity

Step 1. Verify the DHCP configuration.

Each BX-WRS router should already have IP addressing from the DHCP of the BX router for VLAN 88.

Step 2. Configure the Network Setup/LAN settings.

The Router IP on the Status page in the GUI tab should be the first IP of the 10.*x*.40.0 /24 subnet. Leave all other settings at the default.

Step 3. Configure the wireless network settings.

The service set identifiers (SSID) for the routers are **BX-WRS_LAN**, where the **X** is the branch router number.

The WEP key is **12345ABCDE**.

Step 4. Configure the wireless routers for remote access.

Configure the administration password as **cisco123** and enable remote management.

Step 5. Configure the BX-PC4 PCs to access the wireless network using DHCP.

Step 6. Verify connectivity and remote management capability.

Each wireless PC should be able to access the www.cisco.com web server.

Verify remote management capability by accessing the wireless router through the web browser.

Task 13: Network Troubleshooting

Step 1. Break the network.

One student leaves the room, if necessary, while another student breaks the configuration.

Step 2. Troubleshoot the problem.

The student returns and uses troubleshooting techniques to isolate and solve the problem.

Step 3. Break the network again.

The students switch roles and repeat Steps 1 and 2.

APPENDIX

How to Install SDM

In this lab, you will prepare a router for access via the Cisco Security Device Manager (SDM), using some basic commands, to allow connectivity from the SDM to the router. You will then install the SDM application locally on a host computer. Finally, you will install SDM onto a router's flash memory. Figure A-1 shows the topology that will be used for this lab.

Figure A-1 Topology Diagram for This Appendix

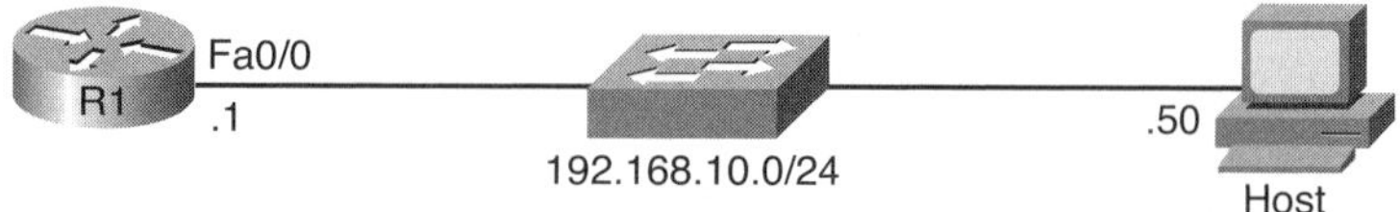

Step 1: Preparation

Start this lab by erasing any previous configurations and reloading your devices. As soon as your devices are reloaded, set the appropriate hostnames. Ensure that the switch is set up so that both the router and host are in the same VLAN. By default, all ports on the switch are assigned to VLAN 1.

Ensure that your PC meets the minimum requirements to support SDM. SDM can be run on a PC running any of the following operating systems:

- Microsoft Windows Me
- Microsoft Windows NT 4.0 Workstation with Service Pack 4
- Microsoft Windows XP Professional
- Microsoft Windows 2003 Server (Standard Edition)
- Microsoft Windows 2000 Professional with Service Pack 4

Note: Windows 2000 Advanced Server is not supported. In addition, a web browser with SUN JRE 1.4 or later or an ActiveX controlled browser must be enabled.

Step 2: Prepare the Router for SDM

First, create a username and password on the router for SDM to use. This login needs a privilege level of 15 so that SDM can change configuration settings on the router:

```
R1(config)# username ciscosdm privilege 15 password 0 ciscosdm
```

HTTP access to the router must be configured for SDM to work. If your image supports it (you need an IOS image that supports crypto functionality), you should also enable secure HTTPS access using the **ip http secure-server** command. Enabling HTTPS generates some output about RSA encryption keys. This is normal. Also, make sure that the HTTP server uses the local database for authentication purposes.

```
R1(config)# ip http server
R1(config)# ip http secure-server
```

```
% Generating 1024 bit RSA keys, keys will be non-exportable...[OK]
*Jan 14 20:19:45.310: %SSH-5-ENABLED: SSH 1.99 has been enabled
*Jan 14 20:19:46.406: %PKI-4-NOAUTOSAVE: Configuration was modified.  Issue "write
memory" to save new certificate
R1(config)# ip http authentication local
```

Finally, configure the router's virtual terminal lines to authenticate using the local authentication database. Allow virtual terminal input through both Telnet and SSH:

```
R1(config)# line vty 0 4
R1(config-line)# login local
R1(config-line)# transport input telnet ssh
```

Step 3: Configure Addressing

Configure the Fast Ethernet interface on the router with the IP address shown in Figure A-1. If you have already configured the correct IP address, skip this step.

```
R1(config)# interface fastethernet0/0
R1(config-if)# ip address 192.168.10.1 255.255.255.0
R1(config-if)# no shutdown
```

Next, assign an IP address to the PC. If the PC already has an IP address in the same subnet as the router, you may skip this step.

From the PC, ping the R1 Ethernet interface. You should receive responses. If you do not receive a response, troubleshoot by verifying the VLAN of the switchports and the IP address and subnet mask on each of the devices attached to the switch.

Step 4: Extract SDM on the Host

Now that the router is ready to be accessed from SDM and connectivity exists between the router and the PC, you can use SDM to configure the router. You should start by extracting the SDM zip file to a directory on your hard drive. In this example, the directory is C:\sdm\, although you can use any path you want.

You are almost ready to use SDM to configure the router. The last step is installing the SDM application on the PC.

Step 5: Install SDM on the PC

Double-click the setup.exe executable program to open the installation wizard. On the installation wizard screen, click Next. Accept the terms of the license agreement, and then click Next.

The next screen, shown in Figure A-2, prompts you to choose where you want to install SDM. You have three options.

Figure A-2 SDM Installation Wizard Options

When installing SDM, you can install the application on the computer and not place it in the router's flash memory, or you can install it on the router without affecting the computer, or you can install it to both. The first two installation types are very similar. If you do not want to install SDM to your computer, skip to Step 7.

For now, click This Computer, and then click Next. Use the default destination folder, and click Next again.

Click Install to begin the installation.

The software installs, and then you are prompted with a final dialog box to launch SDM. Check the Launch Cisco SDM box, and then click Finish.

Step 6: Run SDM from the PC

SDM should start from the installer when you have completed Step 5 if you checked the Launch Cisco SDM option. If you did not, or if you are just running SDM without installing it, click the icon on the desktop labeled Cisco SDM. The SDM Launcher dialog box opens. Enter the router's IP address as a Device IP Address, as shown in Figure A-3. Check **This device has HTTPS enabled and I want to use it** if you enabled the HTTP secure server in Step 2. Then click the Launch button.

Figure A-3 SDM Launcher

Click Yes when the security warning appears. Note that Internet Explorer may block SDM at first. You need to allow it or adjust your Internet Explorer security settings accordingly to use it. Depending on the version of Internet Explorer you are running, one of these settings is especially important for running SDM locally. Choose **Tools > Internet Options**. Click the Advanced tab. Under the Security heading, check **Allow active content to be run in files on My Computer** if it is not already checked.

As shown in Figure A-4, enter the username and password you created earlier.

Figure A-4 Entering the Username and Password

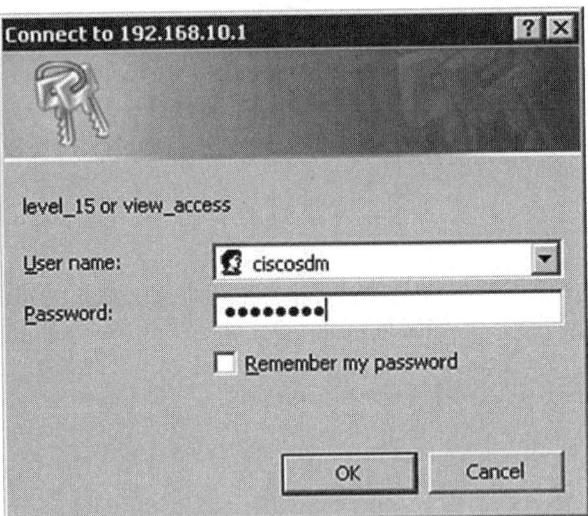

You may be prompted to accept a certificate from this router. Accept the certificate to proceed. After this, give the username and password for the router, as shown in Figure A-5, and click Yes.

Figure A-5 Accepting the Certificate

SDM reads the configuration from the router. If everything was configured correctly, you will be able to access the SDM dashboard, as shown in Figure A-6. If your configuration looks correct, you have successfully configured and connected to SDM. Your information may vary, depending on which version of SDM you are running.

Figure A-6 SDM Dashboard

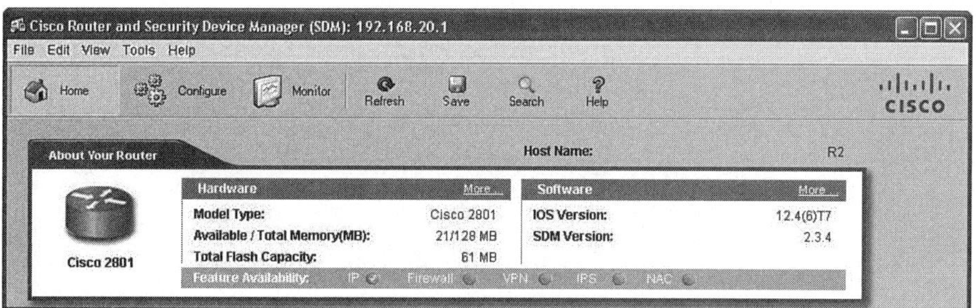

Step 7: Install SDM to the Router

Follow Step 6 until the prompt shown in Figure A-7 appears. When this window appears, click Cisco Router to install SDM to your router's flash memory. If you don't want to install SDM to your router's flash memory, or you don't have the available space on the flash drive, do not attempt to install SDM to the router.

Figure A-7 Installing SDM to the Router's Flash Memory

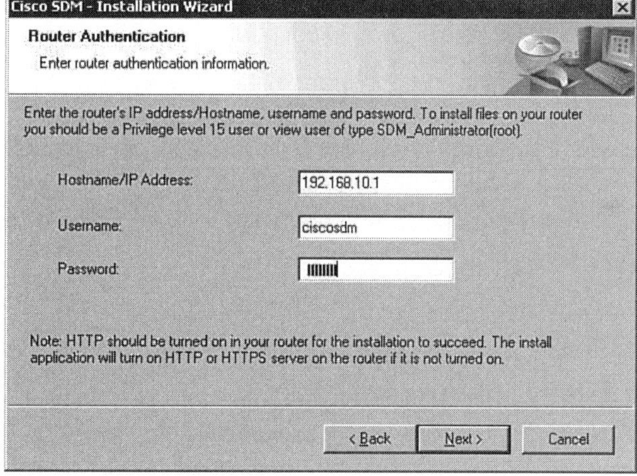

Enter your router's information so that the installer can remotely access and install SDM to the router, and click Next.

Cisco SDM connects to the router. You may notice some messages being logged to the console, such as the following. This is normal.

```
Jan 14 16:15:26.367: %SYS-5-CONFIG_I: Configured from console by ciscosdm on vty0
  (192.168.10.50)
```

Choose Typical as your installation type, and then click Next. In the screen shown in Figure A-8, leave the default installation options checked, and click Next.

Figure A-8 SDM Installation Options

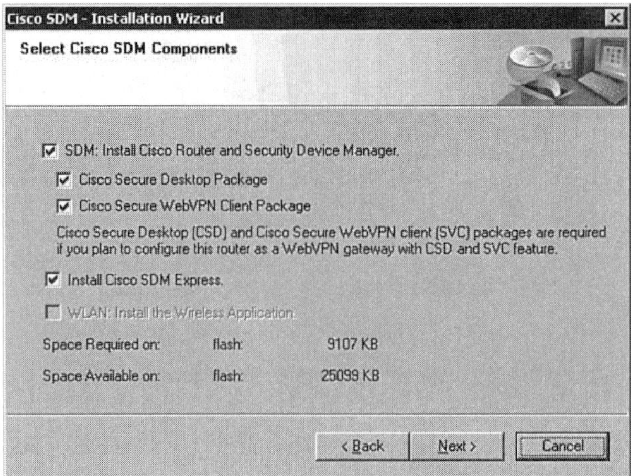

Finally, click Install for the installation process to begin. During the installation, more messages may be logged to the console. This installation process takes a while. (Look at the time stamps in the following console output to estimate the duration on a Cisco 2811.) The time varies according to the router model.

```
Jan 14 16:19:40.795: %SYS-5-CONFIG_I: Configured from console by ciscosdm on vty0
  (192.168.10.50)
```

At the end of the installation, you are prompted to launch SDM on the router. Before you do this, go to the console and issue the **show flash:** command. Notice all the files that SDM installed to flash. Before the installation, the only file listed was the first file, the IOS image.

```
R1# show flash:

CompactFlash directory:
File  Length    Name/status
  1   38523272  c2800nm-advipservicesk9-mz.124-9.T1.bin
  2   1038      home.shtml
  3   1823      sdmconfig-2811.cfg
  4   102400    home.tar
  5   491213    128MB.sdf
  6   1053184   common.tar
  7   4753408   sdm.tar
  8   1684577   securedesktop-ios-3.1.1.27-k9.pkg
  9   398305    sslclient-win-1.1.0.154.pkg
 10   839680    es.tar
[47849552 bytes used, 16375724 available, 64225276 total]
62720K bytes of ATA CompactFlash (Read/Write)
```

Step 8: Run SDM from the Router

Open Internet Explorer and navigate to the URL **https://*IP address*/** or **http://*IP address*/**, depending on whether you enabled the HTTP secure server in Step 2. When you are prompted to accept the certificate, click Yes.

Ignore the security warnings, and click Run.

In the screen shown in Figure A-9, enter the username and password you configured in Step 2.

Figure A-9 Logging in to SDM

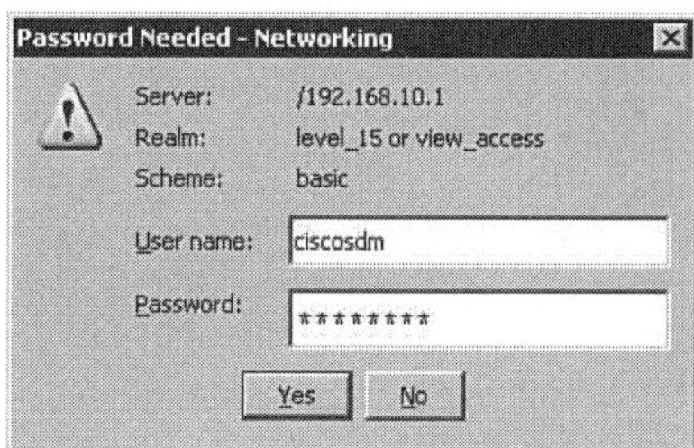

SDM reads the configuration from the router.

When SDM has finished loading your router's current configuration, the SDM home page appears, as shown in Figure A-10. If your configuration here looks correct, you have successfully configured and connected to SDM. What you see may differ from what appears in the figure, depending on the router model number, IOS version, and so forth.

Figure A-10 SDM Home Page

Notes

Notes

Notes

Notes

Notes

Notes

Notes

Notes

Notes

Notes

Notes

Notes

Notes

Notes

Notes

Notes

Notes